JOHN H. HAYES and
†FREDERICK C. PRUSSNER

OLD TESTAMENT THEOLOGY

Its History and Development

John Knox Press
ATLANTA

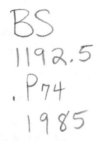

Published simultaneously by SCM Press Ltd in Great Britain and John Knox Press
in the United States of America.

Library of Congress Cataloging in Publication Data

Hayes, John Haralson, 1934–
  Old Testament theology.

  Bibliography: p.
  Includes indexes.
  1. Bible. O.T.—Theology—History.   I. Prussner,
Frederick C., 1917–1978.   II. Title.
BS1192.5.H38   1985   230   84-47798
ISBN 0-8042-0146-3

PREFACE

The present volume is an expansion, revision, and updating of part one (pp. 1–254) of Professor Prussner's doctoral dissertation, *Methodology in Old Testament Theology*, submitted to the Divinity School of the University of Chicago in 1952. Prior to his death on November 24, 1978, Professor Prussner had spoken on numerous occasions about revising and updating the work for publication but unfortunatley was not able to do so. I trust that my revisions and additions remain faithful to what he had envisioned.

Many persons deserve acknowledgement for assistance in bringing the work to completion. I am especially grateful to Mrs. Corinne Prussner for permission to utilize her husband's dissertation as the basis of the present work. Dean Jim Waits of the Candler School of Theology made available released time from teaching for the project. Logan Wright, a Ph.D. student in Old Testament at Emory, has assisted with work on the book throughout its production and Mary Turner, also a Ph.D. student, has aided in reading proofs. To Dorcas Curtis goes thanks for typing the manuscript. The excellent facilities and competent staff of the Pitts Theology Library at Emory University deserve special recognition as does Margaret A. Pitts who helps make it all possible.

J.H.H.

Dedicated to
SIDNEY ISENBERG
who knows all
the reasons why

ABBREVIATIONS

AELKZ	*Allgemeine evangelisch-lutherische Kirchenzeitung*
AJT	*American Journal of Theology*
ASTI	*Annual of the Swedish Theological Institute*
ATR	*Anglican Theological Review*
AUSS	*Andrews University Seminary Studies*
BI	*Biblical Interpreter*
BJRL	*Bulletin of the John Rylands University Library of Manchester*
BO	*Bibliotheca orientalis*
BSac	*Bibliotheca Sacra*
BTB	*Biblical Theology Bulletin*
BZAW	Beihefte zur *ZAW*
CBQ	*Catholic Biblical Quarterly*
CCen	*Christian Century*
CJT	*Canadian Journal of Theology*
CQ	*Church Quarterly*
CTM	*Concordia Theological Monthly*
CuW	*Christentum und Wissenschaft*
EpRev	*Epworth Review*
ER	*Ecumenical Review*
ERE	*Encyclopaedia of Religion and Ethics*
EvQ	*Evangelical Quarterly*
EvTh	*Evangelische Theologie*
ExpTim	*Expository Times*
HBT	*Horizons in Biblical Theology*
HDB	Hastings's *Dictionary of the Bible*
HibJ	*Hibbert Journal*
HTR	*Harvard Theological Review*
IDB	*The Interpreter's Dictionary of the Bible*
IDBSup	Supplementary volume to *IDB*
Int	*Interpretation*
JAAR	*Journal of the American Academy of Religion*
JBL	*Journal of Biblical Literature*
JBR	*Journal of Bible and Religion*
JR	*Journal of Religion*
JSOT	*Journal for the Study of the Old Testament*
JSS	*Journal of Semitic Studies*
JTC	*Journal for Theology and the Church*

JTS	*Journal of Theological Studies*
KatBl	*Katechetische Blätter*
KD	*Kerygma und Dogma*
LCQ	*Lutheran Church Quarterly*
LQHR	*London Quarterly and Holborn Review*
MQR	*Michigan Quarterly Review*
NGTT	*Nederduitse Gereformeerde Teologiese Tydskrif*
NKZ	*Neue kirchliche Zeitschrift*
NSHERK	*New Schaff-Herzog Encyclopedia of Religious Knowledge*
NZST	*Neue Zeitschrift für systematische Theologie*
PMLA	*Proceedings of the Modern Language Association of America*
RelEd	*Religion in Education*
RelLife	*Religion in Life*
RGG	*Die Religion in Geschichte und Gegenwart*
RHPR	*Revue d'histoire et de philosophie religieuses*
RThom	*Revue Thomiste*
RTP	*Revue de théologie et de philosophie*
SJT	*Scottish Journal of Theology*
SVT	Supplements to *Vetus Testamentum*
TBl	*Theologische Blätter*
ThEv	*Theologia Evangelica*
TLZ	*Theologische Literaturzeitung*
TRE	*Theologische Realenzyklopädie*
TRu	*Theologische Rundschau*
TynB	*Tyndale Bulletin*
TZ	*Theologische Zeitschrift*
VT	*Vetus Testamentum*
ZAW	*Zeitschrift für die alttestamentliche Wissenschaft*
ZTK	*Zeitschrift für Theologie und Kirche*
ZZ	*Zwischen den Zeiten*

CONTENTS

I. THE EARLIEST DEVELOPMENTS IN
OLD TESTAMENT THEOLOGY 1

The Dawn of Old Testament Theology 2
The Problem of Defining a Suitable Starting Point 2
Sebastian Schmidt's *Collegium biblicum* 5
The Place of the Bible in Protestant Scholasticism 8
The Nature of Protestant Scholasticism 8
Luther's Thought Concerning Scripture 8
The Scripture in the Estimate of the Other Reformers 10
The Emergence of Protestant Scholasticism 12
Protestant Scholasticism and the Bible 14
The Origin of "Proof-Text" Theologies 15
Dependence Upon the System of Church Doctrine 15
Melanchthon's *Loci communes* 15
The Influence of the *Loci communes* on Church Doctrine 17
Methodology of the "Proof-Text" Theologies 17
Their Salient Features 17
Evaluation of the Approach 19
The Federal Theology of Johannes Cocceius 19
Cocceius: His Life and Activity 19
Appraisal of Cocceius 21
Radical Interpretation of the Old Testament 23
Isaac de La Peyrère 26
Benedict de Spinoza 27
Theological Options in the Period 34

II. OLD TESTAMENT THEOLOGY
IN THE EIGHTEENTH CENTURY 35

The Period's Main Intellectual and Religious Movements 36
General Character of the Century 36

Pietism 38
Rationalism 41
 The Physical Sciences 41
 Arminianism, Amyraldism, and Socinianism 42
 Deism 45
 The Enlightenment 47
Kant's Ethical Idealism 49
Romanticism 51
Concluding Evaluation of the Century 52
Developments in Old Testament Theology in the Eighteenth
 Century 53
The Development of Biblical Theology 53
Significant Developments in Theology and Biblical Studies 56
A Move Toward Independence in Biblical Theology: Zachariä 60
A Program for an Independent Biblical Theology: Gabler 62
The Rationalist Treatment of Old Testament Theology 66
 Christoph Friedrich von Ammon 66
 Georg Lorenz Bauer 68
The Contributions of the Eighteenth Century to Old Testament
 Theology 70

III. OLD TESTAMENT THEOLOGY
 IN THE NINETEENTH CENTURY 73

The Major Movements of Theological Thought 74
 General Character of the Century 74
 Schleiermacher 75
 Hegelianism 77
 The Conservative Reaction: Hengstenberg and von Hofmann 80
 Ritschlianism 84
 The Natural and Social Sciences 86
 Historicism 87
 Estimate of the Nineteenth Century 90
The Study of Old Testament Theology and Religion During
 the Nineteenth Century 90
Old Testament Theology in Early Nineteenth-Century
 Rationalism 90
 Gottlieb Philipp Christian Kaiser 91
 Carl Peter Wilhelm Gramberg 92
 Daniel George Conrad von Cölln 94
Old Testament Theology in Nineteenth-Century Idealism 98
 Wilhelm Martin Leberecht de Wette 98

Johann Karl Wilhelm Vatke 100
Bruno Bauer 103
Old Testament Theology Among Nineteenth-Century
   Supernaturalists 105
Ludwig Friedrich Otto Baumgarten-Crusius 105
Johann Christian Friedrich Steudel 107
Heinrich Andreas Christoph Hävernick 109
Old Testament Theology Among Nineteenth-Century
   Moderate Conservatives 110
Ernst Andreas Heinrich Hermann Schultz 110
Gustaf Friedrich Oehler 114
Heinrich George August Ewald 118
Eduard Karl August Riehm 121
Christian Friedrich August Dillmann 122
Old Testament Theology Outside Germany 123
The Decline of Old Testament Theology and the Dominance
   of the History of Israelite Religion 126
History of the "History of Israel's Religion" 128
The Approach of Histories of Israelite Religion 132
Summary of Developments in the Nineteenth Century 136

IV. THE REBIRTH OF OLD TESTAMENT THEOLOGY 143
The Issue of the Relevance of the Old Testament 144
The Rebirth of Interest in Old Testament Theology 151
   The Call for a Revival of Old Testament Theology 153
   The Impact of New Theological Developments 154
   The Debate over Method and Approach 158
Discussion of Israelite Religion—1920–1950 166
   New Developments in the Study of Israelite Religion 168
   Old Testament Religion Treated in the Form of a History
      of Religious Ideas 171
    Albert Cornelius Knudson 171
    Harry Emerson Fosdick 174
    Yehezkel Kaufmann 175
Old Testament Theology—1920–1950 176
   Eduard König 178
   Walther Eichrodt 179
   Ernst Sellin 184
   Ludwig Köhler 186
   Wilhelm and Hans Möller 187
   Paul Heinisch 189
   Otto Procksch 191

Millar Burrows 192
Otto Justice Baab 195
Robert Claude Dentan 198
Methods and Approaches 201
The So-called Biblical Theology Movement 209

V. RECENT DEVELOPMENTS IN
OLD TESTAMENT THEOLOGY 219

Old Testament Theologies of the 1950s 221
Theodorus Christiaan Vriezen 222
George Ernest Wright 224
Edmond Jacob 226
Paul van Imschoot 227
George Angus Fulton Knight 229
Edward Joseph Young 231
John Barton Payne 232
Gerhard von Rad 233
The Re-evaluation of Features of the Biblical Theology
Movement 239
The Recent Quest for an Adequate Theology 245
Continuing and Contemporary Issues in Old Testament Theology 254
The Problem of a Center of the Old Testament 257
History, Tradition, and Story 260
The History of Israelite Religion and Old Testament Theology 264
The Canon and Old Testament Theology 268
Creation, Cosmology, and World Order 273
Early Judaism and Old Testament Theology 276

Subject Index 281
Person Index 283

I.
THE EARLIEST DEVELOPMENTS IN OLD TESTAMENT THEOLOGY

Don Cameron **Allen**, *The Legend of Noah: Renaissance Rationalism in Art, Science, and Letters* (Urbana: University of Illinois Press, 1949,[2]1963); Henry **Bettenson**, *Documents of the Christian Church* (London/New York: Oxford University Press, 1943,[2]1963); Herbert **Donner**, "Prophetie und Propheten in Spinozas Theologisch-politischem Traktat," *Theologie und Wirklichkeit. Festschrift für Wolfgang Trillhaas zum 70. Geburtstag* (ed. H. W. Schütte and F. Wintzer; Göttingen: Vandenhoeck & Ruprecht, 1974)31–50; Heiner **Faulenbach**, "Coccejus, Johannes," *TRE* 8 (1981)132–40; Hans **Frei**, *The Eclipse of Biblical Narrative: A Study in Eighteenth and Nineteenth Century Hermeneutics* (New Haven/London: Yale University Press, 1974); Jerome **Friedman**, *The Most Ancient Testimony: Sixteenth-Century Christian-Hebraica in the Age of Renaissance Nostalgia* (Athens: Ohio University Press, 1983); Victor Paul **Furnish**, "The Historical Criticism of the New Testament: A Survey of Origins," *BJRL* 56(1974)336–70; David W. **Lotz**, "*Sola Scriptura*: Luther on Biblical Authority," *Int* 35(1981)258–73; Charles S. **McCoy**, "Johannes Cocceius: Federal Theologian," *SJT* 16(1963)352–70; David R. **McKee**, "Isaac de la Peyrère: A Precursor of Eighteenth-Century Critical Deists," *PMLA* 59(1944)456–85; Joseph C. **McLelland**, "Covenant Theology—A Re-evaluation," *CJT* 3(1957)182–88; Otto **Merk**, *Biblische Theologie des Neuen Testaments in ihrer Anfangszeit: Ihre methodischen Probleme bei Johann Philipp Gabler und Georg Lorenz Bauer und deren Nachwirkungen* (Marburg: N. G. Elwert Verlag, 1972); Wilhelm **Pauck** (ed.), *Melanchthon and Bucer* (Philadelphia: Westminster Press, 1969); Jaroslav **Pelikan**, *Luther the Expositor: Introduction to the Reformer's Exegetical Writings* (St. Louis: Concordia Publishing House, 1959); Richard H. **Popkin**, *The History of Scepticism from Erasmus to Spinoza* (Berkeley/London: University of California Press, 1979); James Samuel **Preus**, *From Shadow to Promise: Old Testament Interpretation from Augustine to the Young Luther* (Cambridge: Harvard University Press, 1969); Jack Bartlett **Rogers** and Donald K. **McKim**, *The Authority and Interpretation of the Bible: An Historical Approach* (San Francisco: Harper & Row, 1979); John **Sandys-Wunsch**, "Spinoza—The First Biblical Theologian," *ZAW* 93(1981)327–41; John **Sandys-Wunsch** and Laurence **Eldredge**, "J. P. Gabler and the Distinction Between Biblical and Dogmatic Theology: Translation, Commentary and Discussion of His Originality," *SJT* 33(1980)133–158; Klaus **Scholder**, *Ursprünge und Probleme der Bibelkritik in 17. Jahrhundert* (Munich: Chr. Kaiser Verlag, 1966); Leo **Strauss**, *Spinoza's Critique of Religion* (New York: Schocken Books, 1965); Basel **Willey**, *The Seventeenth Century Background: Studies in the Thought of the Age in Relation to Poetry and Religion* (London/New York: Chatto & Windus Ltd./Columbia University Press, 1934).

THE DAWN OF OLD TESTAMENT THEOLOGY

The Problem of Defining a Suitable Starting Point

In the year 1787, two years before the onset of the French Revolution, a young German scholar, Johann Philipp Gabler (1753–1826), received an appointment to the theological faculty of the University of Altdorf. His inaugural address, delivered on 30 March bore the fairly imposing title of *De justo discrimine theologiae biblicae et dogmaticae regundisque recte utriusque finibus* ("On the Proper Distinction Between Biblical and Dogmatic Theology and the Specific Objectives of Each") and might easily have been consigned to the limbo shared by the majority of such academic discourses (for an English translation, see Sandys-Wunsch and Eldredge, pp. 134–44, which is the text quoted below). The judgment of history, however, has been otherwise, for it is this address which has come to be honored as the first systematic formulation of the basic issues involved in the pursuit of biblical theology.

Gabler's immediate purpose was to offer certain proposals which he hoped would aid theological studies and assist the church and dogmatics in overcoming some of the disputes and divisions which characterized his day. He traced some of the church's problems to an improper understanding of biblical and systematic theology. On the one hand, he emphasized that "the sacred (biblical) books, especially the New Testament, are the one clear source from which all true knowledge of the Christian religion is drawn" (p. 134). On the other hand, he recognized that the biblical materials were not only differently interpreted by various scholars but also that dissension characterized the church's use of the Bible.

> Doubtless this dissension originates in part from the occasional obscurity of the sacred Scriptures themselves; in part from that depraved custom of reading one's own opinions and judgments into the Bible, or from a servile manner of interpreting it. Doubtless the dissension also arises from the neglected distinction between religion and theology; and finally it arises from an inappropriate combination of the simplicity and ease of biblical theology with the subtlety and difficulty of dogmatic theology (pp. 134–35).

Building upon the earlier suggestions of others (especially J. G. Töllner, C. F. Bahrdt, C. C. Tittmann, and G. T. Zachariä), Gabler argued for drawing a clear distinction between biblical theology and dogmatic theology. This was the central thrust of his presentation: "What I should like to establish here is the necessity of making this distinction and the method to be followed" (p. 137).

First of all, he pleaded for the recognition of the difference between biblical religion or biblical theology, *e genere historico*, and theology proper or dogmatics, *e genere didactico*.

> Religion is passed on by the doctrine in the Scriptures, teaching what each Christian ought to know and believe and do in order to secure happiness in this life and in the life to come. Religion then, is every-day, transparently clear knowledge; but theology is subtle, learned knowledge, and by the same token derived not only from the sacred Scripture but also from elsewhere, especially from the domain of philosophy and history (p. 136).

Biblical theology or religion was therefore conceived as "what the holy writers felt about divine matters" (p. 137) which could be articulated if "we hold firmly to a just method for cautiously giving shape to our interpretations of the sacred authors." Such a biblical theology could be utilized by dogmatics if "we rightly establish the use in dogmatics of these interpretations and dogmatics' own objectives" (p. 138).

Gabler outlined a method of arriving at the religion of the Bible or biblical theology. The following are the steps he proposed. (1) The sacred ideas of the biblical materials must be collected after exegetical work on the text based on the best grammatical, literary, genre, and philological interpretation. (2) The biblical ideas must be collected according to the historical periods from which they came.

> That being the case it is necessary, unless we want to labour uselessly, to distinguish among each of the periods in the Old and New Testament, each of the authors, and each of the manners of speaking which each used as a reflection of time and place, whether these manners are historical or didactic or poetic. . . . Therefore, we must carefully collect and classify each of the ideas of each patriarch—Moses, David, and Solomon, and of each prophet with special attention to Isaiah, Jeremiah, Ezekiel, Daniel, Hosea, Zechariah, Haggai, Malachi, and the rest; and for many reasons we ought to include the apocryphal books for this same purpose; also we should include the ideas from the epoch of the New Testament, those of Jesus, Paul, Peter, John and James (pp. 139–40).

(3) One must determine the historically conditioned words or ideas among the biblical writers—"those things which in the sacred books refer most immediately to their own times" (p. 138) or "some opinion that is shaped to the needs of the time" (p. 141). These were to be placed in a different category from "the true sacred ideas typical of each author" (p. 141). (4) The collection of the typical ideas of each author "must be examined for its universal ideas" in "comparison with the help of the universal notions" (p. 142) or "pure notions which divine providence wished to be characteristic of all times and places" (p. 138). (5) The ideas of each period which were not "restricted by God's own intention to a particular time, place, and sort of man" (p. 142) must be compared with one another, properly observed, and carefully ar-

ranged to present what is the common theology or religion of the Bible. This provides "biblical theology in the stricter sense of the word" which manifests "the proper connexion and provable order of doctrines that are truly divine" (p. 144).

> When these opinions of the holy men have been carefully collected from Holy Scripture and suitably digested, carefully referred to the universal notions, and cautiously compared among themselves, the question of their dogmatic use may then profitably be established, and the goals of both biblical and dogmatic theology correctly assigned (p. 142).

In Gabler's essay, we can see him grappling with many issues: the effort required to achieve an understanding of the original meaning of texts, the impact of historical situations and cultural conditions upon the authors of Scripture, the distinction between the historically conditioned material in the Bible and the eternally valid, the need to give expression to the variety of epochs and diversity of viewpoints in the Bible, the problem of organizing and presenting the thoughts and ideas of the biblical writers in a coherent system, and the relationship of such a system to the work of dogmatic theology.

Gabler's observations applied primarily to a theology of the entire Bible and, for that reason, he did not expressly suggest the creation of a separate Old Testament theology. Yet, his emphasis on the existence of distinct stages in the development of the religion of the Bible tended to dissociate the discussion of the Old Testament from that of the New. He, thereby, did actually contribute to laying the foundations for an autonomous Old Testament theology as contrasted with a theology of the New Testament. It is no accident, therefore, that when others adopted his program they soon were led to treat the two testaments individually.

Considerations such as these and the programmatic character of Gabler's presentation carry with them the temptation to open a survey of the history of Old Testament theology with his inaugural discourse. Nevertheless, there are certain disadvantages to such a starting point. The view set forth in the address, for instance, did not come as a bolt out of the blue. In reality, it represented the culmination of a fairly long development in biblical studies in which such important scholars as J. S. Semler, G. E. Lessing, and J. G. Herder had figured prominently. Furthermore, biblical theology of a more limited sort had been pursued under different conditions of thought for over two centuries before his time. Carl Haymann, Sebastian Schmidt, and Johannes Coccejus, to name a few, had in their own peculiar fashion dealt with the religious ideas of the Bible and had organized these ideas into a system. As a matter of fact, a case could undoubtedly also be made for beginning with the Protestant reformers themselves as among the forerunners of biblical theology and, therefore, also of Old Testament theology, for it was their contention that their thought represented nothing less than a recovery of the religion of the Bible. Should one wish to begin with a position that is less ecclesiastically oriented, then Benedict (Baruch) de Spinoza might also serve as a starting point.

Without in any way minimizing the fundamental importance of Gabler's contribution, to which we shall return, it seems better to begin this history of Old Testament theology with his predecessors than with him. Such a course not only will make it possible to recognize the proper significance of his achievement and the importance of his proposed program but also it will make room for a discussion of the first major form which the systematic exposition of biblical concepts assumed, that is, the treatment of the religion of the Bible from the point of view of the dogmas of orthodox Protestantism.

Somewhat arbitrarily, Sebastian Schmidt can be selected to serve as the starting point of our survey, chiefly because his work illustrates the approach of Protestant Orthodoxy in its most characteristic cast and because he stands historically almost midway between Gabler and the earliest attempts at the systematization of biblical thought. The "federal theology" of Johannes Cocceius might have been equally suitable, for it, too, reflects the preoccupation with Protestant dogma and is, chronologically considered, even earlier than Schmidt's venture. At the same time, however, particularly in matters of procedure, it was less rigidly bound to the patterns of thought commonly employed in the study of the dogmas and was, therefore, likewise less typical of the orthodox theologians and the time in which it was written. An additional reason for turning first to a figure like Sebastian Schmidt is the fact that he made use of a method which by the time of his writing was already quite old, having had its origin very largely in the *loci communes* of Philipp Melanchthon and the works of the medieval scholastics.

Sebastian Schmidt's *Collegium biblicum*

Of the numerous books accredited to Sebastian Schmidt (1617–96), a Lutheran theologian and Bible translator from the city of Strassburg, the only one to concern us is his *Collegium biblicum prius, in quo dicta V. T., et collegium biblicum posterius, in dicta N. T. iuxta seriem locorum communium theologicarum explicantur* ("A Biblical Collection of OT and NT Texts Explicated in Relation to the Series of Standard Theological Topics"; 2 vols. in 1; Argentorati: J. Staedeii, 1671). To the casual observer it might seem to consist merely of commentaries on a motley group of biblical passages. Actually, however, it was a well-planned textbook for students engaged in what by then had become one of the recognized pursuits of theological education, the study, namely, of the *dicta probantia* or the *dicta classica*, as they were also called. These were texts chosen from the Scripture for the purpose of supporting and demonstrating the correctness of Protestant church dogma. Schmidt's treatment was arranged in two major sections, one for the Old Testament and the other for the New. Such a division was actually one of convenience and not one based on any recognition of deep-seated differences between the two testaments; however, the practice of employing such differentiation may have contributed to calling attention to the diversity between the testaments and thus to the later creation of the autonomous study of Old Testament theology as a separate discipline. Each of the parts on the two testaments constituted a complete and independent entity, and each, in turn, was subdivided according to the various doctrines of the Lutheran churches. For example, the first topic (or *locus*, as Schmidt preferred to say) dealt with the doctrine of "Holy Scripture." Texts from the Old Testament used to support this doctrine were such verses as Deut. 4:2; 17:8–13; 28:14; 30:11; Ps. 19:9; and Isaiah 8:19–20; for the New Testament the texts came from John 5:39–40 and 20:31. All together there were some twenty-two different doctrines which Schmidt undertook to defend with the aid of scriptural references and exegesis, namely:

(1) Holy Scripture	(12) Repentance
(2) God	(13) Justification
(3) Holy Trinity	(14) Good Works
(4) Christ	(15) Church
(5) Creation	(16) Election
(6) Angels	(17) Ministry
(7) Providence	(18) Magistrates
(8) Sin	(19) Marriage and Celibacy
(9) Free Will	(20) Death and Resurrection
(10) Law	(21) End of Time and Last Judgment
(11) Gospel	(22) Eternal Life and Hell

This description may suffice to indicate the nature of the approach. Such a work as Schmidt's is an example of the earliest model in the history of biblical theology, a model in which the study of the Bible was carried out in terms of the needs, the thought patterns, and the subject matter of dogmatic theology. The formula for such works is simplicity itself. First, take the dogmas, then, select passages from the Bible which seem to support them, and, finally, expound these passages exegetically.

The earliest work comparable to Schmidt's made its appearance over a century before his time. In 1560 and 1563, Johann Wigand (1523–87) and Matthaeus Richter (1528–64) published two collections of biblical proofs to support doctrinal positions. The Old Testament part of their work bears the title *Syntagma seu corpus doctrinae veri et omnipotentis Dei ex veteri Testamento tantum, methodica ratione . . . dispositum* ("A Complete Collection [of texts] on the Doctrine of the True and Almighty God Taken Only from the Old Testament and Arranged in a Methodical Fashion"; Basilaea: Ioannes Oporinum & Hervagium, 1563). Similar works, based on the entire Bible, were later produced by Wolffgang Jacob Christmann (1597–1631) whose *Teutsche biblische Theologie* (1629) was the first work entitled a "Biblical Theology," but no copies of this volume are now extant, and by Henricus à Diest (*Theologica biblica* [Daventriae: Ioannem Janssonium, 1644]) whose work brought together various biblical texts under twenty-three different categories or doctrines. In his *Systema locorum theologicorum* (12 vols.; Witterbergae: [1–4] A. Hartmanni, [5–6, 9–10] C. Schrödtermus, [7–8, 11–12] J. Wilkius, 1655–77), Abraham Calov (1612–86) applied the expression "theologia biblica" to the biblical-exegetical work considered preliminary and subsidiary to dogmatics proper. After Schmidt, volumes on the *dicta probantia* model were produced by Johann Hülsemann (1679), Johann Heinrich Maius (1689), Johann Wilhelm Baier (1716–19), Christian Eberhard Weisman (1739), Emo Lucius Vriemoet (1743–58), Friedrich Samuel Zickler (1754–65), Wilhelm Abraham Teller (1764), and others. (The production of such works was not a purely Protestant exercise. The last major work along the lines of the *dicta probantia* on the Old Testament was produced by the Roman Catholic M. Hetzenauer in 1908 [*Theologia biblica; sive, Scientia historia et religionis utriusque Testamenti* ("Biblical Theology, or the Science and History of the Religion of Both Testaments"), vol. 1: *Vetus Testamentum* (Friburgi Brisgoviae: Herder, 1908)].)

Whatever one may think today of the intrinsic worth of these *dicta probantia* volumes, such as that of Schmidt's, there can be no doubt about their initial value. In terms of the thinking and needs of the religious environment out of which they came, they represented a real contribution and performed both a pedagogical and theological function. Their strong adherence to and support of a rigid dogmatic system must be appreciated against the character of their times rather than simply deprecated in light of later and more critical thinking. They reflect the orthodox assumption that Christian thought and life had to be based on the Bible and the orthodox belief that its version of dogmatics was biblically anchored and that its theological systems were a deduction from Scripture.

This dogmatic approach to Old Testament theology demands fuller explanation and elaboration. It is necessary to determine, for instance, the assumptions which underlie this method and, similarly, to consider its derivation and development. In addition, the milieu out of which it came deserves to be examined more closely. Here we will center specifically on two problems. The first concerns the interpretation of the nature and the meaning of the

Bible in seventeenth-century Protestantism. The other relates to the origin and growth of the method itself.

THE PLACE OF THE BIBLE
IN PROTESTANT SCHOLASTICISM

The Nature of Protestant Scholasticism

Protestant Scholasticism is the not very complimentary phrase used quite commonly today to describe a school of thought which arose among Protestant theologians of the post-Reformation era and which seems to have been distinguished chiefly by its efforts to formulate a logically perfect and impregnable structure of Christian doctrine (see Rogers and McKim, pp. 147–99). Like its medieval counterpart it had much to commend it. It was massive and far-reaching. It took the Reformation cry about the sole authority of the Bible so seriously that it made the doctrine of the Holy Scriptures the pivot around which the entire system moved. It succeeded in keeping Protestantism from disintegrating intellectually during the stress and strain of the Wars of Religion. It also preserved the heritage of the Reformation against the onslaughts of the Counter-Reformation.

The Protestant scholastics, although they differed considerably among themselves, all shared the belief that their chief duty as theologians was to explain and defend the religious legacy left to them by the Reformers. From our own vantage point we may feel that they did not always succeed in their avowed purpose, in fact, that they actually distorted and even disregarded some of the most important perspectives of the Reformation. Yet, they themselves were convinced that the doctrinal structure they were maintaining was entirely the one which Luther, Melanchthon, Zwingli, and Calvin had erected. It is, therefore, always necessary to go back to their roots in the Reformation if one is to understand them at all. This is especially true when one comes to their views about the Bible.

Luther's Thought Concerning Scripture

Luther broke with the Roman Church over two issues in particular. The first is contained in his assertion, often called his *material principle*, that sinful human beings could be saved only by the grace of God which had been revealed in Jesus Christ and which they stood to receive only through self-surrender to God in hope and trust (*sola fide*) rather than through the medium of the sacramental ministrations of the Church. The second issue may be seen in his affirmation, known also as his *formal principle*, which ascribed authority in determining what was Christian faith exclusively to the Scripture (*sola scriptura*) instead of to ecclesiastical tradition, the decisions of the church councils, or the papal decretals. A good part of Luther's genius lay precisely in his insistence that these two principles were correlative. Each had its own independent worth and function but both were inseparable in their inward connection. On the one hand he was, thereby, spared the caprice of unchecked mysticism or of church institutionalism. On the other hand, he was also rescued from a biblical literalism which might easily have stifled the creative inner forces released by the conviction of having gained justification through faith.

The coequality of these two convictions is strikingly illustrated in his ideas about the nature and the significance of the Bible. His stoutly maintained belief in the sole authority of the Scripture was grounded, in the last resort, not on some impersonal or rigid doctrine of divine inspiration but on his discovery there of the good news of the forgiveness of sins through faith in Christ. This good news, he identified with the *Word of God* (*Verbum Dei*). This fundamental perspective explains why he did not simply equate the *Word of God* solely with the canonical body of Scripture or even with just the New Testament but could speak of the personal Word (Christ), the preached Word (gospel), and the written Word (Scripture) (see Pelikan, pp. 48–70, and Rogers and McKim, pp. 75–88).

Another significant result of this position was Luther's well-known, moderately critical attitude toward certain parts of the Bible. The Reformer did not regard all portions of the Scripture as of equal and uniform authority. A case in point is provided by his ideas concerning the inspiration of the various biblical books. His one test for determining true inspiration was whether a given book dealt with Christ. In fact, his principle of *sola scriptura* was in reality the principle of *sola Christus* (see Lotz). In his "Preface to the Epistles of St. James and St. Jude" (1522), he stated: "All the genuine sacred books agree in this, that all of them preach Christ and deal with Him (*Christum treiben*). That is the true test by which to judge all books." On these grounds he could call the letter of James a "right strawy epistle" and could also single out the prophetic writings and the book of Genesis as especially inspired parts of the Old Testament. Equally suggestive of the freedom with which he at times approached the Bible are his misgivings about such claims as the Mosaic authorship of the Pentateuch ("what matter if Moses did not write it") or the ascription of Hebrews to Paul. In other words, when Luther spoke of the sole authority of the Scripture he did not extend that authority indiscriminately to the entire Bible but only to those portions where he found what he thought to be the true *Word of God*.

There is another aspect of Luther's position which needs to be noted. In close dependence on Paul's teachings (Rom. 3:20; 7:7; Gal. 3:24), he differentiated within the Bible between Law and Gospel. To him the saving *Word of God* consisted of Law as well as of Gospel, corresponding to the process of salvation which led from *conviction* to *forgiveness*. The Law was regarded as leading to the recognition of sin, whereas the Gospel brought the good news of the forgiveness of sin. The result was that he considered the Law to be an integral part of the Word of God and, furthermore, he accepted it as good.

Luther had in mind the *ideal* Law, as different from the law of Moses as the Gospel of Christ is from the canonical gospels. In substance, it represents that method of salvation which requires "works" and not "faith," a method which, as Luther himself could testify, led only to further bondage to sin. Only this ideal Law was effective soteriologically. For the mundane version, the law of Moses, Luther had no use, especially for the ceremonial laws, but even the moral laws of the Pentateuch he did not regard as binding for the civic morality of his day. The really significant feature of this view is that he found both Law and Gospel in the Old Testament as well as in the New. The two parts of the Bible he thus held to be a complete whole containing essentially the same Divine Word. This seems all the more remarkable because his emphasis on justification by faith in God's grace and in the redemptive work of Christ might easily have induced him to concentrate all his attention on the New Testament and to take the all too simple step of identifying Law with the Old Testament and Gospel with the New (see Preus, especially pp. 200–211).

Luther's interpretation of the nature and significance of the Bible is arresting because, guided by his own religious experience, he was able to transcend the letter of Scripture and to maintain, at the same time, that the Bible contained all that was necessary in matters of Christian belief. As long as Lutheranism kept the balance between its material and formal principles it retained the vitality with which it had been infused by its founder. It was only when this balance was lost that Lutheran thought developed into the dogmatically fixed orthodoxy of the seventeenth century.

The Scripture in the Estimate of the Other Reformers

In the distinction he had drawn between the saving *Word of God* and the canonical Scripture, Luther seems to have received the general support of the other leaders of the Reformation. Zwingli, for example, made essentially the same differentiation in his emphasis on the distinction between the *internal* and *external* Word. Calvin echoed a similar note by declaring that the proper attestation of the authority of the Bible was through the "internal witness of the Holy Spirit" (*testimonium Spiritus Sancti internum*; *Institutes*, I vii 4). His misgivings about such matters as Davidic authorship of many psalms and the authorship of Second Peter show, furthermore, that he, too, was not a strict traditionalist nor literalist. Melanchthon, especially during the early years of his association with the Saxon reformer, also stood fairly close to the latter in interpreting the nature and significance of the Bible. This is hardly surprising since Luther's influence upon the thinking of the young humanist was at first overpowering. Melanchthon's first statement of the Reformation viewpoint, the *Loci communes* of 1521, was simply an ordered presentation of Luther's teachings concerning justification by faith. It contained no separate section on the doctrine of the Bible, although strikingly he quoted it as if all of its parts were of equal authority and, in so doing, already foreshadowed developments which were to come later. The Augsburg Confession (1530), largely from Melanchthon's pen, contained no separate section on the Bible and appealed to the supreme authority of the Scripture only in three places.

Despite such evidence of their freedom from the letter of the Scripture, it is also possible to detect in the thought of the other reformers an inclination to stress more strongly than Luther the objective and exclusive authority of the Bible and to allow more and more coalescence of the Word of God and the canonical writings. In Melanchthon's case this tendency became particularly noticeable in his later years when, as the result of his controversies with various theological opponents and because of his own efforts to formulate a complete system of Christian doctrine, he came to regard the canonical Scripture as the foundation stone of his theology. Georg Major (1502–74) of Melanchthon's school took an additional step in the direction of a thorough biblical literalism by refusing any admission of differences within the Bible or of the possibility of errors.

Among the Swiss reformers we meet the same inclination to resort to the Scripture as the ultimate norm of Christian faith and practice, thereby, laying the groundwork for the more legalistic trait of later Calvinism. Where Luther, for example, had been relatively conservative about retaining many of the traditional forms of worship because they were not contrary to Scripture, Zwingli had proposed as early as 1520 a far more radical principle, namely, that only that for which a distinct authorization could be found in the Bible might be considered binding or permissible. A similar emphasis on the formal authority of the Scripture speaks through Calvin's pronouncement that no person could stand in the Christian faith prior to being persuaded of the divine authorship of the sacred writings (*Institutes*, I vii 4). Elsewhere he says that he was completely certain that "the Scripture had come to us from the very mouth of God" (*Institutes*, I vii 5).

A partial explanation for their inclination to lay greater stress on the Bible as the source of knowledge for Christian teaching than Luther may be found in the fact that neither Melanchthon, Zwingli, nor Calvin went through a religious crisis comparable to the one experienced by the Saxon and thus did not have as strong an experimental dimension in their theology as he. It is also worth noting that all three came from a background in humanism which was not the case with Luther. It was as humanists that they had first been led to examine the biblical sources of Christian belief and to criticize the existing life and order of the church. A third reason can be found in their greater tendency to intellectualize and to moralize religion and to stress it as a system of belief and an ethical pattern of life, thereby laying the foundations for the later Protestant preoccupation with correct doctrine and, on the Calvinist side especially, with the application of biblical ethics to community and individual life. With such interests motivating their thinking it is not surprising to find them falling back more than Luther on the Scripture as the all-sufficient norm of their theological activity.

In stressing the principle of *sola scriptura*, the Reformers had set the Bible over and against the tradition and authority of the church and used the Bible both in placing the contemporary church under judgment and in giving expression to the reformed faith. A subtle consequence of this position was a separation of the Bible from the living tradition of the church thereby producing a historical distancing between church and Bible. Thus the Bible was viewed as a document anchored in the past which could be used as a means of judging not only the church of the present but also the tradition of the intervening centuries. Thus history and historical consciousness and criticism were built into the reformers' position in a way which they probably did not recognize. This historical distance separating the Bible from the present and its contemporary readers would eventually contribute to the rise of historical criticism. When combined with the Protestant insistence on the right of the individual to interpret the Scripture, the way was opened for a diversity of interpretations and eventually for the criticism of the Bible itself. This exercise of private judgment meant that contemporary ideas, various forms of modernity, and/or theological systems could be read back into or out of the text.

The Emergence of Protestant Scholasticism

The development of Protestant Scholasticism must be understood against this background of the thought of the Reformers. It came into existence most naturally among the reformed groups, for in Calvin's *Institutes*, which rapidly became the theological textbook of western Protestantism, they had an authoritative dogmatic system established on and backed by the canonical books of the Bible. The development of Reformed Scholasticism can be seen in the works of Peter Martyr Vermigli (1500–62), Girolami Zanchi (1516–90), and Theodore Beza (1519–1605). These theologians tended to view theology as a science and relied heavily on the thought and methodology of Aristotle and Aquinas. In many ways, early Reformed Scholasticism reached its apex in the work of the Geneva theologian Francis Turretin (1632–87).

Within the Lutheran churches, however, Scholasticism's growth was not so painless. In the first place, there was nothing comparable to Calvin's *Institutes*. Luther, not being a dogmatician at heart, had failed to formulate a complete and self-consistent structure of doctrine. In the second place, he had also permitted his own personal experience to determine his interpretation of the nature of Christianity to a very large degree. Almost inevitably his followers found themselves, especially after his death, unable to agree on the precise content of several major doctrines. For roughly three decades they were torn into rival factions over a number of hotly controverted questions, notably over free will, the Lord's Supper, the Law, good works, and justification. Efforts at reconciliation failed until 1580 when the *Formula of Concord* succeeded in bringing the hostile groups together. This *Formula* was not a complete statement of doctrine but, rather, an attempt to settle the differences which had led to the controversies in the first place. For the rest of theology, it asserted both the supremacy of the Scripture and the secondary authority of the Apostles', the Nicene, and the Athanasian creeds, the Augsburg Confession and its Apology, the Smalcald Articles, and Luther's Great and Small Catechisms. These, together with the Formula of Concord, were published as the *Book of Concord*, and this, in turn, became the official doctrinal standard of the Lutheran churches.

With the acceptance of the *Book of Concord* and the closed system of doctrine it contained, scholastic tendencies now could develop unhindered among the Protestant theologians. The dogmatic systems, either Lutheran or Calvinistic, were treated as the sum and substance not only of theology but also of all religious life. In them truth was considered to be given fully and fixed unalterably, and salvation was made dependent upon the acceptance of the teachings and interpretations of the version of faith which they declared. Under such circumstances theological activity consisted of elaborating and defending them through logical deduction and proof of scriptural support. It is certainly not too much to say that dogmatic systems completely outweighed any other form of religious authority, even overshadowing that of the Bible or of personal religious experience. What the Protestant churches did was to create their own tradition, in the form of dogmas summarized in the so-called "symbolic books" (confessions and credal statements), which came to have its own authority. This is illustrated no better than by the fact that in the theological schools of the sixteenth century emphasis had been placed on biblical studies whereas in the seventeenth century the study of the doctrines was deemed far more important than biblical subjects. That such a position was far removed from Martin Luther's point of view did not seem to cause too much concern.

In all fairness to this period of extreme orthodoxy, however, it should be remembered that certain external pressures also contributed to this trend toward absolutism. Among these were the combat with the forces of the

Counter-Reformation, the struggle with subjectivistic sects like the Anabaptists, the defense of the faith against the rationalism of the Socinians, the impact of widespread forms of scepticism, and the effort to shore up the faith against the inroads of new philosophical and scientific thought (see Scholder).

Protestant Scholasticism and the Bible

As in the case of their interpretation of the nature of the Christian religion, the orthodox theologians were also not lacking in definite and clear-cut views about the nature and significance of the Bible. In their opinion, it represented the infallible and objective standard which guaranteed the truth of their theologies. To assure people of its inerrancy, all kinds of arguments were advanced. Calvin himself had prepared the way for such a development by arguing for the "sufficiently firm proofs at hand to establish the credibility of Scripture" and had discussed its superiority to human wisdom, its antiquity and preservation, the witness of miracles, and other characteristics (*Institutes*, I viii). In Protestant Scholasticism, the Bible was pictured as a supernatural book, the literal Word of God in all its parts, with the role of the human writers reduced to that of amanuenses. Everything about it was argued to be divine, even down to the precise phraseology, the words, the letters, and, with some theologians, the Masoretic vowel points themselves. It contained no inaccuracies and no discrepancies. Its infallibility extended to all areas upon which it touched, not only in religion and morals but also in history, geography, geology, astronomy, and so forth. In its strictest form, Orthodoxy made no concession to ideas of historic development, of divine accommodation in revelation, or of progression in revelation. Not only were the two testaments considered to contain the same revelation but they were also treated as though they were equally Christian and of equal value. (The influential writings of Francis Turretin provide classical expression for this point of view. See the recent translation of his *The Doctrine of Scripture: Locus 2 of* Institutio theologiae elencticae [Grand Rapids: Baker Book House, 1981].) Yet, in the end, it is hard to escape the suspicion that while the final authority of the Scripture might be maintained in theory, actually it was made subordinate to the doctrinal system itself, for almost the only use to which it was put was that of providing proof-texts for the various doctrines.

Seen against this background of the thought patterns of Protestant Scholasticism, it becomes more readily apparent why Sebastian Schmidt gave his *Collegium biblicum* its peculiar form; why, for example, he treated the Bible as an arsenal of proof-texts for the Protestant dogmas; why his discussion consisted of an exposition of a relatively small number of passages rather than of a full and coherent treatment of biblical religious ideas; and why, finally, he could regard the value of the Old Testament as equal to that of the New. Not only was he doing a valuable service for his students; it was, actually, the only way possible for him to treat the subject in terms of the presuppositions of his thought.

THE ORIGIN OF "PROOF-TEXT" THEOLOGIES

Dependence Upon the System of Church Doctrine

The Lutheran system of doctrine, which, as we have seen gave Schmidt's *Collegium biblicum* its purpose and nature, also determined its method of presentation. In the organization of his subject matter he followed, in other words, simply the outline used in that system itself. Far from being unique with him, this outline of the central doctrines by his time had become standard for all the major works on theology produced by the prominent Protestant Scholastics, for example, Abraham Calov (1612–86), Johann Gerhard (1582–1637), Martin Chemnitz (1522–86), and Leonhard Hutter (1563–1616). For their part, these men too were merely carrying on a method of study which had been adopted fairly generally among the Lutheran theologians since the days of Melanchthon himself. Indeed, it is the latter's famous *Loci communes rerum theologicarum* ("Fundamental Theological Themes"; Wittenberg: Melchior Lotter, 1521) which appears to have set the pattern for all subsequent treatments of dogmatics.

Melanchthon's *Loci communes*

Small in size but enormous in its influence on Protestant thought, Philipp Melanchthon's first edition of his *Loci communes* constituted the first major attempt to set forth and to justify Luther's fundamental ideas in a systematic form. It was by no means a complete statement of his beliefs but, following the example of Paul in Romans, was primarily designed as a discussion of the issue of salvation. It was beautifully written and attractively simple in its exposition of Luther's own new-found gospel. It shows its author in his early role as the Reformer's *alter ego* who served to systematize his master's views. The later editions of the *Loci* (1535 and 1559) were more comprehensive. In fact, their avowed purpose was to deal with the entire field of theology.

What interests us in this compendium of 1521 is, however, the organization of its subject matter. Its origin goes back to Melanchthon's plan, expressed early in 1519, to write a series of comments on the *Sentences* of Peter Lombard (c. 1100–60), the accredited textbook of medieval theology on which the rest of the Scholastics had erected the body of thought so repugnant to the Reformers. He had hoped thereby to criticize, point by point, not only the *magister sententiarum* but the entire medieval system as well. This earlier work never materialized, but it did affect the form of the *Loci* themselves. In its stead, Melanchthon, who had begun to lecture to his students at Wittenberg on the letter to the Romans, undertook to treat the leading ideas of Paul's great epistle. After passing through two preliminary stages, the work was finally published in 1521 as the *Loci communes*.

The title was quite characteristic of Melanchthon's humanistic training and of his own habits of study. The term, *Loci communes*, goes back to Aristotle who in his *Rhetorica* had employed the word *topos* to define a proposition used in syllogistic argumentation. This expression, in turn, had come to the Renaissance humanists through Cicero's *Topica*. Melanchthon himself evidently became familiar with it through his study of the work of the first great German humanist, Rudolf Agricola (1443–85), whose *De inventione dialectica libri tres*; "Concerning Dialectic Invention in Three Books"; Lovanni: T. Martinii [?], 1480 [?]) had served as a basis for Melanchthon's own work on rhetoric, *De rhetorica libri tres* ("Concerning Rhetoric in Three Books"; Basileae: Ioannem Frobenium, 1519). In this last-named treatise he described *loci communes* as the basic concepts belonging to any given area of study or of thought, with the help of which one can adequately discuss or understand it. He even suggested several of these concepts for the field of theology, namely faith, church, Word of God, sin, law, grace, and ceremonies.

It was, therefore, natural for Melanchthon to choose this system for his presentation of the fundamental beliefs of the Lutheran Reformation. The concepts he selected—and their order of treatment—he took largely from Peter Lombard's *Sentences* and from the latter's predecessor in the development of Christian theology, the Eastern Orthodox John of Damascus (c. 675–c. 749). Unlike the former, however, he did not use the dialectical logic of the Scholastics in setting forth the content of each concept but, rather, was satisfied to present the teaching of the Scripture on the various subjects. In the dedicatory letter of the *Loci*, Melanchthon described his approach and purpose in the following way:

> I am discussing everything sparingly and briefly because the book is to function more as an index than a commentary. I am therefore merely stating a list of topics to which a person roaming through Scripture should be directed. Further, I am setting forth in only a few words the elements on which the main points of Christian doctrine are based! I do this not to call students away from the Scriptures to obscure and complicated arguments but, rather, to summon them to the Scriptures if I can (translation from Pauck, p. 19).

This gave his work an anti-rationalistic tone which, in part, accounts for its great popularity and influence. Even a cursory review of the *Loci* shows how closely Sebastian Schmidt's list of doctrines (see above, p. 6) follows the one used by Melanchthon, for we meet the same general scheme, sequence, and selection. Melanchthon's list included twenty-four subjects all told:

(1)	God	(4)	Creation
(2)	One	(5)	Man
(3)	Triune	(6)	Man's Powers

(7)	Sin	(16)	Hope
(8)	Fruits of Sin, Vices	(17)	Charity
(9)	Punishment	(18)	Predestination
(10)	Law	(19)	Sacraments
(11)	Promises	(20)	Human Orders
(12)	Restoration by Christ	(21)	Magistrates
(13)	Grace	(22)	Bishops
(14)	Fruits of Grace	(23)	Condemnation
(15)	Faith	(24)	Blessedness

The most striking difference between the two lists is seen in Schmidt's starting point, the doctrine of "Sacred Scripture." In 1521 Melanchthon, like the Augsburg Confession (1530), did not have such a cardinal doctrine, but Schmidt simply reveals here again his adherence to later orthodox dogmatics and the content of Protestant confessions of the seventeenth century. In Protestant confessions of the sixteenth century the doctrine of Scripture was not given prominence or priority, whereas in the seventeenth century the doctrine tended consistently to occupy the first article of such creeds.

The Influence of the *Loci communes* on Church Doctrine

The appeal made by Melanchthon's book, with its endorsement by Luther, was strong and reaction to it immediate. The later editions, although quite different in scope, content, and purpose, nonetheless retained the same topical outline. Furthermore—and this seems even more significant—it unmistakably influenced the shaping of the *Augsburg Confession* and the *Apology* to that Confession, both of which Melanchthon had been commissioned to write. With the acceptance by the Lutherans of the Augustana as authoritative for their churches and its subsequent enlargement in the *Formula of Concord* the stage was set for a yet greater influence of the *Loci communes*. Thus, when Lutheran Scholasticism set in, the task of the theologians was understood to consist, not of keeping the Reformation's tender plant—the believer's justification by faith in God's mercy—alive and growing, but of interpreting and of defending the body of doctrine collected in these confessions. Their theologies were essentially bound to the confessions and almost of necessity held to the order of content continued in them. From Johann Gerhard's *Locorum theologicorum* (Jenae: Tobiae Steinmanni, 1610–32) it was only a small step farther to such works as Schmidt's *Collegium biblicum*.

METHODOLOGY OF THE "PROOF-TEXT" THEOLOGIES

Their Salient Features

As one strikes the balance of the method adopted by Sebastian Schmidt and his predecessors and successors, its outstanding characteristics seem to be the following. (1) Emerging, as it did, as a child of Protestant Scholasticism, its basic presuppositions reflected the peculiarities of the parent system of thought. It began with the belief that the church dogmas contained the correct interpretation of the Christian religion. These, in turn, were deemed to be sacrosanct, true for all time, and unchangeable. Their authority lay especially in the fact that the Scripture, constituting the literal Word of God, was considered to give them a supernatural approval. Accordingly, the Bible's own inerrancy became a fundamental necessity, and this was assured by claiming its accuracy down to the very last detail, even the letters themselves. It meant, furthermore, that the Bible was regarded as uniformly authoritative and that any notions of the dissimilarity between the Old and New Testaments were completely nonexistent. Yet, it is also quite evident that, despite the prestige attached to the Scripture, the infallible doctrines actually outweighed the infallible Bible whose role, in practice, was reduced to one of providing proofs for the truth of the dogmas.

(2) With assumptions like these, biblical theology could be only a very limited undertaking. Of course, it would not even be correct to speak of Old Testament theology in this case, for no important distinctions were drawn between the Old and the New Testaments. However, because such works generally treated the two testaments separately, these discussions of the *dicta probantia* do constitute rather elementary examples of a theology of the Old Testament. Be this as it may, Old Testament theology thus described may be taken to mean the use of Israel's canonical writings for the purpose of demonstrating the soundness of Protestant doctrine on the basis of certain passages selected for their suitability as proof-texts. Since all of Scripture was deemed to be of equal value, such passages could and were chosen from all sections of the Old Testament, the only requirement being that the texts could be interpreted to agree with whatever doctrine was being considered. Schmidt's work, for example, discussed the doctrine of the Trinity from such widely separated references as Gen. 1:1–3; Exod. 33:12–23; 23:20; Isa. 63:8, 6:3, 8.

(3) Under these circumstances, the method of discussion was an extremely simple one, involving only three steps. It began with the authoritative definition and elucidation of an individual doctrine. It then moved on to choose passages from the Old Testament which might be thought to support that formulation. Finally, it entailed the detailed exposition of those texts in order to show how they actually did provide such support.

(4) The order of the subject matter came bodily from the doctrinal systems themselves. In this respect Schmidt was only following the practice current among the Protestant theologians of his day. This is but another illustration of the evident fact that the *Collegium biblicum* and similar works were essentially designed to expound Christian doctrines instead of the religious thought of the Old Testament or the Bible.

Evaluation of the Approach

The flaws in this method cry out from every side. Its chief faults are its superficiality and its totally inadequate view of the significance of the Bible. Instead of permitting the Scripture to speak for itself, it sought, actually, to compress the Bible within the narrow confines of a dogmatic system. Its assumption of a uniform revelation throughout the Scriptures is an impossible one. Furthermore, by limiting the attention to a very few isolated passages it could hardly do justice to all the religious ideas of the Old Testament. Equally serious is the prevalence of fallacious exegesis whereby meanings were read into a text without any consideration of its obvious sense. The method of arranging biblical concepts was of a kind. Naive and superficial, it was derived not from the Bible itself but from an extraneous doctrinal theology.

Although wholly inadequate in conception as well as in execution, we need, nevertheless, to keep in mind that this approach made at least a beginning in the long history of Old Testament theology. It ultimately led to the recognition of better ways to study Israel's religion. What seems to be of even greater significance is that some of its assumptions have been revived in some scholars' advocacy of a confessional orientation for Old Testament theology, for, in so doing, they have brought the seventeenth century back into the purview of the twentieth-century discussion of the nature and method to be used in treating the Old Testament theologically.

THE FEDERAL THEOLOGY OF JOHANNES COCCEIUS

COCCEIUS: HIS LIFE AND ACTIVITY

Another stream and in some ways a far more impressive and creative contribution to the embryonic study of Old Testament theology came in the seventeenth century when Cocceius (1603–69) used federal or covenant theology as the key for expounding the Old Testament (see Frei, pp. 46–50; McCoy; and Faulenbach). Cocceius (originally Johannes Koch) was born in Bremen in 1603, but his life's work later took him to Holland, first at the University of Franeker, later (from 1650 on) as Professor of Dogmatic Theology at the University of Leiden. His early interests had been in the Oriental and Old Testament fields, and these studies continued throughout his life to exert a strong influence on his thinking. His chief work, *Summa doctrina de foedere et testamento Dei* ("Doctrinal Summary of the Covenant and Testament of God"; Lugduni Batavorum: Elseviriorum), was first published in 1648 and went through several subsequent editions. As a Dutch Calvinist he belonged to the Reformed wing of Protestantism. His following was large; in fact, his school of thought lasted for many decades well into the eighteenth century and its influence spread widely, even into some twentieth-century theologies.

In the preface to his *magnum opus* he saw his purpose to consist of furnishing a *symphonia* or a harmony between Christian doctrine and the total content of Scripture. It is exceedingly important to take note of this statement of purpose, for it shows that he, too, was moving in the atmosphere of dogmatic theology with its emphasis on doctrine as well as on the infallibility of the Bible. At the same time, there is so much which distinguished his theology from those contemporary systems with which we are already familiar that we seem to be dealing with something entirely different. The Bible comes alive to a degree utterly unknown in the discussions of the proof-texts, while truly biblical concepts and viewpoints give to his thought a strikingly biblical flavor.

Instead of slavishly imitating the topical outline of the doctrinal systems, he organized his work around a central principle upon which all other lines of thought converged. This principle he found in the idea of the covenant, and on it he proceeded to raise the structure of his theology in which he brought together not only the outstanding concepts of the Bible but also the doctrines of his Reformed faith. With one blow he thereby sought to take the study of Christian belief out of the realm of abstraction and the search for eternally valid truths and place it upon the level of the historical and living relationship between God and humans. For the idea of the covenant is fundamentally a historically oriented one, stressing, as it does, a series of divine actions whereby humanity has gained the gift of salvation.

Cocceius was not the first theologian to utilize the idea of covenant or to integrate the principle into a system of theology. The covenant idea had played an important role in the thought of many of the Calvinistic reformers but especially that of the Swiss theologian Johann Heinrich Bullinger (1504–75). Federal theology was also taught at Bremen when Cocceius studied there early in his life. It was also popular among Scottish divines and such English Puritans as William Ames (1576–1633). The Westminster Confession (1648) shows many influences of such Federal Theology (see McLelland). Cocceius was the first, however, to apply the concept of covenant to the Bible in minute detail and to include all the divine words and deeds of biblical history under this one viewpoint. In addition to the Father-Son covenant initiated before creation, he actually distinguished between two historical covenants. The first, the *covenant of works* (*foedus operum*), he regarded as having been in force before the fall of Adam. This original relationship was based on a God-given promise of everlasting life as a reward for humanity's obedience to God's will. Since humanity was considered to be able by nature to perform its side of the agreement with deeds pleasing to God, Cocceius also called this the *covenant of nature (foedus naturae)*. The second one, the *covenant of grace (foedus gratiae)*, came into being with Adam's fall when the original covenant could no longer lead to eternal life but only to death. Because Christ, in a special pact with the Father, offered to take upon himself the task of expiating the sins of humanity, God made the second covenant, the covenant of grace, which would last to the end of the world. The scriptural dividing point between the two covenants is placed at Gen. 3:15 which was considered to promise the conquest of Satan and, by implication, also the coming of the mediator.

Within the term of this latter covenant, Cocceius distinguished three economies or dispensations. The first he called the anti-legal or patriarchal one when God's kingdom or church was upheld by a family and when law was given through conscience. The second, the legal one, gained its distinctiveness by the fact that it saw God's kingdom follow national or, also, theocratic lines and the divine grace mediated through the prophets and ceremonial laws. The third he characterized as the post-legal or universal phase when all nations were gathered together in the kingdom and when the highest form of grace, Christ himself, was made available to human beings. The three eras, differing in the manner whereby grace was dispensed, were united by the common trait that not good works but only faith in the redemption by Christ could bring about humanity's salvation. Cocceius included even the Mosaic law in the covenant of grace, his reasons for this being (1) that the law was given at a time when the covenant was in force, (2) that it possessed at least the negative value of reminding people of their sins, and (3) that it separated the Hebrews as the bearers of the kingdom from the surrounding heathen groups and so preserved the people for Christ.

APPRAISAL OF COCCEIUS

Cocceius was one of those persons frequently found in history who stand with one foot in a new era while the other is still firmly implanted in the old. Many of his assumptions were those of the more orthodox theologians. Yet, he is also generally regarded as one of the men who contributed to breaking the sway of contemporary Scholasticism. By centering more attention on the Bible than had been usual he helped to loosen the grip of dogmatic theology. Furthermore, he seems to have been attracted to the then developing Cartesian philosophy. In his concept of the covenant of nature or of works he shared some similarity not only to the deistic thinkers with their emphasis on *natural religion* in contrast to *revealed religion* but also to the Puritans who were influenced by natural theology. Finally, by calling attention, in his distinction between the three economies, to the differences which divide the Old Testament from the New, he effectively challenged the traditional view in which the Bible had been treated as though it were of one level.

Unlike the Lutherans, whose thinking had always been more inspired by the New Testament, particularly by Paul's writings, the Calvinists had tended to be influenced by the Old Testament. In going to the Hebrew Scripture for his cardinal principle, Cocceius thus showed himself to be a true son of the Reformed Church. If anything, his work was, of course, a biblical theology, but actually the Old Testament elements were so prominent in it and their place so central that one is tempted to regard it more as an Old Testament theology. Generally speaking, the study of the religious ideas of the Bible, in the form which he gave to it, is primarily made up of two factors. The first is to be seen in his purpose to effect a harmony between the doctrines and Scripture. The second is evident in his effort to discuss humanity's salvation in terms of a living historical relationship between God and human beings manifest in distinctive temporal stages. His stress on history and its various stages of development as well as on doctrine seem to constitute the chief peculiarity of his entire point of view. His solution to the problem of combining these two somewhat unrelated items into a larger whole lay in selecting one point in which, as he thought, both could be made to meet, namely, the covenant. Consequently, his method for accomplishing his main purpose consisted simply in tracing the course of the covenant relationship between God and humanity and in indicating—by forced exegesis, if need be—how the distinctive beliefs of Christianity had emerged from it.

One of the least satisfactory features of his work is the fanciful exegesis in which he frequently engaged. Not only allegory but also typology (i.e., the interpretation of Old Testament persons or events as having actually foreshadowed Christ or some doctrine and practice of the Christian church) figured prominently. In this he showed himself to be a son of his time and also demonstrated clearly the difficulty of harmonizing in all details the doctrines of his Reformed faith with the materials found in the Bible.

As one attempts to assess the place occupied by Cocceius in the story of the study of Old Testament theology, it is at once apparent that his theology did greater justice to the Hebrew religious outlook than the expositions of the *dicta probantia* were capable of doing. The prominence he gave to the idea of the redemptive activity of God in history and his choice of the covenant as the center point of his entire discussion correspond to some of the most characteristic emphases of the Old Testament. It is a tribute to his insight that these two themes have continued to play a role in the subsequent treatment of Old Testament theology, for we shall meet his definition of biblical religion in terms of a *history of redemption* or, to use the German word, of a *Heilsgeschichte* again and again, and in his selection of the covenant idea he was a forerunner of a dominant approach in nineteenth- and twentieth-century scholarship. Yet, despite these valuable features, his work belongs, of course, only to what could be called the pre-history of our discipline, that is, to that period before Old Testament theology was regarded as an independent study. His interest in the doctrine of his own communion, his inclination to regard everything in the Old Testament as leading up to Christ, and his inadequate methods of exegesis are all signs of an age which did not look upon the religious thought of the Old Testament as having value in its own right.

RADICAL INTERPRETATION
OF THE OLD TESTAMENT

The Reformers' emphasis on *sola scriptura* had developed as an alternative to Catholicism's subordination of the Bible to the church's rule of faith. Cocceius's more holistic and dynamistic federal theology had developed as an alternative to the scholastic and atomistic use of the Bible in Protestantism. Alongside all of these and in some cases only loosely related to institutional religious communities, new attitudes and treatments of the Bible developed in the sixteenth and seventeenth centuries, some of which were only slowly absorbed into the mainstream of biblical interpretation in the eighteenth century.

The bases for these departures from current interpretations of biblical materials were diverse and the degree of their diversion varied. Although some of the innovations in biblical interpretation were reactions to Scholasticism, others were not. Before discussing the most radical of seventeenth-century interpretations and their underlying theologies, those of Isaac de La Peyrère and Benedict de Spinoza, some comments about the intellectual environment in which they developed are necessary.

(1) The Reformer's view of the Bible and how it should be used to establish religious truth had built within it a disposition toward diversity and an ambiguous basis for religious certainty. At the Diet of Worms (1521), Luther had been asked if he would recant his teaching to which he responded with his "simple answer . . . plain and unvarnished."

> Unless I am convicted of error by the testimony of Scripture or (since I put no trust in the unsupported authority of Pope or of councils, since it is plain that they have often erred and often contradicted themselves) by manifest reasoning I stand convicted by the Scriptures to which I have appealed, and my conscience is taken captive by God's word, I cannot and will not recant anything, for to act against our conscience is neither safe for us, nor open to us (Bettenson, p. 201).

This affirmation illustrates that Luther's criterion of certainty in religion was actually based on such factors as reason and conscience as these interacted with Scripture to produce inner persuasion.

A somewhat similar situation existed with Calvin who stressed the double illumination of the Spirit.

> The testimony of the Spirit is more excellent than all reason. For as God alone is a fit witness of himself in his Word, so also the Word will not find acceptance in men's hearts before it is sealed by the inward testimony of the Spirit. The same Spirit, therefore, who has spoken through the mouths of the prophets must penetrate into our hearts to persuade us that they faithfully proclaimed what has been divinely commanded (*Institutes*, I vii 4).

Both Luther and Calvin thus stressed the role of subjective certainty, whether in the form of a convicted conscience or the inner testimony of the Spirit, as a rule of faith (see Popkin, pp. 1–17). Protestant Scholasticism sought to overcome this emphasis on subjective persuasion as the ground of religious certainty by stressing the objectivity of a totally consistent, thoroughly inspired, and completely infallible Bible. When new and different insights and attitudes produced consciences with divergent persuasions and when further study and reflection viewed the Bible in a light incompatible with orthodoxy's assertions, old systems were certain to be challenged.

(2) In addition to this ambiguous principle of religious certainty introduced by the Reformers, the sixteenth century witnessed the revival of extreme philosophical scepticism or Pyrrhonism, so called after the Greek sceptical philosopher Pyrrho of Elis who lived about 360–275 B.C. (see Popkin, pp. 18–41). Such scepticism, with its uncertainty about ultimate truth, led, as in the case of Erasmus of Rotterdam (1467–1536) in his attitude toward the church, to the rather passive acceptance of authoritarian systems. For some thinkers, scepticism led to the failure to affirm truth in any absolute sense. In the case of René Descartes (1596–1650), scepticism led to the location of certainty in a thoroughgoing subjectivity.

(3) The Renaissance and Reformation were partially nostalgic attempts to recover and to reconstitute the ancient past as it was believed to have existed prior to the contaminating developments of the Middle Ages. The Reformation, of course, focused its attention on reconstituting the early Christian church. The recovery of and nostalgia for the ancient past could focus, however, not only on Christian issues and concerns but also on the recovery of ancient pagan thought and Jewish Hebraica (see Friedman). Both of these latter ancient testimonies possessed the potential for challenging aspects of Christian theology and biblical interpretation. In addition, methods developed for the study of both Greco-Roman literature and biblical-rabbinic

Hebraica texts could offer alternatives to traditional approaches to literary and biblical materials.

(4) The development of scientific knowledge and methodology as well as the accumulation of new data through the discovery and exploration of new lands produced an explosion of new knowledge in the sixteenth and seventeenth centuries (see Allen). Such new knowledge offered new paradigms for understanding the world and challenged the current interpretive paradigm which viewed the world primarily through a biblical lens. Much new knowledge and information simply did not fit within the boundaries set by the Bible. New peoples and places, for example, had now to be placed on newly drawn maps but such peoples and places were not even mentioned much less discussed within the pages of the Bible.

The impact of these developments can be seen in the work of various persons and in the rise of several movements, some of which will be further discussed in the next chapter. In the case of Miguel Servetus (1511–53), it produced a denial of a scriptural basis for the doctrine of the Trinity and Servetus's burning at the stake as a heretic in Protestant Geneva. For scientists like Galileo (1564–1642), Johann Kepler (1571–1630), and Francis Bacon (1561–1626), it meant assigning the Bible to the realm of faith and morals and removing it from an authoritative status in other realms of thought (see Furnish; Willey, pp. 65–80). For others, like Thomas Hobbes (1588–1679) in his *Leviathan, or the Matter, Forme and Power of a Commonwealth Ecclesiasticall and Civill* (London: Andrew Crooke, 1651), it meant a challenge to the institutional and clerical claims of religion, a call for a historical-critical approach to the Scriptures, and a new method for reading the Bible (see especially, *Leviathan*, chapter thirty-three). Some of his principles of biblical interpretation can be seen in the following quote:

> In the allegation of Scripture, I have endeavoured to avoid such texts as are of obscure or controverted interpretation; and to allege none, but in such sense as is most plain, and agreeable to the harmony and scope of the whole Bible; which was written for the reestablishment of the kingdom of God in Christ. For it is not the bare words, but the scope of the writer, that giveth the true light, by which any writing is to be interpreted; and they that insist upon single texts, without considering the main design, can derive nothing from them clearly; but rather by casting atoms of Scripture, as dust before men's eyes, make everything more obscure than it is; an ordinary artifice of those that seek not the truth, but their own advantage (quoted from the edition of London/New York: Collier Macmillan Publishers/Collier Books, 1962, p. 436).

The most radical reinterpretations of the Bible during the seventeenth century were produced by La Peyrère and Spinoza whose works, if they cannot be said to constitute biblical theologies, at least opened the door to new theological approaches to the Bible.

ISSAC DE LA PEYRÈRE

La Peyrère (1596[?]–1676) came from Bordeaux of Calvinist backgrounds. Early in his life, before 1626, he was in trouble with his religious authorities and accused of unorthodox beliefs but acquitted. Quite soon in his career he wrote two works which first existed and circulated in a limited fashion only in manuscript. The most significant and influential of these works advanced his "biblically-based" version of the pre-Adamic theory. Initially published in Latin in Amsterdam in 1655, an English version appeared in London the following year. Evidence indicates that the manuscript was completed as early as 1640, when La Peyrère moved to Paris and became associated with a circle of pyrrhonistic intellectuals, since a reference to the work appears as early as 1641 and Grotius published a refutation in 1643 (see Popkin, pp. 292 and 293 notes 5 and 29). The volume in English bore the title *Men before Adam, or, a discourse upon the twelfth, thirteenth, and fourteenth verses of the Epistle of Paul to the Romans. By which are prov'd, that the first men were created before Adam* (London: n.p., 1656).

La Peyrère's works drew upon a personally held and peculiar messianic theory, ancient non-biblical historical documents, and contemporary anthropological data (he was an authority on the Eskimos and wrote works on Iceland and Greenland). In his preface, he wrote:

> It is a natural suspicion that the beginning of the world is not to be received according to that common beginning which says that Adam is the father of all men who have but an ordinary knowledge of things. For that beginning seems inquirable at a far greater distance and from ages past very long before, both by the ancient accounts of the Chaldeans and also by the most ancient records of the Egyptians, Ethiopians, and Scythians, and by parts of the frame of the world newly discovered, as also from those unknown countries into which the Dutch have sailed of late, the men of which, it is probable, did not descend from Adam. I had this suspicion as a child when I read or heard the history of Genesis (see Allen, p. 133).

In La Peyrère's work, one can see two major developments in the treatment and study of the Bible. (1) It was no longer possible for some people to argue against the subjection of the Bible to the same historical-critical examination as given to any other document from antiquity. Thus La Peyrère not only recognized many of the critical problems related to the Bible but also sought to use these for the benefit of his own argument. (It should be noted that Hobbes and Grotius, who were advocates of a historical-critical approach to the Scriptures, were associates of La Peyrère during his early Paris days and that Richard Simon [1638–1712] was a younger fellow Oratorian and personal acquaintance of La Peyrère after the latter "recanted" his views and converted to Catholicism in 1657.) (2) His work demonstrates that developing and accumulating knowledge was no longer capable of being absorbed into the biblical story-line and perspective (see Allen, pp. 132–37). Much historical, anthropological, and other data could not be reconciled with a worldview based solely on the Bible.

Popkin has succintly summarized the basic tenets of La Peyrère's thought.

Among La Peyrère's many heretical theses (he later abjured over one hundred) were the claims that Moses did not write the Pentateuch; that we do not now possess an accurate text of the Bible; that there were men before Adam; that the Bible is only the history of the Jews, not the history of all mankind; that the Flood was only a local event in Palestine; that the world may have been going on for an indefinite period of time; that the only significant history is that of the Jews; that the history of the Jews began with Adam, and Jewish history is divided into three great periods: (a) the election of the Jews covering the period from Adam to Jesus, (b) the rejection of the Jews, covering the time from Jesus to the mid-seventeenth century, and (c) the recall of the Jews that is about to occur; that the Messiah expected by the Jews is about to appear; and lastly that everybody will be saved no matter what they have believed (p. 216).

La Peyrère's work and theses were quickly and vehemently attacked and condemned. At least a dozen refutations were published within a year after the book's appearance and he was condemned by various groups as a heretic. La Peyrère, in spite of his recantation, seems to have continued to hold many of his cherished theories. Some of these he noted, but declared to be rejected opinions, in his annotations to Michel de Marolles's incompletely published French translation of the Bible. After his death, a friend wrote the following as an epitaph:

Here lies La Peyrère, that good Israelite,
Hugenot, Catholic, finally Pre-Adamite
Four religions pleased him at the same time
And his indifference was so uncommon
That after eighty, and he had to make a choice
That Good Man departed and did not choose any of them.
(translation from Popkin, p. 225)

BENEDICT DE SPINOZA

Four factors may be isolated as making major contributions to the understanding and exposition of the Bible represented in the work of Spinoza (1632–77). (1) Of great significance was his Jewish heritage. Spinoza's family, of Portuguese-Jewish background, had settled in Amsterdam to avoid the persecution of the Iberian Inquisition. Both his grandfather and father were prominent leaders in the Jewish congregation and school in Amsterdam. Spinoza was thoroughly educated in and acquainted with not only the biblical materials but also with medieval Jewish scholarship and Hebraica. He rebelled strongly against both the attempt to make Scripture agree with reason and Aristotelian philosophy, as represented in the work of Maimonides (1135–

1204), and the attempt to subordinate reason to Scripture, as represented in the work of many Jewish scholars (see pp. 190–99 of the Elwes translation of *A Theologico-Political Treatise* [New York/London: Dover Publications, Inc./Constable and Company, Ltd., 1951] from which all of Spinoza's citations are taken). His criticism of such approaches applied as well to many uses of the Bible in Christianity.

One of Spinoza's teachers was Manasseh ben Israel (1604–57), a leader in the Amsterdam synagogue. Between 1632 and 1651, Manasseh had published a multivolume work in Spanish attempting to reconcile all of the difficulties in the Hebrew Scriptures. (His work was subsequently translated into other languages and issued in an edited and revised two-volume English edition in 1842 [*The Conciliator, A Reconcilement of the Apparent Contradictions in Holy Scripture. To Which Are Added Explanatory Notes and Biographical Notices*; reissued, New York: Hermon Press, 1972].) Spinoza reacted negatively to such attempts at reconciling the internal contradictions within the Bible as well as the attempt to reconcile biblical and philosophical thought. Instead he affirmed the existence of such problems using these to expound his understanding of the origin and history of the biblical materials.

(2) Spinoza was familiar with and utilized the "radical" thought of such men as Robert Boyle, Francis Bacon, Thomas Hobbes, and, probably, Isaac de La Peyrère. The influence of the first three can be seen in his inductive-scientific interests as well as his political theory. The influence of the latter may be seen not only in some details of his work but also in his willingness to take a stance toward the Bible radically different from many of his contemporaries (see Strauss, pp. 64–85).

(3) The thought of René Descartes, with its strong scepticism, was absorbed, modified, and defended by Spinoza. In 1663 he published a work defending, on mathematical grounds, the principles of Descartes's philosophy (for the influence of Cartesianism on Spinoza's biblical interpretation, see Popkin, pp. 229–48).

(4) Spinoza's opposition to tyranny and dogmatism, in both politics and thought, and his desire for intellectual freedom and hopes for an end to religious and demagogic conflicts and political suppression were significant features of his work which thus must be viewed in light of the particular conditions and controversies of seventeenth-century Europe.

Spinoza, along with others, was expelled for his unorthodox views from the Amsterdam synagogue in 1656. Although he substituted for his Hebrew name, Baruch, the Latin equivalent, Benedict, he never associated himself with any Christian institution but he had some connections for a few years with the Collegiants, a diverse group of freethinking dissenters with millennarian interests and diverse origins.

His approach to and interpretation of the Scriptures were expounded in his book *Tractatus theologico-politicus* published anonymously in Amsterdam in 1670, although bearing both a fictitious place of publication and publisher (Hamburgi: Henricum Künraht [*sic*]; actually Amsterdam: Jan Rieuwertsz). Spinoza's work met with almost universal denunciation. Banned in Holland by the States-General and placed on the Index by the Catholic Church, the book nonetheless was influential as can be seen by the number of works dedicated to its repudiation.

Although Spinoza's purpose or purposes for writing his treatise have been much debated, it seems obvious that he had multiple goals in mind. The three basic positions which he wished to establish are reflected in the headings to chapters XV, XIX, and XX of his work:

XV: Theology is shown not to be subservient to Reason, nor Reason to Theology: a Definition of the reason which enables us to accept the Authority of the Bible (p. 190).

XIX: It is shown that the Right over Matters Spiritual lies wholly with the Sovereign, and that the Outward Forms of Religion should be in accordance with Public Peace, if we would obey God aright (p. 245).

XX: That in a Free State every man may Think what he Likes, and Say what he Thinks (p. 257).

In order to appreciate some of Spinoza's argumentation, it is necessary to note that he understood theology in a rather restricted sense. For him, theology was not what would be designated as systematic theology.

By theology, I mean here, strictly speaking, revelation, in so far as it indicates the object aimed at by Scripture—namely, the scheme and manner of obedience, or the true dogmas of piety and faith. This may truly be called the Word of God, which does not consist in a certain number of books. Theology thus understood, if we regard its precepts or rules of life, will be found in accordance with reason; and, if we look to its aim and object, will be seen to be in nowise repugnant thereto, wherefore it is universal to all men (p. 195).

For Spinoza, faith, theology, religion, word of God, and scriptural truths tended to be used synonymously. Similarly, reason, philosophy, and mathematical certitude were used synonymously. This usage tended both to intensify his polarization of theology and philosophy and to oversimplify the issues by working with a very reduced understanding of or a rather sceptical attitude toward theology but with a very self-confident and self-justifying understanding of reason or philosophical inquiry.

In chapters I–VI of his treatise, Spinoza explores the nature of biblical revelation and its truths or as he says, "I determined to examine the Bible afresh in a careful, impartial, and unfettered spirit, making no assumptions concerning it, and attributing to it no doctrines which I do not find clearly therein set forth" (p. 8). His conclusion about the doctrines of the Scripture, he summed up as follows:

Now, as in the whole course of my investigation I found nothing taught expressly by Scripture, which does not agree with our understanding, or which is repugnant thereto, and as I saw that the prophets taught nothing, which is not very simple and easily to be grasped by all, and further, that they clothed their teaching in the style, and confirmed it with the reasons, which would most deeply move the mind of the masses to devotion towards God, I became thoroughly convinced, that the Bible leaves reason absolutely free, that it has nothing in common with philosophy, in fact, that Revelation and Philosophy stand on totally different footings (p. 9).

Spinoza sought to demonstrate that the Bible, revelation, and biblical truths are in a category completely different from that of philosophy and reason. The "prophets," and here Spinoza used the word in a broad sense meaning the recipients and proclaimers of what is presented in the Bible as revelation (see Donner), were understood as receiving their messages through imagination. "The power of prophecy implies not a peculiarly perfect mind, but a peculiarly vivid imagination" (p. 19) and they "only perceived God's revelation by the aid of imagination, that is, by words and figures either real or imaginary" (p. 25). From such positions, Spinoza argued the following. (1) The truth of the Scriptures and their doctrines are not arrived at through reason, philosophical inquiry, or methodical thought which means that "to suppose that knowledge of natural and spiritual phenomena can be gained from the prophetic books [the Bible], is an utter mistake" (p. 27). This imposed a severe limitation on the type of knowledge which could be gained from the Bible. (2) The teachings and presentations of the prophets "varied not only according to the imagination and physical temperament of the prophet, but also according to his particular opinions; and further that prophecy never rendered the prophet wiser than he was before" (p. 27). Even "the style of the prophecy also varied according to the eloquence of the individual prophet" (p. 31). This meant, for Spinoza, (a) that there is great diversity and even conflicts in the biblical materials (pp. 30–31, 39), (b) that the biblical writers were not omniscient but in fact ignorant of many things (pp. 33–39), and (c) that the authority of the prophets and the appeal of their teachings were primarily ethical and moral (p. 29) and were cast in a form to produce faith and obedience according to the needs of the time and audience (pp. 63–64, 91, 189). (3) The basic doctrines of the prophets were simple.

In a number of places, Spinoza spells out what he understood to be the basic doctrines and eternal truths or the Word of God in the Bible (see especially his chapter XIII). These universal truths, or "precepts which are eternal" as compared with those "which served only a temporary purpose, or were only meant for a few" (p. 103), could be determined in systematic fashion and spelled out in rather clear categories.

> As in the examination of natural phenomena we try first to investigate what is most universal and common to all nature—such, for instance, as mo-

tion and rest, and their laws and rules, which nature always observes, and through which she continually works—and then we proceed to what is less universal; so, too, in the history of Scripture, we seek first for that which is most universal, and serves for the basis and foundation of all Scripture, a doctrine, in fact, that is commended by all prophets as eternal and most profitable to all men. For example, that God is one, and that He is omnipotent, that He alone should be worshipped, that He has a care for all men, and that He especially loves those who adore Him and love their neighbour as themselves, &c. These and similar doctrines, I repeat, Scripture everywhere so clearly and expressly teaches, that no one was ever in doubt of its meaning concerning them.

The nature of God, His manner of regarding and providing for things, and similar doctrines, Scripture nowhere teaches professedly, and as eternal doctrine; on the contrary, we have shown that the prophets themselves did not agree on the subject; therefore, we must not lay down any doctrine as Scriptural on such subjects, though it may appear perfectly clear on rational grounds (p. 104).

To the universal religion, then, belong only such dogmas as are absolutely required in order to attain obedience to God, and without which such obedience would be impossible; as for the rest, each man—seeing that he is the best judge of his own character—should adopt whatever he thinks best adapted to strengthen his love of justice. If this were so, I think there would be no further occasion for controversies in the Church.

I have now no further fear in enumerating the dogmas of universal faith or the fundamental dogmas of the whole of Scripture, inasmuch as they all tend (as may be seen from what has been said) to this one doctrine, namely, that there exists a God, that is, a Supreme Being, Who loves justice and charity, and Who must be obeyed by whosoever would be saved; that the worship of this Being consists in the practice of justice and love towards one's neighbour (p. 186).

All Scripture was written primarily for an entire people, and secondarily for the whole human race; therefore its contents must necessarily be adapted as far as possible to the understanding of the masses, and proved only by examples drawn from experience. . . . The chief speculative doctrines taught in Scripture are the existence of God, or a Being Who made all things, and Who directs and sustains the world with consummate wisdom; furthermore, that God takes the greatest thought for men, or such of them as live piously and honourably, while He punishes, with various penalties, those who do evil, separating them from the good. All this is proved in Scripture entirely through experience—that is, through the narratives there related. No definitions of doctrine are given, but all the sayings and reasonings are adapted to the understanding of the masses. Although experience can give no clear knowledge of these things, nor explain the nature of God, nor how He directs and sustains all things, it can nevertheless teach and enlighten men sufficiently to impress obedience and devotion on their minds (pp. 77–78).

For Spinoza, the Bible taught "religion, universal and catholic to the whole human race, as Isaiah describes it (chap. i.10), teaching that the true way of life consists, not in ceremonies, but in charity, and a true heart, and calling

it indifferently God's Law and God's Word" (p. 169). "From the Bible itself
we learn, without the smallest difficulty or ambiguity, that its cardinal precept
is: To love God above all things, and one's neighbour as one's self" (p. 172).
    Thus, nothing essential was taught in Scripture which, perhaps, could
not have been discovered by reason.

> Not only reason but the expressed opinions of prophets and apostles openly
> proclaim that God's eternal Word and covenant, no less than true religion, is
> Divinely inscribed in human hearts, that is, in the human mind, and that this
> is the true original of God's covenant, stamped with His own seal, namely, the
> idea of Himself, as it were, with the image of His Godhood.
>   Religion was imparted to the early Hebrews as a law written down,
> because they were at that time in the condition of children, but afterwards
> Moses (Deut. xxx. 6) and Jeremiah (xxxi. 33) predicted a time coming when
> the Lord should write His law in their hearts. Thus only the Jews, and amongst
> them chiefly the Sadducees, struggled for the law written on tablets; least of
> all need those who bear it inscribed on their hearts join in the contest (p. 165).

> The morality they teach is in evident agreement with reason, for it is no acci-
> dental coincidence that the Word of God which we find in the prophets coin-
> cides with the Word of God written in our hearts (p. 197).

Nonetheless, Spinoza argued that the Bible played a strategic and important
role, and there is no need to assume that he was speaking tongue in cheek.

> Before I go further I would expressly state (though I have said it before) that I
> consider the utility and the need for Holy Scripture or Revelation to be very
> great. For as we cannot perceive by the natural light of reason that simple
> obedience is the path of salvation, and are taught by revelation only that it is
> so by the special grace of God, which our reason cannot attain, it follows that
> the Bible has brought a very great consolation to mankind. All are able to
> obey, whereas there are but very few, compared with the aggregate of human-
> ity, who can acquire that habit of virtue under the unaided guidance of reason.
> Thus if we had not the testimony of Scripture, we should doubt of the salvation
> of nearly all men (pp. 198–99).

Having investigated the type of truth offered in the Bible and its content, Spinoza proceeded to demonstrate, in chapters VII–XI, the proper method
to be employed in studying the Bible freed from philosophical interests and
presuppositions.

> Scriptural interpretation proceeds by the examination of Scripture, and infer-
> ring the intention of its authors as a legitimate conclusion from its fundamental
> principles. By working in this manner everyone will always advance without
> danger of error—that is, if they admit no principles for interpreting Scripture,
> and discussing its contents save as they find in Scripture itself. . . . The uni-
> versal rule, then, in interpreting Scripture is to accept nothing as an authori-
> tative Scriptural statement which we do not perceive very clearly when we
> examine it in the light of its history (pp. 99, 101).

He then proceeds to lay out a program for studying the Bible, primarily focusing on the Old Testament, which includes questions of authorship, problems of textual criticism, historical exegesis, literary analysis, and even form-critical and sociological concerns ("We must consider who was the speaker, what was the occasion, and to whom were the words addressed"; p. 105).

The consequences of his discussion of biblical interpretation or his examination of the Scripture in the light of its history led to two results. (1) It challenged the traditional views of the biblical canon and the authorship of biblical books. The issue of the canon was posed in clearly historical categories. (2) It called into question any approach to the Scriptures which began with a philosophical orientation, except of course that of Spinoza himself.

In chapters XII–XV he discussed the positive values of Scripture or revelation. This discussion climaxed in his arguments that "we may draw the absolute conclusion that the Bible must not be accommodated to reason, nor reason to the Bible" (p. 195), "that between faith or theology, and philosophy, there is no connection, nor affinity" since "philosophy has no end in view save truth: faith, as we have abundantly proved, looks for nothing but obedience and piety" (p. 189).

The final chapters (XVI–XX) were devoted to political matters, the relationship of religion and religious institutions to civil authority, and the argument for freedom of thought and expression. In these, Spinoza discussed the various stages of Israelite history which for him was no *Heilsgeschichte* but a history from which lessons, mostly negative, may be learned. For him, the postexilic period was a time of dismal consequences, when all affairs were under priestly authority.

> After the high priests had assumed the power of carrying on the government, and added the rights of secular rulers to those they already possessed, each one began both in things religious and in things secular, to seek for the glorification of his own name, settling everything by sacerdotal authority, and issuing every day, concerning ceremonies, faith, and all else, new decress which he sought to make as sacred and authoritative as the laws of Moses. Religion thus sank into a degrading superstition, while the true meaning and interpretation of the laws became corrupted. Furthermore, while the high priests were paving their way to the secular rule just after the restoration, they attempted to gain popular favour by assenting to every demand; approving whatever the people did, however impious, and accommodating Scripture to the very depraved current morals. Malachi bears witness to this in no measured terms (p. 238).

In Spinoza, one can see an attempt to expound the essential content of the Bible, the basic doctrines, or the Word of God. His views stressed their moral and ethical content and authority and the relationship of these to both non-philosophical and philosophical forms of knowledge. In doing so, he sought to liberate the doctrines of the Bible from the ethnocentricity of Judaism and the philosophical-ecclesiastical dogmatism of Christianity.

THEOLOGICAL OPTIONS IN THE PERIOD

By the end of the seventeenth century, four main options or approaches to the theological use of the Bible were being propounded. (1) In Catholicism and mainstream Judaism the Bible was viewed as the fountainhead and source of a living tradition which determined the faith and life of the communities and their members. Here the Bible shared its authority with post-biblical tradition and traditional interpretations. The Bible was the wellspring of an ongoing stream of faith. (2) The Reformers had sought to set the Scriptures over against the tradition and to deny the authority of the ongoing stream. This effort was summarized in the afirmation of *sola scriptura*. Even with Luther, however, this position had led to a canon within the canon, that is, an emphasis on certain portions of Scripture as more authoritative than others. In Calvin it led to the development of a system of theology which claimed to be derived from the Bible. (Many non-Protestants pointed out, however, that such systems and confessional summaries were not identical with Scripture but were inferences drawn from Scripture; see Popkin, p. 267, n. 25.) Protestant Scholasticism set out to defend both the Bible as the infallible source of doctrines and reason as capable of expounding a systematic presentation of these doctrines. (3) Federal theology offered a variation on Protestant Scholasticism. Federalism stressed that the history of God's relationship with humanity, as depicted in the Bible, was as significant as the doctrines found in the Bible. It emphasized the importance of the Bible as a document of history as well as a uniform source book of doctrines. (4) Radical approaches to the Bible, like those of Le Peyrère and Spinoza, sought to offer significant alternatives informed by both a sceptical attitude toward traditional claims about the Bible and a willingness to challenge even the Bible itself in light of non-biblical knowledge or philosophical considerations.

II.
OLD TESTAMENT THEOLOGY IN THE EIGHTEENTH CENTURY

Kenneth W. **Appelgate** (ed.), *Voltaire on Religion: Selected Writings* (New York: Frederick Ungar, 1974); Isaiah **Berlin**, "Herder and the Enlightenment," *Aspects of the Eighteenth Century* (ed. E. R. Wasserman; Baltimore: John Hopkins Press, 1965)47–104 = his *Vico and Herder: Two Studies in the History of Ideas* (New York: Viking Press, 1976)143–216; Hendrikus **Boers**, *What Is New Testament Theology? The Rise of Criticism and the Problem of a Theology of the New Testament* (Philadelphia: Fortress Press, 1979); Edward **Carpenter**, "The Bible in the Eighteenth Century," *The Church's Use of the Bible, Past and Present* (ed. D. E. Nineham; London: SPCK, 1963)89–124; Ernst **Cassirer**, *The Philosophy of the Enlightenment* (Princeton: Princeton University Press, 1951); Henry **Chadwick** (ed.), *Lessing's Theological Writings* (London/Stanford: A. & C. Black Ltd./Stanford University Press, 1956/57); Robert Claude **Dentan**, *Preface to Old Testament Theology* (New Haven: Yale University Press, 1950; rev. ed.; New York: Seabury Press, 1963); Ludwig **Diestel**, *Geschichte des Alten Testamentes in der christlichen Kirche* (Jena: Mauke's Verlag [Hermann Dufft], 1869); Gerhard **Ebeling**, "The Meaning of Biblical Theology," *Word and Faith* (London/Philadelphia: SCM Press/Fortress Press, 1963)79–97; Burton **Feldman** and Robert D. **Richardson**, *The Rise of Modern Mythology 1680–1860* (Bloomington/London: Indiana University Press, 1972); Dean **Freiday**, *The Bible—Its Criticism, Interpretation and Use—in 16th and 17th Century England* (Pittsburgh: Catholic and Quaker Studies, 1979); Peter **Gay**, *Deism: An Anthology* (Princeton: Van Nostrand, 1968); Antonius Hermann Joseph **Gunneweg**, *Understanding the Old Testament* (London/Philadelphia: SCM Press/Westminister Press, 1978)63–77; Paul **Hazard**, *La Crise de la Conscience Européene* (Paris: Boivin, 1935) = *The European Mind (1680–1715)* (London: Hollis & Carter, 1953); Johann Gottfried von **Herder**, *Reflections on the Philosphy of the History of Mankind* (abridged and with an introduction by Frank E. Manuel; Chicago/London: University of Chicago Press, 1968); Gottfried **Hornig**, *Die Anfänge der historisch-kritischen Theologie. Johann Salomo Semlers Schriftverständnis und seine Stellung zu Luther* (Göttingen: Vandenhoeck & Ruprecht, 1961); Otto **Kaiser**, "Johann Salomo Semler als Bahnbrecher der modernen Bibelwissenschaft," *Textgamäss. Aufsätze und Beiträge zur Hermeneutik des Alten Testament* (ed. by A. H. J. Gunneweg and Otto Kaiser; Göttingen: Vandenhoeck & Ruprecht, 1979)59–79; Immanuel **Kant**, *On History* (ed. with an introduction by Lewis White Beck; Indianapolis: Bobbs-Merrill Educational Publishing, 1963); Emil Gottlieb Heinrich **Kraeling**, *The Old Testament Since the Reformation* (London/New York: Lutterworth Press/Schocken, 1955/1969); Hans-Joachim **Kraus**, *Die biblische Theologie: Ihre Geschichte und Problematik* (Neukirchen-Vluyn: Neukirchener Verlag, 1970)1–69; *idem*, *Geschichte der historisch-*

kritischen Erforschung des Alten Testaments (Neukirchen-Vluyn: Neukirchener Verlag, 1956, ²1969); Henning Graf **Reventlow**, "Die Auffassung vom Alten Testament bei Hermann Samuel Reimarus und Gotthold Ephraim Lessing," *EvTh* 25(1965)429–48; *idem, Bibelautorität und Geist der Moderne. Die Bedeutung des Bibelverständnisses für die geistesgeschichtliche und politische Entwicklung in England von der Reformation bis zur Aufklärung* (Göttingen: Vandenhoeck & Ruprecht, 1980) = *The Authority of the Bible and the Rise of the Modern World* (London/Philadelphia: SCM Press/Fortress Press, 1984); *idem*, "Richard Simon und seine Bedeutung für die kritische Erforschung der Bibel," *Historische Kritik in der Theologie: Beiträge zu ihrer Geschichte* (ed. by Georg Schwaiger; Göttingen: Vandenhoeck & Ruprecht, 1980)11–36; Dietrich **Ritschl**, "Johann Salomo Semler: The Rise of the Historical-Critical Method in Eighteenth-Century Theology on the Continent," *Introduction to Modernity: A Symposium on Eighteenth-Century Thought* (ed. by Robert Mollenauer; Austin: University of Texas Press, 1965)107–33; John W. **Rogerson**, *Myth in Old Testament Interpretation* (Berlin: Walter de Gruyter, 1974); John **Sandys-Wunsch**, "G. T. Zachariae's Contributions to Biblical Theology," *ZAW* 92(1980)1–23; Bertram **Schwarzbach**, *Voltaire's Old Testament Criticism* (Geneva: Droz, 1971); Rudolf **Smend**, "Johann Philipp Gablers Begründung der biblischen Theologie," *EvTh* 22(1962)345–57; *idem*, "Lessing und die Bibelwissenschaft," *SVT* 29(1978)298–319; Philipp Jacob **Spener**, *Pia Desideria* (tr., ed., and with an introduction by Theodore G. Tappert; Philadelphia: Fortress Press, 1964); Leslie **Stephen**, *History of English Thought in the Eighteenth Century* (2 vols.; London/New York: Smith, Elder & Co./ G. P. Putnam's Sons, 1876); Paul **Tillich**, *A History of Christian Thought: From Its Judaic and Hellenistic Origins to Existentialism* (New York: Simon and Schuster, 1968); Earl Morse **Wilbur**, *A History of Unitarianism: Socinianism and Its Antecedents* (Cambridge: Harvard University Press, 1945); Basil **Willey**, *The Eighteenth Century Background: Studies on the Idea of Nature in the Thought of the Period* (London/New York: Chatto & Windus Ltd./Columbia University Press, 1940); Thomas **Willi**, *Herders Beitrag zum Verstehen des Alten Testaments* (Tübingen: J. C. B. Mohr, 1971).

THE PERIOD'S MAIN INTELLECTUAL AND RELIGIOUS MOVEMENTS

General Character of the Century

The seventeenth century ended, theologically, with Protestant Orthodoxy firmly entrenched and seemingly impregnable. Yet, under the impact of the following century's revolution in human life and thought, it soon began to fall apart and finally made way for decidedly different sets of ideas and new methodological approaches. It would be surprising indeed had the study of the religion of the Bible remained unaffected by these developments.

The seventeenth century bequeathed to the eighteenth a propitious legacy (see Willey). First of all, the wars that had decimated Europe through much of the seventeenth century had receded sufficiently to allow not only for limited recovery but also for optimism about the future. Secondly, world exploration, epitomized in Columbus's discovery of America, had opened new vistas, introduced the "noble savage" to the world of civilization, and allowed Europeans to understand themselves in new categories. Thirdly, Cartesian philosophy with its anti-authoritarianism and its emphasis on the subjective verification of truth made possible a greater sense of importance and certainty for the individual person and encouraged the role of personal evaluation and judgment. Fourthly, the breakup of Aristotelian and scholastic metaphysics, with its concern for the "why" and ultimate causes, had begun and the old approach was being replaced gradually by a new approach which focused on the "how" and relied on perceptual experience, observation, and inductive reasoning. Humanity and the world of nature in which humanity now felt more at home and which was slowly denuded of its mystery, awe, and fear were gradually moving to center stage. Fifthly, historical consciousness and historiographic concerns were becoming more dominant. Historical criticism had been a polemical weapon in the hands of the Magdeburg Centuriators (1559–74), and in the seventeenth century the works of Herbert Rosweyde (1569–1629), John Bollandus (1596–1665), and Jean Mabillon (1632–1707) displayed a real historical methodology at work. The Frenchman Pierre Bayle (1647–1706) emphasized that "the presentation of historical phenomena must not be hindered by any prejudice or distorted by any religious or political bias" (see Cassirer, p. 208). Sixthly, the eighteenth century inherited a rudimentary biblical criticism and some critique of positions contained in or deduced from the Bible. This can be seen, as we noted in the last chapter, in the work and theories of Kepler, Galileo, La Peyrère, Spinoza, Simon, and others.

The eighteenth century was almost universally greeted with the sense that civilization was moving in radically new and hopeful directions. The nostalgia for the past which had greatly influenced life and culture from the time of the Renaissance was giving way to optimism about and orientation to the future.

> As the seventeenth century wore to its close, Nature and Reason began on the whole to gain upon Aristotle and the Rules. The quiet influence of Descartes, who had taught men to look within for the first certainties, and had spread abroad the clear light of geometric reasoning, told strongly on behalf of 'Moderns' versus 'Ancients'. It was not that one adopted only new standards: supporters of both parties in the controversy seem to have shared the same general scale of values. It was a sense that the world's great age was beginning anew and that pupilage to antiquity was now unnecessary (Willey, 1940, p. 22)

The most obvious significance of the eighteenth century for the total history of Old Testament theology is that the discipline gained recognition for the first time as a separate branch of theological research. This independence, in turn, was the result of two momentous innovations for which the century was responsible. The first of these was closely related to the gradual

disintegration of scholastic Orthodoxy. It grew out of the mounting conviction that the religion of the Scripture was not at all identical with that contained in the dogmas of Protestantism and that, therefore, one ought to
distinguish between biblical and dogmatic theology. The second may properly be called the child of the era's most distinctive movement of thought,
Rationalism. It found expression in the increasing demand for an historical
treatment of the literature and religion of the Bible and was, accordingly, also
intimately connected with the currently emerging study of biblical criticism.
Although these two innovations came into being independently and for a
while, at least, were pursued each in its own special way, ultimately a fruitful
harmony between the two was brought about. On the whole, the age's contribution to the ongoing course of Old Testament theology is to be seen in the
fact that it broke new ground and called attention to hitherto unrealized directions of research. In so doing, it laid the foundations for the work which
was to be done in the following centuries.

The breakdown of the orthodox position involved a multiplicity of factors. Similarly, no one single cause can explain the rise of Rationalism. In
some ways the two processes were interwoven; in others they were separate
and distinct. Together, however, they determined the intellectual and religious life within which the biblical theology of that century moved and had
its being. Our first step, therefore, in tracing out the subject matter of this
chapter, is to understand the environment from which it came.

There are two notes in particular which sound throughout the eighteenth century, sometimes in a fair degree of harmony but frequently in decided discord. Somewhat superficially they can be reduced to two terms,
feeling and *reason*. The first showed itself in those movements of which
Pietism and Romanticism might be considered typical. The other found
expression in a larger variety of ways and with different degrees of intensity.
Deism, the Enlightenment, the physical sciences, the philosophies of Leibniz
and Voltaire—all reflect the emphasis upon reason and are, therefore, generally grouped together under the name Rationalism.

These two movements, Pietism-Romanticism and Rationalism, actually
shared many roots and, in Orthodoxy, a common enemy (see Tillich, pp.
276–93). Both derive from the drive toward autonomy over against the authoritarianism of orthodox systems. This desire for individualistic autonomy
found expression in Pietism's focus on subjective religious experience and in
Rationalism's focus on human reason and its capacity for understanding.

Pietism

Protestant Orthodoxy, having placed religious life and thought within
certain strictly drawn limits and tending to reduce faith to an acceptance of
sound doctrine, proved in the long run too barren to sustain a really vital

religion. The reaction against it set in inevitably with the appearance of a point of view which strongly asserted the right of personal religion, validated by the experiences of the individual. This rival was Pietism. The impulses which gave birth to Protestant forms of Pietism were felt in many of the religious communities at the time. Theodore G. Tappert among others has pointed out the widespread manifestations of this phenomenon:

> Negatively it represented a protest against the formalism in doctrine, worship, and life into which churches and their members had fallen after the original impulses of the Reformation had dissipated. Positively it represented an attempt to cultivate a keener awareness of the present reality of God's judgment and grace and the bearing which these were believed to have on personal and social life. We can observe evidences of all this not only in the English Puritanism of the late sixteenth and early seventeenth centuries and in the Pietism of the European continent during the late seventeenth and early eighteenth centuries, but also in the contemporary Jansenist movement within Roman Catholicism and the Hasidist movement in Judaism. The English Puritan John Bunyan, the Dutch Reformed Willem Teelinck, the German Lutheran Philipp Jacob Spener, the Moravian Nicholas Zinzendorf, the Methodist progenitor John Wesley, the American Presbyterian Gilbert Tennent, and the Roman Catholic Blaise Pascal—all of these were participants in a common historical climate although they reacted differently in their concrete historical situations (introduction to Spener, p. 1).

Protestant Pietism had its immediate antecedents in the work of such men as Johann Arndt (1555–1621), the German mystic and ascetic, whose books, on "True Christianity" (*Wahre Christentum*), published between 1606 and 1610 were some of the most widely circulated devotional books of his time, and Gottlieb (Theophilus) Grossgebauer (1627–61), especially in his *Wächterstimme aus dem verwüsteten Zion* ("Watcher's Voice from the Destroyed Zion"; Frankfurt am Main: Wilden, 1661). Pietism's most devoted and significant exponent was Philipp Jacob Spener (1635–1705), one of the most notable figures of the late seventeenth century. His *Pia Desideria*, which bore the sub-title "Heartfelt Desire for a God-pleasing Reform of the true Evangelical Church, Together with Several Simple Christian Proposals Looking Toward this End," was published in 1676 (Frankfurt am Main: J. D. Zunner).

Pietism's salient features can be listed quickly. Institutionally speaking, while it did not break away from the Lutheran Church, with the one exception of the Moravian Brethren, it did lead to the development of circles or cells within the larger church body—so-called *ecclesiolae in ecclesia*—in which Bible reading, prayer, mutual edification, and ascetic standards of morality were regarded as the foremost qualities of the Christian life. Spener, himself a Lutheran pastor, did not consciously depart from the confessions or the system of dogma; there can, however, be no doubt that the spirit and

ideals motivating these cells were totally unlike the outlook of Lutheran orthodoxy since Pietists tended to locate religious certainty more in experience
than in correct doctrine.

The success of the movement was such that it spread rapidly over all of
Germany and into the Reformed groups as well, then to England where it
played a role in the rise of Methodism, and thence even to the North American continent. It is easy to see that Pietism's stress on *heartfelt religion* was
destined to clash with the orthodox emphasis on *pure doctrine*. Of greater
importance, in terms of our interest, was the kindling of a new concern for
the Bible itself. Spener called for a knowledge of *all* the Scriptures by church
members inculcated through preaching on more texts than the lectionary se-
lections, through private reading and study, through public reading of the
Scriptures *seriatum*, and through public discussion and interpretation of biblical materials (see *Pia Desideria*, pp. 87–92). Wider familiarity with the
Scripture than heretofore served, in effect, to bring about a growing recognition of the differences between it and dogma. Spener was, in fact, highly
condemnatory of Protestant Scholaticism and theological education; he considered both to be lacking an orientation to the Bible. He quoted with approval remarks about how "the scholastic theology which Luther had thrown
out the front door had been introduced again by others through the back
door." This Scholasticism was contrasted with "true biblical theology" (pp.
54–55). According to Spener, scholastic theology, "while it preserves the
foundation of faith from the Scriptures, builds on it with so much wood, hay,
and stubble of human inquisitiveness that the gold can no longer be seen"
and "it becomes exceedingly difficult to grasp and find pleasure in the real
simiplicity of Christ and his teaching" (p. 56).

The influence of Pietism even made itself felt on the more academic
level and in its German form was certainly not anti-intellectual. This appeared first when its other great leader, August Hermann Francke (1663–
1727), with seven other masters, formed a pietistic cell at the University of
Leipzig for the purpose of pursuing biblical studies. The classes taught in
this *collegium philobiblicum* (founded in 1686) soon proved so popular among
townspeople and students alike that the older professors began to resent the
competitor and finally asked for Francke's dismissal from the university. The
failure at Leipzig was more than balanced, however, by the founding of the
University of Halle (1694) where Francke, as dean of the theological faculty,
quickly created a bustling center of Pietism. Interestingly enough, his efforts
were strongly aided by the anti-orthodox Rationalist, Christian Thomasius
(1655–1728), who had been called to lead the law faculty at the new university.

The harmony between Pietism and Rationalism lasted as long as the
two were drawn together by their mutual antagonism to scholastic theology,
but when the disintegration of Orthodoxy became increasingly apparent the

differences between the two points of view duly asserted themselves and turned Halle into a field of battle. The conflict ended with victory for the Rationalists who had the backing of Frederick the Great. Nevertheless, the pietistic spirit lived on as a subsurface current, so that Halle, despite its rationalistic character, continued to be one of the main centers of biblical studies in Germany, with Rationalists like S. J. Baumgarten and J. S. Semler joined by more conservative scholars like C. B. Michaelis and G. T. Zachariä. To this list one might add another Pietist scholar, J. A. Bengel (1687–1752), long head of the theological seminary at Denkendorf in Württemberg and the founder of New Testament criticism in the Lutheran church.

Rationalism

Influential though Pietism became in the religious life of the eighteenth century, its importance pales when compared with the other contender for human spirits in the same period, namely, Rationalism. Unlike the former, which was in essence a religious phenomenon, Rationalism penetrated into all fields of mental activity and thus assumed a position of preponderance which soon left it the real master in the intellectual field. No well-defined single manifestation, it was, rather, an aggregate of relatively separate movements of thought held together by certain kindred attitudes and basic assumptions, notably a belief in the innate goodness and sufficiency of human nature and a reliance on one's own intellectual faculties in opposition to the earlier authorities of revelation and church dogma and Pietism's emphasis on subjective experience. Some of its aspects have practically no bearing on our subject (for example, its economic, political, and social views) and, therefore, are omitted here. Others, however, are deeply relevant, particularly where they affected philosophical and theological discussion.

THE PHYSICAL SCIENCES

In the first place, we need to recall that from its very outset this century had been stirred by the triumphs of the new inductively pursued physical and astronomical sciences. The method employed in these sciences was first systematically advocated by Sir Francis Bacon (1561–1626) in his famous *Novum organum* (Londini: Ioannem Billium, 1620). Knowledge was to be gained by the inductive study of nature, not by deduction from Aristotle or the medieval scholastics.

The effect of this work on the religious thinking of its day was extraordinary.

When Newton bound together in one dazzling synthesis the great and the little, the stars in their courses and the fall of an apple, a thankful generation, at once scientific and pious, could exclaim with its spokesman, Alexander Pope:

Nature and Nature's laws lay hid in night:
God said, *Let Newton be!* and all was Light!
(Willey, 1940, p. 5).

Newton's picture of the universe as a vast mechanism in which gravitation determined the course of the heavenly bodies contradicted completely the generally accepted view of the world as a field of arbitrary divine action and thus of God's intervention in history. Orthodoxy, having derived its picture of the universe from the Scriptures and the ancients of Rome and Greece, was dealt, thereby, a telling blow.

The vital blows struck against Orthodoxy by the new scientific thought should not be understood to mean that the scientific thinkers were impious or anti-religious. The dominant sciences during the eighteenth century were mathematics and astronomy and for most of the practitioners these new sciences pointed to the existence of an ultimate power in the universe. The finds of scientific thought were seized upon by many as apologetic support for theism but often for a theism radically different from that of Protestant Orthodoxy. One of Newton's last undertakings was an effort to reconcile the chronology of the book of Daniel with the latest astronomical and chronological theories.

These theological implications were less significant in the total development of thought, however, than the other contribution of the sciences, namely, the practical proof of the superiority of the inductive method. Increasingly, this method began to be adopted by scholars in all areas of research, the Bible not excepted. Induction from well-established factual data instead of deduction from some authoritative *a priori* marked a veritable revolution in the patterns of thought within which the study of Old Testament religion, for one, had hitherto moved; a revolution which accounts, more than anything else, for the remarkable changes in the character of Old Testament theology witnessed toward the end of the century.

ARMINIANISM, AMYRALDISM, AND SOCINIANISM

At the same time that the sciences were creating a "new heaven and a new earth," the primacy of reason as against the authority of dogma was being asserted with ever increasing vigor in the realm of philosophical and theological reflection. With this went, almost as an inevitable concomitant, a much higher evaluation of people's natural moral powers than had been granted under the traditional views of original sin and depravity. We may detect the faint beginnings of this process in a number of seventeenth-century controversies within the Christian churches. Although in each instance the representatives of the new spirit were effectively censored, many of their ideas came back to life and in differing forms during the eighteenth century.

Two of these movements, Arminianism and Amyraldism, involved the

Reformed churches. Arminianism, the earliest revolt against the Calvinist system, had its home in Holland where humanistic tendencies and a growing mercantile way of life produced a mental atmosphere in which humanity's native abilities might be looked upon with greater favor than elsewhere. Its founder was Jacob Arminius (1560–1609), professor of theology at the University of Leiden. Included among its adherents were such outstanding men as the statesman, Johann van Oldenbarneveldt (1547–1619), and the founder of international law, Hugo Grotius (1583–1645). The Arminian position received its credal statement in the so-called "Remonstrance" of 1610 but was rejected by the Synod of Dort (1618–19) which, at the same time, reasserted the principles of High Calvinism: (1) unconditional election, (2) a limited atonement, (3) the total depravity of humanity, (4) the irresistibility of grace, and (5) the final perseverance of the saints. As a consequence of the synod's decisions, Grotius was sentenced to perpetual imprisonment and van Oldenbarneveldt beheaded on a charge of treason. For a while the Arminians were banished from the country but they later gained permission to return. As one might expect, their religious life was chiefly of an intellectual and ethical kind, betraying a friendliness towards Socinianism and the anti-scholastic philosophy of Descartes.

In their attitudes concerning the Bible Arminians were, however, strikingly akin to the orthodox party, inasmuch as they, too, asserted its exclusive authority. On the whole, their thought did not directly affect the study of Old Testament theology except as it contributed ultimately to the disintegration of Reformed Scholasticism. In one respect, it is true, their treatment of the Bible did constitute a real advance over that of more traditional practice. This we may detect most clearly in the comments or *annotationes* on the text of the Bible and Apocrypha published by Grotius (on his historical and linguistic studies, see Freiday, pp. 51–58). His notes on the biblical text like those of John Locke anticipated the later critical commentaries. His exegesis was quite scientific, for he insisted not only on the need for determining the literal sense instead of a mystical or allegorical meaning but also on the importance of explaining biblical passages historically in terms of the times and conditions in which they had originated. Although his work did not produce a sudden change in the field of Old Testament interpretation, it did act as a fermenting agent and, subsequently, played a role in the reformation of exegetical principles during the eighteenth century.

Another group of dissidents against orthodox Calvinism emerged, several decades later, among the members of the faculty at the French college of Saumur, most notable among whom were such men as Moses Amyraut (1596–1664), Joshua de la Place (1596–1655), and Louis Cappel (1585–1658). Their heterodoxy was of a relatively minor sort and featured chiefly a slightly more favorable estimate of human nature. We might pass over this school rather quickly, were it not for the third member of the trio, Louis Cappel. Although one of the most eminent biblical scholars of his day, his fame rests chiefly on his denial of the verbal inspiration of the Masoretic text of the Old Testament, a stand which was based on a minute comparison of the variants found in both manuscripts and versions and on the fact that the vowel points were not introduced until long after the beginning of the Christian era. Although his conflict, especially with the Buxtorffs, over the sanctity of the Masorah was far more spectacular, it was his contribution to the actual study of textual criticism which proved of more lasting importance (on this debate, see Allen, pp. 41–65). By applying to the Old Testament the rules developed in contemporary efforts to restore the original texts of ancient secular literature, he helped to lay the foundations of the modern study of the Old Testament text and carried out much of the preliminary spadework required before the investigations of "higher criticism" could be undertaken with any degree of confidence.

A third movement which adumbrated Rationalism was that of the Socinians (see Wilbur; Scholder, pp. 34–55). The movement had had its origins among Italian humanists of the sixteenth century, chiefly in the views of Lelio Sozzini (Socinus, 1525–62) and of his more prominent nephew, Faustus (1539–1604). Driven from Catholic territory and later from the Protestant countries, Faustus and others of similar inclinations were given refuge in tolerant Poland and there found wide acceptance. The group's doctrinal standards were laid down in the *Racovian Catechism* (1605), a document which has been described as a remarkable combination of rationalistic reasoning and hard supernaturalism. Catholic reaction, under Jesuit leadership, ultimately broke up the society, and by 1658 it was proscribed on pain of death. Some of its members migrated to Transylvania, others to East Prussia, and a number reached Holland where they helped to liberalize Dutch thought and where they came into contact with English Deists with whose views their own eventually coalesced. Socianism's assumed or actual threat to Orthodoxy can be seen in the fact that over seven hundred polemical dissertations are said to have been produced on the movement between 1595 and 1797 (Wilbur, p. 525).

Socinianism's objections to orthodox Christianity also concerned largely those ideas which had a bearing on the problem of moral living, especially those of predestination and original sin (see Tillich, pp. 288–89). Unlike the two movements previously examined, it applied the principles of free will and of a native ability to choose between right and wrong in a much more thoroughgoing fashion and, in effect, transformed Christianity into an ethical way of life. Its theology was decidedly anti-trinitarian and placed great emphasis on the humanity of Christ whose life was interpreted as one of exemplary obedience and wisdom. Accordingly, Christ's supreme work was not that of a redeemer but of a prophet and revealer of God's will. Yet, strangely enough, although they made much of humanity's moral ability, they did not take what would seem to be the next and inevitable step, namely, to make the claim of an innate human capacity for moral knowledge as well. This is not to say that they deprecated human reason, for they insisted on their right to use rational arguments in their criticism of orthodox belief and, similarly, demanded a rational interpretation of the Bible. They did, however, teach that unaided human reason could never know the will of God and thus could never guide persons in their moral life to salvation and immortality. Only by a revelation proceeding from God could such knowledge be imparted to humanity, and this knowledge was contained in Scripture alone.

On this basis they accorded the Bible a position of authority which was not very different from the point of view of other Protestant thinkers. Since the main avenue of the self-disclosure of God's will had been the life and teachings of Jesus, they were inclined to single out the New Testament as particularly divine, although they also accepted the Old Testament primarily on the testimony of the New. So determined were they in their loyalty to the Bible that they retained concepts (e.g., the Virgin Birth) and practices (Baptism and the Lord's Supper) which bore little relation to their controlling principles. Their lack of interest in the Old Testament is worth noting, particularly because it had a deep-going reason. Not being bound by a postulated notion of the uniformity of Scripture, they were free to discern real differences between the two testaments and to draw from these differences a conclusion which we shall meet again in the following centuries. That conclusion was essentially a repetition of the Marcionite heresy, for it asserted not only that the Old Testament constituted an inferior revelation but also that it had been completely abrogated. The difference between the two testaments seemed to them to be indicated by such matters as: (1) the dissimilarity of the characters of the givers of the two covenants—Moses, a sinful man, Christ, sinless and supernaturally conceived; (2) the difference in moral standards—Moses, for instance, having permitted such practices as polygamy and having laid little stress on the need for loving one's neighbors; (3) the old covenant was given for one people, while the new was universal in scope; and (4) the Old Testament's promise was only for an earthly fulfillment and contained no hope in an eternal life.

DEISM

A far more pretentious constituent of Rationalism emerged in the movement generally known as Deism. It was peculiarly at home in England (see Reventlow, 1984), and it was here that it flourished, but in the middle of the eighteenth century it gained a considerable following in France and Germany. In numerous ways it reminds one of Socinianism, although one would find it very difficult to discover anything corresponding to the Socinian estimate of Scripture. The cause for this more modest appreciation of the Bible is not too far to be sought. It is to be found in Deism's fundamental belief in the adequacy of human reason as the medium for discovering all necessary religious knowledge. The need for a revelation of God's will or purpose lost, thereby, most if not all of its urgency.

The roster of the leading Deists includes such names as John Toland (1670–1772; *Christianity Not Mysterious: or, A treatise shewing that there is nothing in the gospel contrary to reason, nor above it: and that no Christian doctrine can be properly call'd a mystery* [London: n. p. for 1st edition, 1696]), Anthony Collins (1679–1729; *Discourse of Freethinking, Occasion'd by the rise and growth of a sect call'd free-thinkers* [London: n. p., 1713]), and, particularly, Matthew Tindal (1653–1733; *Christianity as Old as the Creation, or, The Gospel, a Republication of the Religion of Nature* [London: n.p., 1730]). Their views were in part based on those of England's most renowned thinker of the closing seventeenth century, John Locke (1632–1704) whose famous *An Essay Concerning Human Understanding* (London: Thomas Basset, 1689) had asserted that knowledge could be attained only by reason, that the existence of God was demonstrated by the argument of cause and effect, that human moral knowledge was as certain as mathematical knowledge and that nothing in religion could be against reason—although he allowed that some religious beliefs might be above reason such as the belief in the resurrection of the dead. Thomas Hobbes provided another profound influence on Deism, for it adopted his mechanistic interpretation of God, an interpretation which, moreover, seemed to receive strong support from the Newtonian conception of the universe as a realm of law, created by a "first cause" and moving in an unchangeable mechanical order.

Although there were moderate and extreme Deists and a wide diversity in the movement, a number of ideas were common to all. Aside from their basic assumptions of the sufficiency of reason and of the moral goodness of humanity, one of their chief tenets asserted the existence of a universal, unrevealed, rational, and natural religion. Common to most Deists was the desire to reduce religion to its basic and universal elements and beliefs or the "common notions of mankind." Already as early as 1624, Edward Lord Herbert of Cherbury (1583–1648) in his *De-veritate* (Paris: Lutetiae) had reduced the essence of religion to five innate ideas: (1) There is a God; (2) This God ought to be worshiped; (3) Virtue is the chief element in such worship; (4) Since all fail to live up to the ideal, repentance from sin is a necessity; (5) There is another life of rewards and punishments (see Willey, 1934, pp. 119–32; Popkin, pp. 151–71). In light of these basic notions of universal, natural religion, Deism looked with disdain upon the ritual and priestly aspects of religion (and in this shared many perspectives with Spinoza).

All deists were . . . both critical and constructive. . . . All sought to destroy in order to build, and reasoned either from the absurdity of Christianity to the need for a new philosophy or from their desire for a new philosophy to the absurdity of Christianity. . . . Deism . . . is the product of the confluence of three strong emotions: hate, love, and hope. The deists hated priests and priest-craft, mystery-mongering, and assaults on common sense. They loved the ethical teachings of the classical philosophers, the grand unalterable regularity of nature, the sense of freedom granted the man liberated from superstition. They hoped that the problems of life—of private conduct and public policy—could be solved by the application of unaided human reason, and that the mysteries of the universe could be, if not solved, at least defined and circumscribed by man's scientific inquiry (Gay, p. 13).

Deists could scarcely be expected to pay much attention to the Bible as a divine and special revelation, and it is no mere accident, therefore, that the Deists were among the first groups to engage in a form of biblical criticism subjecting miracles and prophecies to merciless scrutiny (see Stephen, vol. 1, pp. 179–212; Frei, pp. 66–85). Yet, at least the early Deists did not abandon the Scriptures completely. Their usual practice was, instead, to regard it and the religious ideas contained in it as a "second edition" of the original natural religion and revelation. It had added nothing new (so Tindal); on the contrary, its real purpose was to revitalize the religion of nature for the benefit of those whose innate consciousness of it had grown dim or who were not sufficiently learned to reason matters out for themselves (Locke). Since the Deists felt no special commitment to Scripture, they made no real effort to reconstruct the development of Israelite and early Christian religion along historical-critical lines.

The efforts of the apologists for a more traditional Christianity, such as that of George Berkeley (1685–1753) and of Bishop Joseph Butler (1692–1752), the acute criticism of Deism and its opponents alike by the sceptic David Hume (1711–76), and the revival of a more evangelical piety in the form of Methodism—all brought about a decided weakening of the rather diverse Deist movement in England during the second half of the eighteenth century. By that time, however, it had already crossed over to the continent and had begun to influence Rationalist thought both in France, where it had the ardent support of the anti-Jewish Voltaire (1694–1778; see Appelgate and Schwarzbach), a strong critic and opponent of most religious thought and practices, and in Germany, where it played a role in the so-called *Aufklärung* or *Enlightenment*. In the American colonies, it could number among its adherents such men as Benjamin Franklin (1706–90), Thomas Jefferson (1743–1826), and Thomas Paine (1737–1809).

THE ENLIGHTENMENT

The interests and literature of English Deism had enormous impact in both France and Germany. Communication of English ideas occurred through the visits of continental scholars to England, through the translations of many works into German, and through the journal *Englische Bibelwerk* founded by Siegmund Jakob Baumgarten (1706–57) to keep German scholars posted on developments in England. The period which saw the invasion of deistic thought also witnessed the blossoming of German universities and the vast dissemination of information through new journals. In 1700, there were only three journals being published in Germany devoted to historical studies; by 1790 there were one hundred and thirty-seven.

German Rationalism received its first significant expression in the thought of Gottfried Wilhelm Leibniz (1646–1716). Leibniz's thought was transmitted to theological circles primarily by Baumgarten, but it remained for Johann Christian Wolff (1679–1754) to become the real leader of the movement and to achieve its wide acceptance among Germans. Wolff's theological views remind one of those held by the Deists—God is the "first cause" who has created a mechanistic universe while there are within human beings, as a part of their God-made nature, all the principles of right action needed for a virtuous life. Concepts like "miracles" had no place in his system. He permitted revelation to stand as long as it did not disagree with reason which was given a status higher than empirical experience. In fact, he sought to work out of a position in which there was a reconciliation between reason and revelation with the two seen as complementary and never antagonistic.

Moderate rationalistic philosophers and theologians sought to reinterpret many of the doctrines in terms of natural reason and thought. The German expression was far more temperate and scholarly than the English counterpart and less anti-clerical than the French. Doctrines which were considered an affront to reason, such as original sin, eternal punishment in Hell, and the Trinity, were subject to repudiation and/or reinterpretation.

A far more radical type of Rationalism began to emerge after the middle of the eighteenth century. There was no more characteristic representative of this new tendency than a Hamburg professor of Oriental languages, Hermann Samuel Reimarus (1694–1768; see Reventlow, 1965). In his youth he had traveled in England and in that country had come in touch with deistic thought. During his lifetime he was particularly concerned with the defense of natural religion against both materialism and atheism. His chief claim to fame rests, however, on his work attacking Christianity and the Bible, seven portions of which were published posthumously by the dramatist and critic Gotthold Ephraim Lessing (1729–81). These came to be known as the *Wolfenbüttel Fragmente* (1774–78). Whereas Lessing and the other moderate Rationalists regarded the essence of Christianity as synonymous with natural religion, Reimarus went farther and asserted that Christianity was totally contrary to reason. The fact that it claimed to be based on a certain specific revelation was proof enough that it could not possibly serve as a universal religion.

Furthermore, the records of that revelation were completely incredible because they had been written by persons motivated by dishonesty and fraud. The miracles in the Bible were the main target of his criticism. In the third fragment he undertakes, for example, to demonstrate that three million Hebrews with their belongings could not possibly have crossed the sea during a single night. With respect to the Old Testament, he felt that it could not be a revelation of true religion because it said nothing about a future life (see the selection in Gay, pp. 158–63).

In Germany, Reimarus's rejection of the Bible remained a solitary move. Lessing's own conception of revelation as God's means of educating the human race was more hospitable to the Bible (see Smend, 1978). He advocated the position that no dogmatic creed could be regarded as final and saw every historical religion as contributing to the development of the spiritual life of mankind. "The religion of the Bible," he argued, like Tindal (*Christianity as Old as the Creation*, p. 336), "is not true because the evangelists and apostles taught it; but they taught it because it is true" (quoted in Chadwick, p. 18). Although Lessing argued that the contingent events of history could not form the basis for the necessary truths of philosophy, he was not anti-historical since he argued that history was the arena for the progressive education of humanity. In his book on "the education of the human race" (*Die Erziehung des Menschengeschlechts* [Berlin: C. F. Voss und Sohn, 1780; for the English see Chadwick, pp. 82–98]), Lessing compared the religious education of humanity to the education of individuals. Childhood, like the Old Testament, is motivated by rewards and punishments. Youth—and the New Testament—represents the stage when individuals are willing to sacrifice present ease and lesser goods for future success and happiness. But adulthood and rational religion are ruled by duty and uninfluenced by hopes of reward or fears of punishment.

The chief reason that the point of view of the *Wolfenbüttel Fragmente* did not gain wider favor is that toward the end of the century a new shift in philosophical and theological thinking began to take place and to crowd Rationalism off the field.

Kant's Ethical Idealism

The new directions in which German thought was just starting to move when the eighteenth century came to a close resulted in part from a fundamental reorientation in the realm of philosophy itself. The change was heralded most clearly in the destructive criticism of the Wolffian system by Immanuel Kant (1724–1804) whose *Kritik der reinen Vernunft* (Riga: J. F. Hartknoch, 1781 = *Critique of Pure Reason* [London/New York: Henry G. Bohn/P. F. Collier, 1845–1901]) robbed the human mind of its so-called innate ideas and insisted that knowledge comes to the mind from without, the latter's function being simply that of classifying and organizing the information acquired in such an empirical fashion. On the surface this might appear to be a mere epistemological problem. Actually it implied also the abandonment of the Wolffian argument for God and the close bonds uniting religion and philosophy. Kant, however, succeeded in avoiding scepticism in religion by developing a new foundation for it in his *Kritik der praktischen Vernunft* (Riga: J. F. Hartknoch, 1788 = *Critique of Practical Reason* [London/Chicago: Longmanns/University of Chicago, 1881/1949]). No longer was the mind looked upon as the basis of religion. In its stead he placed, rather, an individual's moral nature. His proof for the existence of God, accordingly, was that the fulfillment of moral life demanded a "moral governor" who would ensure such a fulfillment; and, consistent with this view, he defined religion as obedience to moral commands or imperatives and advocated a "religion within the limits of reason alone."

It may come as a distinct surprise, especially to those who rightly prize the moral emphasis of the Old Testament, to discover that Kant nourished a strong dislike for Israel's Scripture (see Kraeling, pp. 51–54), in spite of the fact that the practical nature of that religion, its freedom from metaphysics, and its stress upon the absolutely binding character of moral laws would seem to agree admirably with his own system. His objections to the Old Testament all converge on one point: Judaism was not a religion but a secular community possessing a body of statutory laws. Its worldly nature, he thought, was indicated by the absence of any belief in a future life and by the restriction of rewards and punishments to the purely mundane level. He even went so far as to assert that polytheism, if it made moral requirements, would be more suitable as a religion than the worship of a God whose commands did not call for an improvement in one's moral life. One of the most important of the consequences arising from these views is to be seen in his claim that Christianity had not developed from traditional Judaism but, rather, from that portion of Judaism which had adopted a large amount of Gentile thought.

It is amazing that so acute a critic as Kant should have been so eminently unjust to the Old Testament. It is evident that what he interpreted as the essential elements in its thought were in reality what today is commonly referred to as the priestly aspects of Israel's religion. Its other achievements, those, namely, which are reflected in the teachings of the prophets, he arbitrarily removed as "non-Jewish" and, quite understandably, was left with a caricature. Kant's attitude could be dismissed as just an isolated phenomenon if it were not for the simple fact that he was actually expressing the opinion of a large number of his contemporaries. We have already seen other instances of it, for example, among the Socinians and in the thinking of Reimarus. Even Schleiermacher shared this disapprobation. Not until Hegel constructed his synthesis of the development of human thought did influential philosophers and theologians again begin to accord the Old Testament a more favorable place and to assert its superiority over the religions of nature.

A different light is, thereby, thrown upon the work of the "higher critics" of the eighteenth century. It has been commonly assumed that they were motivated in their historical-critical investigation of the Old Testament by a desire to prove the inaccuracy of traditional or dogmatic opinion. This, however, tells only a part of the story. For, although they themselves were influenced by Rationalism, in treating the Old Testament according to the accepted canons of criticism they were also endeavoring, almost as strenuously, to save it from some of their fellow Rationalists. Johann Gottfried Eichhorn (1752–1827), for example, took great pains to emphasize the significance of Israel for universal religion and pointed out against the despisers of the Old Testament that it "was destined to be the world's teacher in matters of religion and, as such, to be the patron of world religion" (*Allgemeine Bibliothek der biblischen Litteratur* [Leipzig: Weidmann, 1787–1803] vol. 1, p. 532.

Romanticism

Equally as influential as Kant's philosophy in bringing about a change in the theological atmosphere at the end of the eighteenth century was the growing inclination to trade the dryness and coldness of the Rationalist approach for the warmth and tenderness of feeling. This Romantic protest against Protestant Scholasticism and Enlightenment Rationalism extended into all areas of European culture, and religion was not excepted. Whereas, enlightened Rationalism sought the truth in universals and stressed the role of reason and thought, Romanticism concerned itself with the particulars and stressed the role of empathy, passion, and imagination. One of the first works on the Bible reflecting Romanticism's aesthetic appreciation and analysis was *De sacra poesi Hebraeorum* (Oxonii: Clarendoniano, 1753) by Robert Lowth (1711–87) which was later translated into English along with notes which had been added by the German scholar J. D. Michaelis and others (*Lectures on the Sacred Poetry of the Hebrews* [2 vols.; London: J. Johnson, 1787]). This work had greater influence in Germany, where it had been translated in 1770, than in its earlier Latin dress in England.

Another of the outstanding representatives of the new trend, Johann Gottfried von Herder (1744–1803), deserves to be mentioned particularly (see Willi). An enthusiastic writer, a creative artist, and an eloquent court-preacher, he was a man of many-sided interests, not the least of which were biblical studies themselves (see Berlin). His most noteworthy contribution in this field in his treatment of Hebrew poetry, *Vom Geist der ebräischen Poesie* (2 vols.; Dessau: Verlag-Kasse, 1782–83 = *The Spirit of Hebrew Poetry* [2 vols.; Boston/Burlington, VT: E. Smith, 1833]). In it he sought especially to show the literary beauty of the Hebrew Scriptures and to recover its elemental sublimity and its reflection of Israel's poetic and folkloric faith for an age which was distinctly inclined to search for eternal ideas in the Scripture or else inclined to look upon it as of little value. Furthermore, in his *Briefe, das Studium der Theologie betreffend* ("Letters Concerning the Study of Theology" [4 vols. in 2; Weimar: C. L. Hoffmann, 1780–81]), he used his influence to encourage the historical interpretation of the Bible, and thus became partly responsible for the increasingly common practice to recognize the Bible as a collection of religious literature to which one might apply the same canons of literary and historical criticism as employed in the study of secular writings (a position already advocated by Toland and Lessing; see Chadwick, p. 20; on Herder's hermeneutic, see Frei, pp. 183–201).

Herder's work reflects an eighteenth-century movement characterized by a revered appreciation of ancient cultures (see Tillich, pp. 372–86). While recognizing their differences from contemporary cultures, this movement did not disdain, but if anything idealized, ancient cultural forms as in the case of Jean-Jacques Rousseau (1712–78). Study of the history of classical art by Johann Joachim Winckelmann (1717–68) and the study of ancient mythology by Christian Gottlob Heyne (1729–1812) stimulated this broader appreciation and the recognition that ancient cultures might simply be different rather than inferior (see Feldman and Richardson, pp. 215–23). Thus Herder, like others of his contemporaries, called for empathic identity with the authors and literature of the past. He wrote:

> Become with shepherds a shepherd, with the people of the sod a man of the land, with the ancients of the Orient an Easterner, if you wish to relish these writings in the atmosphere of their origin; and be on guard especially against abstractions of dull, new academic prisons, and even more against all so-called artistry which our social circles force and press on those sacred archetypes of the most ancient days (quoted in Frei, p. 185).

At the same time, Herder argued that each society should be studied in its own individuality. "Each *Volk* contained the principle of its individuality within itself; it was a self-respecting monad. The Christian Pietist conception of souls equal in the eyes of God was extended to peoples throughout world history" (Manuel, in von Herder, p. xvii). The chief exponent of the Romantic movement in the field of theology, Friedrich Schleiermacher (1768–1834), was at this time already engaged in his controversy with Orthodoxy and Rationalism alike, but had as yet not profoundly affected religious thinking nor the study of biblical religion. That did not happen until the following century.

Concluding Evaluation of the Century

It is clear, as we strike the balance of this "Age of Reason," that it was by no means uniform in character. The dominant mood, to be sure, was set by the Rationalists, themselves not always single-minded. Along with them, the religious scene included both Pietists and Orthodox who were to be found in greatest numbers among the clergy and the theological teachers. To these groups we need to add the Kantians and the Romantics. All of these viewpoints left their imprint on the study of Old Testament faith and religion and gave to it a diversity which contrasts remarkably with the overall homogeneity of the work carried out in the preceding century.

We owe to Kant the most clear-cut descriptions of the entire century to be found anywhere. Two of his quotes accurately characterize the temperament of the creative thinkers of the period:

> Our age is the age of criticism, to which everything must be subjected. The sacredness of religion, and the authority of legislation, are by many regarded as grounds of exemption from the examination of this tribunal. But, if they are exempted, they become the subjects of just suspicion, and cannot lay claim to sincere respect, which reason accords only to that which has stood the test of a free and public examination (*Critique of Pure Reason*, p. 15).

> Enlightenment is man's release from his self-incurred tutelage. Tutelage is man's inability to make use of his understanding without direction from another. Self-incurred is this tutelage when its cause lies not in lack of reason but in lack of resolution and courage to use it without direction from another. *Sapere aude!* "Have courage to use your own reason!"—that is the motto of the enlightenment (Kant, *On History*, p. 3).

All of the traditional authorities were brought before the bar of reason and there subjected to the most searching examination. It was normal that religion should come in for its full share of criticism and that it should emerge from the process with new viewpoints and new patterns of thought. In this bold reconstruction carried on in complete reliance on the adequacy of both human reason and human moral ability, there was a general inclination to disregard the past unless the various earlier forms of religious life and thought could be made to agree with the new conceptions of religion's true nature. Kant's attitudes towards the Old Testament serve to illustrate this tendency and to indicate how he was almost as prone to make use of straitjackets as the dogmatism against which he so vigorously protested. The effects of this rationalistic "authoritarianism" on Old Testament theology, with all due credit for the valuable contributions which its criticism provided, were very serious and help to explain why, on the whole, the eighteenth century did little justice to Israel's religion.

DEVELOPMENTS IN OLD TESTAMENT THEOLOGY IN THE EIGHTEENTH CENTURY

The Development of Biblical Theology

As we look over the various forms which the treatment of the religion and thought of the Bible assumed in the eighteenth century, their close ties to the movements of thought of which we have just spoken impress themselves on us at almost every step. Although Rationalism finally achieved a dominant position here, too, and radiated more significant influences than the others, Orthodoxy and Pietism were also well-represented, especially during the first half of the century, and continued to be heard from even after their more aggressive opponent had started to supplant them. This explains why, for example, the "Age of Reason" was likewise the golden age of the *dicta probantia*. For the most part, theological education remained what it had been before, namely, the study of dogmatics, and under these circumstances the proof-text form of presentation had a definite value. The first German universities to abandon the old scholastic type of theological education were those of Halle and Göttingen (the latter founded in 1734). These two schools were, it is worth noting, also the ones to play the most important role in the development of biblical criticism. More striking, however, is the fact that some of the Rationalists themselves bowed to custom and gave this approach their attention. Such a pioneer in the historical and critical examination of the Bible as Johann Salomo Semler (1725–91) was, therefore, to be found among those who discussed these texts, differing from the orthodox treatment in exegesis but not in organization and form. Nor was he the only one, for Wilhelm Abraham Teller (*Topice Scripturae . . . proposita et defensa* [Lipsiae, 1761]) paid the same lipservice to a theological system which was almost the exact opposite of his own.

Nevertheless, despite this external evidence of popularity, the tide of religious opinion was actually running against these collections of proof-texts and their parent, scholastic theology. A major sign of a new spirit in the treatment of the religion of the Bible appeared in the form of several "biblical theologies" early in the eighteenth century. Whereas the older forms and references to biblical theology had denoted that form of theology which could be illustrated from the Bible, these newer biblical theologies were cautious moves toward producing what was considered the theology contained in the Bible (see Ebeling). Carl Haymann published his *Versuch einer biblischen Theologie in Tabellen* (1708) and gave printed expression to the growing conviction that church dogma and the concepts of the Bible were not always identical and that there should be a separate account of dogmatics' biblical foundation produced with some independence from dogmatic systems. This was followed by *Theologia biblica* (Wittenberg: Ludwig, 1709) by Johann Deutschmann (1625–1706) and *Collegium biblicum secundum locos theologicos adorntum* (Copenhagen: J. C. Rothen, 1726) by Franz Julius Lütkens (1650–1712).

The one feature of the new development which strikes a person at once is its bipartisan sponsorship, for its advocates came from the evangelical camp as well as from that of the Rationalists. The purposes of the two groups were, of course, decidedly different. The former's chief concern was to correct and purify the doctrines of the church by comparing them with the Scriptures, hoping, thereby, to strengthen its case in the face of the Rationalist charge that church dogma did not represent the true biblical religion. By contrast, the latter was motivated by the understandable desire to prove its opponents wrong and to show that the ideas of the Bible, especially those of Jesus, agreed with rational religion. The rationalists, Wilhelm Friedrick Hufnagel (1754–1830) (*Handbuch der biblischen Theologie* [2 vols.; Erlangen: J. J. Palm, 1785–89]) and the notorious Karl Friedrich Bahrdt (1741–92), the *bête noire* of Rationalism (*Versuch eines biblischen Systems der Dogmatik* [2 vols. in 1; Gotha/Leipzig: Heinsius, 1769–70]) followed Haymann's lead and helped to naturalize this newcomer to the theological world. Hufnagel encouraged his readers to avoid accepting traditional doctrine and scholarly opinion without serious thought about matters. He argued for reading texts for their plain meaning and that "the proof-texts must be used to correct the theological system, not the system the proof-texts" (see Dentan, p. 20).

Thus the latter half of the eighteenth century witnessed a proliferation of books and discussion of "biblical theology." The phrase, with its roots in Protestant Orthodoxy, originally had been employed to designate the collection and exegesis of biblical texts used to support orthodox dogmas. In Pietism, the idea of biblical theology or biblical thought, even if works bearing the title did not result from pietistic interests, was used to refer to the simplicity and passion of the biblical religion over against orthodox intellectualizations and dogmatic schemes. In moderate orthodox thought, it had come to mean the biblical foundation for dogmatics. Among those of strong rationalistic tendencies with sympathy for natural religion and with less supernaturalistic orientation in their understanding of revelation, biblical theology was the means for offering a religious system and approach to life as an alternative to Orthodoxy.

In 1758 Anton Friedrich Büsching (1724–93) delivered his inaugural address entitled *Gedanken von der Beschaffenheit und dem Vorzug der biblischdogmatischen Theologie vor dem alten und neuen Scholastischen* ("Thoughts on the Nature and Advantage of Biblical-Dogmatic Theology over Scholasticism Old and New"). Büsching proposed replacing dogmatic, scholastic theology with a pure biblical theology which would be itself a dogmatics (Diestel, p. 563). He felt that a biblical-dogmatic system could be produced which would render unnecessary such scholastic systems. He thus advocated biblical theology not as preparatory nor as preliminary to dogmatics but as a substitute.

In the last quarter of the century, "biblical theology" thus became such a widely used phrase until what it denoted became a matter of debate. This context forms the background to the programmatic work of the two most significant figures in biblical theology in the century—Gotthilf Traugott Zachariä (1729–77) and Johann Philipp Gabler (1753–1826). Before turning to these figures, a few remarks about general developments in biblical studies and theology are in order since they will aid in understanding both Zachariä and Gabler.

Significant Developments in Theology and Biblical Studies

In both biblical studies and theology the interests of historiography made significant impact during the second half of the eighteenth century. Historical theology and historical-critical methods had many of their roots in this period (see Hornig and Ritschl). While practically all theologians still considered the Bible to be the basis of theology and shared a general allegiance to inherited theological doctrines, historical perspectives demonstrated that doctrines were not timeless but possessed a history of development. The historical circumstances and conditions under which doctrines had risen and developed became a major concern. This produced a further erosion in Protestant Scholasticism and in the belief that the faith existed once and for all in a form given to the fathers. At the same time this relativizing of traditional faith freed theologians to present theological systems and dogmatics in terms less bound to traditional patterns.

The search for the essential elements or primary characteristics of Christianity—the fundamentals—characterized major theological debates in the late seventeenth and early eighteenth centuries in England, Germany, and elsewhere. This was the consequence of developments not only in theology proper but also in educational pedagogy.

> Since personal faith means everything in Protestantism, the distinction between *fides implicita* and *expliciata* (implicit and explict faith) is impossible for it. But then an impossible task arose: How can every ordinary farmer, shoemaker, and proletarian in the city and the country understand all these many doctrines found in the Bible, which are too numerous even for an educated man to know in his theological examinations? The answer was given by distinguishing between fundamental and non-fundamental articles. . . . Two interests were in conflict with each other. On the one hand, the interest of the systematic theologian is to increase the fundamentals as much as possible; everything is important, not only because he is writing about it, but because it is in the Bible. On the other hand, the interest of the educator contradicts this interest of the systematic theologian. The educator wants to maintain as little as possible, so that what he teaches becomes understandable. He would like to leave out all doctrines of secondary importance. In the end the educator prevails. What we find in the rationalism of the Enlightenment is largely a reduction of the fundamentals to the level of popular reasonableness. Education was partly responsible for the coming of the Enlightenment; it was a central concern of all the great philosophers of that period (Tillich, pp. 282–83).

A primary interest in Deism and its focus on natural religion was the desire to find the basic common denominators in religious thought and thus to produce a set of theological doctrines which could be universally understood and grasped. The expectation was that one of the consequences of such a system that reduced the faith to its simplest and most universal form would be an end to the squabbling and warfare over theological differences and details. In mainline Christianity, the distinction between fundamental and nonfundamental doctrines was an attempt to distinguish between those essential to the faith and those that were peripheral. Such efforts were of special interest to such English writers as Henry Hammond, John Locke, and others. Conservatives in Germany like Johann Melchior Goeze (1717–86) and Johann Lorenz von Mosheim (1694–1755) and more rationalistic liberals like Büsching and Johannes Bernhard Basedow (1724–90) sought to set out the essentials of the faith in quite contrary ways and debated the issue of the biblical basis of doctrine (see Sandys-Wunsch, 1980, pp. 1–12). Gradually it was becoming obvious that the assumed biblical foundation of dogmatics was problematic and the assumption that dogmatics was primarily the systematization of biblical ideas and doctrines was widely questioned.

In the field of biblical studies developments in philology, textual criticism, grammatical analysis, and historical criticism were being applied in exegetical work. These began to make quite clear that views and ideas often attributed to the biblical writers were in actuality not present in the texts but were read back into the texts from and for dogmatic and theological purposes and perspectives.

One reflection of the maturation of biblical study, or "higher criticism," was the great three-volume *Einleitung ins Alte Testament* (Leipzig: Weidmann, 1780–83) by Johann Gottfried Eichhorn (1752–1827). Eichhorn's work stands in the critical tradition of Old Testament introduction represented by such scholars as Richard Simon (1638–1712) and Campegius Vitringa (1659–1722). Simon's *Histoire critique du Vieux Testament* (Paris: V. Billaine, 1678 = *A Critical History of the Old Testament* [London: W. Davis, 1682]) had taken a thoroughly critical attitude toward the Scriptures, for his day, in order to demonstrate that Protestant reliance upon the Scriptures was not as reasonable a posture as Catholicism's reliance upon Scripture and the church (see Hazard, pp. 180–97 and Reventlow, 1980). By 1700, his work had gone through four Latin, two English (London: Jacob Tonson, 1682), and seven French printings but was not translated into German until later (by Semler). Campegius Vitringa's *Sacrarum observationum* (2 vols.; Franequerae: J. Gyselaar, 1683–89) and his commentaries represented a moderately critical approach by an orthodox theologian. Eichhorn's work occupied a position about middleway between these two forms of earlier seventeenth-century critical approaches to the Bible.

Another reflection is to be found in the works of Johann August Ernesti (1707–81) who, coming to biblical study from classical philology, sought to establish the rules and boundaries of hermeneutics. (Ernesti's major hermeneutical work, *Institutio interpretis Novi Testamenti* [Lipsiae: Weidmanniana, 1761], in its fifth edition, was translated into English by the American Old Testament scholar Moses Stuart (*Elements of Interpretation* [Andover: Flagg and Gould, 1822, and subsequently with various titles].) Ernesti argued that the interpreter must assign only one meaning to a text, that is, the grammatical sense or the author's original meaning. Such meaning, he concluded, could be established by focusing on the words of the text, the historical circumstances in which they were employed, and the intention of the author in his use of the words within the given historical context (see Frei, pp. 246–55). For him, the same principles of interpretation apply whether one is working with divine books (Scripture) or human books. His view of inspiration, however, as with many of his contemporaries, prevented him from postulating diversity or contradictions within the canon. Since God is consistent so must be the divine words, and therefore incompatibility of statements within the Bible are only apparent and, where these seem to appear, must be appropriately reconciled. His acceptance of the traditional authorship of the biblical books foreclosed any radical historical criticism.

If one were to single out a particular person in whom the new developments in theology, biblical studies, and historical criticism are best represented, it would have to be Johann Salomo Semler (1725–91). To be sure, the only work in which he actually undertook to deal with biblical religion theologically was, as we have already noted, merely another exposition of the *dicta probantia*. His importance derives, rather, from the service he performed in the field of exegesis. By vindicating what has since come to be known in biblical interpretation as the grammatico-historical method he helped lay the foundation for all modern research in the Scripture, including its religion (see Kaiser and Ritschl).

Coming out of a background of strictest Pietism, Semler studied at Halle. In 1753 he received an appointment as professor of theology at the same university and several years later became head of the theological faculty. His influence was both widespread and consequential in spite of the fact that he wrote in what has been called the "worst German that a German intellectual has ever written." It is not easy to fit him into any of the religious groupings which the eighteenth century produced. There can be no doubt about his Rationalism, although it was of a moderate variety. In harmony with his fellow Rationalists he was concerned for a religion which could be universally accepted, and, for this reason, his quarrel with historic Christianity was that much of its religious content was merely temporal and local. The Bible, he believed, had been "clothed in Jewish garments," and in order to discover its truth it would be necessary first to remove the ancient Jewish shell. The implications of such a view were of greatest importance. In the first place, he did not follow the more extreme Deists in their total rejection of Scripture. Instead, he took a more eclectic attitude by virtue of which he considered some parts of the Bible more valuable than others (especially the teachings of Jesus and of the Apostles). In his four-volume *Abhandlung von freier Untersuchung des Canon* ("Treatise on the Free Investigation of the Canon"; Halle: C. H. Hemmerde, 1771–75), Semler distinguished between the Word of God and the words of Scripture (a procedure already found in Spinoza) and argued "that the question of the unity of the canon is purely historical, to be determined by the consideration of each book in its own historical context and that many of the books, judged by this criterion, are clearly of purely historical and not permanent religious interest, let alone of a uniform and pervasive level of divine inspiration" (Frei, p. 161). Thus he was stimulated to pay greater attention to the conditions of the time and place from which the biblical writing had emerged. This led him not only to adopt the historical approach but also to stress it as the only valid method of interpretation. Such an approach challenges a direct understanding and direct application of the text. Hermeneutics thus becomes a two-stage affair. He wrote:

> The most important thing, in short, in hermeneutical skill depends upon one's knowing the Bible's use of language properly and precisely, as well as distinguishing and representing to oneself the historical circumstances of a biblical discourse; and on one's being able to speak today of these matters in such a way as the changed times and circumstances of our fellow-men demand. . . . All the rest of hermeneutics can be reduced to these two things (quoted in Frei, p. 247).

Thus, for him, the explication and understanding of the meaning of a text are different from the application of the text or its use in theology and dogmatics. "He says that, since Scripture is a historically situation-bound witness to revelation, the Biblical statements cannot directly become dogmatical statements" (Ritschl, p. 125).

In marked contrast to the criticism of traditional Christianity contained in his theological position, his personal religious life stood forth almost as a model of evangelical piety. It is here that the lasting effect of his pietistic upbringing shines through most distinctly. It would be a mistake, of course, to infer that he was a victim of a kind of religious schizophrenia, that he was a Rationalist in the classroom and a Pietist at home. The clue to this apparent discrepancy may well be that his conception of universal religion was grounded, ultimately, in the twin authorities of reason and feeling.

Semler's great service to biblical studies lay, not in creating the grammatico-historical method but, rather, in clarifying its nature and purpose and in demonstrating specifically how it was to be applied to the task of interpreting the writings of both testaments. All of his exegetical principles have their gathering point in the fundamental assertion that the sole meaning of any scriptural passage must be the literal or obvious one, and this, in turn, must be the one intended by the author himself. The real problem, of course, was to determine what that intended sense was, particularly because each writer lived in an age which was marked by customs, attitudes, religious and moral concepts, and living conditions differing greatly from our own. Only a careful and objective analysis of his language and of the social context of his thought can ever bridge the gap which separates him from us. All *a priori* considerations, especially those of a dogmatic or philosophical kind, must be avoided completely in the interest of such objectivity; in fact, most of the vehemence of Semler's argumentation is leveled directly at the exegetical straitjackets imposed by dogma-centered interpretation.

A Move Toward Independence in Biblical Theology: Zachariä

The first major attempt to produce a biblical theology which would stand between and differ from both exegesis and dogmatic theology is to be found in the work of Zachariä (see Sandys-Wunsch, 1980; Merk, pp. 24–27; Kraus, 1970, pp. 31–39). Educated at Halle, where he studied under Baumgarten, Zachariä was a moderate Rationalist in his acceptance of the correlation of Wolffian philosophy with orthodox theology. In exegetical method, he followed Ernesti. His major four-volume work was entitled *Biblische Theologie, oder Untersuchung des biblischen Grundes der vornehmsten theologischen Lehren* ("Biblical Theology, or an Examination of the Biblical Basis of the Principal Theological Doctrines"; Tübingen: C. G. Frank und W. H. Schramm, 1771–75; a fifth volume, edited by J. C. Vollborth [Göttingen: J. D. G. Brose], appeared posthumously in 1786). The title he gave to his work as well as his definition of his intention provide a limited clue to the nature of his work. He wrote that his purpose was "to examine and to compare the ideas of church dogma with those of the Bible, in order to determine what, in the former, is correct or incorrect." This, however, was not his only aim. He was not simply engaged in an assessment of church doctrine but hoped to present a complete exposition of biblical thought. Thus he sought to investigate the biblical materials on their own, to allow them to speak for themselves and not use them merely to express an already formulated structure of doctrines.

Zachariä initially intended to produce a biblical theology along the lines of the old "proof-text" model, that is, an exegetical commentary on the *dicta classica*. A number of factors seem to have diverted this original purpose. First of all, this proof-text approach had received increasing criticism in the 1760s, especially on the part of Basedow, for both pedagogical and theological reasons. Secondly, competent exegesis was beginning to demonstrate, to the satisfaction of many scholars, that the proof-texts frequently did not teach what was deduced from them. For example, Basedow challenged the common view that the doctrine of the Trinity was taught in Genesis 1 and 18. Thirdly, Zacharia's work was to some extent the product of his classroom instruction. At the time Göttingen, where he taught, was innovative in pedagogical and practical concerns in theology. Its academic and scholarly freedom stimulated instruction based on personal conviction rather than the routine presentation and mastery of theological compendia. Zacharia was concerned to teach and write in a form that would encourage firsthand knowledge of the Bible which teachers and clergy could transmit to their students and parishioners and which would be applicable in practical and moral matters.

Zacharia recognized that the Bible does not contain a unified, explicit theology nor is it a storehouse of clearly formulated doctrines. These must be derived from Scripture by the interpreter.

> In his discussion of how doctrine is to be derived from Scripture, G. T. Zachariae lists three ways in which a doctrine is biblical: 1) it can be contained expressly in Scripture in so many words; 2) it can be expressed in Scripture though not in the precise wording we would prefer; and 3) it is not in Scripture but can be derived from it logically. Thus the fact that the doctrine of the Trinity is not in Scripture as a precise formulation does not mean it is unscriptural and G. T. Zachariae comments that he cannot understand why this doctrine is rejected simply on the grounds that a more detailed research into Scripture is necessary to prove it (Sandys-Wunsch, 1980, pp. 15–16).

With such a position, Zacharia obviously did not produce a biblical theology that seriously challenged church doctrines.

His system of biblical theology was structured around the following outline: (1) of God, (2) of the fall and the divine arrangements established as a consequence, and (3) of the total change in the damaged human condition and the resultant conduct of Christians by means of the Christian religion. In some ways, such a scheme of thought is similar to that of Paul in Romans.

For Zacharia the primary concern of the biblical theologian was the ideas of the Bible, the unchanging concepts in their stable and abiding significance. For him as for most rationalists as well as orthodox theologians, truth and revelation were propositional. In spite of this philosophical posture and his commitment to a high view of inspiration, he was sufficiently influenced by historical criticism to recognize that the Bible must be seen in historical perspective and that there is development in the Bible since the thought of various periods of biblical history differed from one another. Some elements of one period may be relevant only for that period or at least not forever binding.

From his awareness of the historical origins of the Bible, G. T. Zachariae points out that while divine providence arranged for the Bible as a whole to be preserved for us as a sure guide, nonetheless the particular circumstances surrounding the writing of each book need to be borne in mind. Not every biblical writer thought he was writing for posterity and therefore it is not surprising that biblical books often pay more attention to the immediate problems of the day rather than to matters that concern theology generally. Thus the extent to which matters are treated in the Bible is no real guide to their importance; the Mosaic law was meant for Israel, not us; St. Paul's concern with the significance of this law is more relevant to his time than to ours (Sandys-Wunsch, 1980, p. 18).

The incidental and historically conditioned are thus to be distinguished from the abiding and the universal. Zachariä never confronts satisfactorily the problem of how one differentiates between the two. He suggests that one assume something is revelation and inspired if it comes directly from God or from a person unquestionably inspired by God but he does not propose how such qualities are determined. One gets the distinct impression that three other factors aided Zachariä in distinguishing, especially in the case of the Old Testament, the abiding from the incidental: (1) the New Testament perspectives on the Old Testament, (2) the main doctrines of the church, and (3) his own convictions and philosophical-theological positions.

A Program for an Independent Biblical Theology: Gabler

Gabler was the first to face theoretically many of the issues already present, even if not always consciously evident, in the work of his predecessors, and especially in that of Zachariä to whom he was heavily indebted (see Sandys-Wunsch and Eldredge; all quotes from Gabler are from their translation). J. G. Hofmann, one of Gabler's predecessors at Altdorf, had delivered his inaugural lecture (1770) on biblical theology but it is uncertain if Gabler utilized this work since he makes no reference to Hofmann (see Sandys-Wunsch and Eldredge, pp. 150–51). The first volume of *Handbuch der biblischen Theologie* (2 vols.; Erlangen, J. J. Palm. 1785–89) by Wilhelm Friedrich Hufnagel (1754–1830) had made its appearance shortly before Gabler's inaugural and may have at least stimulated his thinking along these lines. In his inaugural lecture (see above, pp. 2–4) and other writings, many published as notes in the three successive journals he edited, Gabler sought to outline and establish the boundaries of the various disciplinary tasks and aspects involved in the total movement from the Bible to contemporary dogmatics (see Boers, pp. 23–38; Kraus, 1970, pp. 52–59; Merk, pp. 29–140; Smend, 1962). Three distinct theological disciplines, each with its own methodology and goals, can be distinguished in his program.

(1) *A True Biblical Theology*. In his later writings, Gabler distinguished between what he called true (*wahre*) and pure (*reine*) biblical theology or

biblical theology in a broader and narrower sense. True biblical theology was to be concerned with the comprehensive presentation of the total religion of the Bible and the true sense of the authors arrived at through careful exegesis and interpretation. Such a presentation would have to be done in a historical perspective:

> That being the case it is necessary, unless we want to labour uselessly, to distinguish among each of the periods in the Old and New Testaments, each of the authors, and each of the manners of speaking which each used as a reflection of time and place, whether these manners are historical or didactic or poetic (p. 139).

For him, this meant collecting and classifying the ideas of each of these authors and periods using the ideas actually expressed in Scripture or by the interpreter's fashioning these, when they were not clearly expressed, through the comparison of passages with one another. True biblical theology was thus conceived as a purely descriptive task: a true and accurate description of the religion (= religious ideas) of the Bible in its various periods and contexts and in a systematic and historical presentation.

> If we rightly hold on to all these things, then indeed we shall draw out the true sacred ideas typical of each author; certainly not all the ideas, for there is no place for everything in the books that have come down to us, but at least those ideas which the opportunity or the necessity for writing had shaped in their souls. Nonetheless, there is a sufficient number of ideas, and usually of such a kind that those that have been omitted can then be inferred without difficulty, if they constitute a single principle of opinion expressly declared, or if they are connected to the ideas that are stated in some necessary fashion . . . but according to this rule: that each of the ideas is consistent with its own era; its own testament, its own place of origin, and its own genius (pp. 141–42).

(2) *A Pure Biblical Theology.* Biblical theology in its narrower or pure sense was conceived by Gabler as a systematic presentation of God's eternal truths or the unchanging ideas found in the Bible which were valid for all times. Here the descriptive task moves to the level of the normative task. Gabler suggested that the biblical theologian must distinguish "those things which in the sacred books refer most immediately to their own times and to the men of those times from those pure notions which divine providence wished to be characteristic of all times and places" (p. 138).

Gabler offered several factors which should be noted in isolating the timeless ideas of the Bible from the contingent and historically conditioned ideas. (a) Not all biblical writers stand on the same level:

> And so the sacred authors, however much we must cherish them with equal reverence because of the divine authority that has been imprinted on their writings, cannot all be considered in the same category if we are referring to their use in dogmatics (p. 139).

(b) Many things in the biblical materials were intended by God for only a limited historical time:

> One should investigate with great diligence which opinions have to do with the unchanging testament of Christian doctrine, and therefore pertain directly to us; and which are said only to men of some particular era or testament. For among other things it is evident that the universal argument within the holy books is not designed for men of every sort; but the great part of these books is rather restricted by God's own intention to a particular time, place, and sort of man. Who, I ask, would apply to our times the Mosaic rites which have been invalidated by Christ, or Paul's advice about women veiling themselves in church? Therefore the ideas of the Mosaic law have not been designated for any dogmatic use, neither by Jesus and his Apostles nor by reason itself (p. 142).

(c) Much in the Bible must be seen as the authors' attempts to be understood rather than the expression of timeless truths.

> By the same token we must diligently investigate what in the books of the New Testament was said as an accommodation to the ideas or the needs of the first Christians and what was said in reference to the unchanging idea of the doctrine of salvation (pp. 142–43).

(d) Universal ideas and notions are more reflective of pure doctrine than particular ideas. This criterion which Gabler "adopts from [Samuel Freidrich Nathanael] Morus [1736–92] is based on the philosophical doctrine that universal truths are more real than the particulars from which they are derived; this philosophical assumption is explicit in some of Morus' publications where he compares the process of eliciting universal truth from Scripture with the process of eliciting universals from particulars in philosophy" (Sandys-Wunsch and Eldredge, p. 156).

Gabler does not clarify fully nor demonstrate the operation of moving from true biblical theology to pure biblical theology nor does he fully explain the process of distinguishing the particular from the universal, the historical from the transhistorical, the divine from the human, the inspired from the uninspired. When he says that the Mosaic law can be of no dogmatic use since it has not been so designated "neither by Jesus and his Apostles nor by reason itself," it is clear that reason played a significant role.

(3) *Dogmatic Theology.* Once a pure biblical theology has been produced, that is, a systematic presentation of the universal and changeless ideas of biblical religion in a form understandable by reason, then this could be used by theologians in producing dogmatic systems. Unlike religion, dogmatics was didactic, "teaching what each theologian philosophizes rationally about divine things, according to the measure of his ability or of the times, age, place, sect, school, and other similar factors." Here Gabler recognizes that dogmatic theology, like *true* biblical theology, has a "chronology and geography," as he says, and "is subject to a multiplicity of change along with

the rest of the humane disciplines" (p. 137). Although he had no desire to replace dogmatics with biblical theology, even of the pure sort, Gabler was appalled at the great diversity in the dogmatics of his day, a diversity which he saw as contributing to the disunity and confusion in the church and as the object of attack from enemies outside the church.

> If I may refer to the Lutheran church alone, the teaching of Chemnitz and Gerhard is one thing, that of Calov another, that of Museus and Baier another, that of Budde another, that of Pfaff and Mosheim another, that of Baumgarten another, that of Carpov another, that of Michaelis and Heilmann another, that of Ernesti and Zachariae another, that of Teller another, that of Walch and Carpzov another, that of Semler another, and that of Doederlein finally another (p. 138).

This production of numerous and rather individualized dogmatics was a characteristic of the late eighteenth century and represented a new development in the church, and Gabler hoped that pure biblical theology would produce a great commonality in dogmatics and function as a limiting factor in dogmatic formulations.

Although Gabler never produced a biblical theology and thus never provided a demonstration of his program at work, his recognition of important factors was significant. (1) He clearly argued for biblical theology's freedom and independence from any predetermined dogmatic system. (2) He recognized the legitimacy of dogmatics and argued that dogmatics must be philosophizing about divine matters in light of both biblical perspectives and contemporary life and thought. That is, dogmatics cannot and never has operated on the principle of *sola scriptura*. (3) He recognized that for biblical thought to be available in a usable and foundational form for dogmatics there had to be an intermediate stage or stages between exegesis and dogmatic thought. (4) He affirmed that there is a vast world of difference between on the one hand biblical theology, thought, and expression, which is religious and historical, and on the other hand dogmatic theology, which is didactic and philosophical. He recognized that the latter in its various formulations is very historically time-bound and reflective of the context which gave it birth. (5) He argued that a *pure* biblical theology should provide a system of normative thought, a summation of the timeless ideas of the Bible.

Gabler's program for biblical theology did not specifically endorse a separate study of Old Testament theology. It was probably inevitable, however, that his emphasis on the distinctiveness of the various phases in the unfolding of biblical religion should contribute to the growing awareness of the peculiarity of Israel's beliefs when placed side by side with those of the New Testament. This explains why he can be regarded also as one of the founders of Old Testament theology, although he himself was concerned with a theology of the entire Bible. Since his time the arguments for a historical

treatment of Old Testament religion have generally prevailed in spite of evident disagreements concerning the form which such a historical treatment
should assume. It would also seem, if we judge his strong stress on strict
historical order and on the need for comparative study correctly, that his own
thinking was moving in the direction of a "history of religion." We find him,
therefore, not only laying the foundations for Old Testament theology as a
distinct science, but also anticipating, as it were, the "history of religion"
approach, the very one destined a century or so later to put an end, temporarily at least, to the theological presentation of the religion of the Scriptures.

The Rationalist Treatment of Old Testament Theology

Before the turn of the century, a further biblical theology and the first
strictly Old Testament theology made their appearance. The first was by
Christoph Friedrich von Ammon (*Biblische Theologie* [3 vols.; Erlangen;
Johann Jakob Palm, 1792, ²1801–2]. The second was written by Georg Lorenz Bauer (*Theologie des Alten Testaments oder Abriss der religiösen Be-
griffe der alten Hebräer von den altesten Zeiten bis auf den Anfang der
christlichen Epoche. Zum Gebrauch akademischer Vorlesungen* ["Theology
of the Old Testament or an Outline of the Religious Concepts of the Ancient
Hebrews from the Earliest Times to the Beginning of the Christian Epoch.
For the Use of Academic Lectures"; Leipzig: Weygandsche Buchhandlung,
1796]. Portions of his work were translated into English as *The Theology of
the Old Testament; or a Biblical Sketch of the Religious Opinions of the
Ancient Hebrews* [London: C. Fox, 1838]). Both von Ammon (1766–1850)
and Bauer (1755–1806) were rationalists.

CHRISTOPH FRIEDRICH VON AMMON

In 1792 von Ammon, at the age of twenty-six, published his *Entwurf
einer reinen biblischen Theologie* ("Outline of a Pure Biblical Theology";
Erlangen: Johann Jacob Palm). His biblical theology was written while he
held a chair in the theological faculty at the University of Göttingen. Later
he went to Erlangen and, finally, occupied from 1813 to the end of his life
the position of court preacher at Dresden. He was one of the most influential
and respected rationalist theologians of his day, although Schleiermacher once
accused him of religious and moral vacillation and even insinuated that he
was paying homage to a more confessional form of Protestantism merely to
safeguard his appointment as royal chaplain.

His biblical theology treats the doctrines of God, creation, and providence (volume one), messianic prophecies and the history of Jesus (volume
two), and the ennoblement and well-being (*Beglückung*) of humankind through
Jesus and the prospects of Christians in eternity (volume three).

In many respects von Ammon's treatment constituted a step backwards from the position attained by Gabler and Zachariä (see Kraus, pp. 40–51). His work was, in fact, little more than one of the old discussions of the proof-texts embellished with rationalistic and idealistic perspectives borrowed from Lessing, Semler, and Kant. From the point of view of the Old Testament his presentation was even less satisfactory than the orthodox studies, for while Orthodoxy at least accorded the Old Testament equality with the New, he dismissed what he called the "national books of the Jews" in very short order. Much of what we can expect is already implied in his own statement of the purpose motivating the work. It was to provide, namely, "a means for a better understanding of the so-called proof-texts of dogmatic theology and a manual for academic lectures on the pure theology of the Bible in consideration of the contemporary needs of this age" (I, p. ix).

In the same spirit he defined the essential nature of biblical theology as "a correct understanding . . . of those passages of Scripture from which flow the doctrines of biblical dogmatics" (I, p. 7). Much of his work consists of exegetical comments on selected biblical passages in terms of particular doctrines understood in light of Kantian moralism.

Although he called his study a theology of the Bible, the emphasis he gave to the New Testament far outweighed any consideration of the Old. By and large, when he did make use of the Old Testament, it was to demonstrate its inferiority to the teachings of Jesus or of the Apostles (I, p. 76). After explaining that the Old Testament idea of God was a nationally oriented one, he goes on to contrast it with Jesus' conception which, he argued, had stressed God's love for all people. He frankly admitted his hostile attitudes toward the Old Testament and sought to justify them in a typically rationalistic fashion. First, Israel's writings, he thought, did not meet the test of universalism, whereas the Christian ones did, and secondly, the content of the New Testament was also "more rational, more thoughtful, and more spiritual than that of the national books of the Jews" (I, p. xv). On the same page he states in terms reminiscent of Lessing that "the sacred writers had presented as revealed only what they had come to regard as reasonable." Von Ammon's dislike of the Old Testament may be traced in part to Kantian influences. He eulogized the "Kantische Hermeneutik" which he said had permitted the discovery of new truths in the Bible (I, p. xii). Obviously, under such circumstances, the contributions he made to Old Testament theology were minimal.

The close affinities to the *dicta probantia* are evident throughout his work. The outline of subjects is largely identical, and the proof-texts traditionally assigned to each doctrine are explained in the same logically disconnected manner. One major difference between this version of the proof-text method and that displayed in the scholastic works is its use of a very elementary form of historical interpretation. The passages belonging to each heading were all arranged, for example, according to their chronological sequence as understood by the critics of his day. He was aware of Eichhorn's and Ilgen's work on pentateuchal criticism (I, p. 25). More or less typical of this attention to chronological sequence is his treatment of the "existence of God" where he discussed Pss. 8:2–5; 19:2–5; Acts 14:15–17; 17:23–25; and Rom. 1:19–20 in that order (I, p. 76). In his discussion of Old Testament messianic prophecies he comments on various texts assigning them to five periods: (1) from the earliest time to Moses, (2) from Moses to David, (3) from David to Isaiah, (4) from Isaiah to the Exile and the close of the Old Testament canon, and (5) the apocryphal, Alexandrian, Samaritan, and Rabbinic period. Furthermore, his expository comments strove to embody grammatico-historical principles of exegesis, not solely for the purpose of discovering the literal meaning, but also in order to separate purely local and temporal elements from what could be considered true for everyone at all times. Since his attention was occupied for the most part with individual texts and the relationship they bore to the doctrines of Protestant theology, his historical interests were, of course, fairly limited in their scope. He was not concerned, therefore, to set forth the total development through which any particular concept had passed, nor even to achieve some kind of consciousness of the history of biblical religion in its entirety.

GEORG LORENZ BAUER

Although he died at a relatively young age, Bauer, who taught at Altdorf as professor of Rhetoric, Oriental Languages, and Morality, was a very productive scholar. He wrote a historical-critical introduction to the Old Testament (1794), a volume on Old and New Testament hermeneutic (1799), a New Testament theology (4 volumes, 1800–02), a work on biblical mythology with parallels from other cultures (2 volumes, 1802), books on biblical morality (1802–5), and numerous other works. In the preface to his Old Testament theology he states that the volume had grown out of his responsibility to lecture on the "dicta classica Veteris Testamenti," but that he had been reluctant to limit his courses simply to the task of collecting and interpreting the proof-texts of Protestant dogmatics, and that, therefore, he had been led to follow a historical discussion of Old Testament concepts with a special emphasis on their probable origin and development (see Merk, pp. 157–67).

In Bauer's estimation Old Testament theology was to consist essentially of an analysis of the stages through which Hebrew religious thought had passed. In accordance with this general purpose he divided his subject matter into two sections. In the first one, labeled Theology, he was concerned with the doctrine of God and the divine relationship to humanity and, in two appendixes, also with angels and demons. The second section was devoted to Anthropology and humanity's relationship to God and included, in turn, an appendix on Christology. Each of these major subjects he then endeavored to examine historically in terms of five different periods: (1) the earliest Hebrew religious ideas, (2) the influence of Moses, (3) the influence of subsequent sages and prophets down to the Babylonian Exile, (4) the effect of living in foreign cultures, and (5) the situation at the time of Christ. The source material he used for his survey included, in addition to the Old Testament, the Apocrypha, the Targums, the Talmud, Josephus, and Philo. The title of his book as well as the organization of his material indicate the impact which the historical approach to the Scriptures was making. In fact, Bauer later published, in response to some of his critics, a history of Old Testament religion which he divided into fourteen different periods (*Beylagen zur Theologie des Alten Testaments* ["Supplements to the Theology of the Old Testament"; Leipzig: Weygandsche Buchhandburg, 1801]).

Another sign of the new departure in Old Testament theology was that he consistently tried to compare the religious beliefs of the Hebrews with those of other ancient peoples, notably the Egyptians, Chaldeans, Persians, and Greeks. Bauer, like Gabler, was familiar with the studies of mythology by Heyne and Eichhorn (see Rogerson, pp. 1–15). In many respects his work introduced into biblical theology the materials of comparative religion.

Bauer went to considerable pains to maintain this historical approach and his work reflects the stage which literary and historical criticism had reached in his day. He was familiar with Eichhorn's differentiation between a First and Second Isaiah and between a First and Second Zechariah, but assumed that the Pentateuch was wholly Mosaic, although he granted that Moses had made use of old documents, as had the French physician Jean Astruc (1684–1766) whose work, *Conjectures sur les memoires originaux dont il paroit gue Moyse s'est servi pour composer le livre de la Genese* ("Conjectures upon the Original Memoirs Which Moses Made Use of to Compose the Book of Genesis"; Bruxelles: Chez Fricx), was published in 1753 (for an English translation of much of Astruc's volume, see *BI* 6[1836]218–26; 7[1837]23–31, 80–94). On the basis of this supposition, he posited an early pre-patriarchal and patriarchal monotheism which had then deteriorated into a polytheism from which even Moses had not been able to rescue the Hebrews. Again and again he judged the Old Testament materials by the standards of measurement contained in his rationalistic interpretation of religion. He went out of his way, for instance, to point out the mythological, legendary, or miraculous elements in the Hebrew Scriptures and to dismiss them as the superstitions of a primitive race. Another illustration appears in his treatment of the Old Testament proofs for God's existence. He pointed out that most of these proofs were grounded in divine appearance and revelations or in the fulfillment of prophecy. At the same time, he felt that the cosmological argument was preferable and quoted Kant's *Critique of Pure Reason* to the effect that this is the oldest, clearest, and most convincing proof of all. Yet, he could find evidence for this argument only in Psalms 8, 19, 104 and in Job 38–41. One might expect that he would have recognized here how different his ideas were from those of the Israelite thinkers and that, in the spirit of objectivity, he should have followed the Hebrew conceptions to their roots instead of merely taking note of them and deeming them unworthy of any further attention. In so doing, he was scarcely any better than the dogmatic theologians whom he had bitterly decried.

THE CONTRIBUTIONS OF THE EIGHTEENTH CENTURY TO OLD TESTAMENT THEOLOGY

In retrospect, the importance of the age of Semler, Gabler, and Eichhorn for the study of Old Testament theology is abundantly clear. The questioning of traditional interpretations and the emergence of an entirely new point of view made it a period of complete reorientation and heralded the beginning of developments which have lasted down to our own day. The first sign that a new era was breaking in appeared with the rise of an autonomous discipline of biblical theology. The purpose of this new science was quite simply to uncover the actual content of biblical religion without regard to any supposed *a priori* claims upon it from dogmatic theology. On the Rationalist side, first given expression in the work of Bauer, biblical theology was broken into two fairly distinct divisions, one for each of the two testaments. The reasons for this differentiation were partly a growing realization of the differences between Israel's religion and that of the New Testament and partly the rationalistic emphasis on the inferiority of the Old Testament. This anti-Hebraic bias with its ancient roots was to remain a continuing factor throughout most of the history of Old Testament theology.

The eighteenth century was responsible, likewise, for a second major characteristic of the future study of biblical religion. Whereas Orthodoxy had assumed the uniformity of the Scripture, rationalistic criticism had uncovered numerous discrepancies within biblical thought and pointed out its diversity and looked for its historical origins. In the face of these Christian faith was headed for an impossible dilemma as long as the old mode of defining the nature and unity of biblical religion remained, especially when this was supported by a high theory of the inspiration of Scripture. Men like Semler and Gabler deserve credit for recognizing this fact and for pointing to what they believed to be a possible way out of the impasse. The Bible, they held, was the product of a long process of historical development marked by certain definite stages, and the contradictions, accordingly, were to be accounted for on the basis of the increase and change in Hebrew-Jewish spiritual perception. By the same token, it followed that, in order to be valid, the treatment of biblical religion would have to be a historically conducted one.

Although the historical method thus helped to solve one difficulty, it also raised other problems. The effect of the emphasis now placed on the social-historical nature of the Bible was to humanize it and to sharpen the question of its relationship to divine revelation. This was undoubtedly the greatest issue bequeathed by the eighteenth century to its successor. The historical point of view was, furthermore, bound to focus attention on the problem of the connection between the Bible and the religions of the areas surrounding Palestine. Gabler himself, had suggested—and Bauer had carried out without apparently being directly dependent on Gabler—such comparative studies, and many more were to appear later. Finally, because of the new emphasis on the Bible's historical development and the peculiarities through which its thought had passed, the very possibility of thorough systematization became more and more problematic. The deep-going significance of this question may be judged by the fact that since Gabler the study of biblical religion has moved chiefly in two directions. One has sought to effect a compromise between a systematic and an historical method of discussion, whereas the other has felt itself increasingly forced to sacrifice systematization in favor of a purely historical description of this religion's origin and growth.

III.
OLD TESTAMENT THEOLOGY IN THE NINETEENTH CENTURY

Heinrich **Benecke**, *Wilhelm Vatke in seinem Leben und seinen Schriften* (Bonn: Emil Strauss, 1883); Theodore Dwight **Bozeman**, *Protestants in an Age of Science: The Baconian Ideal and Antebellum American Religious Thought* (Chapel Hill: University of North Carolina Press, 1977); Jerry Wayne **Brown**, *The Rise of Biblical Criticism in America, 1800–1870: The New England Scholars* (Middletown: Wesleyan University Press, 1969); Martin J. **Buss**, "The Idea of Sitz im Leben—History and Critique," *ZAW* 90(1978)157–70; Joseph Estlin **Carpenter**, *The Bible in the Nineteenth Century* (London: Longmans, Green, and Co., 1903); T. K. **Cheyne**, *Founders of Old Testament Criticism: Biographical, Descriptive, and Critical Studies* (London/New York: Methuen & Co./Charles Scribner's Sons, 1893; M. A. **Crowther**, *Church Embattled: Religious Controversy in Mid-Victorian England* (Newton Abbot/Hamden, CT: David & Charles/Archon Books, 1970); T. W. **Davies**, *Heinrich Ewald: Orientalist and Theologian* (London: T. F. Unwin, 1903); Simon John **De Vries**, *Bible and Theology in the Netherlands: Dutch Old Testament Criticism Under Modernist and Conservative Auspices 1850 to World War I* (Wageningen: H. Veenman & Zonen, 1968); Charles Coulston **Gillispie**, *Genesis and Geology: The Impact of Scientific Discoveries upon Religious Beliefs in the Decades Before Darwin* (Cambridge: Harvard University Press, 1951); Willis B. **Glover**, *Evangelical Nonconformists and Higher Criticism in the Nineteenth Century* (London: Independent Press, 1954); Hugo **Gressmann**, *Albert Eichhorn und die religionsgeschichtliche Schule* (Göttingen: Vandenhoeck & Ruprecht, 1914); Hermann **Gunkel**, "The Religio-Historical Interpretation of the New Testament," *The Monist* 13(1903)398–455; *idem*, "The 'Historical Movement' in the Study of Religion," *ExpTim* 38(1926–27)532–36; *idem*, "Biblische Theologie und biblische Religionsgeschichte: I. des AT," *RGG* 1(1927)1089–91; *idem*, *What Remains of the Old Testament and Other Essays* (London/New York: George Allen and Unwin/Macmillan, 1928); Herbert F. **Hahn**, *The Old Testament in Modern Research* (London: SCM Press, 1956); Walter **Kaufmann**, *Hegel: A Reinterpretation* (Notre Dame: University of Notre Dame Press, 1978): S T **Kimbrough**, Jr., *Israelite Religion in Sociological Perspective: The Work of Antonin Causse* (Wiesbaden: Otto Harrassowitz, 1978); Werner **Klatt**, *Hermann Gunkel: Zu seiner Theologie der Religionsgeschichte und zur Entstehung der formgeschichtlichen Methode* (Göttingen: Vandenhoeck & Ruprecht, 1969); Douglas A. **Knight** (ed.), *Julius Wellhausen and His Prolegomena to the History of Israel* (Chico: Scholars Press, 1983); William A. **McKane**, *Studies in the Patriarchal Narratives* (Edinburgh: Hansel Press, 1979); George Foot **Moore**, "Christian Writers on Judaism," *HTR* 14(1921)197–254; Robert A. **Oden**, Jr., "Hermeneutics and Historiography: Germany and America," *Society of Biblical Literature 1980 Seminar Papers* (ed. by

Paul J. Achtemeier; Chico: Scholars Press, 1980)135–57; Lothar **Perlitt**, *Vatke und Wellhausen. Geschichtsphilosophische voraussetzungen und historiographische Motive für die Darstellung der Religion und Geschichte Israels durch Wilhelm Vatke und Julius Wellhausen* (Berlin: Alfred Töpelmann, 1965); Christian **Preus**, "The Contemporary Relevance of von Hofmann's Hermeneutical Principles," *Int* 4(1950)311–21; J. W. **Rogerson**, *Old Testament Criticism in the Nineteenth Century: England and Germany* (London/Philadelphia: SPCK/Fortress Press, 1984); John **Sandys-Wunsch**, "G. P. C. Kaiser; La theologie biblique et l'histoire des Religions," *RHPR* 59(1979)391–96; E. S. **Shaffer**, *'Kubla Khan' and the Fall of Jerusalem: The Mythological School in Biblical Criticism and Secular Literature 1770–1880* (Cambridge: Cambridge University Press, 1975); Rudolf **Smend**, *Wilhelm Martin Leberecht de Wettes Arbeit am Alten und am Neuen Testament* (Basil: Helbing & Lichtenhahn, 1958); *idem*, "De Wette und das Verhältnis zwischen historischer Bibelkritik und philosophischen System im 19. Jahrhundert," *TZ* 14(1958)107–19; *idem*, "Universalismus und Partikularismus in der Alttestamentliche Theologie des 19. Jahrhunderts," *EvTh* 22(1962)169–79; *idem*, "Heinrich Ewalds Biblische Theologie," *Festschrift für Wolfgang Trillhaas* (ed. by H. W. Schütte and F. Wintzer; Göttingen: Vandenhoeck & Ruprecht, 1974)176–91; *idem*, "Wellhausen und das Judentum," *ZTK* 79(1982)249–82; Karl Gerhard **Steck**, *Die Idee der Heilsgechichte: Hofmann, Schlatter, Cullmann* (Zollikon: Evangelischer Verlag, 1959); S. W. **Sykes** (ed.), *England and Germany. Studies in Theological Diplomacy* (Frankfurt: Peter D. Lang, 1982); R. J. **Thompson**, *Moses and the Law in a Century of Criticism Since Graf* (Leiden: E. J. Brill, 1970); Ernst **Troeltsch**, "The Dogmatics of the 'Religionsgeschichtliche Schule,'" *AJT* 17(1913)1–21; *idem*, "Historiography," *ERE* 6(1914)716–23; Walther **Zimmerli**, *The Law and the Prophets: A Study of the Meaning of the Old Testament* (Oxford/New York: B. H. Blackwell/Harper Torchbooks, 1965/1967).

THE MAJOR MOVEMENTS OF THEOLOGICAL THOUGHT

General Character of the Century

Following the pattern of the preceding chapter, we shall begin this treatment of the nineteenth-century developments in Old Testament theology with a survey of the major theological movements of the period since these strongly impinge on all aspects of biblical studies. Concerned as it primarily is with furnishing a picture of the chief religious and philosophical tendencies which affected the course of Old Testament theology during the nineteenth century, the ensuing sketch is frankly eclectic. In the first place, it is heavily weighted in favor of German Protestantism for the simple reason that, with a few exceptions, all the major innovative work in this field was done in Germany. Furthermore, even within German Protestant thought only those elements will come into our purview which have had an outstanding bearing on our subject matter. Only in so doing has it seemed possible to maintain a proper balance between the rich variety of this century's contributions and the purpose of the present study.

Theologically speaking, the nineteenth century may be best understood as a period of reconstruction, made mandatory by the breakdown of Protestant Orthodoxy as well as by the repudiation of the rationalistic theology which had been the chief agent of Orthodoxy's collapse. The forces destined to fill the vacuum left by the dissolution of these previous thought patterns were extremely varied. Romanticism, Idealism, the impact of the findings of the natural and the newly created social sciences, the heightened interest in non-Christian cultures and religions, a mounting attention to the problem of applying Christian social principles, in addition to at least one determined effort to revive Lutheran confessionalism—all these explain why the theological picture presented by this century takes on the color and variety of a kaleidoscope. Even Rationalism and Pietism, in some academic circles, continued for a while to live on and to make their influence felt.

Schleiermacher

The most important theologian at the beginning of the century was indisputably Friedrich Daniel Ernst Schleiermacher (1768–1834), one of the towering giants in the history of theological studies. Reared in a home of pronounced pietistic inclinations, he had consecutively come under the spell of Wolff, Plato, Spinoza, Kant, and the Romantics. In 1810 he was installed as the first professor of theology at the new University of Berlin. His mature thought was set forth in his *magnum opus, Der christliche Glaube* (Berlin: G. Reimer, 1821–22 = *The Christian Faith* [Edinburgh: T. & T. Clark, 1928]), but his fundamental ideas had already found expression in a much earlier work, originally published anonymously, *Über die Religion, Reden an die Gebildeten unter ihren Verächtern* (Berlin: J. F. Unger, 1799 = *On Religion: Speeches to Its Cultured Despisers* [London: K. Paul, Trench, Trübner & Company, 1893]). Rejecting the authority of dogma, scriptural revelation, and reason alike, he located the heart of his system in the Christian religious experience itself, of which he considered the essential ingredient to be a "feeling of being absolutely dependent, or, which is the same thing, of being in relation with God" (*The Christian Faith*, p. 12). He may be described as a Romantic in his emphasis on feeling, as bordering on being a pantheist in the importance he gave to divine immanence, and as a mystic who regarded the aim of all religion to be an immediate union between God and people. In his *Speeches* he describes this mystical union as "the holy wedlock of the Universe with the incarnated Reason for a creative, productive embrace. It is immediate, raised above all error and understanding. You lie directly on the bosom of the infinite world. In that moment you are its soul" (p. 43). He was an individualist who nevertheless valued the church as a fellowship of kindred sprits. He believed that by founding theology on religious experience he had placed Christianity upon a firm foundation from which neither changes in the realm of thought nor new discoveries in the realm of science could ever shake it. Christ, himself the embodiment of the immediate union between God and humanity, he considered to be the mediator of this reconciliation to others. Little wonder that this theology was strongly Christocentric.

The implications of his views for Old Testament theology are evident (see Kraeling, pp. 59–67; Kraus, 1970, pp. 210–20). The Scripture had no prior claim on Christian faith and certainly was not to be used as the source material of Christian doctrine. Its only authority was a derived one, valid insofar as it reflected the central religious experience of communion with God. With this rule to guide him his interest in the Bible was confined chiefly to the New Testament. Like Kant, he did not regard the Old Testament very highly and for the same reasons. He disliked its religion because of its basis in the external authority of law and commandment and, in addition, criticized its nationalistic particularism which, by limiting the divine love to Abraham's tribe, he felt was little better than fetishism. He recognized the historical connection between Christianity and Israel's faith, but, at the same time, also insisted that Christianity was just as close to paganism as to Judaism. Some have seen this antipathy toward the Old Testament as a reflection of his strong classical education and his failure to have studied any Semitic language.

Writing as a Christian theologian, Schleiermacher argued that Christian theology should not be based on the Old Testament since overall its content does not reflect the level of Christian teaching.

> Even the noblest Psalms always contain something which Christian piety is unable to appropriate as a perfectly pure expression of itself, so that it is only after deluding ourselves by unconscious additions and subtractions that we can suppose we are able to gather a Christian doctrine of God out of the Prophets and the Psalms. . . . Further, the history of Christian theology shows only too clearly on the one hand how gravely this effort to find our Christian faith in the Old Testament has injured our practice of the exegetical art, and how on the other it has submerged the later development of doctrine and the controversies regarding its more exact definition under a flood of useless complications. Thus a thoroughgoing improvement is only to be looked for when we utterly discard Old Testament proofs for specifically Christian doctrines, preferring to put aside what chiefly rests on such support (*The Christian Faith*, pp. 609–10).

He argued that in spite of the presence of the Old Testament in the Christian canon, it cannot be assigned a normative function and even its presence in the canon can be best understood as the result of certain historical factors. His position was summarized in his heading to § 132 of *The Christian Faith*:

> The Old Testament Scriptures owe their place in our Bible partly to the appeals the New Testament Scriptures make to them, partly to the historical connexion of Christian worship with the Jewish Synagogue; but the Old Testament Scrip-

tures do not on that account share the normative dignity or the inspiration of the New.

For Christians, the Old Testament must occupy a very subordinate position.

Historical fidelity and completeness of view demand that what Christ and His first preachers appealed to should be preserved. This, however, scarcely covers more than the prophetic books and the Psalms; which would justify the practice of adding these to the New Testament as an appendix. But in the time of Christ these books did not exist separately, but only as parts of the sacred collection; they are often cited exclusively in that character; certain quotations, moreover, occur from other books. Hence, although for us the Old Testament cannot be an indivisible whole as it was for the Jews, there can be no objection to its being added in its entirety to the New Testament. None the less, the real meaning of the facts would be clearer if the Old Testament followed the New as an appendix, for the present relative position of the two makes the demand, not obscurely, that we must first work our way through the whole of the Old Testament if we are to approach the New by the right avenue (*The Christian Faith*, p. 611).

The result of this indifference and near hostility toward the Old Testament in a man of his significance was tremendous. Neither he nor those who accepted his leadership saw any real value in according Old Testament theology a place among the other theological disciplines and so prevented the forces of reconstruction and regeneration, in evidence everywhere else, from affecting it. It is not strange, therefore, that during the first third of the century Old Testament theology made little or no advance and had primarily the attention of only the traditional Supernaturalists and of the Rationalists.

Schleiermacher's contribution was, however, somewhat constructive in a different direction. Since the test whereby the worth of religion could be determined was its effectiveness in bringing about the union between God and humans, he believed that the various religions should not be divided into true and false ones, but according to the degree to which they accomplished this main purpose. Although he accepted the superiority of Christianity, he also showed a great interest in the non-Christian religions in the sense that he regarded them, too, as manifestations of the immanent God to the human consciousness. The stimulus he gave to the historical and comparative study of religion was, for this reason, very pronounced and helped to pave the way for an evergrowing acceptance of what eventually was to become the historical and genetic treatment of Old Testament religion.

Hegelianism

Schleiermacher's influence extended far and wide. Its effect appeared most prominently in the so-called "Mediating School" (Johann August Wilhelm Neander [1789–1850], Friedrich August Gottreu Tholuck [1799–1877], Isaak August Dorner [1809–84], and others) and, to a lesser degree, among the Ritschlians. It was by no means, however, the only force at work in the theological world. Almost concurrently with Schleiermacher's career at the University of Berlin, the most important philosopher of the first part of the nineteenth century was teaching there as well. Georg Wilhelm Friedrich Hegel (1770–1831), as an absolute idealist, stood in a philosophical tradition which went back by way of Friedrich Wilhelm Joseph von Schelling (1775–1854) and Johann Gottlieb Fichte (1762–1814) directly to Kant but was also influenced by Johann Christoph Friedrich von Schiller (1759–1805) and Johann Wolfgang von Goethe (1749–1832). His thought gained peculiar form from the dialectical logic upon which it was based. It presented the process of reflection in a continuous movement leading from one idea (thesis) to its opposite (antithesis) and, hence, to a higher union of both (synthesis). The newly gained insight became another thesis to be superseded by another synthesis, and so forth. The ultimate ground for this logic he discovered in human experience itself, the rhythmic pattern being evident in the career of all things: scientific concept, literary movement, national policy, religious creed, political institution, economic system, or philosophical principle.

Hegel's metaphysics, accordingly, represented the universe as a constant development of the Absolute, or God, through struggle and effort. True to his Idealism, he interpreted this Absolute to consist of Spirit or Mind (the German word *Geist* carries both meanings) in which all of reality including matter was embraced. Everything that happened, therefore, tended to occur in conformity to laws of thought, the same laws, namely, which we have come to know as dialectical logic. For example, spirit, the thesis, and matter, the antithesis, unite in a synthesis, the human being, who is a union of both.

It is plain that the notion of development occupied a very important position in his system, although it should also be clear that he characterized it as a dialectical process. For this reason, history very naturally was one of his favorite subjects by which he again and again sought to shed light on the validity of his whole point of view. Considerable distortion of fact and a narrow perspective enabled him to reduce universal history to the following sort of triadic sequence.

> Of world history . . . it may be said that it is the account of the spirit, how it works to attain the *knowledge* of what it is *in itself*. The *Oriental* peoples do not know that the spirit, or man as such, is free in himself. Because they do not know it, they are not free. They only know that *one* is free; but for that very reason such freedom is merely arbitrariness, savagery, dimness of passion, or at times a gentleness, a tameness of passion which is also a mere accident of nature or arbitrariness. This *one* is therefore only a despot, not a free man, a human being.
>
> Only in the *Greeks* did the consciousness of freedom arise, and therefore they were free; but they, as well as the Romans, knew only that some are free, not man as such. Plato and Aristotle did not know this; therefore the Greeks

did not only have slaves, and their lives and the subsistence of their beautiful freedom were tied to this, but their own freedom, too, was partly only an accidental, undeveloped, ephemeral and limited flower, partly at the same time a harsh servitude of man, of what is humane.

Only the *Germanic* nations [the Protestant nations of northern Europe] attained the consciousness, in Christianity, that man as man is free, that the freedom of the spirit constitutes his most distinctive nature. This consciousness arose first in religion, in the inmost region of the spirit; but to build this principle also into the affairs of this world, this was a further task whose solution and execution demands the long and hard work of education. With the acceptance of the Christian religion, slavery, e.g., did not stop immediately; even less did freedom immediately become dominant in states, or were governments and constitutions organized rationally and founded on the principle of freedom. This application of the principle to worldly affairs, the penetration and permeation (*Durchbildung*) of the worldly condition by it, that is the long process which constitutes history itself (*Die Vernunft in der Geschichte*; tr. in Kaufmann, pp. 249–50).

Entirely aside from the question of the truthfulness of such a reading of history, there is one implication of his attitude toward history worthy of note. Each phase of humanity's historical experience, while ultimately displaced by another, higher one, is at the same time a part of the new synthesis. Every age was thus recognized to have a real importance for its successor and, hence, finally also for the present, not simply because it happened to belong to the development out of which the present has emerged, but rather, because in some measure it constituted a genuine ingredient of the present. Thus Hegel did much to stimulate an interest in and an appreciation of all past forms of human life and thought, especially in the matter of discovering the inner principles by which each was governed.

This explains partially at least why Hegel's influence played a prominent role in the nineteenth century's treatment of Old Testament theology. When applied to the Old Testament, his views effectively vindicated its place within Christianity, and it is no accident, therefore, that Wilhelm Vatke, to name but one of his disciples, devoted himself to the study of its religious thought with a zeal and an understanding far above anything shown by either the Rationalists or Schleiermacher's followers.

There is, however, an additional and an even more important reason for the concern of the Hegelians with Old Testament theology. Hegel had used his dialectical scheme to classify the world's religions and to rank them in an ascending scale of value. According to him, at first religion had been nature worship. This, in turn, had given way to religions in which God had taken on individuality, particularly among the Hebrews, Greeks, and Romans. The whole process had, in the end, found its completion in the absolute religion, Christianity, where God and Nature had been combined in the incarnation. The Hebrew conception of God, he thought, had been characterized by the idea of *sublimity* (*Erhabenheit*) because of its peculiar stress on the separation of God from the world. Greek and Roman religions, for their part, had shown equally distinctive features, the one having its center in the idea of beauty, the other in that of utility (*Zweckässigkeit*). It is typical of his liking for classical culture that Hegel considered both of these superior to the religion of the Hebrews, a bias which some of his followers subsequently sought to correct by demonstrating how close the Greeks and the Romans had actually remained to nature worship. Even so, his views had two significant results. By assigning Hebrew faith to the second level of development, he in effect recognized it as an essential presupposition of Christianity itself. Similarly, in singling out the concept of sublimity, he also sought to provide a clue to this religion's innermost nature and thereby suggested lines of investigation which were to advance the study of Old Testament theology very appreciably.

Hegel's philosophy, as a rounded interpretation of experience, did not outlive him by many years. This was especially true in Germany where the major philosophical and theological tendencies later moved into other directions. Nevertheless, certain of his ideas continued to exert an influence long after the parent system had ceased to find widespread acceptance. His dialectical logic, for instance, through the medium of Ludwig Feuerbach (1804–72), was put to a completely new use in the philosophy of Karl Marx (1818–83). In addition, his interest in history ultimately gained an echo in the *Historismus* of the Christian social philosopher, Ernst Troeltsch (1865–1923).

The Conservative Reaction:
Hengstenberg and von Hofmann

At about the same time that Schleiermacher and Hegel were dominating the liberal wing of German theological thought, the conservative side, in turn, was undergoing a strong transformation as well. The expression of this change was a strong revival of Lutheran orthodoxy and a return to the historic creeds. Side by side with these "Confessionalists," as they are commonly called, a second group of theologians, connected chiefly with the University of Erlangen and, hence, known as the "Erlangen School," attempted to revitalize Lutheran thinking in a somewhat less confessional manner by what they considered to be a Bible-centered approach and by a singular emphasis on the Christian experience of rebirth.

The first of the conservative movements just listed arose during the time of reaction and German national renewal which followed the downfall of Napoleon, although some of the ardor displayed by its adherents derived from their opposition to the union between Lutherans and Calvinists proclaimed in Prussia under governmental sponsorship in 1817—the three-hundredth anniversary of the inauguration of the Lutheran Reformation. Still reeling from the blows it had received at the hands of the Pietists and the Rationalists alike, Lutheranism had entered the nineteenth century with an almost complete loss of its distinctive character. To some the situation appeared to call for a revival of the orthodox or confessional position with all its stress on the creeds, the regular use of the sacraments, the authority of the church, and ecclesiastical discipline. Several important results of this new concern with the past were a fresh study of Luther's life and thought and a republication of his works in the so-called *Erlanger Ausgabe* (1826 and succeeding years).

From the point of view of Old Testament studies one person deserves special mention. He is Ernst Wilhelm Hengstenberg (1802–69) who, as a member of the theological faculty at the University of Berlin and as the founder and editor of the journal *Evangelische Kirchenzeitung*, occupied a place which enabled him to wield an extraordinary influence (see Kraus, 1969, pp. 222–26). He had been appointed to the Berlin post succeeding the liberal de Wette after the latter was dismissed for expressing sympathy for a political assassin.

The clearest expression of Hengstenberg's ideas is found in a work entitled *Die Christologie des Alten Testaments* (4 volumes; Berlin: L. Öhmigke, 1829–35 = *Christology of the Old Testament and a Commentary on the Messianic Predictions* [4 volumes; Edinburgh: T. & T. Clark, 1854–58]) in which he sought to throw light from the Old Testament on the confessional doctrines about Christ. Except for a brief concluding section which deals with such subjects as "Importance of the Messianic Prophecies," "The Divinity of the Messiah in the Old Testament," and "The Suffering and Atoning Christ in the Old Testament," the bulk of his work—fully seven-eighths—was given over to exegetical studies of passages traditionally thought to contain messianic prophecies, all the way from the *Protoevangelium* in Gen. 3:15 to Mal. 4:5. As might be expected, a large number of his assumptions and ideas are those which we have come to associate with earlier Lutheran orthodoxy. The Bible is fully inspired Scripture, the two testaments, therefore, are on the whole of equal value, and Christian doctrine may be found in completed form throughout. The kinship which he shows, both in method and in viewpoint, to the proof-text theologies of the scholastic period is, in other words, unmistakable. Needless to say, he was also one of his day's most outspoken opponents of the newly emerging historical-critical treatment of the Bible, and his *Christology* clearly intended to combat the interpretations of various critics who challenged the conclusion that the Old Testament taught a doctrine of the vicarious atonement of a suffering and dying messiah.

It is a striking fact that this resurgence of Lutheran orthodoxy and revivalism did not join in the efforts to treat the theology of the Old Testament. The most likely explanation for this is that the group's primary interest was always focused on church doctrine instead of on the Bible and thus on a defense of the conservative reading of the Bible against its interpretation by the critics. By contrast, the Erlangen School with its avowed biblicism offered a much more congenial atmosphere for the study of biblical theology. An examination of its ancestry reveals that it bore its closest affinities to Pietism. One of its acknowledged forebears was J. A. Bengel, the Swabian Pietist of the previous century. Among its leaders it counted such men as Gottfried Thomasius (1802–75), F. R. von Frank (1827–94), and Adolf von Harless (1806–79). Its guiding spirit, however, was Johann Christian Konrad von Hofmann (1810–77) in whose important works, *Weissagung und Erfüllung im alten und neuen Testamente. Ein theologischer Versuch* ("Prophecy and Fulfillment in the Old and New Testaments. A Theological Investigation"; "Nördlingen: C. H. Beck, 1841–44) and *Der Schriftbeweis. Ein theologischer Versuch* ("The Proof of Scripture. A Theological Investigation"; Nördlingen: C. H. Beck, 1852–56), the movement's fundamental line of thinking received its clearest formulation.

The last named of the two works, in accordance with von Hofmann's dominant emphases on regeneration and the need for a biblically oriented theology, consisted basically of a statement of the pietistically conceived doctrine of rebirth, which he then undertook to prove copiously from the Bible, Old and New Testament alike. This concern to root all his ideas in the Scripture finds expression also in his *Weissagung und Erfüllung*. His general approach to biblical interpretation can be seen in his *Biblische Hermeneutik* (Nördlingen: C. H. Beck, 1860 = *Interpreting the Bible* [Minneapolis: Augsburg Publishing House, 1959]).

The theme of much of his work was the unity of the Bible, the integrating principle being defined in terms of a divinely guided history of redemption, a *Heilsgeschichte*, which had as its ultimate goal the establishment of the kingdom of God (see Steck; Kraus, 1969, pp. 209–41, 1970, pp. 240–53). The Old Testament contained the prediction or foreshadowing, in ever increasing intensity, of the fulfillment of God's purpose in the salvation eventually brought about in Christ. Its religion, in turn, he characterized as a progressively revealed saving truth which, it is important to note, was to be found not in the actual teachings of the Old Testament but, rather, in the events heralding the realization of the kingdom of God. Some quotes from his *Interpreting the Bible* demonstrate his approach:

> We divide the study of the Old Testament into two different subjects, Old Testament History and Old Testament Theology. The former reproduces the series of events recorded in the Old Testament as a continuous history. The latter describes the history of the proclamation of salvation implied in that history. The former one teaches the intrinsic connection of the revelatory facts, the latter one that of the divine revelation by Word. While in both disciplines the understanding of the Bible as the document of salvation must precede its

historical interpretation, yet the latter cannot be dispensed with either. The records of those events demand to be read as the record of the realization of actual salvation, yet of one which tends towards its full realization. . . . The history recorded in the Old Testament is the history of salvation (*Heilsgeschichte*) as proceeding towards its full realization. Hence the things recorded therein are to be interpreted teleologically, i.e., as aiming at their final goal; and thus as being of the same nature as the goal yet modified by their respective place in history (pp. 134–35).

Scripture is not a text book teaching conceptual truths but rather a document of an historical process, and . . . has originated within the history recorded therein. This fact implies that the Biblical witness of salvation partly records things past, partly refers to things present, partly foretells things future (p. 204).

The historical fact of salvation in Christ had an historical preparation; and . . . the Biblical proclamation of salvation originated step by step in the course of Holy History (*Heilsgeschichte*). As a result of these facts, the process of salvation itself and the Biblical witness concerning it are to be differentiated (p. 236).

We must always ascertain the viewpoint in Holy History from which the narrative has been told, in order to be able correctly to evaluate both the arrangement of the narrative as a whole and also the significance which its details have for the whole. By doing so we shall understand not only why these features of the narrative were selected but also why this manner of presentation was chosen (p. 210).

The suggestiveness of much of von Hofmann's thought is apparent. In many respects one is reminded of the views introduced into the seventeenth century by the covenant or federal theology of Johannes Cocceius. We might single out, because they seem to have more than ordinary value, such points as the idea of a progressive revelation, the interpretation of Israel's history as a history of redemption, the really novel concept of revelation through the medium of historical events, and his serious concern to discover the inner unity of the Bible.

The translator of his only work to appear in English, Christian Preus, has described von Hofmann in the following manner:

With orthodoxy he saw that the interpreter must operate within the traditions and confessions of the Church. With the critical schools he taught that the interpreter must employ proper methods of literary and historical criticism, and he showed that such studies need not be destructive to faith. With pietism he agreed that the interpreter must himself be a man of faith; and with Schleiermacher he held that the personal religious experience of the individual is indispensable for a congenial understanding of the Scriptures. From the reformers he learned that the testimony of the Holy Spirit in the Scripture, in the Church, and in the life of faith is basic for a genuine appreciation of Revelation (*Interpreting the Bible*, p. xiii).

This description highlights the fact that von Hofmann was influenced by and granted concession to many of the major theological and philosophical currents of his day. One other point however must be stressed. He recognized the impact of historical studies on biblical interpretation and seized\ upon history (*Heilsgeschichte*) as the clue to understanding both divine revelation and the Bible. As a student of Leopold von Ranke (1795–1886), von Hofmann was interested in empirical history, the actual course of events,which in the biblical tradition he read as a story of salvation. Nonetheless, he placed the Bible and its story in a respected position and refused to apply to it the rigorous methodology which von Ranke applied to his sources. Only those who had really experienced the new birth through Christian faith could really sense and identify with the biblical story as a *Heilsgeschichte* with Christ at its center.

Ritschlianism

Despite their undeniable liveliness, these conservatives, among whom one may also count Michael Baumgarten (1812–89) and Franz Julius Delitzsch (1813–90), never lost what can be called their sectarian coloring. The dominant theological mood of the century, particularly as it progressed into its second half, was simply against them. That mood was distinguished by its thoroughly empirical orientation and by its reinterpretation of religion in terms of its social value. The task of theology, under these new circumstances, was not to exhibit the content of a divinely revealed body of truth but, rather, to explain the Christian religious experience and view of life. The importance attached to human social relationships, in turn, had their deepest effect on the concept of salvation. The redemption of humanity, so long considered a matter of the individual soul, came to be understood in social terms. The resultant interest in the present social and moral salvation of humanity correspondingly reduced the preoccupation with any future deliverance, especially in the form of an apocalyptic eschatology such as that with which von Hofmann had been concerned.

This concern with social issues, classes, and institutional structures over against concern with the individual and the unique can be seen in many areas: in the rise and impact of the social sciences such as anthropology, sociology, and ethnology, in the writings of Karl Marx (1818–83) and Nikolai Lenin (1870–1924), and in the roots of the "social gospel" later to be popularized by Walter Rauschenbusch (1861–1918).

This mood of the late nineteenth century found one of its clearest theological expressions in the thought of Albrecht Benjamin Ritschl (1822–89). Successively a Pietist, an Hegelian, and the author of a system which was sufficiently distinctive to merit being called an independent position, this professor of theology at Göttingen (from 1864 to his death) undoubtedly molded the theological life of Germany, England, and America more than any other individual of his day. His *magnum opus* was *Die christliche Lehre von der Rechtfertigung und Versohnung* (3 vols; Bonn: Adolph Marcus, 1870–74 = *The Christian Doctrine of Justification and Reconciliation* [2 vols.; Edinburgh: T. & T. Clark, 1872, 1900]). The title is somewhat misleading, for the work was more than a mere discussion of the doctrine of justification. Actually it set forth a complete system of theology grouped around this teaching. Traditionally, the usual procedure, from the days of the medieval schoolmen on, had been to begin with the doctrine of God and, thence, to move on to an exposition of the doctrines of humanity, of sin, and of salvation. This order Ritschl reversed in perfectly empirical fashion. He started with the facts of Christian experience, such as sin, the consciousness of forgiveness, the awareness of a restoration of the power of goodness, the gift of love, and a confidence that this life is not all. To this consciousness of salvation he then related all other topics of Christian belief.

In a survey of this nature it is unnecessary to dwell on Ritschl's peculiar epistemology which made religious knowledge a matter of value judgments (*Werthurteile*), but it is important to gain an understanding of the place he and his followers accorded the Bible in their theology. Humanity, sick with sin, has had an historical demonstration of the way by which sin may be overcome, namely, through the person of Jesus. This same personality, of whose effect on the lives of those about him there can be no doubt, still seizes and uplifts people today and makes it possible for them to partake with him in the highest good through their full surrender to God and their life and love for their fellows. The life and spirit of the historical Jesus thus assumed central significance in the Ritschlian school.

The implications of this position for the status of the Bible are evident. The divine revelation was provided in the person of Jesus of Nazareth and not in the book which constitutes the Christian Bible. The latter is only a record mediating a knowledge of Jesus. The New Testament is more important than the Old because it contains the account of his life and of the impression he left upon his immediate followers. Yet, the Old Testament, too, has value because it furnishes information about his social and religious background. To understand the religious consciousness presented in the Bible one need have no recourse to a theory of inspiration. All that is actually required is a strictly historical and inductive investigation. The Ritschlian approach stressed the practical and ethical essence of religion, and its biblical research centered on those basic ideas of practical religion especially as they found embodiment in the teachings of Jesus. In many ways, it was both unphilosophical and anti-philosophical and was a halfway house between radical historical criticism and a naive acceptance of the biblical documents as completely historically reliable.

Ritschl's theology thus offered a rationale for the purely historical treatment of biblical religion. Not a theology of the Old Testament, for instance, but a history of Israel's religious life and thought was what seemed to be really necessary.

The Natural and Social Sciences

For all its effort to express the essence of Christian faith in a form acceptable to the point of view and interests of the intellectual life which had gradually emerged in the nineteenth century, Ritschlianism was never more than a "middle of the road" movement, another "mediating" school, trying to hold in balance traditional supernaturalism with its theocentric emphasis and a new type of naturalism whose purview was quite frankly limited to the natural area of experience. It is sufficient to call attention to the phenomenal growth both of the natural sciences, especially in the fields of geology and biology, and of the social sciences to recognize the mainsprings of this new naturalistic and positivistic line of thought. Such publications as the *On the Origin of the Species* (London: J. Murray, 1859) by Charles Darwin (1809–82), the *Cours de philosophie positive* (Paris: Bachelier, 1830–42), by Auguste Comte (1798–1857), *A System of Synthetic Philosophy* (London: Williams & Norgate, 1862–93) by Herbert Spencer (1820–1903), and *The Geological Evidences of the Antiquity of Man* (London: J. Murray, 1863) by Charles Lyell (1797–1875) either reflected this growing mood or effectively intensified it. To many it seemed that such an empirical interpretation of nature and the world provided a far more rational explanation of all aspects of human experience than either philosophical Idealism or religious Theism had or could.

Writing just after the turn of the century, Ernst Troeltsch (1865–1923) described the new situation within which theology and biblical studies found themselves:

> The profound changes which have so drastically altered the whole situation in the religious thought and practice of modern times make their appearance in various spheres, and assail the traditional Christian view of the world from the most diverse quarters and with the most manifold results. To begin with, there is the modern conception of Nature, which, as comprised in the mathematico-mechanical method, has dissolved the purely metaphysical teleology of Nature given by Aristotle, demolished the cosmology of the Bible, and provided modern philosophy with all its essential problems. There is, secondly, the new conception of history, which has radically altered our whole attitude to the past and the future, and with which the present is a link in the whole concatenation of things. Thirdly, there is the modern ethics of humanity, which, besides the unworldly virtues of love to God and one's neighbour, has emphasized the intrinsic excellences of artistic and scientific culture—treating them indeed, as

peculiar and indispensable ideals—and has also recognized the positive ethical imperatives involved in political, social, economical, and industrial problems. There are, finally, the new conditions of social life on its economical and industrial sides, and the sociological mode of thought issuing from them, which, in contrast to mere abstract speculation, insists upon the novelty of the whole situation in its social and economical aspects. The first three movements sprang from the Renaissance, while the fourth is a product of the Illumination [Enlightenment] and, under the influence of 19th century thought, has become a force that towers above all else (p. 716).

The impact of this evolutionary and sociologically minded naturalism extended to all branches of Christian theology and was particularly devastating as far as Old Testament theology was concerned. Israel's teachings about the creation, for example, were deemed by many to be completely untenable, at least in the form in which they were presented. The idea of a divinely guided history, a *Heilsgeschichte*, or of a view of life somehow communicated by God to humankind seemed to evaporate into utter nothingness because the facts of Israel's history and beliefs appeared to be explicable as products of social factors alone. The practice of combining the new learning based on inductive methodologies with some form of supernaturalism, which had characterized most "mediating theologies" since the seventeenth century, was dealt a devastating blow by the new developments in the social and natural sciences. Needless to say, any form of out-and-out supernaturalism fared even worse. In 1860 Thomas Henry Huxley (1825–95), Darwin's "bulldog," who was sometimes prone to advocacy in the name of description, argued that "Extinguished theologians lie about the cradle of every science as the strangled snakes beside that of Hercules" (quoted in Gillispie, p. 3).

Historicism

Within the context of German philosophy one movement, by virtue of its relationship to the new naturalistic point of view and to the study of Old Testament religion as well, had more than ordinary impact. This was the school of thought known as *Historismus* (historicism). Inspired chiefly by the method of historical investigation first propounded by Leopold von Ranke, historicism represented essentially an attempt to understand all human experience in terms of the interaction of social forces throughout the long course of history. Its ultimate goal was to display the total development (*Gesamtentwicklung*) of all culture and so to bring about a kind of historical synthesis which, however, did not have the purpose of exhibiting general laws, such as Hegel's system had sought to demonstrate, but only of setting forth the relationship of each separate moment of history to the rest. Nothing, it held, could be assumed to be permanent except the progress of life itself; therefore, it would also be useless to try to find a rational or logical order, much less a divine purpose, running through history.

The history of mankind merges in the evolutionary history of the earth's surface; it takes its rise in the prehistoric life of primitive peoples; it is determined throughout by the general laws of geographical conditions, and by the various phases of social life, and forms an unspeakable complex, yet altogether coherent, whole of immeasurable duration both in the past and in the future. It is as a part of this array and system that we must survey and estimate our own existence, and find its rationale and origin. On the analogy of the events known to us we seek by conjecture and sympathetic understanding to explain and reconstruct the past. From this point, again, we advance to the criticism of extant traditions and to the correction of generally accepted historical representations. Since we discern the same process of phenomena in operation in the past as in the present, and see, there as here, the various historical cycles of human life influencing and intersecting one another, we gain at length the idea of an integral continuity, balanced in its changes, never at rest, and ever moving towards incalculable issues. The causal explanation of all that happens, the setting of the individual life in its true relations, the interpretation of events in their most intricate interaction, the placing of mankind in a rounded system of ceaseless change—these constitute the essential function and result of modern historical reflexion. The latter, viewed as a whole, forms a new scientific mode of representing man and his development, and, as such, shows at all points an absolute contrast to the Biblico-theological views of later antiquity (Troeltsch, p. 718).

Relativism and scepticism in this position are evident and, for that matter, did not fail to lay hold of many who adopted it. No one displayed more awareness of these pitfalls nor labored more strenuously to overcome them than Troeltsch himself. Troeltsch, who had been a student of Paul Anton de Lagarde (1827–91) and Ritschl, seems to have been influenced especially by his contacts at Heidelberg with the sociologist, Max Weber (1865–1923). Out of this association came a remarkable treatise on *Die Soziallehren der christlichen Kirchen und Gruppen* (2 vols.; Tübingen: J. C. B. Mohr, 1912 = *The Social Teachings of the Christian Churches* [2 vols.; London/New York: George Allen & Unwin/Macmillan Company, 1931]) easily his most famous work, in which he noted the strong interdependence of Christian religion and the surrounding social culture. Although many of his seminal publications belong to the early years of the twentieth century, Troeltsch's work illustrates both the dilemmas of historicism and an attempted path beyond these dilemmas but without the abandonment of historicism's basic presuppositions. Recognizing the reality of social determinism, he argued that there was nonetheless a distinct place for personal freedom in the processes of history, indeed, that the effect of human personalities seemed to outweigh the social factors. Christianity, he remarked quite pertinently, was after all "not a theory, but a life, not a social order, but a power."

Within Troeltsch's understanding of historical causation, history itself was open-ended and certainly not totally determined. The scientific model of causation was seen as in need of modification when utilized in understanding history.

> The causality of natural science implies the absolutely necessary principle that events are bound together by a changeless, all-pervading, and, in all particular cases, identical law of reciprocity. . . . Now, historical causation is something entirely different, being almost exclusively a matter of psychological motivation. In the historical sphere nearly everything passes through the medium of consciousness, and in the last resort all turns upon the constant interaction of conscious efforts, into which even the unconscious elements tend to resolve themselves. Thus the peculiar irrational quality and initiative of the individual consciousness make themselves felt in the ultimate result, alike in the individual life and in the life of groups. Here, therefore, it is not permissible to reduce events to non-qualitative forces, or to explain effects by causal equivalence. Then we must also bear in mind the infinite complexity of the motives that arise on all sides and act upon one another—a complexity which gives a special and peculiar character to every particular case, and so defies all calculation and experimental proof. Further, all occurrences, whether in the individual life or in the life of groups, are so affected by the entire psychical condition of the individual or the group that another quite incalculable element is introduced. In the historical process, moreover, there ever emerges the fact of the new, which is no mere transformation of existent forces, but an element of essentially fresh content, due to a convergence of historical causes (p. 719).

In this milder form of Troeltschian "non-sceptical relativism," historicism gained entry into a large segment of German theological thinking around the turn of the century and became the philosophical foundation of the so-called *religionsgeschichtliche Schule* (history-of-religion school). Nowhere is this more apparent than in the work done during the last years of the nineteenth century and the first two or three decades of the twentieth century in the study of Old Testament religion. About 1890, several younger scholars organized at Göttingen what came to be called "the little faculty." Among this group were such biblical scholars as Hermann Gunkel (1862–1932), Albert Eichhorn (1856–1926), Wilhelm Bousset (1865–1920), and William Wrede (1859–1906). They considered themselves to be historians primarily, not theologians. Their task was to exhibit, in so far as the Old Testament is concerned, through strict application of the principles of historical investigation, the origin and growth of Israel's literature and religion and to call attention, within the limits of available knowledge, to the social milieu from which it had developed (see Hahn, pp. 83–103). The achievement of their purpose was facilitated by an astonishing increase in information about the life and thought of ancient Palestine and of the entire ancient Orient. Archaeology, the writers of classical antiquity, and the large body of material contributed by the science of comparative religion were all drawn upon to furnish the data considered indispensable for an understanding of the history of Old Testament religion.

Estimate of the Nineteenth Century

Theologically speaking, the nineteenth century did not come to a close until after the first World War, for the first quarter of the present century was actually a continuation or a fulfillment of tendencies which had their origin or had run a large part of their course in the preceding century. A clearly articulated change in theological climate did not occur until the early twenties when it was heralded most conspicuously by the rise of the Barthian movement. Barthianism, although only one instance of the reawakened interest in the earlier Protestant interpretation of Christianity, sought to turn contemporary theological thought away from the emphases and thought patterns of the late nineteenth century.

Nevertheless, the legacy of the nineteenth century lingers on, and there are few among those engaged in the study of Old Testament religion, for example, who are not profoundly grateful for its rich contributions to our better understanding of biblical literature, history, and faith. In spite of the Barthian reaction against its definition of the nature of biblical religion and revelation, these gains retain a genuine value. Nonetheless, the view of biblical faith and literature which developed in the late nineteenth century, probably did more than any other factor to bring about the temporary demise of Old Testament theology in the decades before and after the turn of the century.

THE STUDY OF OLD TESTAMENT THEOLOGY AND RELIGION DURING THE NINETEENTH CENTURY

Old Testament Theology in Early Nineteenth-Century Rationalism

The fundamental principles which had emerged concerning biblical theology near the end of the eighteenth century, and which we noted at the end of the last chapter, received serious consideration at first only among the Rationalists. Supernaturalism's attachment to Protestant church doctrine and Schleiermacher's disregard of the Old Testament are perhaps the main reasons why the study of Old Testament theology remained for the initial three decades of the new century mainly the private domain of Rationalism. Three works call for attention. Each one followed more or less the pattern set by G. L. Bauer and reflected in varying degrees the same perspectives.

GOTTLIEB PHILIPP CHRISTIAN KAISER

Years after the publication of its first volume in 1813, the conservative Hävernick could still speak of the "great sensation" which Kaiser's biblical theology had created. This work, *Die biblische Theologie oder Judaismus und Christianismus nach der grammatisch-historischen Interpretationsmethode und nach einer freymüthigen Stellung in die kritisch-vergleichende Universalegeschichte der Religionen und in die Universale Religion* ("Biblical Theology or Judaism and Christianity According to the Grammatical-Historical Method of Interpretation and According to a Frank Position in the Critical-Comparative Universal History of Religions and in Universal Religion"; 3 vols.; Erlangen: J. J. Palm, 1813–21), has often been placed in the same rationalistic category as the work of Samuel Reimarus. It would be hard, indeed, to imagine anything more shocking to the sensibilities of orthodox Christians than Kaiser's "Universalism" which not only claimed to be superior to Christianity but also valued "the honest worshiper of the Divine in every age and clime." Hardly less surprising was his statement that he had written the work for those who, refusing to believe that any one church is in sole possession of salvation, had adopted as their religion "neither Judaism, Christianity, Mohammedanism, nor Paganism, but religious Universalism, Catholicism in the true sense of the word, what our theologians call perfectible Christianity" (I, p. 12).

One novelty of Kaiser's discussion lay particularly in the prominence he gave to comparative studies by which he sought to establish the place of biblical religion within the context of all other religions (see Sandys-Wunsch, pp. 393–95). Both Gabler and Bauer had underscored the value of such a comparative treatment before him but had never considered it the essential purpose or characteristic task of biblical theology. This is precisely what Kaiser proceeded to do. He began with a survey of the major features of the various religions (typical of his depreciatory attitudes towards most empirical forms of religion is the importance he accorded here to fetishism) and then drew upon biblical materials to illustrate these features. His work thus had the character of a critical survey of religions into which Judaism and Christianity were fitted.

His tendency throughout was to reduce Old Testament religion to the low level of fetishism and idolatry and, thereby, equalizing its entire content as the orthodox theologians before him, only, of course, with the opposite effect. Where he had to admit the existence of higher elements (for example, the idea of a universal god), he usually dismissed them as borrowings from Persian thought. The tenor of his attitudes may be gathered from a few quotations selected from various pages.

The whole of the Pentateuch is a strange mixture of a later Persian enlighten-ment acquired during the Exile and a blind veneration of Moses, although the latter had often been repudiated in his own day, blended with earlier supersti-tions and even with Persian mythology which continues to shine through the entire Old Testament in connection with real history. . . . Abraham's god was an idol like the idols of the other tribal leaders. . . . He came from Chaldaea with fetishism and astral worship. . . . Jacob's stone at Bethel was a stone-fetish, Moses' god a commanding general who was jealous of other gods. He (Moses) permitted the nation to offer sacrifices, not because of the brutality of the Israelites but because he himself was convinced of their necessity (I, pp. 58, 59, 79, 23).

Kaiser's distinctiveness did not lie in the fact that he called attention to the primitive nature of Israel's earliest beliefs—that had been more or less the accepted view in practically all references to the history of Hebrew reli-gion—but, rather, in his inclination to assert that Israel never got beyond the stage of animism and narrow nationalistic particularism.

A second feature in Kaiser's work is the importance which he gave to the cult and cultic practices and institutions (see Sandys-Wunsch, pp. 395–96). His second volume was devoted to this topic.

Needless to say, he could find little that was of permanent value in the Old Testament. Later he passed sentence upon his own book and offered a far more favorable interpretation of Hebrew morality in volume three written after he became professor of theology in Erlangen. Nonetheless, his biblical theology stands as a monument to the sort of hyper-rationalistic treatment of the Bible which was characteristic of his day.

He hoped through his work to separate those ideas in the Bible which are universally true from those which are merely *Zeitideen*, and so to lay the foun-dations for the universal religion of the future—a religion whose temples would be consecrated to such things as Mother Love, Married Bliss, Friendship, etc.; whose feasts would celebrate the annual round of nature as well as the birth-days of the founders of great religions; and whose canon of Scripture would be large enough to include all the great spiritual writings of the past, present, and future (see II, pp. 232–42; the quote is from Dentan, pp. 28–29).

CARL PETER WILHELM GRAMBERG

A definite improvement over Kaiser's "frightening caricature" (Diestel, p. 713) appeared when Gramberg (1797–1830) published his *Kritische Ge-schichte der Religionsideen des Alten Testaments* (2 vols.; "Critical History of the Religious Ideas of the Old Testament"; Berlin: Duncker und Humblot, 1829–30), upon which Wilhelm Gesenius (1786–1842), by way of an exten-sive preface, may be said to have placed the *imprimatur* of the best of con-temporary biblical criticism. In its original design the work was divided into four parts, dealing, in order, with (1) Hierarchy and Cultus, (2) Theocracy and Prophecy, (3) a History of Doctrines (*Dogmatik*), and (4) a History of

Morality. Gramberg, a teacher for a time in a boarding school in the Prussian city of Züllichau, did not, however, live long enough to complete more than the first two parts which themselves contain over twelve hundred pages.

A theology of the Old Testament, in this author's view, was taken to mean a history of its religious ideas and in this he was greatly indebted to de Wette (see below pp. 98–100). The primary categories which he employed in his treatment were the various concepts he thought he could abstract from Israel's literature. Accordingly, the two volumes he was able to finish classify the appropriate material along topical lines. In the first one, under Hierarchy and Cultus, he was concerned with (1) places of worship, (2) gifts and offerings, (3) and priesthood, (4) feasts, (5) cultic practices (vows, prayer, fasting, and circumcision), and (6) the worship of God and gods. The second one, on Theocracy and Prophecy, discussed (1) theocratic rulers, (2) prophets, and (3) messianic hopes. The last two parts of his work, on Old Testament dogmatics and ethics, were never finished because of his unfortunate, premature death.

Gramberg, utilizing the work of de Wette, tried to maintain a strict historical approach, and so we find him adopting a second set of categories, namely, an historical framework in which he distinguished, all told, seven different stages in Israel's religious history. Since the pre-Davidic era constituted for him very largely an unknown quantity, he felt justified in beginning his inquiry with David, whence he then carried it forward to the days of the Maccabeans, rounding out his presentation by a brief consideration of the Apocryphal writings. His seven periods are: (1) David to Hezekiah, (2) Hezekiah to Josiah, (3) the years immediately preceding the Exile, (4) the early part of the Exile, (5) the remainder of the Exile, (6) the postexilic or Persian period, and (7) the Greek period to the Maccabeans. To each of these periods he assigned what he understood to be the appropriate books of the Old Testament, depending for the most part on the second edition of de Wette's introduction (1822). (The work of Gramberg and his predecessor de Wette allowed Johann Friedrich Ludwig George [1811–73] to write his *Die älteren jüdischen Feste mit einer Kritik der Gesetzgebung des Pentateuch* ["The Older Jewish Festivals with a Critique of the Pentateuchal Legislation"; Berlin: E. H. Schroeder, 1835] in which he sought to reconstruct the history of Israelite religion giving special attention to the issue of centralization of worship, the nature of the priesthood, and religious festivals.) Gramberg's literary chronology was, understandably, reflective of the scholarship of his age which still stood in the initial phases of Old Testament criticism. Joel, for example, was placed in the eighth century with Amos and Hosea; Genesis, Exodus, and Ruth he thought belonged to the period between David and Hezekiah. First and Second Chronicles were separated from Ezra and Nehemiah and placed in his seventh period (I, pp. xxv–xxvi).

Methodologically speaking, Gramberg's work represents a blending of topical and inductive-historical approaches. Its object was to show the origin, as far as it could be ascertained, and the development of the religious ideas and practices contained in the Old Testament and the Apocrypha. Strange aş it may seem, especially when we consider the importance attached to the matter by his predecessors, he paid no attention to the religions of the rest of the Orient and their bearing upon the Hebrews. The absence of "comparative-historical" considerations struck Gesenius, too, and led him to underscore the significance of such investigations, in typically rationalistic fashion, by claiming that they would provide "a fruitful elucidation by analogy to the rest of antiquity, especially in its Oriental varieties, and, what is intimately connected with it, a reduction of empirical historical and religious phenomena to the general ideas and conceptions held by all races" (I, pp. xiii–xiv).

One other apsect of Gramberg's study deserves special comment, namely, the peculiar distinction he drew between Hierarchy and Cultus on the one hand and Theocracy and Prophecy on the other. In so doing, he intended to point out the two opposing forces which, he believed, had controlled the development of Hebrew thought. He was particularly unsympathetic towards the hierarchical stream, characterizing it, true to the Deistic tradition, as "the unlimited dominion of a holy caste over a thoughtlessly obedient laity" (I, p. 2). The theocratic and prophetic side, by contrast, received from him a more favorable hearing, apparently because he felt that it had fostered a more valuable type of religion. Whatever else we may think of this juxtaposition, the higher appreciation of the prophetic influence implied in it had the advantage of turning attention to the difference between prophetic faith and popular Hebrew religion and thus raised the problem of the prophets' contribution to the development of Israelite thought and religion. It is unfortunate that Gramberg was not able to pursue his insight beyond the point of merely having stated it. It was precisely along this line, through the growing recognition of the impact made in Hebrew religion by prophetic leadership, that ultimately the common rationalistic view of the almost total worthlessness of the Old Testament was attacked.

DANIEL GEORGE CONRAD VON CÖLLN

The last of the significant rationalistic discussions of the religion of the Old Testament was the *Biblische Theologie* (ed. by David Schultz; 2 vols.; Leipzig: J. A. Barth, 1836) prepared by von Cölln (1788–1833) and published after his death. We have here the first instance of what was eventually to become an almost steady pattern in the history of the nineteenth-century discussion of Old Testament theology, namely, the singular fact that most of the works were published posthumously. We may perhaps recognize here a mute testimony to the difficulty which even then was felt by many in the matter of developing a proper methodology for approaching the subject and which kept many from engaging in this endeavor.

Von Cölln, a "moderate Rationalist," had spent the major part of his career as a professor of theology at the University of Breslau. On the whole, his treatment contains little of the partisanship which we have come to associate with his predecessors, and it is understandable, therefore, why it enjoyed the reputation for a long time of being the best in its field, and why it even received a qualified commendation from such conservatives as Hengstenberg. The title may be slightly misleading. The work did not offer an integrated biblical theology but, rather, dealt with each of the Testaments separately and without too much effort to correlate the two. Accordingly, the first volume contains the theology of the Old Testament and the second one that of the New.

The value of his study is enhanced particularly by the fact that he began it by reviewing the history of biblical theology and the methodological principles which he had employed (I, pp. 18–35). In the first place, he asserted, the investigation must be carried out in complete freedom from philosophical or doctrinal interests. In no case is one permitted to do what had been practiced hitherto almost universally, namely, to allow any system of thought to govern the selection of the biblical passages which were to be considered. Then, accepting Gabler's view of the historical nature of Old Testament theology, he listed what should be the basic rules of such an historical study:

(1) a careful differentiation of times and writers;
(2) a strict attention to the viewpoint and opinions of the biblical authors when determining their religious concepts;
(3) the presentation and explanation of the symbolic and mythical forms and of their relation to the pure ideas and convictions of the writers;
(4) the explanation of the relation of their teachings to the external conditions of the people;
(5) the search for the origin of the various concepts as it appears from the earliest sources.

Within the Old Testament he found two distinct phases of development, separated from one another by the Exile. On that basis, he divided his discussion into two sections, defining the first as Hebraism and the second as Judaism, following de Wette. In dealing with each of these periods he proposed the following procedure. It would be necessary to start with a critical sifting of the source material, meaning thereby that he wished to determine the time from which each writing actually came, the condition of its text, and its general trustworthiness. His next step was to describe the historical conditions of the nation during the particular era. Finally, he had in mind to ascertain those concepts which were common to all writers in a given period in order to discover what could be considered their "common opinion" (*all-*

gemeine Ansicht). This, then, would give the basic character of the religion prevailing at the time (*religiöser Grundcharakter*) and would constitute partly a standard whereby all details and individual peculiarities could be measured and partly a bond holding everything together and so making systematic treatment possible.

These methodological ideas are faithfully mirrored in the body of his discussion and, in general, fix its outline. After a critical characterization of the biblical sources and an extensive survey of Israel's history as it is related to the nation's religious development, he came to the third and major portion, an attempt to present, in a logically organized form, the theological concepts of Hebraism and, later, of Judaism. The source material for Hebraism was derived, of course, solely from the Old Testament, but in his section on Judaism he included non-canonical sources, e.g., the Apocrypha, Josephus, Philo, the Mishnah. His policy of prefacing the theological part of his inquiry with an historical review of the development of Israel's religion was actually not his own but one borrowed from de Wette's *Biblische Dogmatik* of 1813. We call attention to it now, however, because it became a fairly common practice among later investigators in the field, notably Steudel, Hermann Schultz, Dillmann, and, more recently, Sellin and others.

In keeping with his general principles, von Cölln took his point of departure in the systematic sections from what he thought had been the fundamental ideas of the individual periods. That of Hebraism he described as "a particularly strict form of monotheism or the idea of the unity of the Divine Being" (I, p. 89), whereas in the case of Judaism he described it as the belief "that the divine revelation was completely included in the nation's old sacred writings and that no new revelations would be imparted" (I, p. 360).

There is a further methodological peculiarity in these sections, one which presumably grew out of his own religious interests, although here again it is possible to discover a precedent in de Wette's work. At this point he interjected another type of classification based on the distinction between universalism and particularism (on this issue, see Smend, 1962). Theologically understood, universalism had to do with God and his relation to humanity as such, while particularism meant God's relation to the Jewish people in the form of a theocracy. Thus when he came to examine the separate concepts of Hebraism and Judaism, he divided them into "general religious ideas or religious particularism." Under the first grouping he listed (1) the teachings about God (the divine nature, names, unity, spirit, will, holiness, goodness, justice, and majesty) and God's relationship to the world as its creator, sustainer, and ruler and (2) the teachings about rational creatures (angels and human beings) and humanity's religious and moral relationship to God. In the second category he dealt with (1) theocratic concepts, (2) the theocracy in its historical manifestations, (3) the theocratic interpretation of religious teachings, and (4) the theocracy and its idealization in the future.

Although von Cölln gave no explicit definition of his conception of Old Testament theology, from his work we may infer that it signified the systematic discussion of the religious thought current in each of the two periods of Israelite history, Hebraism and Judaism, both of which he seems to have considered sufficiently homogeneous to make such a treatment possible. His procedure, in other words, was a combination of historical analysis and logical integration, the former furnishing the source materials in proper chronological arrangement, a picture of the origin and growth of Israel's religion, and the means for differentiating between Hebraism and Judaism; the latter undertaking to show how each of these stages had possessed a coherent theology.

The validity of his entire approach turns on three questions, namely, the correctness of his critical reconstruction, the validity of his strict dichotomy between preexilic and postexilic thought, and the adequacy of his thoroughgoing differentiation between universalism and particularism. True to the common opinion of his day he assigned the whole Pentateuch and Job to the period before the Exile and, by so doing, was justified in defining monotheism as the central concept of preexilic religion or of Hebraism.

Equally debatable is his attempt to distinguish between universalism and particularism as two distinctive realms within which the Old Testament moves. That these tendencies existed and that they figured, for example, in the controversies between the prophets and their opponents is generally admitted. Yet, it is doubtful whether they were ever sufficiently separated for each to produce a special type of religion still distinguishable in the Old Testament. The truth seems, rather, that they were frequently found side by side in the thinking of one and the same author (Amos and Second Isaiah). Even von Cölln was forced to agree that in those writings which offer the clearest expressions of the Hebrew religious spirit (Psalms and the Prophets) the two elements interpenetrated.

Despite his strong insistence on objectivity, he, too, did not escape the pitfalls of *a priori* opinions. He is perhaps the least guilty of the Rationalists we have examined. Designating angels and human beings as God's "rational" creatures is probably an offence of little consequence. However, it is a serious matter when he did not make room among his major categories for the ideas of Sin and Salvation as if these were of little concern to biblical writers and, instead, spoke only of "man's spiritual nature" and "religious-moral relation to God."

Old Testament Theology in Nineteenth-Century Idealism

The low esteem in which the intellectuals of the early nineteenth century held the Old Testament is amply demonstrated by the almost total disregard displayed by the period's most influential philosophical school, Idealism, for the new study of Old Testament religion. Kant's criticism of the Hebrew tradition appears to have been accepted by the majority of his followers—the only exception was de Wette, and his views cannot be classed as pure Idealism—until the movement entered upon its Hegelian phase. Seen in this light, Hegel's contribution becomes all the more significant, for by placing Hebrew religion on the second level of development in his categorizing and by differentiating it from the nature worship of paganism, he paved the way for a more appreciative attitude. Tangible evidence of the change were two works on Old Testament theology by Vatke and Bauer, both directly inspired by Hegel's thought.

WILHELM MARTIN LEBERECHT DE WETTE

In the same year that Kaiser published the first part of his infelicitous *Biblische Theologie*, a far more thoughtful discussion of biblical theology was offered by de Wette (1780–1849) then a young professor on the theological faculty of the new university in Berlin. His work bore the title of *Biblische Dogmatik des Alten und Neuen Testaments, oder kritische Darstellung der Religionslehre des Hebraismus, des Judentums und Urchristentums* ("Biblical Dogmatics of the Old and New Testaments, or a Critical Presentation of the Religious Teachings of Hebraism, Judaism and Early Christianity"; Berlin: Realschulbuchhandlung, 1813; 3rd ed., G. Reimer, 1831). The term "dogmatics" in the title was deliberately chosen because he wished to present biblical doctrines and to exclude morals and ethics as well as such matters as cultic practices. The former he treated in a work on ethics (1823) and the latter in a volume on Hebraic and Judaic archaeology (1814). The popularity of his biblical theology is evidenced by the appearance of two subsequent editions (1818 and 1831).

Successively professor at Jena, Heidelberg, Berlin, and Basel, de Wette was one of the most influential Old Testament scholars of the nineteenth century (for biographical data, see Cheyne, 31–54). A life-long friend and sometime colleague of Schleiermacher, de Wette was strongly influenced quite early in his studies by Jakob Friedrich Fries (1773–1843). Fries sought to construct a philosophical system far less skeptical than that of Kant, arguing that the human mind could apprehend transcendent reality directly by means of a kind of intuition (*Ahnung*). Earlier, as a student of Herder, de Wette had absorbed many romantic ideas. The influences of Herder and Fries were combined with de Wette's personal evangelical appreciation of Christianity and a vigorous historical-critical attitude. This rare combination of historical-critical interest, philosophical motivations, and theological perspectives is reflected in his treatment of the religion of the Bible (see Smend, 1958, pp. 72–105; Kraus, 1970, pp. 70–78; Rogerson, 1984).

For historical reasons, he divided his biblical dogmatics, which was actually the first volume in his Christian Dogmatics, into two separate sections, but at the same time took pains to underscore their interrelationship. Within the Old Testament, he further distinguished two phases, Hebraism, or the beginning and flowering of Hebrew faith, and Judaism, a more degenerate form of religion which Ezra initiated. This distinction between Hebraism and Judaism with the Exile as the significant watershed was fairly widespread in his day having already appeared in the work of such diverse interpreters as Spinoza and Eichhorn (for the latter, see Smend, 1958, p. 103). Methodologically, we have already seen this division in the work of von Cölln who was borrowing from de Wette.

De Wette began his volume with a discussion of anthropological considerations in which he discussed such topics as the nature of knowledge, faith and intuition, and religious feeling. He distinguished between symbols and myths on the one hand and dogma and convictions on the other. The former he saw in the Old Testament as the reflection of the activity of the Spirit operating upon the human intuition with intimations of the Unconscious. This spiritual life experienced and expressed itself in feeling whose forms were primarily esthetic, that is, symbolic and poetical (1831 ed.; p. 20).

According to de Wette, every religion possessed a basic idea (*Grundidee*) upon which all else was dependent and which had to be ordered in accordance with it (p. 38). For him, the basic principle or foundational idea in Hebraism was the ethical and non-mythical idea of one God as holy will (p. 63). In his discussion of the main teachings of Hebraism, he distinguished between the general teachings of faith or "ideal universalism" and "symbolic particularism" or the basic ideas and institutions of the theocracy. Under the former were located the topics of God, Angels, and Men. Under the latter he discussed the idea and institutions of the theocracy, the theocratic worldview, and the ideal theocracy or messianism.

Like most of his nineteenth-century counterparts, de Wette held a low opinion of Judaism or postexilic life and faith. (The roots of this German vilification of Judaism during the nineteenth century were manifold; undoubtedly Luther's animosity toward the Jews did not contribute to a fair appraisal of Judaism in German circles anymore than did Deistic deprecations in English circles.) The following is de Wette's assessment of Judaism which he based not only on late Old Testament writings but also on Philo, Josephus, and the Mishnah:

Judaism is the unfortunate reinterpretation of Hebraism and the mixture of the positive ingredients of the former with foreign mythological-metaphysical teachings wherein a reflective understanding without the living animation of feeling held sway: a chaos which awaited a new creation. The characteristic features are: (1) in place of an ethical tendency, a metaphysical orientation and therein many developments. (2) In addition to the misunderstanding of symbols, written sources of religion without the power of autonomous productivity. (3) Therefore, while Hebraism was concerned with matters of life and animation, Judaism was concerned with matters of concept and the essence of the written (p. 114).

JOHANN KARL WILHELM VATKE

The first instance of an Hegelian reading of the religion of the Old Testament was *Die Religion des Alten Testaments nach dem kanonischen Büchern entwickelt* ("The Religion of the Old Testament Presented According to the Canonical Books"; Berlin: G. Bethge, 1835) by Vatke (1806–82), an abstrusely written work which, nonetheless, was destined to become one of the epoch-making books in the treatment of the subject. Its author had learned his lessons in Old Testament criticism from such masters as Gesenius, Gramberg, and Ewald, and at the Gesenius's instigation had completely familiarized himself with all the books of de Wette from whom, be it said, he took as his own the principle that "every truth is better than even the most edifying error, and a faith which is inconsistent with the truth cannot possibly be the right one" (Cheyne, p. 132). The all important inspiration for the further course of his thinking and of his career came with his entrance into the University of Berlin in 1828, for here he found himself attracted rapidly not only by Schleiermacher and the university's other philosophical theologian, Philipp Konrad Marheineke (1780–1846), but especially by Hegel. Another influence must be noted. In 1832 shortly after the great philosopher's death, he began his life-long friendship with David Friedrich Strauss (1808–74), the young theologian who so soon afterwards was to find himself one of the most controversial figures of the century. Their common interest in the Hegelian point of view eventually led them to undertake a thoroughgoing criticism of the religion of the Bible, each in his own particular field. So it was that in 1835, with but a few months between them, there appeared Strauss's *Das Leben Jesu, kritisch bearbeitet* (Leipzig: F. A. Brockhaus = *The Life of Jesus Critically Examined* [3 vols.; London: Chapman Brothers, 1846]) and Vatke's *Religion des Alten Testaments*.

Strauss's book was addressed to ordinary educated readers and, therefore, achieved a popularity—and notoriety—to which its many subsequent editions are ample testimony, whereas Vatke's work, intended solely for his theological colleagues and those who understood his Hegelian terminology, could still at the end of the century be obtained new in its original edition (Cheyne, p. 136). The storm created by Strauss's critical posture toward the gospel records was in a measure shared by Vatke also. The orthodox faction, under Hengstenberg's powerful leadership, following the death of Schleiermacher in 1834, demanded Vatke's dismissal from the university, although unsuccessfully, but it did have the satisfaction of preventing his appointment to anything more than an extraordinary professorship without compensation.

The limited acclaim Vatke received was to a large degree his own doing. His use of forbidding Hegelian terminology must carry a part of the blame. But far more effective a deterrent to a just appraisal of his achievement was the lengthy introduction in which he set out to initiate his readers into the complexities of Hegelian speculation and which was enough to keep even an Eduard Reuss (1804–91) from paying any further attention to the book despite the fact that it offered a critical theory of the development of Israel's religion admirably close to his own. Reuss's own words on the matter are:

> On the appearance of the book, the table of contents, with its Hegelian formulae, of itself terrified me to such an extent that I remained at the time unacquainted with it. A speculative treatment of history I trust no farther than I can see. Since then indeed I have seen that theory and formula in this book were really only an addition which might be dispensed with, and that my inquiries might have been materially assisted if I had not let myself be deterred by them (*Die Geschichte der heiligen Schriften Alten Testaments* [Braunschweig: C. A. Schwetschke, 1881] p. ix).

The best way to appreciate its real merits is to accept the advice given by Vatke himself to his brother: "should the introduction of my book bore you, pass over it and read the critical history which, in this form, is the first of its kind" (Benecke, p. 150).

There is another reason for the difficulty one has in grasping the meaning of this introduction. It was intended not only as a means of stating the author's philosophical point of view but also as a preparation for the whole "biblical theology" which was to follow. Considerations of expediency, namely, to prevent the orthodox party from achieving Vatke's complete removal from the theological faculty, seemed at the time, however, to demand a postponement of all further work on the subject, and postponement eventually became cessation (Benecke, p. 271). That circumstance, of course, only adds to the confusion and makes it doubly hard to perceive the direction in which Vatke's interpretation of biblical theology was ultimately moving. So it is that, as far as a systematic presentation is concerned, we have only his abstract dissertations on the nature of biblical theology, on the differences between the fundamental notion (*Begriff*) of Old Testament religion and its concrete historical appearance (*Erscheinungsform*), on the Hegelian concept of revelation as the slow self-realization of pure Spirit in history gradually coming to conscious expression in the religious thought of the Hebrews, and, finally, on the basic idea of that religion itself.

Into these philosophical discourses Vatke inserted his critical history of the religion of the Old Testament. It constitutes by far the largest portion of his volume and is also the part which has had the greatest influence of any of the studies we have examined so far on the matter of constructing a critical history of Israel's religious development. This in itself was an achievement sufficient to ensure the work's permanent significance. But, be it remembered, for Vatke's larger purposes, it was simply preliminary in nature, intended to provide him with the empirical data by which he would be enabled to carry on his systematizing efforts.

This critical history was not a mere enumeration of facts placed in their proper chronological order. Its primary purpose was, rather, to demonstrate the basic development of Israelite religion, by showing how the Old Testament reflected the gradual movement from nature worship (with which the Hebrews became familiar in Egypt and which continued to engage them in Canaan) to a religion of spiritual individuality where God was "unlimited power . . . absolute wisdom and holiness" (pp. 594–95). The entire history of Old Testament religion, from its beginning, through its maturity, and to its disintegration, he divided into eight different periods, starting with Moses and ending with the Maccabeans. The level of maturity was reached shortly before and during the Exile, chiefly in Jeremiah and Deutero-Isaiah (p. 501), but this higher phase continued on into the Persian period, when prophetic enthusiasm finally attained its highest fulfillment in the reflections of the wisdom movement with its transcendence over nationalistic particularism and in the lyrical movement which had managed to combine within itself cultus and prophetic spirituality (p. 552). Vatke thus differed radically from most of his predecessors and contemporaries who saw Israelite religion beginning a decline at the time of the Exile.

Where do Vatke's real contributions lie? We note first the most important one, his theory shared by de Wette, George, and Gramberg that the culmination of the process which produced the law came after the prophets, not before them. He retained Moses as an historic personage, but held that he was responsible only for increasing the reputation of the old national god, for attempting to banish the worship of other gods, for spiritualizing the natural elements in the cultus, and for establishing a purer moral life among the Hebrews. Moses did not give a national constitution such as is represented by the law of later years, and the beliefs of a later time were also present merely in germinal form (pp. 184–85). The significance of this for the history of Israel's religion is patent. Monotheism was late. The line of development had not been: monotheism—a relapse into polytheism—a slow recapturing of the earlier purer faith, but, rather: polytheism—monotheism.

Hebrew religion had started as star-worship, Yahweh being identical with Saturn (pp. 198–99; see Cheyne, p. 139), but had gradually evolved into a religion of pure spirituality. This is the remarkable shift which helped in the formulation of a literary theory concerning the chronology of the composition of documents in the Pentateuch which sought to make the whole development of Israel's religion psychologically and historically more plausible.

Another feature needs to be mentioned as well. By stressing the distinction between *Begriff* and *Erscheinungsform*, Vatke attacked the common rationalistic practice of defining Hebrew faith in terms of the superstitions and polytheism of the masses and, instead, insisted that if one wanted to find the real essence of that religion, one would have to look for it in prophetic consciousness, not in Mosaism or in popular worship (p. 593).

It is clear, then, that the chief value of Vatke's work must be seen in his contributions to the history of Old Testament religion, but that as far as Old Testament theology is concerned, either in terms of method or content, he offered little. Nor does it seem likely, given his preoccupation with Hegelian speculation, that he would have even if he had been permitted to complete his plan. Two statements in Vatke's work may be noted because of their bearing on Old Testament theology. The first concerns his interpretation of the nature of biblical theology: "the fundamental idea of biblical theology as a science is determined by its purpose which is to present the living movement of the main elements of biblical religion, namely, its general concept (*Begriff*), its subjective and historical appearance, and its idea." The second contains his formulation of the fundamental idea of Old Testament religion: "God is defined as pure subjectivity which, as unlimited power, is distinguished from everything particular but which, as absolute wisdom and holiness, nevertheless includes within itself these differences between itself and the particular in a simple, yet concrete identity" (pp. 147, 594–95).

BRUNO BAUER

Equally Hegelian but of far less ultimate importance was *Die Religion des Alten Testaments in der geschichtlichen Entwicklung ihrer Principien* ("The Religion of the Old Testament in the Historical Development of its Principles"; 2 vols.; Berlin: F. Dümmler, 1838) by Bruno Bauer (1809–82). A licentiate first at Berlin (he had been one of Vatke's earliest students) and then at Bonn, Bauer had begun his intellectual odyssey as a member of the conservative Hegelian right wing but had gradually turned to the other extreme where he joined the ranks of the radical atheists and, henceforth, would grant the existence, not of an absolute spirit, but only of a human and a subjective spirit. The immediate result of this change was an attack on the historical reliability of the four gospels as documents for the life and teachings of Jesus. They contained, he concluded, no picture of the historical

Jesus but only of the imagined Christ of the early Christian church. Little wonder that he lost (in 1842) all further right to teach and found himself forced, for the rest of his life, to confine his activities to free-lance writing and pamphleteering. Still, the questions he raised would not go away.

The work with which we are concerned belongs to his convervative period (1838). Although it, too, is a part of an extensive critique of the history of revelation and so is at least formally related to his later criticism of the gospels, it included no radical reconstruction of the religion of the Old Testament such as Vatke had offered. As a matter of fact, it left the traditional views almost intact. Historical criticism, he thought, could be dispensed with for the simple reason that in any attempt to recover the actual content of the Hebrew religious beliefs it makes little or no difference whether any particular idea is early or late. This does not mean that Bauer had no appreciation of historical development. What he did do, however, was to accept at face value the course of development outlined in the Bible itself.

His formidable definition of Old Testament theology is completely Hegelian in character and reminds one of Vatke's.

> The fundamental idea of our science . . . may be defined as the presentation of the self-consciousness of the absolute Spirit in its free, historically mediated development. Its content is the historical movement in which the notion of revelation is carried to completion in a living idea. The method of our science is to reproduce . . . this movement of the notion in its historical expressions . . . (I, pp. xciii–xciv).

History, as we see, is a definite ingredient of his definition, but it is uncritical history. He distinguished four different periods, (1) the patriarchal, (2) the legal, (3) the time of the struggle between external Law and inner Spirit, and (4) the prophetic. It is peculiar, however, that he found the Hebrew religious spirit to be present equally in all these stages. Abraham's views were those of a monotheist. For him, as for all the succeeding representatives of Hebrew thought, God's unity, power, holiness, and authority over the whole earth stood unquestioned (I, pp. 83–84).

Where, then, for him does history lie? It cannot be found in a gradual evolution of the Hebrew religious consciousness, for that always remained essentially the same. It is to be discovered, rather, in the historical fate of this consciousness as it passed through conflicts with other, inferior types of belief. Israel's religion during the days of the patriarchs existed under almost idyllic conditions but, thereupon, entered into a struggle with nature worship (in Egypt) and, in order to save itself, had eventually crystallized in a strong sense of national unity and in the law (I, pp. 101, 143–47). Unfortunately, this proved to be a doubtful blessing and inevitably led to a second struggle, in this instance, between externalism and spirituality, for which the history of the monarchy, the Psalms, and the wisdom literature still provide evidence. Finally, a new synthesis emerged in the prophetic movement.

Such, briefly, is the method and content of Bauer's study. Its contributions, either historically or theologically, can hardly be called significant. The most that may be said for it is that it effectively disproved Hegel's theory of the subordination of Hebrew faith to the religions of Greece and Rome, particularly as far as the prophets were concerned. Mosaic legalism, he granted, might possibly justify the Hegelian interpretation, but certainly not the prophets (I, p. lxxxi).

As we strike the balance of the effect which these followers of Hegelian Idealism had on the history of Old Testament theology, one thing is strikingly clear. Thoroughly enmeshed in their philosophical system and convinced that it alone could offer the proper point of view for understanding biblical thought, their very presuppositions made them inherently incapable of doing justice to that thought. The benefit Old Testament theology received from them was, accordingly, rather small. Still, through Vatke's efforts Hegelianism deserved the credit of having contributed to a more adequate reconstruction of Hebrew religious development and of having exerted, thereby, a most telling influence on the work of the historical school later in the century.

Old Testament Theology Among Nineteenth-Century Supernaturalists

The confessionalists of Hengstenberg's variety, as has already been noted, paid only the slightest attention to the problems and subject matter of Old Testament theology. Nevertheless, there were a few conservative scholars who, perhaps because their attachment to the traditional dogmas was less complete, showed a genuine interest in this area of study and added to its already growing body of literature. In general, it must be said, they did not advance the discussion appreciably, but their presence is witness to the fact that, slowly but surely, the old monopoly of the Rationalists was coming to an end. Three men, in particular, deserve separate consideration, Baumgarten-Crusius, Steudel, and Hävernick. All three disclose how deeply Gabler's historical principle had by now (i.e., the second quarter of the century) penetrated even into the orthodox camp.

LUDWIG FRIEDRICH OTTO BAUMGARTEN-CRUSIUS

The earliest and also the least satisfactory of the conservative treatments is the *Grundzüge der biblischen Theologie* ("Basic Features of Biblical Theology"; Jena: F. Frommann, 1828) of Baumgarten-Crusius (1788–1843), professor of dogmatic theology at Jena from 1812 to his death. By theological position he represented a "rationalistic supernaturalism," which in es-

sence meant that, like the earlier English anti-deistic apologists, he attempted
to defend Supernaturalism with the weapons of Rationalism.

The title of his work serves to make one thing clear immediately. His is
a biblical theology, an integrated examination of the religious thought of both
testaments together. The basic unity of the Scripture was for him, in other
words, an established fact. Immediately, of course, the question of the unifying elements arises. His answer was to propose as the central principle of
biblical religion the idea of the "expectation of the kingdom of God" (p.
146). Such a definition carries with it two implications. His standpoint reveals a similarity to the *Heilsgeschichte* approach of the Erlangen School. It
also indicates that he had some grasp of historical process.

His definition of the nature and method of biblical theology shows the
influence of Gabler's major principles.

> The task of biblical theology is to present the ideas and teachings of the Old
> and New Testament writers about God and the destiny of man, according to
> their inner relationship to one another and their inner development. . . . The
> idea and execution of biblical theology are intrinsically connected with histor-
> ical exegesis, and both, therefore, have recently developed in close relation to
> one another (pp. 1, 4).

At the same time, he also felt that biblical theology owed a distinct
obligation to dogmatic theology, although that obligation was more in the
nature of a critique of doctrine rather than of a validation of church dogma.
It was his intention, he tells us, to "set up a system of purely biblical concepts, in order that it might be used as a basis and a norm of dogmatics and
as a starting point for the history of doctrine" (p. vii).

The bulk of his discussion falls into two sections, a general and a special one. In the first, the historical perspective receives considerable prominence, for it includes (1) a characterization not only of the literature of the
Bible but also of extra-canonical writings like the Apocrypha, the works of
hellenistic Judaism, and even those of the Kabbalah, (2) an account of Mosaic religion and its relation to patriarchal faith, (3) a description of the nature
and meaning of Christianity, and (4) a comparison of the biblical to other
forms of religion in antiquity. Significant is his omission of the prophets in
his historical survey (their importance seems to have been limited to the
prediction of the kingdom of God), for because of the unimportance he attached to them, he thought it necessary to distinguish only two main periods
in the total development of biblical religion, the Mosaic and the Christian.

It is the second, special section which, of course, is of greatest interest
for it is here that he undertook to systematize the concepts of the Bible. His
categories were the familiar ones of systematic theology: God, Man and Salvation. Throughout this portion of his treatment he was careful to distinguish

between the Old and the New Testaments and, in so doing, took account of historical development. Nevertheless, his attention was mainly directed to the New Testament, for it was there that he located all the basic ingredients and standards of biblical thought. His discussion of the Old Testament was, for this reason, uniformly brief and superficial. Nowhere, so it seems, did it occur to him that there might be a distinct value in analyzing the inner nature of its religion. The treatment he accorded the Old Testament was deficient in another respect as well. At no point, namely, did he distinguish different levels of development in its religious views but, instead, left his readers with the impression that the religion he had defined as Mosaism was to be found in all of its various writings.

JOHANN CHRISTIAN FRIEDRICH STEUDEL

Like Baumgarten-Crusius, Steudel (1779–1837) also belonged to the "rationalistic supernaturalists" and had the distinction of being the last representative of the "old Tübingen school" before Swabian Protestantism's venerable seminary was taken over by the Hegelians under Ferdinand Christian Baur (1792–1860). Brought up in pietistic biblicism (he was J. A. Bengel's great-grandson), afterwards professor of theology and dean at the seminary, one of his last acts was to serve as the spearhead in the attack against Strauss's *Leben Jesu*, even though Strauss had not only been one of his students but, at the time, was also a member of the faculty. He enters our purview through his *Vorlesungen über die Theologie des Alten Testaments* ("Lectures on Old Testament Theology"; Berlin: G. A. Reimer, 1840), which were edited and published following his death by one of his closest disciples, G. F. Oehler.

Oehler, in his preface, tells us that Steudel had been in the habit of introducing his lectures with a "detailed presentation of the history of the Old Testament revelation in order to bring to light the ongoing development of its religion" (p. v). For a while the editor seriously considered the advisability of reproducing that survey of the "progressive movement of the Kingdom of God under the Old Covenant" but finally desisted because of the difficulty attached to the task (p. vi). Fairness to Steudel requires us to take note of this. It shows that he, too, recognized the need for an historical perspective and made certain that his students were familiar with the historical development of Hebrew religion before engaging in a systematic study of that religion's concepts.

His interpretation of the idea of revelation bears out this historical orientation. The Old Testament, in his opinion, contained a "communication from God" which had been mediated, however, not as a ready-made body of doctrine but through a series of historical facts from which it is possible to derive a religious interpretation of life and a knowledge of God's nature (p.

19). Revelation so considered was, to repeat the statement already quoted from the preface, a "progressive movement" which had culminated in the appearance of Jesus Christ. The most instructive expression of his views may perhaps be found in a passage where his immediate concern was to trace the inner unity of the Old Testament.

> A divine purpose moves down the whole period which these books traverse. On its strength, the people, to whom God's educating influence is extended, are brought to the pure perception of the true God and are strengthened in it. At the same time, the way is prepared for making this purer perception the possession of all humanity (p. 44).

Elsewhere he speaks of a "divine plan of salvation" which, while promised in the Old Testament, did not reach its full completion until the appearance of Jesus Christ (p. 47). The affinities between his thought and the viewpoint we have come to know as *Heilsgeschichte* are, as they were in the case of Baumgarten-Crusius, once more unmistakable.

Certain other influences of a *heilsgeschichtliche* nature can be detected in his work. He, for example, made use of typology in order to define the relationship between the Old and the New Testament. Not only were the two linked together by "most appropriate agreements and parallels," but the Old Testament had also possessed "from its origins the purpose of depicting Christ and Christ's work, nor would it ever have taken the form it did, had it not been destined to serve as such a prototype" (p. 58). To his credit, perhaps, it should be said that this concern with *types* is not prominently reflected in his discussion. One discovers a far more valuable indication of his contact with *Heilsgeschichte* in the importance he accorded, in his definition of Old Testament theology, to the problem of salvation. He looked upon Old Testament theology as "a systematically ordered arrangement of what the Old Testament declares concerning God and the relationship which takes place between God and man" (p. 73). Nothing could be more characteristic of the Old Testament than the emphasis it places upon God's ongoing relationship with humanity and the redemption which is rooted in that relationship. It is this grasp of the vital quality of the Old Testament religious point of view which lifts Steudel's treatment above the works we have examined so far and which, one might add, also constitutes one of the more acceptable insights of the *Heilsgeschichtler*. His topical outline followed the foregoing definition quite closely and, accordingly, was divided into three major sections, (1) man, (2) God, and (3) the relationship taking place between God and man.

His method of treatment within these systematic categories took account of the development and even modification of the Old Testament's religious ideas (p. 65). The significance he attached to a coupling of systematic and historical forms of presentation speaks from a sentence such as this one:

"The recognition that there occurs in the Old Testament revelation a gradual but sure development of religious understanding is of great importance for the treatment of Old Testament theology" (p. 66). He favored the "grammatico-historical" method of interpretation (p. 69)—although his use of typology presents some difficulty at this point—and even granted that comparative studies between biblical and non-biblical religions could be instructive provided one did not lose sight of the real task at hand, namely, to determine the character of the Old Testament ideas (pp. 68–69).

Steudel's principles were thus, on several counts, surprisingly sound. It is true that in the main portion of his discussion the historical principle fades into the background, but the fact remains, nevertheless, that his study offers the clearest evidence of the manner in which the historical point of view had begun to permeate the ranks of even the conservative writers on Old Testament theology by the end of the first third of the century.

HEINRICH ANDREAS CHRISTOPH HÄVERNICK

The most conservative of the supernaturalists was Hävernick (1811–45), a professor of Old Testament in Königsberg. He is best known as the author of a large number of biblical commentaries. The theological position he espoused is defined for us in Diestel's note that he was Hengstenberg's "most loyal disciple" (p. 719). Posthumously, his lecture notes on Old Testament theology were published in an edition produced by H. A. Hahn and later enlarged by Hermann Schultz through the addition of corrective notes (*Vorlesungen über die Theologie des Alten Testaments* [Erlangen: Heyder & Zimmer, 1848, ²1863]).

Although the largest part of his study reflects Lutheran orthodoxy with great consistency, there are also passages—particularly in the sections devoted to methodology—in which it is hard to recognize the work of a man supposedly attached to Hengstenberg's school. The definition he gave of biblical theology can scarcely be called extraordinary—its task is "to present the biblical teachings organically and scientifically" (p. 2)—but one is taken by surprise when one reads further of his plans to carry on his investigations in a thoroughly historical and objective spirit. The principles he adopted were similar to those of Gabler.

> Biblical theology must be treated with a sound historical disposition and interest. Any treatment according to an *a priori* system, be it strictly ecclesiastical or philosophical, must, therefore, be excluded. . . . The treatment must be in strict accord with its object and must be derived from it. Similarly, one may not allow a purely systematic principle to predominate at this point but only a purely historical one. Many a Christian dogma, for example, is contained in the Old Testament either not at all or only germinally or only undeveloped and

unfinished. The different periods of the development must be distinguished (p. 3).

That he, too, was inclined to describe the essential nature of Old Testament religion in terms of *Heilsgeschichte* may be deduced from his short characterization of the principle of Hebrew faith:

> God witnesses of himself in a certain community, his Kingdom, which stands in a certain moral relationship to him (covenant relationship), and in a series of deeds which form a connected, organically developing sequence (pp. 19–20).

Yet, here again one finds that theory was different from practice. His actual treatment of the theology of the Old Testament was essentially systematic and betrayed the interests and subject-matter of Protestant dogmatics. Note, for example, his outline of the section on humanity: (1) original condition of man, (2) evil and sin, (3) origin of evil, (4) original sin, (5) guilt, (6) consequences of evil, and (7) immortality. The major categories he adopted were the familiar trilogy: God, man, and salvation. At this point alone he departed from a purely topical procedure and organized the material according to four main periods: the patriarchs, Moses, David, and the prophets.

Old Testament Theology Among Nineteenth-Century Moderate Conservatives

It is freely admitted that this portion of our survey is almost in the nature of a miscellany and that studies are here grouped together which show, in spirit as well as in execution, a great deal of diversity. That there are differences, even profound ones, between Ewald on the one hand, and Oehler on the other, cannot be denied. These moderate conservatives did not belong to any single school of thought. Nevertheless, one would have to be blind indeed to overlook their deep-going resemblances. All stood, theologically speaking, somewhere between the strictly orthodox confessionalists or supernaturalists and the decidedly liberal adherents of a purely historical point of view. In the true sense of the word they were "mediating theologians" whose concern it was to steer a middle course between the two extremes and to retain the essential elements of the traditional faith while they, at the same time, took account of the implications of biblical criticism. Such, then, were the conditions under which they labored and the task which they set out to perform.

ERNST ANDREAS HEINRICH HERMANN SCHULTZ

The turn of the seventies saw the greatest flowering of Old Testament theology during the entire century. In rapid succession three massive and profound studies made their appearance and, for a while, all but dominated the scene. The first of these was *Alttestamentliche Theologie: Die Offens-*

barungsreligion auf ihrer vorchristlichen Entwicklungstufe (Frankfurt: Heyder & Zimmer, 1869) by Schultz (1836–1903). Four subsequent editions (the last in 1896) attest to its popularity and value, but also to its author's changing critical views. The first edition (1869) followed Ewald's critical theories and so distinguished three major periods: Mosaism, Prophetism, and Levitism. The second and third, because Schultz by then had accepted the views of Vatke and Karl Heinrich Graf (1815–69), discussed the whole religion in two periods with Ezra serving as the dividing point. With the fourth edition he abandoned this procedure because the material seemed too drawn out and, instead, adopted the plan of tracing first the history of Hebrew-Jewish religion and, then, of developing its content systematically. The fourth edition was translated into English as *Old Testament Theology: The Religion of Revelation in its Pre-Christian Stage of Development* (2 vols.; Edinburgh: T. & T. Clark, 1892). Schultz was a Ritschlian and a professor of theology at Göttingen, and so it was from this wider perspective that he approached the narrower field of the Old Testament. In order to round out our brief picture, one further biographical note needs to be reported. As a student he had spent some time at Erlangen, drawn there especially by von Hofmann. That early association continued to influence the content and form of his discussion even in the latest editions.

The translator, J. A. Paterson, recommended the work to the English-speaking world as "a *via media* between the positions of biblical scholars like Delitzsch on the one hand and Stade on the other" (I, p. v). Equally descriptive of Schultz's standpoint is the subtitle he gave to his work, *The Religion of Revelation in Its Pre-Christian Stage of Development*, for it openly made clear his intention of combining traditional concepts such as revelation, Word of God, and inspiration with the more recent ideas of organic or genetic development and change. Nor was this merely a theory with him. His whole presentation clearly bespeaks that purpose and proves how seriously he was striving to integrate two patterns of thought which, when taken by themselves, differ considerably from one another.

At the very beginning Schultz made it plain that he proposed to treat Old Testament theology as an integral part of biblical theology. This he justified by insisting that in the Bible there is unfolded "a single religion" with "a homogeneous character of its own," and not a conglomerate of "various forms of religion which have merely an external connection of time and place" (I, p. 2). It is, furthermore, the "revealed religion" and thus possesses distinctive features which set it apart from all other religions.

Almost in the same breath, however, after stressing the unity of biblical religion, he goes on to describe another characteristic, for him quite as important as the first, namely, that this religion is also found only in various stages of development. Each stage, although it is organically related to the next and to all the others, has its own peculiar features and is certainly not to be equated with the final one where the whole process of progressive revelation came to an end. Drawing upon a simile from the world of nature, he tried to picture that interrelationship in terms of the affinity between seed and plant: "In the product of each stage in the biblical religion, the germ of the latest and highest stage was present, but still only the germ" (I, p. 6). The final stage is located in the New Testament, and the Old Testament, consequently, contains simply an incomplete version of the "revealed religion." But there is also an opposite side, for at the same time that the principle of organic growth points to the uniqueness of the specifically Christian or New Testament revelation, it likewise underscores the real importance of the Old Testament, for "there is not a single Christian conception but has its roots in the Old Testament" (I, p. 6). Elsewhere he points to the old saying, *Vetus testamentum in nove patet, novum testamentum in vetere latet*. He cautions against taking it to mean that the religion of the New Testament is already present in the Old as esoteric teaching. The saying was correct for him if it means that "the germinal principles of the Christian salvation are present in the Old Testament in various forms as yet incomplete and undefined and that only in the New Testament does the Old Testament salvation attain its eternal and truly saving significance. In both religions there is an inner unity of life, an unfolding of the same power" (I, p. 59).

The trait which binds the religion of the Bible together is for him, as it was for Baumgarten-Crusius, Steudel, and Hävernick, the Kingdom of God. It is not, to name but one earlier suggested alternative, the concept of monotheism, for that is only a "tolerably late development" (I, pp. 34–35). This fundamental principle, in every respect the same for the Old Testament as for the New, he formulated in these words:

> The perfect spiritual God wishes in love to realise His holy will in communion with man . . . a loving communion of the people with a God who is self-communicative, and whose object it is, through, and in spite of human sin, in other words, by redemption and reconciliation, to produce a divine life, to set up a kingdom of God. Hence the history of this religion is the history of the kingdom of God, of redemption and of reconciliation (I, pp. 55–56.).

In another connection he defined the religion of the Old Testament more specifically:

> The Old Testament religion is the religion of the Kingdom of God in the process of growth, the Kingdom still being confined within the bounds of a political community, that is, restricted to a single nation (I, p. 58).

To this sketch of Schultz's interpretation of biblical—and of Old Testament—religion one more element needs to be added. How did he visualize the process of revelation? Here again it is possible to detect the interpenetration of historical viewpoint and more traditional considerations. The faith of the Old Testament, like the Christian, "did not come forth out of humanity . . . but as a result of the working, upon Israel's spiritual life, of that divine, self-communicating spirit which aims at establishing the Kingdom of God among men" (I, p. 53). It is not simply the idealization of the empirical but a communication of the spirit "to such members of the human family as are privileged to become interpreters to their brethren of the heavenly life" (I, p. 54). Such people, by "natural susceptibility to moral and religious truth, developed by the course of their inner and outer lives," grasp the will of God intuitively as a power which presses in upon their souls with irresistible might (I, pp. 53–54).

This is, of course, not the old theory of plenary inspiration which pictured God as communicating knowledge through otherwise passive amanuenses. Schultz's media of the revelation are active participants in the process and translate their own experiences of the divine spirit into terms which are understandable to their fellow participants. By the same token it follows, however, that their interpretations are historically conditioned and so amenable to the laws of historical development as is everything else the world produces (I, p. 54). Hence, belief in the Bible as a revelation and a historical perspective were for him fundamentally compatible. He even considered it permissible to compare the religion of the Old Testament with other pre-Christian religions and "to take account of the attempts that have been made to bring this religion into connection with the general religious development of mankind" (I, p. 32).

Old Testament theology, as Schultz defined it, had a twofold purpose. First, it consisted of "a historical presentation of revealed religion during the period of its growth" (I, p. 2). Its second subject was "the moral and religious views which the sacred books contain, considered in their historical development and in their inner living connection" (I, p. 2). What this meant for the actual arrangement of such a theology is clarified by the fact that Schultz divided his study into two major sections, the first one actually a history of Israel's religion setting forth "the development of religion and morals in Israel down to the founding of the Asmonaean state," and the second one a systematic presentation of "Israel's consciousness of salvation and religious view of the world."

Certain other ingredients of Schultz's method need to be noted as well. His method of discussion was, as one might expect, consistently historical and genetic, that is to say, he not only took account of historical development but also endeavored to make plain the inner relations between the various stages of development and to justify, thereby, one of his earliest contentions, namely, that biblical religion was a "single religion." The question of source materials he answered by limiting these to the canonical writings, but they, in turn, required careful chronological sifting before they could be used in determining the religious and moral content of every stage of development. One other principle of his methodology may be found in his insistence that only those elements ought to be considered which "eventually proved them¬ selves the successful exponents of a healthy development." He thus frankly admitted his *Christian* viewpoint and even declared that his sole interest was "to give a history of the development of revealed religion as consummated in Christianity" (I, p. 11).

The plan of his systematic account of Old Testament religion deserves a special though hurried mention. It began with a discussion of the "consciousness of salvation," then moved on to Israel's "religious view of the world," and included under this section a study of the subjects "God and the World," "Man and Sin," "Hope of Israel," and the "human instruments for establishing the Kingdom of God." One striking fact presents itself: Schultz began, as a true follower of Ritschl, with a description of Israel's empirical experience of salvation (exemplified chiefly in the Covenant) and then related all other ideas to this central experience. Within these various topical subdivisions he carefully took note of historical development and frequently even went beyond the canonical limits he had earlier drawn so strictly to show how certain ideas had fared in the apocryphal and pseudepigraphic literature.

Schultz's theology, even when one considers it methodologically, is not without its faults, but as a sincere effort to interpenetrate historical and systematic methods, it is one of the best and most suggestive and certainly has earned its place among the most valuable of the Old Testament theologies written during the nineteenth century.

GUSTAF FRIEDRICH OEHLER

Schultz was a Ritschlian from northern Germany. Swabian Pietism had its turn when Theodor Oehler published posthumously (1873) the lectures on Old Testament theology delivered by his father, G. F. Oehler (1812–72), when the latter was still professor of theology and dean of the seminary at Tübingen. His work, immediately translated into English, bore the title of *Die Theologie des Alten Testament* (2 vols.; Tübingen: Heckenhauer, 1873–74 = *Theology of the Old Testament* 2 vols.; Edinburgh/New York: T. & T. Clark/Funk & Wagnalls, 1874–75/1883). For fullness of discussion, attention to detail, and consistency of viewpoint Oehler's work stands second to none. We have already seen that he had been singled out to prepare Steudel's lectures for publication. In addition, his own ideas about the subject of Old Testament theology had received their first formal expression as early as 1845 in a study entitled *Prolegomena zur Theologie des Alten Testaments* ("Prolegomena to Old Testament Theology"; Stuttgart: Samuel Gottlieb Leisching). His *magnum opus* had the enthusiastic approval of many of his contempories; it also enjoyed the distinction of being regarded for many years as the standard textbook in its field.

The chief feature of Oehler's study was its close adherence to the patterns of thought of the *Heilsgeschichte* approach with which von Hofmann's Erlangen School was so concerned but which also had roots in Swabian Pietism itself (J. A. Bengel in particular). As for Schultz so for Oehler: the religion of the Bible was fundamentally one and yet also historically developmental. He spoke of it as "one great economy of salvation—*unum continuum systema*, as Bengel put it—an organism of divine acts and testimonies which, beginning in Genesis with the creation, advances progressively to its completion in the person and work of Christ, and is to find its close in the new heaven and earth predicted in the Apocalypse" (p. 1). It was from this basic understanding of biblical religion that he derived the central principle of his whole Old Testament theology. The Bible, he pointed out, did not simply offer teachings; it likewise contained a record of a series of divine deeds and institutions which formed an integral part of the revelation. These facts of the history of salvation could under no circumstances be divorced from the didactic material. The two ingredients, rather, constituted a coherent and indivisible totality, and it was the business of Old Testament theology to exhibit them as such (pp. 5–6).

Notwithstanding this agreement with Schultz over the unity of biblical religion, there were deep-seated differences between the two, for example, over the question of the nature of revelation. For Schultz's view of a divine self-communication through individuals inspired of God who were able to grasp the divine will intuitively, he had nothing but scorn. What would be the difference, he asked, between a prophet and a heathen sage under such conditions? Revelation must be something more objective than intuition if one is to remain true to the biblical interpretation of the matter. On this account he preferred to speak of revelation as an "objective presentation of Himself by God" (p. 16), who has disclosed Himself to humanity through the objective media of name, presence, glory, voice, *malakh*, *shekhina*, miracle, and the entry of the divine spirit into the human heart (p. 124). Furthermore, because the Bible was the record of this objectively given revelation (p. 8), it was not for human beings to destroy the validity of that record either through a radical criticism of its writings (a thrust aimed particularly at Graf, his theories of pentateuchal criticism, and his reconstruction of the development of Hebrew religion) or through a denial of the historicity of the central events described there (p. 12). Oehler also strongly insisted on the difference between the views he held on the subject of revelation and those of the older Protestant theology. That difference he stated in two terms: (1) the older views thought of revelation almost exclusively as a *communication of doctrine*; (2) they had ignored the *gradual development* through which revelation passes in the Bible itself (pp. 17–18). His own rather conservative source-criticism of the Pentateuch gave him the following results. Certain portions were written by Moses himself (Exod. 20–24; 34:11–27; and the legal portions of Deuteronomy). The so-called "legislation of the middle books" was delivered orally by him but committed to writing afterwards by priests, perhaps as late as the first centuries of the period of the Judges (p. 47). All the facts described in the Old Testament he considered definitely historical, not mythological. "The thing believed was also a thing which took place" (p. 10).

The parallels to von Hofmann's *heilsgeschichtliche* views show themselves at other points. To the question, for example, why it would not have been simpler for God to send from heaven a ready-made system of doctrine, comparable to the Muslim claim for the form of its revelation, his answer was to fall back on the idea of a divine tuition. Primitive and sinful people had to undergo a lengthy preparation before they could be ready to receive the final and complete revelation in Jesus Christ. "We discern the educational character of the divine forms of revelation. To mankind in its childhood God's existence must be taught in theophany from without, and then from that point revelation advances toward the manifestation of the reality of this God in the spirit" (p. 16). With due caution he even accepted typological interpretations (p. 61).

Needless to say, he repudiated the sociological (i.e., environmental) point of view which makes historical conditioning explain the rise and change of human ideas. Of attention to the religious life in the countries surrounding Palestine there is very little. Where one does find it, it is limited to an argument for the difference between biblical religion and the other contemporary religions (pp. 18, 50). Any dependence of biblical religious thought upon foreign ideas was for him out of the question.

Oehler's general theological position finds its reflection in the definitions he gave to the subject of Old Testament theology. Its function, he stated, was to offer an "historical exhibition of the development of the religion contained in the canonical books of the Old Testament" (p. 5). A little later, he characterized it more specifically as the "exhibition of the whole of the Old Testament dispensation" (p. 6). It could be dealt with only from a Christian theological standpoint—"it does not treat its subject as the *Jewish religion*, but as the divine revelation of the Old Covenant" (p. 13)—for, while the Old Testament is not to be equated with the New Testament, its significance can be understood only in terms of its fulfillment in Christ. He even asserted that "the Old Testament teachings and institutions, divested of their fulfillment in Christ, sink down into poor and beggarly rudiments" (p. 19).

His method of treatment he described as *historico-genetic*. Its purpose was to comprehend the various stages of the divine revelation as members of an organic process of development (p. 41). In this matter he stood, of course, on much the same theoretical ground as Schultz. Related to this question is his statement that "the theology of the Old Testament has to handle as such *what is only in germ*" (p. 7). The stages he distinguished corresponded roughly to the three parts of the Hebrew canon—Law, Prophets and Writings—and were defined as Mosaism, Prophetism, and Wisdom. The inner connection between them he pictured in the following manner. Mosaism, itself divided into two phases, the patriarchal covenant of promise and the Mosaic covenant of Law, represented the establishment of God's kingdom on a theocratic basis. Once it was established (i.e., with the conquest of Canaan), two developments ensued. The first, which he designated as the objective development, was marked by the course taken by the covenant relationship during the remainder of Hebrew history both in the external progress of history (former prophets) and in the pronouncements of the prophets themselves (latter prophets). This movement he called Prophetism. The second, the subjective or reflective development, he found in the meditations of divinely guided sages whose interest lay not in theocratic institutions (hence their relation to the history of the chosen people is only slightly in evidence) but in the contemplation of God's cosmic ordinances and the general aspects of the ethical life. The Psalms, although they belong to the Hagiographa and contain subjective elements, he assigned to Prophetism because they are "cognate in subject to the section on prophecy" (p. 43).

So important did Oehler deem this "genetic" view of the unfolding of the Old Testament revelation that he carried it into the very structure of his *Theology*. Instead of following topical or systematic considerations in the basic outline of his work, he preferred, rather, to proceed historically and to treat separately what he adjudged to be the theological content of each of the three stages in Israel's religious experience. Consistent with his belief that the revelation had been given not only in communicated doctrine but also in events, he added a further peculiarity to his method of presentation in that he opened the treatment of each period with a survey of its history and of God's efforts to guide the people progressively to a closer communion (only in the section on Wisdom is history omitted for the reason already mentioned, namely, that historical concerns had little or no connection with the reflection of the sages). Only then did he undertake a systematic treatment of the religious concepts and theocratic institutions which belonged in the particular period in question (e.g., God, humanity, covenant, theocracy, public worship, etc.).

Oehler's work stands in the history of Old Testament theology as a prominent example of the *heilsgeschichtliche* approach and of the endeavor to retain the doctrine of "special revelation" as a valid concept in an age which was becoming increasingly conscious of the element of development in the Bible. Yet, the role and content assigned to the period of "Mosaism" meant that there was little room for much substantive development in Israelite religion. The extraordinarily large place he assigned to Mosaism (it embraces almost three-fifths of the book) was, it is true, typical of his time when even Ewald was convinced of the chronological priority of the law in the history of Israelite religion. Far from being "a germ," Mosaism, as it emerges in his discussion, was more like a full-grown tree, in comparison to which the succeeding stages, Prophetism and Wisdom, were almost anti-climactic. One cannot help but wonder why he went to the trouble of insisting on the necessity of interpreting the Old Testament in terms of genetic development, for the changes he noted between the various periods were quite minor in character. The main developments between Mosaism and Prophetism were, as he saw them, only the following: (1) "The idea of Jehovah develops into the Divine name of the LORD of hosts (*Jehovah Sabaoth*), with which is connected a further expansion of *angelology*." (2) "The intrinsically *moral* nature of the Law is further developed by Prophecy." (3) "*The communion of man with God* culminates in Prophecy." (4) "*The progress of the kingdom of God* forms the essential matter of prophecy" (p. 437).

A criticism of a different kind has to do with his practice of including within a purview of Old Testament theology also a discussion of Israel's historical experiences and of the various institutions of the people's public, private, and cultic life. Such a detailed review of the nation's history or of its institutions as he offered is perhaps best left to other disciplines. A third weakness of Oehler's method is more of form than of content. His policy of treating Old Testament theology in three separate historical stages has produced a disjointed presentation which requires the reader to turn from section to section if one is to discover what the Old Testament says on any of the religious ideas isolated by Oehler.

A final note on this work needs to be recorded, especially because it bears relation to the history of Old Testament theology in the English-speaking world. It was the first of the important German theologies to be translated into English (first in England by E. D. Smith and S. Taylor, 1874–75, and almost a decade later, in America by G. E. Day, 1883) and thus contributed to the awakening of interest in this subject among English-speaking theological and biblical circles.

HEINRICH GEORGE AUGUST EWALD

In the group of those who during the nineteenth century sought to solve the problem of Old Testament theology there occurs also the famous name of Ewald (1803–75), "the great, the faulty, but the never-to-be-forgotten Heinrich Ewald," as Cheyne once wrote of him (p. 67; another biographical sketch is found in Davies). The claim to such distinction rests chiefly on his work as a Semitic grammarian (the first edition of his Hebrew grammar appeared in 1827 and he published studies on Arabic grammar as well as Sanskrit literature), as commentator (Psalms, 1835; Job, 1836; Proverbs and Ecclesiastes, 1837; the Prophets, 1840–41; the New Testament, 1871–72), and as historian (his multivolume history of Israel is easily his most monumental achievement). The largest part of his life was spent at Göttingen, but fiery temperament and fearless opposition to injustice, even in the highest places, twice cost him his position, the last time in 1866 when he bitterly denounced Prussia's annexation of his native Hannover.

The personal impression Ewald made on many who met him was that of an Old Testament prophet come back to life. When he was asked on one occasion why he was always engaged in some form of controversy, his answer was: "I cannot act otherwise than I do: it would be against my conscience if I did: . . . Men may laugh at me, mock me, insult me, and imprison me: I will lead a pure life before God and posterity" (Davies, pp. 42–43). He belonged to no particular theological school of thought, and it is characteristic of his independence that the Orthodox (against whom in 1836 he helped to found the *Protestantenverein*) and Rationalists were alike repugnant to him. Some of the greatest Old Testament scholars—Ernst Bertheau (1818–88), August Dillmann (1823–94), Theodor Nöldeke (1836–1930), and Julius Wellhausen (1844–1918), to name but a few—came out of his tutelage and helped to carry his influence to other generations.

We are not now concerned with Ewald the critic and historian but with Ewald the theologian. The work to be considered is his massive *die Lehre der Bibel von Gott, oder Theologie des Alten und Neuen Bundes* ("The Biblical Doctrine of God or the Theology of the Old and New Covenants," 4 vols.; Leipzig: F. C. W. Vogel, 1871–76). Volume one of this work was translated into English as *Revelation, Its Nature and Record* (Edinburgh: T. & T. Clark, 1884) and volumes two and three as *Old and New Testament Theology* (Edinburgh: T. & T. Clark, 1888). Long, wordy, and devoid of anything except the most general structural outline and consequently difficult to grasp, it nonetheless represents an imposing attempt to synthesize all of biblical thought (see Smend, 1974). Nor was this synthesis the only end he had in mind, for he also hoped that the work might rehabilitate "this source of Christian knowledge" for his own day among those who because of philosophical, theological, or scientific reasons had come to ignore it (I, pp. 8–10).

Ewald belonged to those who firmly believed in the Bible as revelation. He would not have been true to himself as critic and historian if he had not been thoroughly conscious of the element of diversity in the Scripture, but like Schultz he, too, was convinced that ultimate unity predominated over whatever variety it might contain (I, pp. 433–38). The revelation the Bible embodied was centered, he thought, in two focal points, in religious teachings and in history, neither of which should be divorced from the other. History constituted, in the first place, the warp and woof on which gradually the whole completed pattern of biblical thought had been woven. In other words, he was quite insistent on the need of seeing the teachings of the Bible in their historical development. History, however, was also a series of events which validated these teachings—the resemblance to von Hofmann and Oehler is apparent on this point—and consequently was as much a part of revelation as the doctrines which had been communicated. His own words on the matter say:

> Everything we rightly call revelation consists, in its content, of words about God and the relationship of the world as well as of man to Him and to His will . . . and in deeds and events which accompany this revelation and which stand in close connection with those words as clear witnesses to the world concerning their truth (I, p. 316).

In order to gain a fair view of Ewald's method one should not look to his *Lehre* alone but recognize, rather, that the work was planned to fit into a larger framework. His whole treatment of Israel's religion, he tells us, was to fall into the following three parts: (1) an Introduction on the nature of revelation and the Word of God, (2) a History of the Hebrew people down to the days of Jesus in which he intended to show not only the evolution of biblical thought but also the course of God's redemptive purposes, and (3) a system of biblical thought. What is today known as his *Lehre* actually embraces only the first and third parts; the second is to be found, instead, in his *History of Israel*. Justice to him requires that one remain aware of this larger interrelationship.

Within the *Lehre* his method was a combination of systematic treatment and historical presentation. The topics of systematic theology provided the major divisions. Volume I contained the biblical doctrine of the Word of God, volumes II and III, bearing the title "Glaubenslehre," discussed the doctrine of God, and the fourth volume considered "the life of man and the kingdom of God," or, to put the matter differently, it dealt with humanity, ethics, and salvation. Yet, while he placed his greatest emphasis on exhibiting the structure and theological content of biblical religion, he also gave considerable attention to the role which historical process had played in the creation of that religion and showed how every single concept had grown until it reached its full and final definition in the New Testament. As far as the Old Testament was concerned, he distinguished four major periods of development: (1) the pre-Mosaic prophets, i.e., the patriarchs, (2) Mosaism or theocracy, (3) prophecy, and (4) a degeneration of prophecy, "a prophetless time," which he called hagiocracy. Ewald always held to the chronological priority of the law over the prophets and consequently never accepted Graf's— later Wellhausen's—reconstruction of Hebrew religious development.

On the whole, the *Lehre der Bibel von Gott* was not Ewald's greatest work, nor does it appear to have exercised much influence. His biographers are usually prone to apologize for it, especially in the light of his more famous history of Israel. It is pointed out, by way of an excuse, that he "almost alone among famous theologians had no special philosophical training" (Cheyne, p. 117). The major shortcomings are its lack of clear expression and exposition, of a plain definition of purpose and method, and of coherence and integration.

EDUARD KARL AUGUST RIEHM

The concluding years of the nineteenth century saw a new upsurge in published studies of Old Testament theology, but this revival was more in the nature of a deathwatch over a dying discipline than of a vigorous advance beyond the frontiers which Schultz and Oehler had reached. Symptomatic of the decline which had set in is the fact that none of these treatises were printed during their authors' lifetimes and owed their final form instead only to the editorial labors of devoted friends and students. One of those who attempted to stay the tide was Eduard Riehm (1830–88), a student of Hermann Hupfeld (1796–1866) and later professor at Halle. In viewpoint he, too, was a "mediating theologian." A year after his death Karl Pahncke published the lecture notes he had left in his legacy under the title *Alttestamentliche Theologie* ("Old Testament Theology"; Halle: Eugene Strien, 1889).

Old Testament theology he defined as "the historical presentation of the divinely revealed religion of Israel with reference to its nature, its inner development, and the growth of its content in Israel's spiritual consciousness. It has to pursue the historical development of Israelite religion to the point where the latter finds its higher fulfillment in Christianity" (p. 1).

The content of the Old Testament revelation was essentially that of a revealed body of knowledge. And it is that knowledge which he considered to be the proper subject of Old Testament theology. He did grant the place of "events" as an accompanying factor in revelation and even accepted them as a medium of revelation, but he also thought that Oehler had gone too far in the attention he had given to these events and to the external side of Israel's religion (i.e., sacrifices, purifications, festivals, etc.; see p. 2).

For him, as it had been for Schultz and Oehler, the method of study was "historico-genetic." He thought that he could discover one central principle running through the entire Old Testament—that principle was, briefly, the creation of God's kingdom in Israel—and the purpose of his work was, accordingly, to follow that principle through the various periods of Hebrew history. His definition of the principle reads:

> The peculiar nature of Old Testament religion consists in the belief that the one, purely spiritual, personal, and morally perfect god, who is infinitely exalted over a world absolutely dependent upon him, but who nevertheless re-

veals himself in the world, has founded in Israel, his chosen people, through the medium of a series of special revelations and deeds, a kingdom in which he desires to demonstrate to the people the whole wealth of his grace and in which his will is to be the sole, all-determinative norm (p. 20).

The patriarchs already had worshiped the true, one God. Mosaism's function was to give concrete expression to the kingdom of God by establishing the "Law of the theocracy." Prophecy represented, first, a consolidation of the theocracy, and, second, a further spiritualization of Israel's religious consciousness. Finally, in Judaism, a deterioration set in. Religion became legalistic, disintegrated into various forms, and took into itself foreign elements.

His method of discussion was to advance period by period, beginning each period with a survey of the main historical events which had occurred during its time and then systematizing its thought under topical headings. We have seen enough to draw one conclusion. His approach was basically that used by Oehler, with perhaps slightly less attention being given to the events of *Heilsgeschichte* and to external religious forms.

CHRISTIAN FRIEDRICH AUGUST DILLMANN

August Dillmann (1823–94), who taught at the University of Berlin and who was known chiefly for his Ethiopic studies and his commentaries on the Pentateuch, Joshua, and Isaiah, belongs in the history of Old Testament theology by virtue of his posthumous *Handbuch der alttestamentlichen Theologie* ("Handbook of Old Testament Theology"; ed. by Rudolf Kittel; Leipzig: S. Hirzel, 1895). The task of Old Testament theology, in his interpretation, was "to discuss scientifically the religion contained in the Bible" (p. 1), and by "scientific" he meant systematic as well as historical. He, too, centered the religion of the Old Testament in the concept of revelation which, in its contents as well as in its external theocratic and cultic manifestations, was mediated by Moses, but which also underwent further developments under specially guided prophets.

Dillmann's first problem was to determine the essential characteristic of Old Testament revelation. Strangely, the principle he chose was almost the very one which Hegel had used to describe the religion of the Hebrews. Only, instead of "sublimity," Dillmann preferred the typically Old Testament term "holiness." The basis for this principle he found in Lev. 19:2: "You must be holy; for I, the Lord your God, am holy." This idea he regarded as the quintessence of the revelation, and to it he related all other ingredients of Hebrew faith and practice. He argued that the following ideas in particular were implied in the concept of "holiness" where it applied to God;

> Sublimity, the removal from all that is creaturely, eminence, therefore also uniqueness, omnipotence, and eternity, . . . also purity, the alienation from evil and sinfulness, goodness, and ethical perfection . . . at the same time the

idea of a self-disclosing, revealing God . . . who as a person stands over against everything and as a self-conscious personality desires that all unholiness vanish (pp. 27–28).

Having thus defined the nature of the religion, he proceeded in a second section to survey its history from the patriarchal period to Moses and, thence, to the prophets. Finally, in his third and major section, he presented the doctrines of the Old Testament in systematic fashion under the headings of God, world, man, and salvation. Here, too, the historical viewpoint was ever-present and accounted for the emphasis which the study placed on a proper understanding of each concept's development. The attention he gave to historical growth should not, however, blind one to the fact that he always considered the religion as fundamentally one. Dillmann was not a *Heilsgeschichtler* and for that reason did not explain Israel's religion within the context of the establishment of the kingdom of God. His interest was limited almost exclusively to the religious ideas of the Old Testament, their content and their history, and omitted any treatment of theocratic events or institutions.

Old Testament Theology Outside Germany

Interest in Old Testament theology as well as the development of critical approaches to biblical studies were primarily located in Germany during the first three quarters of the nineteenth century. This does not mean either that France, Holland, Great Britain, and the United States were devoid of competent biblical scholars or that German scholarship was completely unknown outside its native land. As a rule, however, scholars in other countries tended to be far more conservative and orthodox in their theology and more traditional in their methodologies than the Germans. Although the Frenchman Eduard Wilhelm Eugen Reuss (1804–91) was a clear exception to the rule, he published little in the field until late in his career. Surveys of Old Testament studies in France (Kimbrough, pp. 17–42), Holland (De Vries), Great Britain (Glover, pp. 11–70; Crowther, pp. 40–81; and the early chapters in Shaffer), and the United States (Brown) during this period point to a number of reasons for the lag of biblical studies outside Germany (see also the various studies in Sykes). Some of the reasons proposed as explanations for this contrast include the following: the more radical use of philosophical speculation in explicating the Bible and its thought in German circles, the greater academic freedom of German intellectuals which allowed the employment of innovative methodologies, the greater importance assigned to lectures and publications in Germany both in educational programs in general and in the established means of acquiring teaching posts, the greater number of teaching positions and students in German theological schools with their accompanying differences in philosophical orientation and regional competitiveness, the higher educational level and philosophically oriented character of the German reading public, and the Lutheran emphasis on *sola scriptura* in the interpretation of Christian faith which necessitated a hermeneutics based on the meaning and relevance of biblical materials. At any rate, in the last two decades of the nineteenth century, German biblical scholarship became domesticated in many circles outside Germany, and non-German nationals, although frequently still more cautious and traditional than their counterparts, became contributors to the critical and historical study of the Scriptures. When Old Testament theologies came to be published outside Germany, most of these were clearly influenced not only by their German counterparts but also by historical-critical considerations. This can be seen in the work of the Frenchman Charles Piepenbring (1840–?) whose *Theologie de l'Ancien Testament* (Paris: Fischbacher, 1886 = *Theology of the Old Testament* [New York: Thomas Y. Crowell & Company, 1893]) was oriented to "the exegetical and historical method" rather than "the dogmatic method" (p. 1). The impact of the historical approach can be seen in the author's division of his work into three periods within which was stressed the historical development of each particular topic.

> The first, from Moses to the beginning of the eighth century, is distinguished by the preponderating influence exercised by traditional ideas and usages, modified only in part by early prophecy. The second, from the appearance of the oldest prophetical books to the end of the Exile, is marked by the great influence of prophecy, now at its apogee. The third, from the Exile to the first century before the Christian era, is characterized by the extraordinary influence of the written law and the priesthood (p. 2).

Signs that the English-speaking world was beginning to awaken to the importance and value of Old Testament theology made themselves known well before the end of the century. Translations of the works of Oehler, Ewald, and Schultz are cases in point. Alongside these efforts one must also place the works of Archibald Duff (1845–1934): *Old Testament Theology or the History of Hebrew Religion from the Year 800 B.C.* (2 vols.; London: A. & C. Black, 1891–1900) and *The Theology and Ethics of the Hebrews* (New York: Charles Scribner's Sons, 1902). A manual-like *Theology of the Old Testament* (London/New York: Hodder & Stoughton/Thomas Whittaker, 1896) was published by William Henry Bennett (1855–1920). Additional evidence of this interest and its incorporation into the general field of biblical studies are the chapters on the history and method of biblical theology in *The Study of Holy Scriptures* (New York: Charles Scribner's Sons, 1899; pp. 596–606) by Charles Augustus Briggs (1844–1913).

It was, however, in a large measure the work of an evangelical Scotsman, Andrew Bruce Davidson (1831–1892), of the United Free Church Seminary (New College) in Edinburgh, that the discipline of Old Testament theology entered the domain of English and American theologians. His own contemporaries, such as Cheyne, recognized the pioneer role played by Davidson in the field of English-language Old Testament scholarship. Yet, although his grasp of the grammatical and historical were abreast of the times, it is also true that he displayed a certain "hesitativeness" about accepting the more radical results of criticism (Cheyne, p. 227). These are precisely the characteristics one finds in his *Theology of the Old Testament* (ed. by S. D. F. Salmond; Edinburgh: T. & T. Clark, 1904), namely, a strong insistence on the need for an historical viewpoint combined with an unwillingness to depart very far from the paths of traditional theology, characteristics also shared by Duff, Bennett, and Briggs.

To do justice to Davidson's work one must again bear in mind that he, like so many of his predecessors, was very hesitant to publish his work and did not leave it to posterity in as definitive a form as he himself might have wished. The editor reports that he found much of the material in as many as six different editions, all undated—ample proof that Davidson still was not satisfied with his treatment of the subject when death ended his labors. Nor is one permitted to regard it as unfinished merely with respect to its content, for the same editor states quite frankly:

> One thing that gave Dr. Davidson much concern was the question of the plan on which a work of this kind should be constructed. His object was to bring the history and the ideas into living relation, to trace the progress of Old Testament faith from stage to stage, and to exhibit the course along which it advanced from its beginnings to the comparative fulness which it obtained at the end of the prophetic period. But he never carried out his scheme (p. vi).

If, therefore, his introductory statements about the nature of Old Testament theology lead us to expect one form of procedure, while the actual presentation exhibits another, we should in all fairness lay it to the fact that the question of method was a problem over which he, like many of his contemporaries, agonized and never came to a definite conclusion.

The task of Old Testament theology he regarded as "the presentation of the great operation of God in bringing in the kingdom of God, so far as that operation was carried out in the Old Testament period" (p. 6). The similarity to Oehler's conception is at once apparent and, for that matter, was pointed out by Davidson himself almost in the next sentence. Nor is this his only connection with Oehler. He, too, spoke of the "progressive" character of God's revelation which had come to an end only in "the Coming of the Son of God" (p. 2). There are passages that suggest the idea of the education of the human race (pp. 13, 35). One finds, furthermore, the same insistence that the method of discussion must not only be historical but also genetic, i.e., it must exhibit how the "succeeding truth rose out of the former truth," or, to state it differently, it must show how the same revelation developed and yet always remained fundamentally the same.

Still Biblical revelation being an organism, Old Testament theology is not a torso. It is a growth which, though it has not attained perfection, has attained a certain proper development. All its parts are there, though none of it is yet in full stature. There is perhaps no truth in the New Testament which does not lie in germ in the Old; and conversely, there is perhaps no truth in the Old Testament which has not been expanded and had new meaning put into it in the New (p. 10).

His *Theology*, however, is not a "presentation of the great operation of God in bringing in the kingdom of God." That Davidson may have had even a third plan in mind than the one suggested in the introduction or the one actually employed in his presentation might be deduced from his discussion of the "Divisions of the Subject." Rejecting the ordinary threefold division, God, Man, and Salvation, as "too abstract for a subject like ours," he then proposed a distinction between the four main types of thought, "prophecy, or religious politics; legislation, or the ritual of worship; devotion; and reflection," and suggested that each be treated historically (pp. 12–15). Whether one may see here another sign of the different "editions" with which the editor Salmond had to cope is, of course, impossible to know. It is striking, however, that the division he indicated at this point does not show itself in the body of his treatment. The only evidence of a *Heilsgeschichte* are a few pages in which he tried to sketch "the general course and drift of the history" (p. 22). His work contains no broad sweep of the history of the kingdom of God into which Israel's doctrines are integrated such as Oehler had presented. It is, rather, another discussion of the religious concepts of the Old Testament in four major groupings: God, Man, Redemption, and Last Things. The fact of historical development receives some recognition, not so much in terms of strictly defined periods as in the distinctions he drew between earlier and later thought or between individual writers.

THE DECLINE OF OLD TESTAMENT THEOLOGY AND THE DOMINANCE OF THE HISTORY OF ISRAELITE RELIGION

Near the close of the nineteenth and the beginning of the twentieth century, there occurred a remarkable decline in and temporary eclipse of concern with traditional forms of Old Testament theology. The constructive and systematic presentation of Old Testament theology was widely and almost completely replaced by a purely historical treatment of Israel's religion. This represented a different mode or organization of the material; a mode— the historical—which was widely characteristic of all forms of humanistic research at the time. The causes for this radical change were rooted in two separate areas, in the broader general theological and intellectual situation of the second half of the nineteenth century and in the narrower field of Old Testament research itself. The first of these is reflected in the widespread liberal and humanistic attitudes that became more characteristic of general and religious life during the latter half of the century. The second factor is represented in the triumph and pervasiveness of the historical-critical and history-of-religion methodologies. The crucial element in bringing about the transformation was simply that profound developments in both areas converged to take the Old Testament out of the realm of revelation.

Even so moderate a theologian as Ritschl had, in effect, excluded the Old Testament from the realm of revelation when he allowed only the person and teachings of the historic Jesus to stand as the norm of Christian theology. Nor was this condition altered by his willingness to retain Israel's literature and religion as background material from which Jesus might be better understood. His specific views on revelation were an integral part of the widespread tendency to move away from a supernatural interpretation of God and to stress, instead, divine immanence within the world. God was in nature, in the historical experience of humankind, and in the human conscience. There was, so it appeared, no need to look for God in a special revelation mediated through a specially chosen people.

To this change in theological orientation one might add certain innovations in the general intellectual life of the century. Under the impact particularly of the social sciences religion was treated more and more as an expression and reflection of human culture and human experiences. The growing prevalence of the practice to resort to environmental forces or to creative human personalities for the explanation of all forms of thought, including religious beliefs, was bound to exert a deep-going influence on the study of the religion of the Old Testament as well.

Within the more limited area of Old Testament scholarship, nothing had a more far-reaching effect than the revolution which was produced by the historical-critical work of Karl Henning Graf (1815–69), Abraham Kuenen (1828–91), and Julius Wellhausen (1844–1918). Mosaism or the law, once considered as in the biblical traditions themselves to be the great starting point of the divine revelation, came to be seen as a late development which had been ultimately dependent upon the prophets for its theological views. The position that came to dominate late nineteenth-century scholarship was expressed by Reuss in the formula: "The prophets are older than the law and the psalms are later than both" (*Die Geschichte der Heiligen Schriften Alten Testaments* [Braunschweig: C. A. Schwetschke, 1881] p. vii). With that conclusion, the most definite literary entity to which the idea of a divinely communicated doctrine could be attached, namely, the Torah, now had lost its connection with Moses and the exodus. It was above all Wellhausen, whose first volume of his *Geschichte Israels* (Berlin: G. Reimer, 1878 = *Prolegomena to the History of Israel* [Edinburgh: A. & C. Black, 1885]) summed up the literary and historical arguments for the late date of the Mosaic legislation, who forced totally new interpretations of the religious and political history of Israel (see the contributions in Knight).

A logical result of this new approach was an inevitable underscoring of the primitive character of Israel's pre-prophetic religion, while, on the other hand, the prophets came to be looked upon as the real creators of the religious beliefs of the Old Testament. Parallels to primitive religion elsewhere (animism and primitive polytheism) were found to be more conspicuous in the Old Testament than had hitherto generally been considered possible. The work of Near Eastern archaeologists demonstrated, moreover, with increasing clarity that Hebrew faith had not developed in isolation but had stood in contact with and had been stimulated by the other religious cultures of the ancient Orient.

Thus the histories of Israelite religion had as one of their purposes to provide a religious and historical context within which the Old Testament could be read and understood. They sought to provide a description of the religious and thought worlds of ancient Israel that were considered essential for an understanding of the Old Testament itself. Since Israelite religion was reflected in but not identical with Old Testament traditions, such histories sought to expound this larger world and its development and thus offer a larger canvas against which to study the text. Let us try to illustrate the function of such histories with reference to some of Gabler's discussion. He spoke of "true biblical theology" which was a faithful description of the religion of the Old Testament divided into its different periods. He also spoke of "pure biblical theology" or a constructive systematization of the important and abiding religious teachings of the Bible which would utilize the "true biblical theology" and in turn be utilized by systematic theology. In terms of Gabler's program the histories of Israelite religion which proliferated at the end of the nineteenth century were what might be called "prior biblical theology." That is, they sought to provide a description of Israel's religion and its Near Eastern backgrounds and connections which would make possible an intelligent reading of the Bible. The focus on this "prior" theology tended, of course, to eclipse or reduce the production of "true" and "pure" theologies and at the same time to reduce any claims made for the Old Testament as revelation or as essential to the work of systematic theology.

History of the "History of Israel's Religion"

The science of the "history of Israel's religion"—the name most generally assigned this approach—had behind it a long formative period when it supplanted Old Testament theology at the end of the nineteenth century. Many of its principles and procedures may, in fact, be traced back to Gabler's discourse and the work of G. L. Bauer but it was not until the work of Vatke, George, and Gramberg that it began to show any real identity. Vatke's *Religion des Alten Testaments*, if one ignores the philosophical framework into which it was placed, was the first real "history of Israelite religion" and the first treatise also to reconstruct the development of that religion in what came to be widely regarded as its proper sequence. Being so far ahead of its time, it was followed by a period of dormancy which lasted a little over thirty years. This interlude, from our larger perspective today, might be looked upon as a period of preparation. In the first place, the critical analysis of the source materials for such a history, the books of the Old Testament themselves, was not yet completed, nor was it to come to any kind of conclusion until the publication of Graf's theories and the subsequent analysis by Wellhausen. In the second place, during these years method as well as point of view of the general "history of religion" received their clarification through the comparative studies undertaken especially among the Indo-European religions of India, Persia, and the Teutonic peoples.

When, after this interlude, the thoroughgoing historical form of treatment again made its appearance, it was in *De godsdienst van Israël tot den ondergang van den Joodschenstaat* (2 vols.; Haarlem: A. C. Kruseman, 1869–70 = *The Religion of Israel to the Fall of the Jewish State* [3 vols.; London: Williams and Norgate, 1874–75]) by the Dutch critic, Abraham Kuenen (1828–91). Nothing is more expressive of his attitude toward the religion of the Old Testament than the assertion, "For us the Israelitish religion is one of those (principal) religions, nothing less, but also nothing more" (I, p. 5). This position was echoed in his *De Profeten en den profetie on der Israel* (2 vols.; Leiden: Engels, 1875 = *The Prophets and Prophecy in Israel* [London: Longmans, Green, & Co., 1877]): "Prophecy . . . a phenomenon, yea one of the most important and remarkable phenomena, in the history of religion, but just on that account a human phenomenon, proceeding from Israel, directed to Israel" (p. 4). The traditional claims made for Israelite religion as divinely revealed and everlastingly relevant were thus summarily rejected.

Kuenen wrote soon after Graf's epochmaking criticism of the historical books of the Old Testament with its critical attempt to validate Vatke's and Reuss's earlier surmise that the prophets had preceded the law and after Bishop John William Colenso (1814–83) had criticized the historical value of the so-called P-narrative in the Hexateuch (in his *The Pentateuch and Book of Joshua Critically Examined* [5 vols.; London: Longmans, Green, and Co., 1862–65]). Kuenen's work was the first to implement the Grafian theory by beginning the survey at the point where historical certainty in the Grafian approach seemed to demand it, namely, with the eighth-century prophets. The revolutionary results of the Grafian theory for the history of the Hebrews become particularly clear when we compare the confidence with which the Pentateuch had been used by the more conservative critics like Ewald, Riehm, and Dillmann with such a sentence as "Of the first centuries of Israel's existence as a people, we possess either no contemporary memorials at all, or but very few" (Kuenen, *Religion of Israel*, I, p. 28).

Less comprehensive in the area it covered, but methodologically far more instructive, was Berhnard Duhm's *Die Theologie der Propheten als Grundlage für die innere Entwicklungsgeschichte der Israelitischen Religion* ("The Theology of the Prophets as the Basis for the Inner Developmental History of Israelite Religion"; Bonn: Adolph Marcus, 1875). Duhm (1847–1925) devoted considerable attention to the entire question of method and, therefore, performed much of the fundamental spadework needed in developing the procedures which were eventually adopted by the whole historical-critical approach. Published at a time when the controversy over what has come to be known as the Graf–Wellhausen theory was coming to a head— Wellhausen's articles on the composition of the Hexateuch and the historical books of the Old Testament began to appear only a year later—its main purpose was to prove that the real basis for the inner development of Israel's religion had been laid in the thought of the prophets. Prophecy had not grown out of Mosaic religion (p. 10); rather, it had to be understood in terms of itself (p. 18). A theological presentation of the religion of the Old Testament in its entirety he regarded as an inherent impossibility "because of the absence of temporal, formal, and factual unity" (p. 27), and, instead, wanted it replaced by a "history of Israelitish religion" (p. 28). At the same time, he was confident that the prophets had possessed a sufficiently unified religious outlook to justify the expression "a theology of the prophets" (p. 29).

Duhm's other principles were no less determinative. The very first sentence established the mood in which he planned to carry out his description of prophetic thought: "The following studies . . . are inductive, not didactic, in nature" (p. 1). Equally illustrative of his temper are the two frequently used phrases "presuppositionless investigation" and "pragmatic history-writing." The findings of source criticism, because they constituted for him the very basis of his study, were to be rigidly adhered to (p. 18). Even for such a relatively homogeneous group as the prophets the outline of the discussion could only be historical, never systematic. Only so, he thought, would it be possible to make clear the "particular situation" of each prophet, to emphasize "the active, dynamic, personal contribution of each prophet as he meets that situation," and, finally, to demonstrate that the prophets, despite their general agreement, also had exhibited individual differences (pp. 29–30). Typical, again, of the new attitude towards the Bible is his interpretation of the prophets, not as mediators of a divine revelation, but as *religiöse Volks-redner* ("religious orators"; p. 31).

Kuenen and Duhm paid little or no attention to the pre-prophetic period in Israelite history and religion. This now became a major center of interest and with that shift we enter the next phase in the history of the new study. The first area in which the traceable origins of the religion were sought was that of primitive Semitic paganism. Here again we meet the famous name of Wellhausen whose *Reste arabischen Heidentumes, gesammelt und erläutert* ("Remnants of Arabic Paganism Collected and Explained"; Berlin: G. Reimer, 1887) provided a long list of data on pre-Islamic Arabic religion which he continued to argue should be used to understand and explain the earliest beginnings of Hebrew religion. His approach was continued by the Scotsman William Robertson Smith (1846–92), a student of A. B. Davidson, whose Burnett lectures became one of the standard treatments of the subject (*Lectures on the Religion of the Semites* [London: A. & C. Black, 1889]).

The enlarged compass which Wellhausen and Smith had furnished to the new historical school was fully represented in the first comprehensive history of Old Testament religion, Rudolf Smend's *Lehrbuch der alttestamentlichen Religionsgeschichte* ("Textbook of the History of Old Testament Religion"; Freiburg: J. C. B. Mohr, 1893). Where Kuenen and Duhm had begun the survey with the prophets, Smend (1851–1913) sought to take the origins of the religion of the Hebrews back to the primitive beliefs and cults of the early Semites and, thereby, set a pattern frequently adopted in subsequent discussion. In English, *Hebrew Religion: Its Origin and Development* (London: SPCK, 1930) by William Oscar Emil Oesterley (1866–1950) and Theodore Henry Robinson (1881–1964) may be said to represent a classical expression of this particular thrust in the history of Old Testament religion.

The second direction into which the historical treatment moved is associated especially with the members of the *religionsgeschichtliche Schule*, the history-of-religion school. First of all, aided by the remarkable increase in the knowledge about the religious life of the whole Near East during biblical times, this group turned its attention to the question of the influence of ancient Near Eastern religion on the Hebrews throughout their entire history. Hugo Gressmann (1877–1927) one of the prominent representatives of the school, has aptly described this phase as the effort to discover the "pre-history" of all Old Testament concepts (pp. 30–39). To establish the literal meaning of an idea or the analysis of a particular genre of literature as a certain biblical writer had used them was not considered sufficient. Strict regard for historical method and the complexities of the historical and literary process also demanded that the historian be concerned with the development before it entered the Bible. Hermann Gunkel, in the subsequent controversy with Wellhausen which developed over the issue of searching for pre-biblical antecedents, expressed this radical historical orientation in the following words:

> Wellhausen falls into conflict with fundamental principles which are everywhere recognized in historical science. . . . The cardinal principle of historical study is this: that we are unable to comprehend a person, a period, or a thought dissociated from its antecedents, but that we can speak of a real living understanding only when we have the antecedent history (1903, p. 404).

The history-of-religion school thus criticized Wellhausen, and other literary critics, for not being "sufficiently historical because he was too mechanical in his emphasis on source analysis, too little concerned with connections between the religion of Israel and the religions of the surrounding nations, and too little aware of the deeper origins which define the truest spirit of Israelite religion" (Oden, p. 144; on the controversy between Gunkel and Wellhausen, see McKane, pp. 225–28).

Both Gunkel and Gressmann wrote of the *truly* new departure which a *truly* historical approach would bring to Old Testament studies (see Klatt, p. 74; Oden, p. 143). Yet, at the same time, the history-of-religion school saw itself as "nothing but a new wave of the mighty historical current set in motion by our great idealist thinkers and poets, which has affected our entire mental life, and has now long influenced our theological outlook also" (Gunkel, 1926–27, p. 533). Gunkel spoke of the new insights gained from what he called neo-Romanticism which saw new colors and heard new sounds which manifested the inner life of ancient people, from comparative religion which brought new vistas to bear in biblical texts, from *Literaturgeschichte* ("history of literature") which stressed form-critical analysis and the location of materials in their original *Sitz im Leben* or Situation in Life (see Buss), and from psychology which allowed the investigator to seek for and appreciate an immediate perception of the ancient person. Such elements reflect the second major component in the treatment of the Old Testament by this movement: an empathetic and aesthetic appreciation of the biblical materials and the concrete religious and social contexts in which they were employed.

> Scholars began in about 1890 to argue again that historical understanding was an art, and an art which demanded of the historian a personal relationship with the material investigated. . . . An awareness of the artistry of the Old Testament carried with it for Gunkel and others an important hermeneutical implication, for it meant that the exegete must himself participate in the feelings the text evokes (Oden, p. 145).

The Approach of Histories of Israelite Religion

During the last decade of the nineteenth century and the first two decades of the twentieth century, numerous histories of Israelite religion were published. Their authors were from several countries and represented Jewish, Protestant, and Catholic traditions. In addition to those already mentioned, the following is a representative but far from exhaustive list of such authors and the dates of their publications: Claude Joseph Goldsmid Montefiore (1892),

Karl Ferdinand Reinhardt Budde (1899), Thomas Kelly Cheyne (1899), Alfred Firmin Loisy (1901, privately printed because of fear of church censure), Wolf Wilhelm Friedrich von Baudissin (1903), William Edward Addis (1906), Max Richard Herman Löhr (1906), Eduard König (1912), John Punnett Peters (1914), Henry Preserved Smith (1914), Henry Thatcher Fowler (1916), and Rudolf Kittel (1921).

The widespread impact of the new development is evident in the fact that even so conservative a scholar as Eduard König (1846–1936) found it necessary to give lip service to the movement even though he took great pains to retain at least a remnant of the old concept of revelation by distinguishing between the "legitimate" religion of Israel—chiefly prophetic in nature and in existence at all stages from patriarchal to late postexilic times—and "illegitmate" religions of Israel which the Hebrews had acquired from their pagan ancestors or neighbors. Several works still retained the term "biblical" or "Old Testament theology" in their titles but in reality were actually histories of Israelite religion. This was the case with *Biblische Theologie des Alten Testaments* (2 vols.; Tübingen: J. C. B. Mohr, 1905–11) begun by Bernhard Stade (1848–1906) and a work with the same title (Tübingen: J. C. B. Mohr, 1911) published by Emil Friedrich Kautzsch (1841–1910) which was a German translation of his "Religion in Israel," originally published in English (in *HDB*, volume 5, pp. 612–734). The same was the situation with the earlier noted works by Duff, Bennett, and Piepenbring. The editors of the posthumously published *Die Theologie des Alten Testament in ihrer geschichtlichen Entwicklung dargestellt* ("Theology of the Old Testament Presented in its Historical Development"; Strassburg: C. F. Schmidt & F. Bull, 1886) by August Kayser (1821–85) chose, in its third edition, simply to delete any reference in the title to Old Testament theology and renamed the work a history of Israelite religion.

The purpose to which the vast majority of these "histories" were dedicated had its basis, ultimately, in the roles they were assigned to play as "prior theologies" for understanding the Old Testament itself. It is not necessary to repeat here what has already been said at the beginning of this section about the theological point of view which gained dominance toward the end of the nineteenth century. Suffice it to reiterate that when the idea of a special scriptural revelation was no longer considered to have central importance, the Old Testament itself moved into the position of a book whose relationship to modern religious thought was actually negligible except for its historical connections with Christianity.

The primary objective of works of this genre was to trace the history of Israel's religion from the earliest discoverable stages down to the Christian era. They were thus preoccupied with *genetics* and *development*. It should be clear, of course, that the emphasis which these studies placed on describ-

ing the evolution of Old Testament religion and their corresponding disregard
of the nature of that religion in its structural coherence and characteristic
viewpoints were not the fault of the historical method *per se*. For this method
is just as much concerned with the problem of *wie es eigentlich gewesen* as
it is with the problem of *wie es eigentlich geworden*. In other words, the
most serious mistake of the historians was a kind of myopia which led them
to believe that once they had traced the origin and development of an idea or
of the entire religion, they had said fundamentally what needed to be or could
be said. It might be well to recall, in passing, that the necessity of using
historical categories had been fully recognized by those who earlier during
the century had labored in the field of Old Testament theology proper. They,
too, were conscious that development had occurred and had sought to do
justice to this very evident fact by distinguishing, some more thoroughly than
others, between different stages or periods. Where they had deviated from
the historians in this respect was in their inclination to minimize the extent
of the developments and to move beyond the portrait of the development to
some form of systematic presentation.

As historical and objectively conducted studies, the "histories" showed
complete agreement with Gabler's principle of the need for independence
from the authority or influence of any writer's own particular theological or
philosophical preferences. In order to discover what the religion of the Hebrews had been only such a course could be possible. That they actually
showed the effect of the religious attitudes held by their authors was to be
expected, since, especially in investigations which deal with human thought,
total objectivity can scarcely be hoped for. Within the limits of their concern
with the evolution of Hebrew religion they were, however, objective enough.
How, otherwise, can one explain the remarkable uniformity, in form of treatment as well as in results achieved, which they revealed?

The historians considered their work as a scientific endeavor and like
all scientific endeavor it involved two essential steps, the gathering of material through induction and the integration of these findings in orderly pattern.
Applied to the study of the history of Israel's religion, the principle of an
inductive collection of reliable data inevitably raised the twin questions of
where and *how* such data were to be found. Because it was interested in the
religion of the Hebrew people and not merely in the religious views of the
Old Testament, the historical school answered the first problem by going
farther afield than had the earlier theologies. The literature of the Old Testament constituted the major source, of course, but other sources of information were tapped as well, particularly the intertestamental writings, archaeology,
and the findings of the comparative study of religions. Anything that was
relevant, no matter whence it came, was taken into consideration. Gunkel

gave succinct expression to the commonly shared perspective that Israelite religion must be understood in terms larger than the Old Testament itself:

> This widening of the horizon took place very slowly, and has only now become generally known. If it cannot be said to have fundamentally changed the attitude of Biblical scholarship, it has at least changed its direction. Just as a man who knows only one language does not really know any language; just as he who studies the history of one state requires to know something of what the life of a state means; so it is our conviction that all religions constitute an essential unit, and that the student of the Bible must needs know in addition something of Religion as such. As a matter of fact, therefore, Biblical study opens out at this point into the Universal History of Religion (1926–27, p. 535).

As for the second problem, which was *how* reliable data could be discovered, it is worth noting that in this century the historians and theologians both agreed that it would have to be by means of grammatico-historical exegesis. The meaning assigned to any biblical passage would have to be the originally intended one. One is struck today by the fact that even the conservatives of that time subscribed quite generally to this form of exegesis and resorted to typology or allegory only on rare occasions. Grammatico-historical interpretation, however, demanded by its very nature that the historical circumstances from which any given portion of the Old Testament had emerged or to which it had been addressed be known. At once this brought up the vexing question of historical criticism, and it is no accident, therefore, that the critical movement was represented among conservatives and liberals alike although, of course, the answers provided by the first group often differed sharply from those of the second.

Historical criticism was, of course, the lifeblood of the historical school, first because it furnished the means of determining the actual sense of the material provided by the sources, and, second, because the historians needed it for their principle of integration. Where the theologies had sought for organic unity in a logical structure of thought, the histories found it in the ongoing process of history. But to establish what the exact course of that process had been, historical criticism was necessary. If one wanted to know, for example, the nature of Hebrew religion before the settlement in Palestine, it was imperative to discover first whether the Pentateuch could be relied on in any way to give an accurate picture of religious conditions in that period.

With the collection of accurate data, the next step was that of relating them to one another in some form of coherence. The instrument of organization was, as was noted in the preceding paragraph, the process of history itself. True to their basic premise that Israel's religion was deeply influenced by the political, social, economic, and intellectual conditions of the Hebrew people, the historians took their framework from the secular history of the nation. On the whole, the number of periods into which the religion's development was divided cannot be called excessive. There were certainly no more than the ones recognized in the theologies. Smend had three, as did Stade, and H. P. Smith four. To be sure, within each period subsidiary stages were commonly differentiated, but never to the point of overshadowing their larger unity.

There is one very far-reaching result which the historical presentation produced. Its picture of the development of Israel's religion was not one of unilineal progress but one of astonishing differences and contrasts. Priest and prophet were shown as glaring antagonists, while pre-prophetic religion was reduced, in many presentations, to nature worship. The impression that the Old Testament contained not one but various religions, was, consequently, quite prevalent. Harnack, therefore, must have expressed the opinion of many when, parodying Max Müller's famous "He who knows one, knows none," he said of the Bible, "He who does not know this religion knows none, and he who knows it together with its history, knows all" (*Reden und Aufsätze* [Giessen: A. Töpelmann, 1906] II, p. 168).

SUMMARY OF DEVELOPMENTS IN THE NINETEENTH CENTURY

In the preceding sections of this chapter we have noted several significant developments in Old Testament study. As we have seen, foremost among these, at least in academic circles, were the dominance of the historical-critical approach and a significant decrease in the authority ascribed to the Bible in general and the Old Testament in particular. A number of other consequences related to these larger issues should be noted as a way of summarizing the status of research at the end of the nineteenth and the beginning of the twentieth century.

(1) Religion and religious practices rather than ideas or teachings had become the primary focus of attention especially in German research. This characteristic is rather obvious, being reflected in the fact that "religion" tended to replace "theology" in the titles of published volumes. The focus on religion meant that the Bible was no longer treated as the inspired word of God, the recorded revelation of the divine, nor even the literary deposit of theological reflections. Neither was the religious history reported in the Bible understood primarily as a history of theology or doctrines nor of doctrinal or theological development. The Old Testament, instead, was treated primarily as a collection of religious documents which had been produced by a living religion (for similar developments in New Testament studies, see Boers, pp. 39–66). Religion, unlike doctrines and theology, does not lend itself readily to systematization and thus defies being presented in the form of logical and coordinated ideas or systems.

(2) Religious truths and insights or, for those who chose to speak in such terms, God's self-revelations were seen as the product and function of human history and human experience rather than objective divine and timeless communication. This was a special emphasis in the *religionsgeschichtliche Schule* which sought to go beyond purely historical and literary studies, associated with Wellhausen and his closest followers, in order to penetrate the world of experience undergone by those who produced the contents of the Scriptures. Throughout his writings this point was constantly made by Gunkel and may be seen in the following quotation:

> We know from the Pietists, and from the teaching of German theology since Schleiermacher's day, that all religious teaching arises in the hearts of men and is only the expression of a far deeper feeling; that the actual well-spring, out of which religion eternally flows, is the heart of the pious man touched by God. Objective truth comes into the consciousness of humanity through persons, who have been mightily stirred and lifted above themselves. If then, we wish to understand religion in its innermost recesses, we must try to understand the inner life of good men. It is, therefore, the problem of Old Testament science to become acquainted, as intimately as possible, with those who best represent the religious atmosphere of the Old Testament. We must penetrate so deeply into their experiences that we can sympathise with them, that we can repeat them in ourselves, and become the interpreters of them to our own generation (1903, p. 119).

Such a position stressed the necessity of the modern interpreter to become contemporary with the original context of the author or the material being studied and to relive the experience of the biblical personages:

> To appropriate the divine message for our wants, we need no help of ecclesiastical tradition, no authoritative churchly exegesis. All that we need is to put ourselves by the side of the psalmist, the prophet, or the apostle, to enter by spiritual sympathy into his experience, to feel our sin and need as he felt them, and to take home to us, as he took them, the gracious words of divine love (William Robertson Smith, *The Old Testament in the Jewish Church* [Edinburgh: A. & C. Black, 1881] p. 14).

This focus on "empathy with the originals" functiond both as a hermeneutical principle and as an apologetic argument. As a hermeneutical principle it had parallels to the position of the early reformers who had used the Bible to critique the church thus demonstrating that the Bible was not a book contemporary with or identical to the faith and tradition of the present. Understanding and appropriation thus required a bridging of the gap between the biblical and the present. The historical-critical method had not only demonstrated this to be the case, thus intensifying the distance between the contemporary and the biblical, but also had shown that frequently the contents of the Bible were not contemporary with the setting the Bible itself had given them. As an apologetic argument, the necessity for "empathy with the originals" meant that biblical criticism was an indispensable requirement. Otherwise how could the original setting and wording with which the interpreter must become contemporary be determined? Gunkel spoke of this use of criticism as the "deepening" of the interpreter's knowledge.

> Let us take the first point; that of deepening our knowledge. If every historical phenomenon represents something particular, something which cannot be repeated, then the problem for investigation must be looked upon as itself individual and peculiar. This explains the object kept in view by the more recent school of thought: not only to give prominence to the chief outlines of these phenomena, that which is understood at the present day and which we can lay before our community as worthy of their careful attention, but also that which is peculiar in it, and which cannot be repeated—its birthmark, so to say, the smell of its mother earth (1903, p. 122).

(3) Both the final form of the canonical materials and the limits of the canon were no longer considered as mandatory boundaries within which the study of Israelite religion and thought had to operate. First of all, the desire to understand biblical materials and religious expressions within their original contexts or life situations meant that the final form of the text—which was the product of long and diverse, later editorial and redactional processes—had to be bypassed. To do this, the interpreter had to rediscover and reconstruct the original contents and contexts within the historical processes of ancient Israelite life which were seldom considered identical with the final or canonical wording and placement of the materials. This can be seen, for example, in the case of the laws of the Pentateuch which are placed within the Bible in the context of the Mosaic period but which practically all interpreters related to later times and conditions. The original form, not the canonical form, became the focus of research.

Even the formation of the canon itself could be viewed as an unfortunate episode in the history of Israelite religion.

> Finally we come to the tragedy of Hebrew literature. The spirit loses power. The forms are exhausted. Imitations begin to abound. Redactions take the place of original creations. Hebrew ceases to be the living language of the people. By this time the collections are grouped together into larger collections. The Canon has come into being (Gunkel, 1928, p. 66).

In the second place, investigations moved beyond the limits of the canon and into not only the world of general Semitic and other Near Eastern religions but also, on occasion, into the larger world of universal religion. This meant that the Old Testament became one component, although a significant one, in a larger complex. This feature of the study of religion, Gunkel referred to as the "widening" of our knowledge:

> Now to the second point: the widening of our knowledge. If everything of importance in history is connected with many other things, the problem must

be to understand them in connection with these other things. . . . The historian of religion must in perfect simplicity overstep the boundaries of his special subject, and must be able to recognize everywhere the actual special relation of the parts to the whole, and the truly significant analogies. In opposition to the spirit of this endeavour we have that old negligent comfortable feeling—a power of incredible strength—and the incapacity of the individual worker which may perhaps be overcome, if many co-operate; but above all the dogmatic prejudice, which regards the religion of the Bible and Christianity as some-thing so peculiar to itself that it cannot possibly be explained on the analogy of other religions. It is not my present business to ask how we are to answer the question of dogma which thus arises, which means ultimately the problem of the "absoluteness" of Christianity. The question I raise at present is that the historian in whose eyes the history of mankind is a Unity, cannot separate into two halves the evolution of what is Christian and what belongs to other reli-gions (1903, pp. 123–24).

(4) The priority and prominence of the prophets in Israelite religion became almost a universal theme in Old Testament studies during the last half of the nineteenth century. The historical-critical approach, as we have seen, had reasoned itself to the conclusion that "the prophets are older than the law and the psalms are later than both" (so Reuss). Such a position cata-pulted the prophets into the center of research where they were understood as the real creators of the authentic religion of Israel. It was they who shifted the focus of Hebrew religion from nature and nationalism to individual mo-rality and universal monotheism and who stressed personal experience as more expressive of genuine religion than institutional forms based on sacri-fice and priestly ritual (see Zimmerli, pp. 17–30).

A number of reasons probably contributed to this strong emphasis on prophecy and prophets. (a) Historical-critical studies had challenged the bib-lical picture of Mosaic religion—embodied in the laws of the Pentateuch—as the fountainhead and continuing authority throughout Israelite history. Thus some other period and source had to be located as the formative era and influence. (b) Assigning creativity to the prophets was a way of avoiding out-and-out historicism which sought to explain everything as the consequence of socio-cultural influences. At least the prophets could be seen as creative individuals in conflict and dialogue with their contemporary culture and as persons pointing to a more excellent way. (c) The prophetic literature seemed, at least in its main features, to be assignable to particular historical contexts and thus provided a body of literature which could be understood "histori-cally." (d) The teachings and message of the prophets, as understood by the interpreters, seemed to be more in harmony with the theology and outlook of the same interpreters and thus struck a responsive and sympathetic chord. (e) The prophets seemed to offer the opportunity for that "empathy with the originals" which was of so much concern for the history-of-religion ap-proach. Thus it was assumed that the religious and inner world of the prophets—their ecstatic experiences—in which they received their "revelations" of the divine could be recreated and empathetically understood. A spate of studies focused on this concern (for a classical statement, see Gunkel, "The Secret Experiences of the Prophets," *Expositor* XI/1[1924]356–66; 427–35; 2[1924]23–32). (f) The strong anti-priestly and anti-cultic emphasis of much nineteenth-century Old Testament study—actually, of course, much older, primarily of Christian rootage, and particularly characteristic of Protestantism—was able to utilize the prophets and prophetism to disparage the traditional and cultic aspects in the religion of the Hebrew Scriptures.

(5) Widely characteristic of nineteenth-century studies, widespread in Christian circles, was the disparagement of postexilic Judean religion in general and later Judaism in particular. We have noted this sentiment in many of the above surveys of particular works. Such sentiments were not original to the nineteenth century but seem to have reached an apogee during this period (see Moore). Wellhausen's attitude toward Judaism (see Silberman's essay in Knight, and compare Smend, 1982) may be considered as typical although his anti-Judaism was not the consequence of a *heilsgeschichtliche* approach in which Judaism was disparaged in order to argue for the fulfilling quality of Christianity. Following the typical interpretation in German scholarship of his day, Wellhausen understood Judaism as a purely legalistic system and described it as "a mere empty chasm over which one springs from the Old Testament to the New" (*Prolegomena*, p. 1). Judaism was the final product of the codification of the law begun with Deuteronomy which inaugurated the end of religious spontaneity and prophecy. The theocratic church (Wellhausen was also opposed to the course which orthodoxy took in early Christianity!) which developed on the basis of the law was presented as an unattractive, unedifying institution:

> Judaism is everywhere historically comprehensible, and yet it is a mass of antinomies. We are struck with the free flight of thought and the deep inwardness of feeling which are found in some passages in the Wisdom and in the Psalms; but, on the other hand, we meet with a pedantic asceticism which is far from lovely, and with pious wishes the greediness of which is ill-concealed; and these unedifying features are the dominant ones of the system. Monotheism is worked out to its furthest consequences, and at the same time is enlisted in the service of the narrowest selfishness; Israel participates in the sovereignty of the One God. The Creator of heaven and earth becomes the manager of a petty scheme of salvation; the living God descends from His throne to make way for the law. The law thrusts itself in everywhere; it commands and blocks up the access to heaven; it regulates and sets limits to the understanding of the divine working on earth. As far as it can, it takes the soul out of religion and spoils morality. It demands a service of God, which, though revealed, may yet with truth be called a self-chosen and unnatural one, the sense and use of which are apparent neither to the understanding nor the heart. The labour is done for the sake of the exercise; it does no one any good, and rejoices neither

God nor man. It has no inner aim after which it spontaneously strives and which it hopes to attain by itself, but only an outward one, namely, the reward attached to it, which might as well be attached to other and possibly even more curious conditions. The ideal is a negative one, to keep one's self from sin, not a positive one, to do good upon the earth; the morality is one which scarcely requires for its exercise the existence of fellow-creatures. Now pious exercises can dam up life and hold it in bounds, they may conquer from it more and more ground, and at last turn it into one great Sabbath, but they cannot penetrate it at the root. The occupation of the hands and the desire of the heart fall asunder. What the hands are doing has nothing in common with the earth, and bears no reference to earthly objects; but with the Jews the result of this is that their hope assumes a more worldly complexion. There is no connection between the Good One and goodness. There are exceptions, but they disappear in the system (*Prolegomena*, p. 509).

The above noted characteristics and consequences were typical of the history-of-religion movement—defined broadly enough to include such scholars as Wellhausen and Stade. One here, of course, must exclude from this group practically all Jewish and Catholic scholars (for a survey of representative figures, see Thompson, pp. 78–91). Conservative scholars sought to offer alternatives to or to refute the reconstruction of Israel's religious history represented by most of the writers noted above. Notable in this defense of more traditional views are *The Early Religion of Israel as Set Forth by Biblical Writers and by Modern Critical Historians* (Edinburgh/New York: W. Blackwood & Sons/T. Whittaker, 1892) by the Scottish orientalist James Robertson (1840–1920) and *The Jewish Religion* (London: K. Paul, Trench, Trübner & Co., 1891) by the principal of the Jews' College in London, Michael Friedländer (1833–1910).

Most British and American scholarship, with its cultural and philosophical heritage radically different from that of Germany, did not fully adopt either the methodology or the conclusions of the historical-critical approach. The theological-philosophical climate in England, and the same holds for the United States, during the first half of the nineteenth century has been described "by saying that Christianity consisted of truths conveyed by revelation, approved by reason, accepted by faith, and put into effect by moral conduct and by worship and prayer. Since the Bible was a principal source of that revelation, its substantial trustworthiness was to be, and could be defended, even though slight doubts could be entertained about parts of the Old Testament" (Rogerson, in Sykes, p. 66). As the century wore on, intensification of the "doubts" increased and expansion of the "parts" occurred, but the general approach still held sway, with of course some notable exceptions. Many British scholars retained confidence in the Bible as a divinely given book containing the revelation of God but sought to combine this with a historical-critical approach which studied the Bible as a human document. In his passionate evangelical plea on behalf of biblical criticism, William

Robertson Smith, in distinguishing the outer and inner aspects or the human and divine components in Scripture, wrote:

> In the Bible, God and man meet together, and hold such converse as is the abiding pattern and rule of all religious experience. In this simple fact lies the key to all those puzzles about the divine and human side of the Bible with which people are so much exercised. . . . The first condition of a sound understanding of Scripture is to give full recognition to the human side, to master the whole situation and character and feelings of each human interlocutor who has a part in the drama of Revelation. *Nay, the whole business of scholarly exegesis lies with this human side* (*The Old Testament in the Jewish Church*, pp. 18–20).

For many in this broad conservative tradition there was little difference between systematic and biblical theology especially when biblical study was conducted in inductive fashion—on the basis of Baconian common-sense philosophy—supported by the assumption that the Bible, like the world of nature, was a great reservoir of facts and truths waiting to be combined and integrated in their organic relationships to produce a harmonious system. This latter attitude was particularly widespread in Old School Presbyterianism in the United States and can be seen in the writings of such scholars as Charles Hodge (1797–1878) and Benjamin Breckinridge Warfield (1851–1921) (see Bozeman, especially pp. 132–59).

IV.

THE REBIRTH OF
OLD TESTAMENT THEOLOGY

A. A. **Anderson**, "Old Testament Theology and Its Methods," *Promise and Fulfillment* (ed. by F. F. Bruce; Edinburgh: T. & T. Clark, 1963)7–19; O. **Betz**, "Biblical Theology, History of," *IDB* 1(1962)432–37; R. E. **Clements**, *A Century of Old Testament Study* (London: Lutterworth Press, 1976) = *One Hundred Years of Old Testament Interpretation* (Philadelphia: Westminster Press, 1976)118–40; Robert C. **Dentan**, *Preface to Old Testament Theology* (New York: Seabury Press, ²1963)61–71; C. T. **Fritsch**, "New Trends in Old Testament Theology," *BSac* 103(1946)293–305; H. F. **Hahn**, *The Old Testament in Modern Research* (London/Philadelphia: SCM Press/Muhlenberg Press, 1954)226–49; W. J. **Harrington**, *The Path of Biblical Theology* (Dublin: Gill and Macmillan, 1973)25–40; Emil G. **Kraeling**, *The Old Testament Since the Reformation* (London/New York: Lutterworth Press/Harper & Row, 1955)265–84; H.-J. **Kraus**, *Geschichte der historisch-kritischen Erforschung des Alten Testaments* (Neukirchen-Vluyn: Neukirchener Verlag, 1956, ²1969)393–434; *idem*, *Die Biblische Theologie. Ihre Geschichte und Problematik* (Neukirchen-Vluyn: Neukirchener Verlag, 1970)126–31, 254–96; Norman W. **Porteous**, "Old Testament Theology," *The Old Testament and Modern Study* (ed. by H. H. Rowley; London: Oxford University Press, 1951)311–45; H. G. **Reventlow**, *Hauptprobleme der alttestamentlichen Theologie im 20. Jahrhundert* (Darmstadt: Wissenschaftliche Buchgesellschaft, 1982)1–64.

The third decade of the twentieth century witnessed a revival of interest in the more traditional form of Old Testament theology. This reawakening of concern spawned, first in Germany and then in other countries, not only the production of new systematic presentations of the subject-matter but also a heated debate over its nature and form. For a time the new movement made little or no impact on English-speaking scholarship which, through repudiation or assimilation, was still reacting to the approach and consequences of historical criticism. Eventually, changes in the larger theological environment brought biblical exegesis, interpretation, and theology back into the center of the entire theological enterprise throughout the Christian world.

Before examining the course of this new development, we should take some note of the way in which scholars during the period from about 1890 to 1920 spoke of the relevance of the Old Testament for theology, the life of the church, and contemporary culture.

The Issue of the Relevance
of the Old Testament

R. **Abramowski**, "Von Streit um das Alte Testament," *TRu* 3(1937)65–93; Matthew **Arnold**, *Literature and Dogma* (London/Boston: Smith, Elder, & Company/J. R. Osgood, 1873); *idem*, *God and the Bible* (London/New York: Smith, Elder, & Company/Macmillan Company, 1875); Martin J. **Buss**, "The Study of Forms," *Old Testament Form Criticism* (ed. by J. H. Hayes; San Antonio: Trinity University Press, 1974)1–56; Friedrich **Delitzsch**, *Babel und Bibel* (Leipzig: J. C. Hinrichs, 1902) = *Babel and Bible* (Chicago: Open Court Publishing Company, 1902); Hermann **Gunkel**, "The History of Religion and Old Testament Criticism," *Fifth International Congress of Free Christianity and Religious Progress: Proceedings and Papers August 5–10, 1910* (ed. by Charles W. Wendte; London: Williams & Norgate, 1910)114–25; *idem*, *What Remains of the Old Testament and Other Essays* (London/New York: George Allen and Unwin/Macmillan Company, 1928); Johannes **Hempel**, "The Religious Value of the Old Testament," *LCQ* 6(1933)225–45; Herbert H. **Huffmon**, "*Babel und Bibel*: The Encounter Between Babylon and the Bible," *MQR* 22(1983)309–20; Emil F. **Kautzsch**, *Die bleibende Bedeutung des Alten Testaments* (Tübingen: J. C. B. Mohr, 1902); Robert Hatch **Kennett**, "The Contribution of the Old Testament to the Religious Development of Mankind," *The People and the Book* (ed. by A. S. Peake; London: Clarendon Press, 1925)383–402; Charles Foster **Kent**, *The Origin and Permanent Value of the Old Testament* (New York: Charles Scribner's Sons, 1906); Justus **Köberle**, *Zum Kampfe um das Alte Testament* (Wismar: H. Bartholdi, 1906); Wilhelm **Lotz**, *Geschichte und Offenbarung im Alten Testament* (Leipzig: J. C. Hinrichs, 1891); John Edgar **McFadyen**, *Old Testament Criticism and the Christian Church* (London/New York: Hodder & Stoughton/Charles Scribner's Sons, 1903); Richard Green **Moulton**, *The Literary Study of the Bible* (London/Boston: Isbister & Company/D. C. Heath, 1895); *idem*, *The Modern Reader's Bible* (London/New York: Macmillan & Company/Macmillan Company, 1895); James **Orr**, *The Problem of the Old Testament: Considered with Reference to Recent Criticism* (London/New York: J. Nisbet/Charles Scribner's Sons, 1906); Arthur Samuel **Peake**, *The Bible: Its Origin, Its Significance, and Its Abiding Worth* (London/New York; Hodder & Stoughton/G. H. Doran, 1913); H. Wheeler **Robinson**, *The Religious Ideas of the Old Testament* (London: Duckworth, 1913); H. W. **Schütte**, "Theologie als Religionsgeschichte. Das Reformprogramm Paul de Lagardes," *NZST* 8(1966)111–20; George Adam **Smith**, *Modern Criticism and the Preaching of the Old Testament* (New York: A. C. Armstrong and Son, 1901); *idem*, "The Hebrew Genius as Exhibited in the Old Testament," *The Legacy of Israel* (ed. by E. R. Bevan and Charles Singer; Oxford: Clarendon Press, 1927)1–28; Helmut **Weidmann**, *Die Patriarchen und ihre Religion im Licht der Forschung seit Julius Wellhausen* (Göttingen: Vandenhoeck & Ruprecht, 1968).

The application of the historical-critical and history-of-religion approaches to the Scriptures effectively undercut the traditional claims which had been made about the unity, authority, inspiration, revelatory quality, and distinctiveness of the Old Testament. Instead of an inspired work full of infallible statements, reliable historical depictions, truths transcending the ages, unified perspectives, and unique contents, the Old Testament, as seen through the lens of historical criticism, turned out to be a very human book time-bound to contexts of long ago, diversified and contradictory in its contents,¹ scientifically primitive in its outlook, often inaccurate in historical details, and frequently surprisingly parallel to the literature of other ancient cultures. An apology for the abiding value of such a work seemed to many to be a serious need. Of course, for those in the church and synagogue who were unaffected by critical approaches and for those scholars and theologians who denied the validity and repudiated the application of historical criticism to the Bible, the traditional arguments and older approaches still held value.

Scholars and critics grappled with the question of the relevance of the Old Testament, or the value of the history of Israelite religion, in various ways and provided a spectrum of answers. For most Christian scholars, who dominated the discipline of biblical studies, the Old Testament and its religion, along with non-canonical Jewish and Hellenistic literature, functioned primarily as a background for understanding the New Testament and the origins and early history of the church and thus performed an indispensable role in this capacity. This particular approach, which we noted throughout the chapter on the nineteenth century and which was probably the most characteristic attitude of the time, has already been sufficiently discussed.

Many critics sought, however, to expound the intrinsic values of the Old Testament and Israelite religion without excessive appeal to their relationship to the New Testament and Christianity. Members of the history-of-religion movement spoke in more religious, humanistic, and experiential than in theological or revelatory terms:

> now one places the history of religion, with ever-increasing confidence, in the place of "Biblical theology." . . . And perhaps one day the time will come when the Christian community will realize that this study is really capable of serving it, in as much as it makes the treasures of the Bible dearer and more valuable than ever, and places the wonderful picture of the history of Biblical truth ever more luminously before it (Gunkel, 1910, pp. 122, 125).

In his famous essay written in 1914 and published in English in 1928 on "What Remains of the Old Testament?," Gunkel addressed the question of the relevance of the Old Testament from the perspective of the history-of-religion approach. His sensitive views are best represented by offering his own reflections on the matter:

> Whoever pays attention to what is being thought and said in our day cannot fail to hear the eagerness with which the question is asked, "What is left to us of the Old Testament?" To this question Old Testament Science is prepared to give a frank and clear reply. For a century and a half scholars have been busy, first groping uncertainly, then progressing with increasing confidence, till they have now worked out a clear conception of what the Old Testament is. Among

the scholars who have helped to achieve this result Julius Wellhausen will always be named with honour. Old Testament scholarship, by means of great acumen, patient detailed investigation, and a power of intuition amounting to genius, has sketched a splendid picture of the history of the people of Israel, its religion and its literature. In so doing it has definitively given up the *old* conception of Inspiration. To Old Testament Science the Bible is in the first instance a book produced by human means in human ways. Science has brought it down from heaven and set it up in the midst of the earth. It treats the Old Testament and the people of Israel with the same methods as would be applied to any other book and any other people. And by doing so Old Testament Science justly claims to be a fully qualified member of the circle of historical Sciences. A University which gives no place to this Science cannot claim to be in full sense a *universitas literarum*. Just because we have dealt with the Old Testament in this manner, we have rediscovered its true significance for the history of the world; and to the question, "What do we have in the Old Testament?" we reply, soberly and definitely: "We have a great treasure, a very great treasure, in the Old Testament" (pp. 18–19).

For the Old Testament has a wealth of thoughts and conceptions which form the imperishable achievements of the Hebrew spirit. These are not, and never can become, obsolete, for they lie at the root of all modern thinking, whatever attitude men may take up towards Church and religion. Besides, the Old Testament contains conceptions which, although they have not been outgrown in the history of thought, can never be forgotten, because they were necessary stages in the path of evolution; and again, the Old Testament has, among its peculiar thoughts, some which form a valuable counterpoise to certain injurious tendencies of our time.

Of the numerous points to which reference might be made in this connection, a few may be here mentioned. We have already spoken of the *simplicity* of Hebrew thought as mirrored in the ancient sagas. This simplicity is a fundamental feature of Hebrew religion. Thoughts that are at the root of all religious and moral civilization have been rammed like posts into its soil. For example, take the principles of morality as expressed in the *Ten Commandments*, with their majestic and inviolable "Thou shalt." Words like these, with the breath of the primeval world upon them, tower up like giant mountain peaks. Empires disappear; nations pass away; even modern nations and States have no promise of permanence; all external civilization is in constant movement, but foundations like these moral principles abide (p. 37).

Our own day, with its marvellous technical achievements and its comprehensive organization of labour, may bear comparison with the civilizations of Egypt and Babylon, but the complaint is heard more and more loudly that the personalities which the idealistic age produced so abundantly are beginning to die out, and that it is becoming more and more difficult for independent men to maintain their ground in face of the mighty machine that reduces everyone to the same pattern. Would not a dash of the spirit of ancient Israel be good for our spiritual life to-day? If the prophets would but awake!

And now one word to gather together all the various points which have been raised in the foregoing pages. We have shown that it is only when we have made up our minds to surrender unreservedly the ancient doctrine of Inspiration that the Old Testament reveals its true greatness. We have brought it down from heaven to earth, and now it rises majestically before our eyes from earth to heaven. We have also seen that it contains much that appears to us far from admirable, many things that would be dangerous and destructive to our religion and morality, if they were carried over unintelligently into our time; and scientific honour demands that we do not, like a bad advocate, lay emphasis only on the one side, but that, like a just judge, we frankly set forth both sides (p. 53).

For Gunkel, emphasis then was placed on certain religious conceptions but also on certain religious attitudes and spiritual and aesthetic sensitivities. For him, a properly executed biblical theology was actually identical with a presentation of religious realities or, to say the same thing as he implied, an elucidation of the religious realities should function in the same capacity as the earlier biblical theologies. In fact, Gunkel felt and predicted that no more Old Testament theologies would be written. Others, like Karl Marti (1855–1925) focused on the value of the prophets as paradigms and forerunners for understanding Jesus; while others, like Kautzsch, stressed the Old Testament's moral and religious irreplaceability. The *Heilsgeschichte* emphasis along the lines of von Hofmann's position was to be found in the writings of such scholars as Wilhelm Lotz (1853–1928) and Justus Köberle (1871–1908) while Johannes Hempel (1891–1964) defended the religion of the Old Testament in terms of the piety and devotion reflected throughout Israel's history.

The Bible as literature movement which blossomed in British and American scholarship beginning at the end of the last century was another way of dealing with the relevance of the Bible, in this case, without necessarily making overt claims about its theological utilization (see Buss, 1974, pp. 40–46). Of special significance in this field were the Britishers Matthew Arnold (1822–88) and Richard Green Moulton (1849–1924) and the work of William Rainey Harper (1856–1906) at the University of Chicago. Most of the contributors to this field were not trained biblical scholars but specialists in literature and other fields. In his book, *The English Bible as Literature* (Boston: Houghton, Mifflin, & Co., 1931), Charles Allen Dinsmore (1860–1941) summed up the intent of the treatment of the Bible as literature and sought to relate it to other approaches:

> The Bible in recent times has passed through two distinct phases and is entering upon a third. There was a period when it was regarded as an infallible authority, the divine element was emphasized and the human overlooked; then came the age of the critic with his eager search for authors, dates, and documents; his main contentions having been established, his battle is losing its heat and absorbing interest. Now we are entering upon the era of appreciation. Educators are beginning to realize that Hebrew literature is not inferior to Greek and Roman in cultural value (p. v).

Most English-language scholarship produced by biblical specialists was still concerned with adjusting to the impact of the historical-critical method and its implications. The same was true for Roman Catholic scholarship in general where the Modernist Movement sought to bring Catholic beliefs more into line with contemporary philosophy, historical studies, and other disciplines as well as historical-critical approaches in biblical interpretation. Among Catholic biblical scholars who were leaders in this effort were Marie-Joseph Lagrange (1855–1938) and Alfred Firmin Loisy (1857–1940). The movement seemed to be temporarily supported by Leo XIII's encyclical *Providentissimus Deus* (1893) but was condemned by Pope Pius X in 1907 papal decrees describing it as "the compendium of all heresies."

Moral and ethical aspects and some religious ideas of the Old Testament were especially emphasized in English-language works produced as apologies both for the abiding significance of the Old Testament and for the employment of and inevitability of the historical-critical approach. The best of such works were produced by Charles Foster Kent (1867–1925), John Edgar McFadyen (1870–1933), Arthur Samuel Peake (1865–1929), Henry Wheeler Robinson (1872–1945), and George Adam Smith (1856–1942). The following quotes from Robinson and Smith illustrate how appeal to the religious ideas and moral content could move to an appeal to accept the Old Testament as revelation.

> The religious ideas of the Old Testament are studied most naturally when they are regarded as organic elements in the one comprehensive idea of religion. They were slowly developed in closest relation to the history, and in response to the successive demands of Israel's experience. The religion of Israel underwent many changes, but faith in the fellowship of God and man gave unity to its eventful history, and supplied that inner continuity which is the mark of a true development. The most characteristic feature of the religion was its moral emphasis. Under the influence of that emphasis, the ideas of God and of man gained in meaning and majesty, until they demanded a wider arena than the political history of a single nation. The God of Israel was recognized as the one God of all the world on whom human nature and destiny everywhere depended. Religion brought the divine personality into such effective relation with the human, and the human with the divine, that the fellowship of God and man became a living fact of experience. God made Himself known to man, particularly through the spoken word of the prophet and the written law of the priest. Man could venture to approach God through particular places, times, persons, and offerings. But two disturbing elements were felt within this fellowship of God and man. There were human acts which were believed to alienate God; there was human suffering, regarded as the evidence of His alienation. Here lay the peculiar problems of Israel's religion. But the hope of Israel rose beyond sin and suffering into confidence in the covenanted help of God, into the vision of His effective intervention in the affairs of Israel and the world, into the consciousness of a divine purpose to be realized even through human sorrows. These are ideas which are embodied in the religion of Israel. If their intrinsic worth, their permanent value, their universal application, can be maintained against all possible objections, then

the history of Israel which created these ideas constitutes a revelation of divine truth (Robinson, pp. 26–27).

> We have seen how thoroughly Semitic the religion of early Israel was in frame and fibre; and not less how in it alone of all Semitic faiths there dwelt an ethical spirit—the only promise in all that Semitic world of a true monotheism, and a promise which was actually fulfilled by the great Hebrew prophets. We have seen how all attempts to account for this religious uniqueness of Israel by their physical or historical conditions have failed, because these conditions were equally shared by Israel's Semitic kinsfolk. We have seen that the gradual ethical development, which thus differentiated Israel from her neighbours, appears to have begun with the introduction to the nations of Jahweh as their God; and that every stage of its progress was achieved in connection with some impression of His character.
>
> It seems to me that there are here the lines of an apologetic, for a Divine Revelation through early Israel, more sure and clear than any which the traditional interpretation of the Old Testament ever attempted to lay down (Smith, p. 142).

Many in Germany certainly would not have agreed with even a reduced assessment of the relevance of the Old Testament to contemporary life. Numerous scholars were calling for the repudiation of Israelite religion, both on its own terms and as the antecedent to Christianity, and for the removal of the Old Testament from the status of canonical Scripture. The roots for this virulent anti-Old Testament attitude were numerous.

(1) One root lies in the general animosity toward traditional religion, whether Jewish or Christian, which was widespread at the time. Prominent figures in this development were the earlier Arthur Schopenhauer (1788–1860) who advocated atheism and depreciation of reason in favor of emphasis on the will; Friedrich Wilhelm Nietzsche (1844–1900) who opposed religion's emphasis on and concern for the weak and thus its disparagement of the drive toward the superhuman; Eduard von Hartmann (1842–1906) who argued that even Christianity should die to give way to a religion of absolute and concrete monism which transcended all religions; and Arthur Drews (1865–1935) who denied the historicity of many of the biblical events including the existence of the man Jesus and argued that religion should represent humans' consciousness of themselves as supra-individual beings.

(2) A second root can be seen in reductionist attempts to interpret religion in purely human categories, generally in positivistic and naturalistic terms. One thinks here of the earlier Ludwig Andreas Feuerbach (1804–72) who saw religion as illusionary human projections without any transcendental authentication or support; of Emile Durkheim (1858–1917) who viewed religious symbols as societal representations and warrants; of Karl Marx (1818–83) for whom religion was reflective of ideological deceits on the part of privileged classes; and of Sigmund Freud (1856–1939) for whom religion was primarily the reflection of neurotic projections.

(3) A further contributor to this attitude toward the Old Testament were approaches based on racial considerations and prejudices. Already in 1878, the pioneer Greek Old Testament scholar, Paul Anton de Lagarde (1827–91), had spoken of the new German national religion in which the Hebrew Scriptures would have no place (see Schütte). His proposal seems to have verbalized widely held opinions. The situation was exacerbated by the sentiments and philosophy of Aryan superiority expressed by the English-born Houston Steward Chamberlain (1855–1927).

(4) A particular reading of the general conclusions arrived at by historical critics was also turned against the Old Testament. The so-called "Pan-Babylonian" school, represented by such scholars as Hugo Winckler (1863–1913), Alfred Jeremias (1864–1935), and Peter Jensen (1861–1936), stressed the dependence of the Old Testament on Near Eastern parallels to the point of denying much creativity to biblical authors. Widespread controversy over this view was inaugurated by the lecture *Babel und Bibel* by the highly respected and influential assyriologist, Friedrich Delitzsch (1850–1922), and raged for more than two decades (see Weidmann, pp. 65–88, and Huffmon). The younger Delitzsch, son of the conservative Old Testament scholar Franz Julius Delitzsch (1813–90), not only emphasized the Near Eastern background of Old Testament materials but also drew the least favorable conclusions from the results of historical criticism as can be seen in the following quote:

> That the Old Testament is full of deceptions of all kinds: a veritable hodge-podge of erroneous, incredible, undependable figures, including those of biblical chronology; a veritable labyrinth of false portrayals, misleading reworkings, revisions and transpositions, therefore also of anachronism, a constant intermixture of contradictory particulars and whole stories, unhistorical inventions, legends and folktales—in short, a book full of intentional and unintentional deceptions, in part self-deceptions, a very dangerous book, in the use of which the greatest care is necessary. I repeat: the Old Testament in all its books is full of linguistic beauties, of archaeological information, and retains its value as a historical document in spite of its defects, but it is in all directions a relatively late and very cloudy source, a propagandistic document from the first chapter of Genesis to the last of Chronicles (translation in Kraeling, p. 158).

Delitzsch was not alone in his utilization of the results of scientific criticism to denounce the Old Testament and its religion. Almost equally influential were the works of Arthur Bonus (1864–1941).

(5) As we noted at the end of the last chapter (see pp. 140–41), nineteenth-century Old Testament scholarship was widely characterized by a tendency to downplay the value of Old Testament cultic and levitical laws and to disparage the Judaism of the second-temple period (from 515 BCE onward). This pervasive sentiment, based ultimately on a Christian reading of

the Old Testament supported by a heightened emphasis on justification by faith, lay ready at hand for those who would extend such feelings to the whole of the Old Testament.

This anti-Judaism and anti-Old Testament movement, of course, reached its apogee under Nazi propaganda and was joined by many respected biblical scholars (see Reventlow, 1982, pp. 31–47 for the pro-Aryan arguments, the ensuing debates, and full bibliography). The oft-quoted remark of the great liberal church historian Adolf von Harnack (1851–1930) gave classical expression to the widespread Germanic antagonism toward the Old Testament:

> To reject the Old Testament in the second century was a mistake the church rightly repudiated; to retain it in the sixteenth century was a fate which the Reformation could not yet avoid; but to continue to keep it as a canonical document after the nineteenth century is the consequence of religious and ecclesiastical paralysis (*Marcion. Das Evangelium vom fremden Gott* [Leipzig: J. C. Hinrichs, 1921] pp. 248–49).

For Harnack, the Old Testament should be placed among other works with a heading to the list that noted these were "good and useful to read," as Luther had said about the apocrypha, but he felt this should be the case only with portions of the Hebrew Scriptures. The Old Testament could no longer be treated as either holy or infallible and in fact to give up such a position was "the great deed which today—although almost too late—is demanded of Protestantism" (pp. 254–55). Harnack felt that Christianity was losing ground because "the largest number of objections which people raise against Christianity and the truthfulness of the church stem from the authority which the church still gives to the Old Testament" (p. 254).

THE REBIRTH OF INTEREST IN OLD TESTAMENT THEOLOGY

Karl **Barth**, "Das Schriftprinzip der reformierten Kirche," *ZZ* 3(1925)215–45; *idem*, *The Word of God and the Word of Man* (London/Boston: Hodder and Stoughton/ Pilgrim Press, 1928); Dietrich **Bonhoeffer**, "Schöpfung und Fall. Theologische Auslegung von Genesis 1—3 (Munich: Chr. Kaiser, 1937) = *Creation and Fall: A Theological Interpretation of Genesis 1—3* (New York/ London: Macmillan Company/ SCM Press, 1959); Geoffrey W. **Bromiley**, *Introduction to the Theology of Karl Barth* (Grand Rapids: Wm. B. Eerdmans, 1979); Raymond E. **Brown**, *The Sensus Plenior of Sacred Scripture* (Baltimore: St. Mary's University, 1955); Clarence T. **Craig**, "Biblical Theology and the Rise of Historicism," *JBL* 62(1943)281–94; Jean **Daniélou**, *From Shadows to Reality: Studies in the Biblical Typology of the Fathers* (Westminster, MD: Newman Press, 1960); Francis N. **Davey**, "Biblical Theology," *Theology* 38(1939)166–76; Walther **Eichrodt**, *Ist die altisraelitische Nationalreligion Offenbarungsreligion?* (Gütersloh: C. Bertelsmann, 1925); *idem*, "Hat die alttestamentliche Theologie noch selbstständige Bedeutung innerhalb der alttestamentlichen Wissenschaft?" *ZAW* 47(1929)83–91; Otto **Eissfeldt**, "Israelitisch-jüdische Religionsgeschichte und alttestamentliche Theologie," *ZAW* 44(1926)1–12 = his *Kleine Schriften* I (Tübingen: J. C. B. Mohr, 1962)105–14; David **Ford**, *Barth and God's Story: Biblical Narrative and the Theological Method of Karl Barth in the "Church Dogmatics"* (Frankfurt/Bern: Peter Lang, 1981); Karl **Girgensohn**, *Der Schriftbeweis in der evangelischen Dogmatik einst und jetzt* (Leipzig: A Deichert, 1914); Werner **Gruehn**, *Die Theologie Karl Girgensohns* (Gütersloh: C. Bertelsmann, 1927); Gwilym O. **Griffith**, *The Theology of P. T. Forsyth* (London/Chicago: Lutterworth Press/A. R. Allenson, 1948); Walter **Harrelson**, "Bonhoeffer and the Bible," *The Place of Bonhoeffer* (ed. by M. E. Marty; New York: Association Press, 1962)113–39; Arthur Gabriel **Hebert**, *The Throne of David: A Study of the Fulfilment of the Old Testament in Jesus Christ and His Church* (London/New York: Faber & Faber/Morehouse-Gorham Co., 1941); Horace D. **Hummel**, "Christological Interpretation of the Old Testament," *Dialog* 2(1963)108–17; William A. **Irwin**, "The Reviving Theology of the Old Testament," *JR* 25(1945)235–46; Martin **Kähler**, *Der sogenannte historische Jesus und der geschichtliche, biblische Christus* (Leipzig: A. Deichert, 1892) = *The So-called Historical Jesus and the Historic, Biblical Christ* (Philadelphia: Fortress Press, 1964); *idem*, "Biblical Theology," *NSHERK* (1908)2. 183–86; Rudolf **Kittel**, "Die Zukunft der alttestamentlichen Wissenschaft," *ZAW* 39(1921)84–99; Ludwig **Köhler**, "Alttestamentliche Theologie," *TRu* 7(1935)255–76; 8(1936)55–69, 247–84; Eduard **König**, "Der gegenwärtige Zustand der 'Biblischen Theologie Alten Testaments,' sein eigentlicher Anlass und die Wege zu seiner Verbesserung," *AELKZ* 55(1922)242–45; Martin **Kuske**, *Das Alte Testament als Buch von Christus, Dietrich Bonhoeffers Wertung und Auslegung des Alten Testaments* (Berlin: Evangelische Verlagsanstalt, 1970) = *The Old Testament as the Book of Christ: An Appraisal of Bonhoeffer's Interpretation* (Philadelphia: Westminster Press, 1976); G. W. H. **Lampe** and K. J. **Woollcombe**, *Essays on Typology* (London: SCM Press, 1957); Christopher R. **North**, "Old Testament Theology and the History of Hebrew Religion," *SJT* 2(1949)113–26; Wilhelm **Pauck**, *Karl Barth, Prophet of A New Christianity?* (New York: Harper & Brothers, 1931); Norman W. **Porteous**, "Towards a Theology of the Old Testament," *SJT* 1(1948)136–49; *idem*, "Old Testament Theology," *The Old Testament in Modern Study* (ed. by H. H. Rowley; London: Oxford University Press, 1951)311–45; Otto **Procksch**, "Ziele und Grenzen der Exegese," *NKZ* 36(1925)715–30; *idem*, "Über pneumatische Exegese," *CuW* 1(1925)145–58; *idem*, "Die kirchliche Bedeutung des Alten Testaments," *NKZ* 42(1931)295–306; Henning Graf **Reventlow**, "Der Konflikt zwischen Exegese und Dogmatik. Wilhelm Vischers Ringen um den 'Christus im Alten Testament,'" *Textgemäss. Festschrift E. Würthwein* (ed. by A. H. J. Gunneweg and Otto Kaiser; Göttingen: Vandenhoeck & Ruprecht, 1979)110–22; Alan **Richardson**, "The Nature of Biblical Theology," *Theology* 39(1939)166–76; H. Wheeler **Robinson**, "The Philosophy of Revelation," *Record and Revelation: Essays on the Old Testament by Members of the Society for Old Testament Study* (Oxford: Clarendon Press, 1938)303–20; James M. **Robinson** (ed.), *The Beginnings of Dialectic Theology* (Richmond: John Knox Press, 1968); James D. **Smart**, "The Death and Rebirth of Old Testament Theology," *JR* 23(1943)1–11, 125–36; Willy **Staerk**, "Religionsgeschichte und Religionsphilosophie in ihrer Bedeutung für die biblische Theologie des Alten Testaments," *ZTK* 4(1923)289–300; Carl **Steuernagel**, "Alttestamentliche Theologie und alttestamentliche Religionsgeschichte," *Vom Alten Testament* (ed. by Karl Budde; Giessen: A Töpelmann, 1925)266–73; Wilhelm **Vischer**, "Das Alte Testament und die Verkündigung," *TBl* 10(1931)1–11; *idem, Das Christuszeugnis des Alten Testaments* (2 vols.; Zürich: A. G. Zollikon, 1934–1942) = *The Witness of the Old Testament to Christ I. The Pentateuch* (London: Lutterworth Press, 1949).

The Call for a Revival of Old Testament Theology

In the 1920s a move began in Germany to revive the classical discipline of Old Testament theology as well as a more "theological exegesis" of the Scriptures. Although this was related in many ways to the changed outlook developing in the field of general theology, to be discussed in the next section, it would be a mistake to attribute this revival solely to the outside stimulus of Christian theology. Its rebirth was just as much a result of developments taking place within the ranks of Old Testament scholars themselves. The revival may be seen, in broad terms, as the desire to allow the Old Testament to address the contemporary situation more on its own terms, to give expression to the theological dimensions of the biblical traditions that were underdeveloped in history-of-religion and purely historical-critical presentations, and to defend the relevance of the Old Testament against its despisers. The call for a new development of Old Testament theology was not, of course, a call for the total repudiation and surrender of current ways of interpreting the Old Testament, such as those represented by the histories of Israelite religion, but for a movement beyond them. Nor was it a call for a mere return to earlier conservative postures unaffected by historical criticism.

In the same year (1921) that Harnack called for the removal of the Old Testament from the Protestant canon, Rudolf Kittel (1853–1929), addressing a meeting of "Alttestamentler" at Leipzig on the topic of "the future of Old Testament science," declared that the time had now come to express a greater concern than previously for the truth content and lasting value of the Old Testament and for an elucidation of its specifically religious values in a systematic rather than historical form. He felt that only such a systematic presentation of the essence of Old Testament religion could give the discipline of Old Testament study some relationship to theology as a whole. The forcefulness of Kittel's challenge was underscored by the fact that it came from a scholar who had himself just published a history of Israel's religion.

Just as Kittel argued for the systematic presentation of Old Testament religion, so Karl Girgensohn (1875–1925) issued a special plea for theological or spiritual exegesis of the Bible (see Gruehn; Reventlow, 1982, pp. 14–21; Kraeling, pp. 173–74). Girgensohn was attuned to the fact that much historical-critical exegesis did little to help and often hindered, he claimed, those going into the ministry who were required to preach on the Scriptures. (In this regard, it should be recalled that Wellhausen had resigned his theological post in Greifswald in 1882 when he realized his teaching was not really preparing ministers for their homiletical and ecclesiastical use of the Scriptures.) In addition, Girgensohn felt that purely historical-critical exegesis was of no service to systematic theology. He proposed reviving what was called a "pneumatic" or spiritual exegesis in which "the exegete should extract the timeless element in Scripture from its historical shell and transpose it to a higher plane" (Kraeling, p. 174). Girgensohn's appeal for pneumatic exegesis was joined by Otto Procksch, a conservative professor in Greifswald who was especially interested in the relation of the Scriptures to the life of the church.

The Impact of New Theological Developments

Much of late nineteenth- and early twentieth-century theology was built on a synthesis of theological and philosophical approaches. As a rule, it reflected the period's confidence, optimism, and belief in progressive development—in historical, social, and personal realms. (In the eleventh edition of the *Encyclopaedia Britannica*, published in 1911, the article on "Torture" suggests something of the spirit of the age: "The whole subject is now one of only historical interest as far as Europe is concerned.") In addition, theology was markedly tilted toward interest in morals and ethics. Characteristic of this thrust was the work of Harnack—the shipment of whose books was said to congest German railroad stations—who summed up the essence of the teachings of Jesus, and thus real Christianity, as the fatherhood of God, the infinite worth of the human soul, and the ethical ideal of the kingdom of God. At the height of its triumph, however, moralistic liberalism was dealt a serious blow.

The impact of cultural turmoil, embodied in the First World War, the loss of nerve by optimistic progressives and the growth of widespread pessimism, and the continuing scientific and philosophical reduction of theology shattered the liberal theological consensus. It was in this context that a theology with strong emphasis on the Bible, revelation, and supernaturalism burst on the scene. Especially associated with Karl Barth (1886–1968), this theology has gone under numerous labels—theology of the word, crisis theology, dialetical theology, neo-orthodoxy, and neo-Reformation theology. Several of its features are noteworthy and eventually influenced significantly both biblical exegesis and biblical theology. Its emphasis on the separation of speculative reason and theology and thus its anti-metaphysical and anti-mystical character was heavily indebted to neo-Kantianism especially as embodied in the work of Wilhelm Herrmann (1846–1922), one of Barth's teachers. Other emphases, the importance of the word of God and the identity of the task of theology and the task of preaching, were taken over from the Reformers, especially Luther. (Predecessors in some of these emphases can be seen in some of Barth's forerunners—especially the British Congregationalist theologian Peter Taylor Forsyth [1848–1921; see Glover, pp. 272–82, and Griffith] and Martin Kähler [1835–1912; see Braaten's introduction to the English translation of Kähler's volume].)

The basic assumptions of Karl Barth's theology, always argued with great vigor and earnestness, might be set down as (1) the infinite transcendence of God and (2) the inability of human beings through their natural faculties to comprehend God. For him, this separation between God and humankind was unqualified, and on this matter he differed even with his colleague in the new movement, Heinrich Emil Brunner (1889–1966) who, for his part, was willing to admit a degree of contact between God and humanity—between natural and special revelation, religion(s) and Christianity, and philosophy and theology. It would be wrong, however. to read into Barth's juxtaposition of God and humanity a metaphysical dualism such as that held by traditional supernaturalism. The concern of Barth's theology was not with the cosmological differences between Creator and creature but with the far more important question of the *knowability* of God.

God, as far as the natural person is concerned, is unknowable. God is the *Totally Other* (*totaliter aliter*) and the *Hidden God* (*Deus absconditus*). Borrowing a phrase from the nineteenth-century Danish religious thinker, Søren Kierkegaard (1813–55), he defined this point of departure as "the infinite qualitative difference between time and eternity." Barth's avenue of escape from the agnosticism implicit in this dialectic was through a third postulate. The *Deus absconditus* is also the *Deus revelatus*. God has bridged the gulf by offering a revelation which human beings may appropriate through faith after having had their spiritual eyes opened, so to speak, by an act of divine grace. Here, in his doctrine of revelation, we have, as Wilhelm Pauck has pointed out, the very core of Barth's thinking.

The centrality of the concept of revelation in his thought was made clear by Barth himself when he devoted the first volume of his systematic discussion of Christian theology to the "Doctrine of the Word of God." What we have in Barth's thought is not a repetition of Orthodoxy's "plenary inspiration" but an interpretation of revelation which in some ways reminds one of Luther's but which also takes account of a century and a half of biblical criticism (see Bromiley, pp. 3–53). The *Word of God* assumes with him a threefold form. First, there is the "proclaimed" Word in the preaching and the sacramental ordinances of the church. Then, he distinguishes the "written" Word which consists of the prophetic and apostolic "word, witness, proclamation, and preaching" found in the Bible. Finally, he points out a third, also the most important, form of the Word, the "revealed" Word, namely, Jesus Christ. Nothing shows the profound difference between Barth and the Ritschlians better than the manner in which he looks upon Jesus as the revelation. Ritschl and Herrmann had focused attention upon the historical Jesus, his personality and his teaching. For Barth, however, it is not even this historical Jesus but only the crucified and resurrected Christ, as in Kähler, who may occupy the center of the Christian revelation. His death and resurrection are at once the negation of humanity, the disclosure of the absolute *otherness* of God, and the revelation of God's mercy.

We will do well to pause a moment and to examine some of the implications for biblical interpretation inherent in his position. In one of his earliest lectures, delivered in 1916 while he was still a pastor in Safenwil, Barth spoke of the "strange new world within the Bible, the world of God" (1928, pp. 28–50). Within the Bible, "there are no transitions, intermixings, or intermediate stages. There is only crisis, finality, new insight. What the Bible brings us from beyond the grave is the perfect, the absolute miracle" (1928, p. 91). Quite clearly, when Barth spoke of revelation he did not mean the Bible as a whole nor even just the New Testament. For him, one does the Bible a bad kind of honor, one which it does not welcome, by identifying it with this other, the revelation itself, he said at one point in his *Dogmatik*. Pauck has summarized the situation neatly by employing the formula "the Word in the words" to characterize the relationship between the actual divine revelation and the record contained in the Bible (p. 94). It is, furthermore, apparent that in his use of the concept of revelation he was placing the emphasis not on a body of divinely communicated doctrines or truths but primarily on a solitary event, namely, the death and resurrection which transformed Jesus into the Christ of Christian faith. That event is not even historical in nature but "supra-historical" and can, therefore, be understood only through faith. In this conception of revelation the Bible has a part because it contains the prophetic and apostolic "word and witness" to that event. It is also, however, essentially no more than a testimony of Christ.

Barth's interpretation of the significance of the Bible leaves, one may readily see, full room for historical and textual criticism. All that is human and historically conditioned in it constitutes for him no fundamental problem since it in no way can affect the heart of the revelation itself. As a matter of fact, all evidence of the relativities of religious thought in it is but further grist for his mill. It makes all the clearer why the Bible cannot be equated with the revelation but only contains a human testimony to it. In a fashion this left Barth practically free to ignore historical criticism. In the foreword to his Romans commentary, first published in 1919, Barth wrote:

> Paul spoke to his contemporaries as a child of his age. But much more important than this truth is the other, that he speaks as a prophet and apostle of the Kingdom of God to all men in all ages. The differences between then and now, there and here, must be considered. But the purpose of this consideration can only be the recognition that these differences have no significance for what really matters. The critical historical method of biblical research has its place; it points to a preparation for understanding that is never superfluous. But if I had to choose between it and the old doctrine of inspiration, I would resolutely choose the latter. It has a greater, deeper, more important place because it points directly to the task of understanding, without which all prep-

aration is worthless. I am happy that I do not have to choose between the two. But all my attention has been directed toward seeing through the historical into the spirit of the Bible, which is the eternal Spirit. What was once a serious matter is still serious today, and what today is serious, and not just arbitrariness and whim, stands also in direct relation to what was formerly serious (in Robinson, p. 61).

The role of the Bible as only an intermediate document between the interpreter and the subject-matter was made even clearer in the foreword to the third edition of his Romans commentary.

> In contrast to all this, I intend now for this first primitive attempt at paraphrase and what belongs with it to constitute only the starting point for a dialectic movement as inexorable as it is elastic, using all the crowbars and wrecking tools needed to achieve *relevant* treatment of the text. The historical critics must be *more critical* to suit me. For how "what is there" is to be understood cannot be established by an appreciation of the words and phrases of the text, strewn in from time to time from some fortuitous standpoint of the exegete, but only through an entering, as freely and eagerly, as practicable, into the inner tension of the concepts presented by the text with more or less clarity. . . . As little as possible should be left over of those blocks of merely historical, merely given, merely accidental concepts; as far as possible the connection of the words to the Word in the words must be disclosed. As one who would understand, I must press forward to the point where insofar as possible I confront the riddle of the *subject matter* and no longer merely the riddle of the *document* as such, where I can almost forget that I am not the author, where I have almost understood him so well that I let him speak in my name, and can myself speak in his name. I know that these sentences will bring me another severe reprimand but I cannot help myself (in Robinson, p. 93).

Barth came very close to a reaffirmation of the old doctrine of verbal inspiration, especially as this was expressed by some of the Reformers. In the third edition of *Der Römerbrief* he had this to say about the charge that has his work based on a modern dogma of inspiration: "From the first edition on I have not denied the certain analogy between my procedure and the old teaching of verbal inspiration. . . . This doctrine, in the form in which Calvin presented it, seems to me at least very ingenious and worthy of discussion. . . . I cannot understand how there could be any other way to the spirit of a writing (whatever it is) than the hypothetical expectation that its spirit would speak to our spirit precisely through the letter" (in Robinson, pp. 128–29).

The real question for us to consider is, of course, the bearing Barth's views have on the discussion of Old Testament theology. Two simple observations of fact may help to bring this matter into focus. In the first place, Barth's direct influence on Old Testament theology was not overwhelming, in fact it was rather nominal in the early years of his career. In the second place, the first major discussion of the Old Testament to come from this school was concerned with pointing out the Old Testament testimony to Christ (the work of Vischer which we shall note below).

While Barthianism's influence on the revival of Old Testament theology was not immediate and direct, it did at least serve to raise the issue of the study's validity and did, perhaps by the very extremeness of its position, call on those who would still retain the Old Testament as a worthwhile source of religious ideas to set forth what they considered so valuable in it. The challenge it offered was all the more acute because it originated, not with the liberal left wing of *Religionsgeschichte*, but with the conservative side itself. It may, furthermore, not be entirely amiss to point out that, whether justified by his principles or not, Barth actually appropriated into his thinking, through the roundabout way of his concern with Calvin perhaps, many ingredients which were derived in reality from the Old Testament. The *holiness* of the Old Testament may not be the same as his concept of the *totaliter aliter*, but the two are also not too far removed from one another. And what the Old Testament has to say about sin certainly found its reflection in his own system. Thus, he gave contemporary theology questions to consider which served to bring the thought content of the Old Testament, not just its *Christuszeugnis* (witness to Christ), back into theological currency.

The Debate over Method and Approach

Once acknowledgment of the need to revive Old Testament theology became widespread, numerous issues and problems presented themselves. What was the relationship between this rebudding discipline and its nineteenth-century and earlier counterparts? How was Old Testament theology to be distinguished from the history of Israelite religion? What form should a presentation of Old Testament theology take and how should it be structured? What was the relationship between historical-critical studies and Old Testament theology? The debate over these topics began in Germany in the 1920s, made some appearance in England in the 1930s, and became a widespread topic in the United States in the 1940s.

Some of the issues involved can be seen in the dispute between Otto Eissfeldt (1887–1973) and Walther Eichrodt (1890–1978) on the topic. Other German scholars such as König, Hempel, Staerk, and Steuernagel participated in the debate (see Köhler, 1935 and 1936) but most of the issues appear in the former. When Eissfeldt and Eichrodt wrote, they were fully cognizant of the nature and growing importance of Barth's work.

Eissfeldt's essay, published in 1926, was very controversial and quite expressive of the expanding influence of Barthianism. The basic question under consideration was the nature of the relationship between a "history of Israel's religion" and a "theology of the Old Testament." In its larger context within contemporary Christian thought that problem was a part, as Eissfeldt correctly saw, of the more general problem presented by the tension between history and revelation, between immanence and transcendence, between the relative and the absolute. But instead of attempting to reduce that tension, he allowed it to stand and, as a matter of fact, even magnified it. The history of Israel's ongoing religious experience with its social conditioning and its development from lower to higher belonged, he thought, to the domain of *Religionsgeschichte*, or to use Gabler's terminology, to the arena of "true biblical theology." On the other hand, the concern of Old Testament theology was only with God's revelation, the true and absolute religion, insofar as it could be found in Israel's Scripture. Again this corresponds somewhat to Gabler's interest in a "pure biblical theology" although with some differences. The two forms of study he considered, therefore, to be irreconcilable; all forms of compromise between them were unsatisfactory. One must acknowledge their difference and bear the tension resulting therefrom.

> Of a different sort [from that of the historical investigator] is the theological treatment of the religion of the Old Testament. Here we are concerned with the presentation of results which have become Old Testament revelation and the word of God for the individual scholar and his religious community— for he will always be in some way the organ of his religious community. These results, while thoroughly scientific, will then bear the character of a testimony to his faith; and their value is limited to the circle of those whose piety is similar to or identical with that of the scholar concerned; that is, it is denominationally conditioned. Here, then, is no corporate activity of members of diverse religious communities, who perhaps side by side through investigation and evidence may be able to advance their knowledge, but instead it is here possible only that one shall overpower the other, and one religious community the other, by the stronger evidence of "The Spirit and the Power" (translation from Irwin, p. 239).

This dichotomy he carried still further. The reason that historical analysis and theological formulation cannot be harmonized is that they represent two separate activities of the human mind, namely, intellectual understanding and religious faith.

> The historical and the theological approaches belong on two different planes. They correspond to two different functions of our spirit, knowing and believing. . . . The knowing mind is conscious that in spite of all its efforts it cannot reach out beyond the limited world of space and time; Faith knows itself laid hold upon by an eternal reality. . . . Thus the necessity of both methods of approach is rooted in our spiritual nature and we have only the choice either to make a compromise between the two or to recognize and prosecute each of them in its own place and in its own way (translation from Smart, pp. 131–32).

Understanding means an unceasing activity to discover what really is or was. Faith is passivity, expressed in a willingness to give oneself to the higher and purer without stint, and as such is a personal, ever renewed venture which becomes greatest where one does not see and yet believes. Both understanding and faith are fully legitimate, although distinct from one another, and so one should recognize the legitimacy of both history of religion and Old Testament theology. (Gabler would, of course, have argued for the second, the pure form, in more rationalistic and universal categories.) The historian prepares the groundwork of factual material, but never asks the question of its value or its truthfulness. One does not have to assume a viewpoint outside the text as a vantage point to determine what is true. It follows also that one need not belong to any particular confessional group, i.e., one may be either Christian or non-Christian. Old Testament theology, on the other hand, can be appropriated only through faith. Here the theologian must present what is considered to be the divine revelation or God's word within a confessional group. The proper task is to witness. One cannot convince an opponent by factual proof, but only by a stronger display of "spirit and power."

Eissfeldt also touched briefly on the method involved in such a presentation of Old Testament theology. It would need to be systematic, not in the sense of developing a system on the basis of some general principle, but in terms of a stringing together of statements about the nature of Yahweh, humanity, sin, and salvation, apparently somewhat like the older *dicta probantia* in Protestant Scholasticism. The New Testament would serve in the majority of cases as the standard for measuring whether a given idea belonged to the divine religion, but not everything would have to be related to it. The Old Testament contains much which has no counterpart in the New, such as the descriptions of God's glory and creative activity in the Psalms. At these points the Old Testament clearly adds to the New and should be treated, accordingly, not as subordinate but as co-ordinate.

Another prominent voice addressing the issue of the revival of Old Testament theology was Walther Eichrodt. In an important article written in 1929, he responded to the new surge in theological and pneumatic exegesis, to the demands of the dialectical theologians, to Eissfeldt's proposals about the shape and interests of histories of Old Testament religion and theology, and sketched his own program for an Old Testament theology. As far as he was concerned, Eissfeldt's dichotomy between *Religionsgeschichte* and theology was an impossible one. Instead, he preferred to think of them as more nearly akin to one another. For, although history of religion has in the past been permitted to stop with an analysis of origin and development, there is no reason why it should preclude an interest in a synthesis of Old Testament religion or why, in other words, it should not fathom the innermost nature of that religion for the purpose of discovering its inner structure, its constant features, and the interrelatedness of its component elements. Such a function demands some form of systematization, but systematic study is, of course, precisely also the business of Old Testament theology. In stressing this kinship between these two types of study, Eichrodt laid bare, moreover, another disagreement with Eissfeldt. The latter, we remember, had defined Old Testament theology as a normative pursuit. This view Eichrodt rejected and, instead, asserted that Old Testament theology could and should remain an empirical, descriptive science and not encroach upon the field of normative or systematic theology. While admitting that the biblical theologian might occasionally find it necessary to step outside the domain proper and make judgments more *a propos* the dogmatic theologian, he felt this should be the exception rather than the rule.

As for Eissfeldt's correlated declaration that the subject matter of Old Testament theology could be apprehended by faith alone, Eichrodt considered it far too extreme while granting, at the same time, that it contained important elements of truth. First, it was justified in calling attention to the impossibility of purely objective historiography because every historian cannot help but bring to one's work a subjective ingredient in the form of a personal specific interpretation of history. Furthermore, a second subjective element is present in any effort to understand and explain historical phenomena because of the need, on the part of the historian, to develop a sense of affinity with the material being investigated. It is this subjective appreciation alone which enables a person to become one with the historical event, to infuse it with life, and to raise the past to new actuality for the present. Such a sense of affinity is, however, more akin to intuitive than to factual knowledge. Finally, he felt that Eissfeldt's insistence on faith was valid in a third respect, insofar, namely, as the Christian theologian, for whom Christ's revelation is the supreme value, must look to the New Testament for the real meaning of the Old. For the same reason, one of the theologian's foremost interests should also be to show how the Old Testament formed the historical basis for the Christian revelation.

Methodologically considered, the most important point of Eichrodt's article was its statement of the purpose of Old Testament theology and the emphasis it placed on the need for exhibiting not only the nature but also the structure of Old Testament thought.

In addition to the proposals of Eissfeldt and Eichrodt, we should note the christological interpretation of the Old Testament which was proposed as a means of expounding its theology (see Hummel; Kraeling, pp. 219–26). Growing out of the Barthianism of the time, the messianic-christological re-reading of the Scriptures reminds one somewhat of the older position of Hengstenberg (for the issues and bibliography of this approach pro and con, see Reventlow, 1982, pp. 23–30). The two most significant voices advancing christological exegesis were Wilhelm Vischer (1895–) and Dietrich Bonhoeffer (1906–1945). Even for Barth the Hebrew Scriptures witness primarily to Christ or at least to the "primal history" or the centrality of the preexistence of Christ. For most Christians, and especially for Barth, it was difficult to speak of the message and value of the Old Testament without reference to Christ and Christianity.

For Vischer, Christians certainly could not dispense with the Old Testament. Like Barth, he saw its theme as the piety and morality of God not the piety and morals of humans. Since the church rests on the Scriptures, Christians must reclaim the Hebrew Scriptures from the realm of general Semitics. The Old Testament is like an arch, where the whole is understood in light of the parts and the parts in the light of the whole, and that arch is the Christ. All of this, of course, requires a degree of christianization of the Old Testament in a form similar to that of the Reformers who, even though they argued for the literal meaning of biblical texts, still adhered to a christianization of its content. To this extent, "Vischer avails himself of a thought of Luther: the *obtaining* of forgiveness took place only once, but the *distribution* of it took place often, both before and after Christ. For since God had decided upon forgiveness, it mattered not whether He dispensed it previously or subsequently through His Word: as He subsequently dispensed it in the sacrament through the Word, so He previously dispensed it in the Old Testament sacrifices through the Word" (Kraeling, p. 223).

The following quotes from the introduction to the first volume of Vischer's two-volume work on the witness of the Old Testament to Christ, of which only the first was translated into English, gives some feeling for Vischer's interests and approach:

> The Bible testifies beyond doubt, with the attestation of the Holy Spirit, that Jesus of Nazareth is the Christ. This is what makes it the Holy Scripture of the Christian Church. For the Christian Church is the company of all those who, on the basis of the biblical testimony, recognize and believe that Jesus is the Christ, i.e., the Messiah of Israel, the Son of the living God, the Saviour of the world.
>
> The two main words of the Christian confession "Jesus is the Christ"— the personal name "Jesus" and the vocational name "Christ"—correspond to the two parts of the Holy Scriptures: the New and the Old Testament. The Old Testament tells us *what* the Christ is; the New, *who* He is—and indeed in such a manner as to make it clear that he alone knows Jesus who recognizes Him as the Christ, and he alone knows what the Christ is who knows that He is Jesus. So the two Testaments, breathing the same spirit, point to each other, "and there is no word in the New Testament that does not look back to the Old, in which it is foretold" [Luther], and all the words of the Old Testament look beyond themselves to the One in the New in whom alone they are true.
>
> Strictly speaking only the Old Testament is "The Scripture", while the New Testament brings the good news that now the meaning of these writings,

the import of all their words, their Lord and Fulfiller, has appeared incarnate. Every book of the New Testament, each in its own way, makes this pronouncement (pp. 7–8).

A historical fact can only be established by *historical documents*. If Jesus Christ were a purely superhistorical figure historical documents would be superfluous. In token that He is not superhistorical, but a fact of history to be known only through the medium of historical documents, we have received the Old and New Testaments. They form the selection of "genuine" documents, approved by the Church and attested by the Holy Spirit which, with their "dead" letters, authentically define the historical event, "Christ Jesus," who through His death has become historical.

Christians who think that the Bible can only be "Holy" Scripture if it be, so to speak, fallen from heaven, are mistaken. The contrary is true; the Bible is the Holy Scripture only in so far as it speaks of Christ *Jesus*, the incarnation of the Son of God. It can only do so if its writings consist of the words of men. It is the abiding merit of the historical-critical investigation of the nineteenth century to have revealed the error of the seventeenth-century doctrine of inspiration, and to have shown the historical-human aspect of scripture. The Word became flesh. In their fleshliness, in their temporal contingency and historical fortuitousness, the writings of the Old and New Testament bear witness to this incarnation. "This shall be the sign; ye shall find the babe wrapped in swaddling clothes, lying in a manger." For us the Scriptures are these swaddling clothes, given us as a sign (p. 14).

Although not wishing to belabor the point of the christological interpretation of the Hebrew Scriptures—in spite of its enormous past and present impact on Christian interpretation—the following description of Vischer's position given by Kuske is worth quoting:

Necessitated by the new consciousness which Barth brought to Protestant theology, Wilhelm Vischer tried "to interpret the Bible again as Bible, and in its own strange sense quite foreign to us." That means for the Old Testament that he sought to lift up its "witness of Christ," for "Jesus Christ is the cornerstone and keystone" of the Old Testament. The Old and New Testaments testify to him like two choirs facing each other in a church and pointing to the same center, to the mediator between God and man. Therefore, Vischer resisted all attempts to disqualify the Old Testament witness as opposed to the New Testament. A "church" which does that will no longer be a church, for the "Christian church stands and falls on the acknowledgment of the unity of both Testaments" (p. 16).

A less extreme christological approach to the Old Testament is found in the work of Bonhoeffer, also heavily indebted to Karl Barth (see Hummel, pp. 109–10, and Kuske). Although primarily a theologian and an ethicist, Bonhoeffer's influential book, *Creation and Fall*, gives some indication of his Christian reading of the Old Testament:

The Church of Christ bears witness to the end of all things. It lives from the end, it thinks from the end, it acts from the end, it proclaims its message from the end. . . . The church does all this because it is grounded upon the testimony of the Holy Scripture. . . . Therefore it reads all Holy Scripture as the book of the end, of the new, of Christ (pp. 7–8).

Bonhoeffer could thus speak of the Old Testament as the book of Christ. For him, in interpretation there must be a movement from the Old Testament to the New Testament and from the New Testament to the Old and both movements must interact. But Bonhoeffer could go farther and forthrightly speak of finding Christ in the Old Testament, very much in the manner of Vischer with whom he became acquainted in 1933.

For the sake of better understanding, it must again be noted that scholars like Vischer and Bonhoeffer were writing in a historical context within which the Old Testament had come under severe Nazi attack even within the church itself. They were fighting, with weapons tipped with christological barbs, to defend the Old Testament as Scripture within the life of the church. At a meeting of Berlin Christians on 13 November 1933 in a Sport Palace demonstration, the leaders of the group had called for, indeed demanded, "the liberation from the Old Testament with its Jewish money morality, from these stories of livestock handlers and pimps," because true Christianity and clinging to the Old Testament would be mutually exclusive (Kuske, p. 8). This conflict over the role and place of the Old Testament in the church was eventually to color much of the later depictions of Old Testament theology in Germany. As early as 1938, for example, Gerhard von Rad could pose the issue as a matter of either-or: "Either the Old Testament speaks 'with the New of the Christ revelation of God . . . or we deny that; then in spite of its highly noteworthy particularities we must assign it to the remaining religions . . . but *tertium non datur*'" (Kuske, p. 33).

The christological, as well as the pneumatic-spiritual, exegesis of the Old Testament which we have noted earlier was not the only attempt made to read a "fuller" Christian message out of the Hebrew Scriptures, and thus "preserve them for the church." Other efforts were made to go beyond the literal meaning of the Hebrew Scriptures, sometimes reviving earlier medieval approaches. When the *sensus literalis* seems to offer nothing valuable or nothing sufficiently theological, some Christians have never been at a loss to utilize forms of exegesis to bridge the gap between past text and present reality and needs. Vischer's interpretation came very close to allegorical reading. Two other interpretative methods should be noted at this point although they tended to become much more widespread and controversial in the 1940s and 1950s and may be seen as radical modifications of Vischer's type of approach while preserving some of his interests. We refer here to what is called the typological approach and the search for the *sensus plenior*.

The typological approach, widely used in the patristic period, seeks to locate events, patterns, and personages in the Old Testament who are then viewed against the anti-types of similar events, patterns, and personages in the New Testament in a promise-anticipation and fulfillment-realization scheme (see Lampe and Woollcombe). In many ways, of course, such a scheme is more concerned with biblical theology as a whole than with Old Testament theology per se although it nonetheless leads to the interpretation of the Old Testament in terms of the New (see Jean Daniélou and Gabriel Hebert).

The *sensus plenior* approach, while not identical to, bears many similarities to christological and typological interpretations. It seeks to uncover deeper intentionalities in the text than a surface or literal-historical reading would suggest. Brown has described this plenary sense in the following way:

> The *sensus plenior* is that additional, deeper meaning, intended by God but not clearly intended by the human author, which is seen to exist in the words of a biblical text (or group of texts, or even a whole book) when they are studied in the light of further revelation or development in the understanding of revelation (p. 92).

The resort to pneumatic, typological, christological, allegorical, and plenary approaches to the Old Testament may thus be seen as reflective of the felt need to produce theological interpretations that would transcend the purely historical-critical approach and thus make the biblical materials relevant and defendable, especially in the Christian community. As such, they were fed by the same concerns that gave birth to the revival of systematic theological approaches to the Hebrew Scriptures in the 1920s and 1930s. The former represented more of a resort to earlier modes of interpretation—New Testament, patristic, and medieval—while the revival of the systematic presentation of Old Testament theology represented an attempt to recover an expression of interpretation characteristic of the time prior to the dominance of the historical-critical and history-of-religion approaches, that is prior to the dominance of the completely "scientific" approach to scriptural interpretation.

Interest in biblical theology and debate about the proper method to approach the issue was not limited to the German scene although it was in Germany that the issue was infused with anxiety, polemic, and *angst*. It was here that scholars were struggling not only to proclaim but also to preserve. When the reader moves to the British discussion of the topic, as in the essays by Davey, Richardson, and Robinson, one feels more the animated atmosphere of an afternoon high tea with well modulated conversation than the drama of a battlefield with screaming, ricocheting bullets. In the essays by these three British scholars, however, one can already see a common theme that would shortly become a major issue in biblical interpretation, namely, the relationship of revelation and history. The following quotes from Richardson and Robinson illustrate some of the British reflection on the issue:

Professor Quick has called attention to the ambiguity of the word "revelation," which may mean either *revelatio*, the act of revealing, or *revelatum*, the thing revealed. He rightly points out that this ambiguity conceals a fatal confusion in what is usually considered to be the "Barthian" view of the subject—namely, the assumption that "because in revelation the revealing act is God's, not man's, therefore the reality revealed cannot become the object of human thought, or be acknowledged as true by the rational or philosophic judgment of the human mind. The reply to this argument must simply be, *Non sequitur*." The *revelatum* must be capable of rational and philosophical criticism just as it must be capable of expression (however imperfectly) by human beings in human language.

But what is the nature of the *revelatum*? According to biblical theology, it is certainly not a series of truths in propositional form, such as that "God is love" or that "Jesus Christ came into the world to save sinners." Admittedly, the *revelatum* must be expressed by us in propositional forms of this kind, but it is not itself *given* to us in a series of propositions. It is not a system of doctrine or a metaphysic. Nor is it an historical event, or a series of historical events. Nor, again, is it an ineffable mystical experience. Let us attempt a tentative definition of what the *revelatum* is in the biblical conception. It is an historical event, or series of events, apprehended by faith as having a certain definite significance. In this definition the words "apprehended by faith" are of crucial importance, because where faith is lacking, even when a large measure of intellectual understanding of the historical event and its alleged significance is present, revelation has not occurred, or, in other words, no *revelatum* has been received. The deficiency of . . . other . . . conceptions of the nature of theology which we have previously considered is now seen to be that each of them omits that which is crucial for the biblical view—namely, faith. Faith is something which God gives, not something which man creates through any "will to believe" on his part. *Revelatum* is inseparable from *revelatio*, since no one can receive the former save through God's activity in the latter (Richardson, pp. 171–72).

The record constituted by the Old Testament is itself dominated by particular theories evolved in the course of the development of the religion. These theories—such as the prophetic doctrine of retribution which has shaped the 'Deuteronomistic' view of the history, and the Jewish conception of the Torah as given completely and once for all through Moses at the very beginning—have affected both the elements of which the Old Testament is composed and their final arrangement. The work of critical scholarship . . . is to get behind these theories to the original history of both events and ideas. This, so far as we can reach it, is the datum for a philosophy of revelation. Only when we have decided on a probable series of events, and a parallel series of human reactions to those events, can we usefully begin to ask how far and in what way they both *in their blended unity* serve to reveal God (Robinson, p. 304).

DISCUSSION OF ISRAELITE RELIGION—1920–1950

G. W. **Anderson**, "Hebrew Religion," *The Old Testament and Modern Study* (ed. by H. H. Rowley: London: Oxford University Press, 1951)283–310; John **Baillie**, *The*

Idea of Revelation in Recent Thought (New York: Columbia University Press, 1956); John **Baillie** and Hugh **Martin** (eds.), *Revelation* (London: Faber & Faber, 1937); Friedrich **Baumgärtel**, *Die Eigenart der alttestamentlichen Frommigkeit* (Schwerin: Bahn, 1932); James **Barr**, *The Semantics of Biblical Language* (London: Oxford University Press, 1961); Martin **Buber**, *Das Kommende* (Berlin: Schocken Verlag, 1932); S. C. **Carpenter**, *The Bible View of Life* (London: Eyre and Spottiswoode, 1937); Johannes **Hänel**, *Die Religion der Heiligkeit* (Gütersloh: C. Bertelsmann, 1931); Christian **Hartlich** and Walter **Sachs**, *Der Ursprung des Mythosbegriffes in der modernen Bibelwissenschaft* (Tübingen: J. C. B. Mohr, 1952); Johannes **Hempel**, *Gott und Mensch im Alten Testament. Studie zur Geschichte der Frommigkeit* (Stuttgart: W. Kohlhammer, 1926); *idem, Das Ethos des Alten Testaments* (Berlin: A. Töpelmann, 1938); S. H. **Hooke** (ed.), *Myth and Ritual: Essays on the Myth and Ritual of the Hebrews in Relation to the Culture Pattern of the Ancient East* (London: Oxford University Press, 1933); *idem, The Labyrinth: Further Studies in the Relation between Myth and Ritual in the Ancient World* (London/New York: SPCK/Macmillan Company, 1935); *idem, Myth, Ritual, and Kingship: Essays on the Theory and Practices of Kingship in the Ancient Near East and in Israel* (Oxford: Clarendon Press, 1958); William A. **Irwin**, "Revelation in the Old Testament," *The Study of the Bible Today and Tomorrow* (ed. by H. R. Willoughby; Chicago: University of Chicago Press, 1947)247–78; Johannes **Lindblom**, *Den gemmaltestamentliga religionens egenart* (Lund: C. W. K. Gleerup, 1935); Paul S. **Minear**, *Eyes of Faith: A Study of the Biblical Point of View* (Philadelphia: Westminster Press, 1946); Sigmund **Mowinckel**, *Psalmenstudien* (6 vols.; Kristiania: Jacob Dybwad, 1921–24); H. Richard **Niebuhr**, *The Meaning of Revelation* (New York: Macmillan Company, 1941); John William **Rogerson**, *Myth in Old Testament Interpretation* (Berlin: Walter de Gruyter, 1974); *idem, Anthropology and the Old Testament* (Oxford/Atlanta: Basil Blackwell/John Knox Press, 1978/1979); John Coert **Rylaarsdam**, *Revelation in Jewish Wisdom Literature* (Chicago: University of Chicago Press, 1946); Paul **Volz**, *Das Neujahrsfest Jahwes* (Tübingen: J. C. B. Mohr, 1912).

The renewed interest in the theological interpretation and exegesis of the Old Testament and the revival of Old Testament theology contained some elements and interests that were new as well as interests which had been continuing staples in Old Testament study or else had been characteristic of an earlier era. The renewal of theological interest cannot be judged merely by the works that were called Old Testament theology since many volumes not bearing such titles began to focus again and with new depth on what was called the religious point of view in the Bible. One could think here of the works by Johannes Hempel on Old Testament piety and ethics, the attempt to outline the "biblical point of view" on certain issues by Spencer Cecil Carpenter (1877–1959) and Paul Sevier Minear (1906–), and the study of piety by Friedrich Baumgärtel (1888–1981).

Such a rapid listing of works would be incomplete without a mention of three other signs of changed conditions, all of which we shall encounter again later. The first of these is the reviving interest in the question of revelation and its bearing on the Old Testament (see Rylaarsdam and Irwin). The next is indicated by several important investigations into the problem of the central idea of the religion of Israel; Johannes Hänel (1887–?), for example, located that idea in the concept of *holiness*, whereas Martin Buber (1878–1965) and Johannes Lindbolm (1882–1974) have defined it as *Yahweh's kingship*. A third illustration offers itself in various attempts to outline certain fundamental concepts of the Bible around the study of particular semantic roots or terms (see Barr, 1961, for the history of this development).

New Developments in the Study of Israelite Religion

The method employed for the study of Israelite religion, which developed in the nineteenth century, continued during this period with most works showing little perceptible change in methodology. In most of these more traditional works the most noticeable difference from such earlier ones was the greater availability of ancient Near Eastern material which could be incorporated into the discussion. Works very similar to older studies, and here we can provide only a partial list of authors, were produced by George Aaron Barton (1919), George Foot Moore (1919), Rudolf Kittel (1921), Gustav Hölscher (1922), Edward George Pace (1924), Bernardus Dirk Eerdmans (1930), Alfred Bertholet (1932), and Isaac George Matthews (1947). As we noted earlier, the major and standard English-language work on Israelite religion by Oesterley and Robinson appeared in 1930 and dominated the market for years.

A new departure in the analysis of Israelite religion developed in the 1920s and 1930s with the introduction of what has been broadly called the "myth and ritual" approach which represented an extension of the *religionsgeschichtliche* interests. There were actually two separate centers in which similar but not identical applications of the approach developed. The one, in Scandinavia, typified by Sigmund Mowinckel (1884–1965), drew upon the studies of Teutonic and Nordic cultures by the Danish anthropologist Vilhelm Grønbech (1873–1948) (see Anderson, pp. 292, 295 and Widengren, in Hooke, 1958, p. 154). The second center, in England, typified by Samuel Henry Hooke (1874–1968), was initially stimulated by the studies on kingship by a number of British scholars (see Hooke, 1958, pp. 1, 237). Mowinckel had been a student of Gunkel and thus shared in the interests of the German *religionsgeschichtliche Schule* and its emphasis on form criticism. Hooke had worked under a number of anthropologists at the University of Manchester.

Many of the older histories of Israelite religion had related that religion to its Near Eastern counterparts in what has been loosely called a developmentalist paradigm which looked for remnants or survivals of older or foreign forms of religion which could be seen developing or dying out in the course of the transformation and growth of Israelite religion. These older elements were generally traced back to a particular cultural phase—nomadism for example—or to a particular religious phase—animism or polytheism for example. The myth and ritual approach tended to follow a diffusionist paradigm (for the two approaches, see Rogerson, 1978, pp. 22–45). In its purer form, diffusionism sought to trace most religious practices back to a major cultural center from which it had become diffused to other areas. The earlier Pan-Babylonian school and the *Babel und Bibel* controversy had involved features of the diffusionist approach, although this earlier debate had focused primarily on literary matters rather than the larger realm of religious practices.

The diffusionist approach argued for the existence of a widespread pattern of similarity in the religion, mythology, and ritual of the various cultures of the Near East. This pattern and its reflection in Old Testament religion were seen as having a setting not so much in primitive Arabic cultures, where such scholars as Wellhausen and Robertson Smith had searched for parallels, but in the more developed monarchical states particularly those of Mesopotamia. In the myth and ritual approach the central elements of the religious faith of the cultures were viewed as concentrated in major annual rituals or festivals. Hooke spoke of this widely shared ritual pattern in the following manner:

> The annual festival which was the centre and climax of all the religious activities of the year contained the following elements:
> (*a*) The dramatic representation of the death and resurrection of the god.
> (*b*) The recitation or symbolic representation of the myth of creation.
> (*c*) The ritual combat, in which the triumph of the god over his enemies was depicted.
> (*d*) The sacred marriage.
> (*e*) The triumphal procession, in which the king played the part of the god followed by a train of lesser gods or visiting deities.
> These elements might vary in different localities and at different periods, some being more strongly stressed than others, but they constitute the underlying skeleton, so to speak, not only of such seasonal rituals as the great New Year Festivals, but also of the coronation rituals, initiation ceremonies and may even be discerned in occasional rituals such as spells against demons and various diseases (Hooke, 1933, p. 8)

T. H. Robinson (1881–1964) offered the following conjectual reconstruction of the central festival of the myth and ritual pattern in pre-exilic Israel:

> It necessarily began with the removal of Jahweh and Anath [Yahweh's female consort] from their home in the Temple, and with their occupation of a sacred hut in the neighbourhood of the sanctuary, probably in a vineyard. Then began the story of Creation, opening with the great contest of Jahweh against the powers of Chaos. This probably took different forms in different sanctuaries, but the issue was everywhere the victory of Jahweh. The divine marriage followed, consummated in the sacred hut, and this was succeeded by the death of Jahweh. After a period of lamentation He was restored to life, and, with his

consort, was led to His home in the Temple, there to reign until the changes of the year brought back again the festal season (in Hooke, 1933, pp. 188–89).

Mowinckel's prior reconstruction, already anticipated independently by Paul Volz (1871–1941), of the great autumn or New Year Festival with its myth-ritual pattern, while similar in many of the general features, differed considerably from the formulations of Hooke and his associates. Mowinckel was never willing to modify his views to accept the ritual enactment of a dying and rising Yahweh.

Interest in biblical and comparative mythology, of course, was not inaugurated by Mowinckel and Hooke. For generations, since the days of Eichchorn and Gabler, myth and its role in Israelite life and literature had been of some general concern (see Hartlich and Sachs, and Rogerson, 1974). The great compilation of world folklore in the multivolume *The Golden Bough* and *Folklore in the Old Testament* by the Scottish anthropologist Sir James Frazer (1854–1941) was one way of dealing with comparative mythological and folklore materials but without much of a deep and appreciative perspective. In addition, Frazer was dependent on a particular scheme of cultural development in which society was assumed to move progressively through various stages—from magic to religion to science (see Rogerson, 1978, pp. 47–51).

The work of the myth and ritual approach—if we may use this designation to cover the larger movement—marked a radical reinterpretation of Israelite religion. The movement and its conclusions as a whole enjoyed only marginal acceptance initially—primarily among some Scandinavian scholars and the circle of British scholars loosely associated with Hooke. Many of its conclusions and perspectives challenged the more traditional ways of understanding Israelite religion. The following represent some of the most significant. (1) First of all, the movement stressed the commonality of religious experiences, faiths, and practices throughout the Near East and thus identified Israelite religion as a member of a larger family of related religions. (2) Rather than relying upon primitive Semitic religions for comparative data, the myth and ritual approach drew upon the developed religious systems of advanced cultures. (3) The common pattern presupposed for the various religions located religious beliefs and practices within what might be called the sphere of nature and creation as opposed to the sphere of history. (4) The central celebrations of religion were assumed to reflect, reenact, and reenforce the cyclical pattern of the natural and climatic seasons. (5) Institutions and personages in Israel, such as the king, were endowed with sacral and religious significance that made comparison of them with modern secular counterparts much more difficult. (6) The cult was seen as the context, carrier, and creator of significant factors and features, including eschatology, in the religion of Israel which meant that lesser roles had to be assigned to creative individuals such as the prophets. As we shall see, many of these issues became central concerns and problems in later discussions of Old Testament theology.

Old Testament Religion Treated in the Form of a History of Religious Ideas

For many nineteenth-century scholars, such as Wellhausen and Duhm, the history of the religion of Israel was closely joined to the history of certain religious ideas—the centralization of the cult, ethics as a primary aspect of the service of Yahweh, and so forth. After the first World War, a number of studies appeared showing a fairly close relationship to a theological form of discussion inasmuch as their concern was to set forth, not the origin and development of Israel's religion as a whole, but the history of its important individual and interrelated ideas. From the larger perspective of our interest in the revival of Old Testament theology, they might be looked upon as points of transition away from the viewpoint of the *Religionsgeschichtler*. Although they were thoroughly characterized by the accepted canons of historical investigation, they were also born—not always in the same degree, however—of a liberal desire to present a constructive system of Old Testament ideas, something approaching Gabler's "true biblical theology," that is, eternal truths freed from the contamination and conditions of historical limitations.

One other fact bears singling out at the outset. Most of these studies came from the English-speaking world and betray—this is even more important—no noticeable influences from contemporary continental theological thought, that is, the impact of Barthian theology. Indeed, one of the most penetrating among them, also the one which is most critical of the typical histories of the nineteenth century, i.e., Knudson's, was published a year before Barth's *Römerbrief*. Their mere existence indicates that the growing demand for a systematic discussion of the theology of the Old Testament was not wholly the product of forces emanating from Europe.

ALBERT CORNELIUS KNUDSON

One of the earliest of such works was *The Religious Teachings of the Old Testament* (New York: Abingdon Press, 1918) by Knudson (1873–1953), a member of the so-called New England Personalist school of philosophy. The book's purpose, he tells us, was "to give an account of the origin and development of the leading religious ideas of the Old Testament," and also, "incidentally . . . to relate these ideas to modern thought" (p. 13).

One does not have to read very far into his book to discover that Knudson's method, despite his intention to deal with questions of "origin and development," was not a mere alternative to the method commonly adopted among the historians of Israel's religion. He might, for instance, have carried out his purpose by a simple modification of the historical school's usual procedure, namely, by treating the religion's individual ideas in chronological order instead of following the entire religion through its development; that is, he could have followed the earlier approach of Gramberg. The emphasis would still have been placed on the *growth* of these ideas, and the final result would still have underscored the disjunctive character of the religion. The notable feature of his work is, however, that in his hands the religion of the Old Testament emerged as a much more unified phenomenon than was normally the case among the critical historians.

The main reasons for the homogeneity he succeeded in giving to the religion of the Old Testament were, it seems, twofold. In the first place, his major interest was not in discovering the pattern of each concept's development, but in determining the content it had possessed for Israel's thinkers and the relation it bore to contemporary thought. Altogether, fifteen different concepts were selected for separate treatment and were grouped, in turn, in two major areas of thought, (1) God and Angels and (2) Man and Redemption. The fifteen were: God's Personality, God's Unity, God's Spirituality, God's Power, God's Holiness, God's Righteousness, God's Love, Angels and Other Divine Beings, Man, Sin, Suffering, Forgiveness and Atonement, Nationalism and Individualism, Messianic Hope, and Future Life. A fine example of his concern for the relevance of Old Testament thought for present-day religion occurs at the close of his chapter on the personality of God. After first calling attention to the manifest difference between the naturalistic, immanentistic philosophies of the later nineteenth century and the stress of the Old Testament on the transcendent personality of God, he pointed with evident approval to the change, in his own day, toward a more personal conception of deity with a consequent "renewed appreciation of the Old Testament" (p. 66). This concern first and foremost, with the nature, implications, and relevance of the various concepts was what gave his work its peculiarly theological quality. Yet, it would be wrong to assume that he lacked a historical perspective. Again and again he pointed out the primitive starting points of Israel's religious ideas and the growth which these ideas had undergone. An illustration of the manner in which he viewed such primitive antecedents is found in his discussion of the concept of holiness. He recognized that the primitive Semitic ideas of "a mysterious, indefinable, fear-inspiring characteristic of Deity" were part of the religious background of Old Testament teaching and that they appear "to some extent" in the Old Testament itself. However—and here he borrowed a quotation from Cornill—"Israel resembled in spiritual matters the fabulous King Midas who turned everything he touched into gold." The heathen associations gradually "gave way to higher spiritual and ethical conceptions. Of these conceptions three may be distinguished: power, purity, and righteousness" (pp. 145–46). The fact remains, nevertheless, that these questions, the very ones with which the historians of religion were wont to occupy themselves most, were left by him in the background.

In the second place, Knudson could never have maintained the general unity of Old Testament thought quite so strongly had he adhered to the critical position of a Duhm or a Wellhausen. What fundamentally enabled him to stress that unity was a theory of Israel's religious development according to which there was no appreciable gap between the pre-prophetic and the prophetic periods. His opening chapter on the development of Old Testament religion was, in a large measure, a repudiation of Wellhausen's interpretation. "The prophets," we are told, "are, then, to be regarded not as innovators, but as reformers. For the source of Israel's higher faith we must go back to Moses" (pp. 31–32). Wellhausen's mistake, he felt, was to be so thoroughly imbued with the Hegelian scheme of human evolution that he disregarded the creative influence of Moses and so reduced the pre-prophetic period to little more than primitive nature worship (p. 29).

On the basis of this theory Knudson found it possible to assign the origin of every one of the Old Testament doctrines about God to Moses (pp. 59, 68, 89, 123, 157, 178). Whatever the advances during the ensuing periods of Hebrew religious history, they were to be interpreted, not as deepgoing changes, but as the outcome of a "clarification and deepening of convictions already present" and, furthermore, of a growing understanding of the "implications" contained in the religious views which Moses had first formulated (pp. 110, 123).

Knudson's work might be looked upon, in other words, as a kind of revival of the "Mosaism" which had been such a favorite with the nineteenth century's conservative theologians (Oehler, Ewald, Riehm, Dillmann, and others, but especially A. B. Davidson with whom he seems to have felt his greatest kinship; pp. 83, 86, 123). There was one important difference, however. Unlike these predecessors, he did not attempt to present "Mosaism" in terms of a complete system of thought. He recognized that the status of knowledge at the time could not permit anything but the most general conclusions about the religious ideas which Moses had held, although, again, he was quick to warn against the opposite assumption that Moses had made no appreciable contribution whatever (p. 32).

For this reason Mosaism emerged from his discussion as a somewhat nebulous and almost hypothetical quantity which had no important function except to serve as the gathering point to which all lines of development in Israel's religious history were to be traced back. Because this was so, his critical theory was actually of little ultimate significance in his effort to state the content, the inner unity, and the present relevance of the teachings of the Old Testament. Fundamentally, what he did present was a description of the thinking of Israel's prophets. It was the coherence of their ideas which enabled him to find a large measure of unity, and to see in them a deep meaning for his own day.

HARRY EMERSON FOSDICK

To discover the characteristics of a pure history of religious ideas in the Bible is the goal of *A Guide to Understanding the Bible: The Development of Ideas within the Old and New Testaments* (New York: Harper and Brothers, 1938) by Fosdick (1878–1969). The work differed significantly from the book by Knudson since the latter came close to presupposing the identity of the pre-prophetic and prophetic eras whereas Fosdick's work presupposed a genuine evolution from the most primitive—the earliest—to the assumed higher level evident in the later books. Unlike most histories of Israelite religion, however, his work concentrated on ideas rather than a broader spectrum of issues. The subtitle indicates that the main interest of the work was with the course of the growth of each idea. Six major ideas—God, Man, Right and Wrong, Suffering, Fellowship with God, and Immortality—were traced in their progress through the two testaments and the intertestamental literature. The contrasts between the earliest and latest phases of each idea's history were stated quite strongly, but without the hypercritical attitude of someone like Harnack who wished to repudiate the entire Old Testament, as we have already noted.

Fosdick, a staunch defender of the liberal cause and of the historical-critical study of the Bible in the American Fundamentalist-Modernist controversy, believed himself to be presenting "an objective, factual picture of unfolding Biblical thought" (p. xv). He called his work "not primarily a book on biblical theology but a genetic survey of developing biblical thought"; "not expository but genetic; it tries to trace the highroads traversed by Biblical ideas from their origin to their culmination; when they have reached their culmination it makes no endeavor to give a systematic and adequate exposition of them" (p. xii). In the final analysis, the unity he found within the Bible was to be measured not in terms of coherence of thought but "on the factually demonstrable basis of a coherent development" (p. ix). Nothing could more aptly describe his historical outlook than the assertion that "the story of developing Scriptural ideas . . . makes of the Bible a coherent whole, understood, as everything has to be understood, in terms of its origins and growth" (p. x).

In spite of Fosdick's emphasis on the genetic development of the ideas he discussed, his schema of ideas carried with it a rather full presentation of what had historically been considered the central doctrines of the Christian faith.

YEHEZKEL KAUFMANN

Kaufmann (1889–1963), a Ukrainian immigrant to Palestine and later professor of Bible at the Hebrew University in Jerusalem, labored for years to produce a multivolume work on the religion of Israel that would refute the views of Wellhausen as well as those of the history-of-religion movement. His work, written in modern Hebrew, appeared between 1937–57 in eight volumes. The first seven volumes were condensed and translated by Moshe Greenberg as *The Religion of Israel: From Its Beginnings to the Babylonian Exile* (Chicago: University of Chicago Press, 1960).

Although very comprehensive and informative, Kaufmann's work sought to support several very basic interpretations of Israelite religion. The following are some of his more important emphases. (1) In his anti-Wellhausenian stance Kaufmann argued that the law (the Torah) "is the literary product of the earliest stage of Israelite religion, the stage prior to literary prophecy. Although its compilation and canonization took place later, its sources are demonstrably ancient—not in part, not in their general content, but in their entirety, even to their language and formulation" (p. 2). (2) From its beginnings Israelite religion was thoroughly monotheistic and *sui generis* and therefore did not represent a gradual development out of paganism nor was its monotheism the child of classical prophecy (although Kaufmann spoke of classical prophecy as the later climax of Israel's religion).

> Israelite religion was an original creation of the people of Israel. It was absolutely different from anything the pagan world ever knew; its monotheistic world view had no antecedents in paganism. Nor was it a theological doctrine conceived and nurtured in limited circles or schools; nor a concept that finds occasional expression in this or that passage or stratum of the Bible. It was the fundamental idea of a national culture, and informed every aspect of that culture from its very beginning. It received, of course, a legacy from the pagan age which preceded it, but the birth of Israelite religion was the death of paganism in Israel. Despite appearances, Israel was not a polytheistic people. . . . Israel's world was its own creation, notwithstanding its utilization of ancient pagan materials. To fathom the meaning of this world, we must interpret its symbols from within; the attempts to explain it in the light of pagan models only obscure its real character and bar the way to a true appreciation (pp. 2–3).

(3) Israel was so immersed in her monotheistic outlook and so separated by a religious gulf from her neighbors that the Israelites never understood the nature of paganism: "the Bible is utterly unaware of the nature and meaning of pagan religion" (p. 7). Although the Hebrew Scriptures and the prophets condemn the people for idolatry, it is obvious from their attacks that neither they nor the people had any real understanding of pagan religion but considered it instead to be fetishism.

> The Bible's ignorance of the meaning of paganism is at once the basic problem and the most important clue to the understanding of biblical religion. It underscores as nothing else the gulf that separates biblical religion from paganism. . . . [The Bible shows no understanding of] the distinguishing mark of pagan thought: the idea that there exists a realm of being prior to the gods and above them, upon which the gods depend, and whose decrees they must obey. Deity belongs to, and is derived from, a primordial realm (pp. 20–21).

(4) Given the preceding conclusions, Kaufmann, of course, denied that Israelite religion and Yahwism ever possessed any character or qualities associated with mythology.

> The basic idea of Israelite religion is that God is supreme over all. There is no realm above or beside him to limit his absolute sovereignty [as would be required if Israelite religion was in anyway mythological]. He is utterly distinct from, and other than, the world; he is subject to no laws, no compulsions, or powers that transcend him. He is, in short, non-mythological. This is the essence of Israelite religion, and that which sets it apart from all forms of paganism. . . . The Bible, while stressing the oneness of God and his supremacy, nowhere articulates the contrast between its new concept and the mythological essence of paganism. The new religious idea never received an abstract, systematic formulation in Israel. It expressed itself rather in symbols, the chief of which was the image of an omnipotent, supreme deity, holy, awful, and jealous, whose will was the highest law. Taking on popular forms, the new idea pervaded every aspect of Israelite creativity. . . . The store of biblical legends lacks the fundamental myth of paganism: the theogony [an account of the origin of the god]. All theogonic motifs are similarly absent. Israel's god has no pedigree, fathers no generations; he neither inherits nor bequeaths his authority. He does not die and is not resurrected. He has no sexual qualities or desires and shows no need of or dependence upon powers outside himself (pp. 60–61).

At this point, we are not concerned with either the accuracy or the cogency of Kaufmann's position but only with the fact that the idea of monotheism, along with a conservative attitude toward the biblical traditions, provided him with a clue and the key for understanding the nature and history of Israelite religion. In this regard, Kaufmann's position comes close to a systematic exposition of the monotheistic theology of the Hebrew Scriptures written in terms of his view of the history of Israelite literature.

OLD TESTAMENT THEOLOGY—1920–1950

Otto J. **Baab**, "Old Testament Theology: Its Possibility," *The Study of the Bible Today and Tomorrow* (ed. by H. R. Willoughby; Chicago: The University of Chicago Press, 1947)401–18; *idem, The Theology of the Old Testament* (New York: Abingdon-Cokesbury Press, 1949); Millar **Burrows**, *An Outline of Biblical Theology* (Philadelphia: Westminster Press, 1946); Robert C. **Dentan**, *Preface to Old Testament Theology* (New Haven: Yale University Press, 1950; rev. ed.; New York: Seabury Press, 1963); Walther **Eichrodt**, *Theologie des Alten Testaments* (3 vols.; Leipzig:

J. C. Hinrichs, 1933–39) = *Theology of the Old Testament* (2 vols.; London/Philadelphia: SCM Press/Westminster Press, 1961–67); Norman K. **Gottwald**, "Recent Biblical Theologies. IX. Walther Eichrodt's 'Theology of the Old Testament,'" *ExpTim* 74(1963)209–12; *idem*, "W. Eichrodt, *Theology of the Old Testament*," in Laurin, pp. 23–62; Wilfrid **Harrington**, *The Path of Biblical Theology* (Dublin: Gill and Macmillan, 1973); Paul **Heinisch**, *Theologie des Alten Testaments* (Bonn: Peter Hanstein, 1940) = *Theology of the Old Testament* (Collegeville: Liturgical Press, 1950); Ludwig **Köhler**, "Alttestamentliche Theologie," *TRu* 7(1935)255–76; 8(1936)55–69; 247–84; *idem*, *Theologie des Alten Testaments* (Tübingen: J. C. B. Mohr, 1935) = *Old Testament Theology* (London/Philadelphia: Lutterworth Press/Westminster Press, 1957); Edward **König**, *Theologie des Alten Testaments kritisch und vergleichend dargestellt* (Stuttgart: C. Belser, 1922); Robert B. **Laurin** (ed.), *Contemporary Old Testament Theologians* (Valley Forge: Judson Press, 1970); Wilhelm and Hans **Möller**, *Biblische Theologie des Alten Testaments in heilsgeschichtlicher Entwicklung* (Zwickau: Johannes Herrmann, 1938); W. G. **Nesbit**, *A Study of Methodologies in Contemporary Old Testament Biblical Theologies* (Ph.D. dissertation, Marquette University, 1968); Otto **Procksch**, *Theologie des Alten Testaments* (Gütersloh: C. Bertelsmann, 1950); John N. **Schofield**, "Otto Procksch, *Theology of the Old Testament*," in Laurin, pp. 91–120; Ernst **Sellin**, *Alttestamentliche Theologie auf religionsgeschichter Grundlage*. Vol. I: *Israelitisch-jüdische Religionsgeschichte*. Vol. II: *Theologie des Alten Testaments* (Leipzig: Quelle & Meyer, 1933); Cuthbert A. **Simpson**, "Professor Procksch's Theology of the Old Testament," *ATR* 34(1952)116–22; D. G. **Spriggs**, *Two Old Testament Theologies: A Comparative Evaluation of the Contributions of Eichrodt and von Rad to our Understanding of the Nature of Old Testament Theology* (London: SCM Press, 1974); Ernst **Würthwein**, "Zur Theologie des Alten Testaments," *TRu* 36(1971)185–208.

At this point we return to the topic of the renewed production of Old Testament theologies following the first World War. Our discussion, in the meantime, has digressed to note some developments in the study of Israelite religion and the attempt of some scholars to present a history of that religion in terms of certain basic ideas. We noted examples of the latter type of such histories which themselves are very close to Old Testament theologies. Some of the new developments in the study of Israelite religion, such as the impact of the myth and ritual school, did not become integral to discussions of Old Testament theology until a later period, but we have chosen to note these at this point since they do form part of the larger background for the writing of Old Testament theologies in the decades between 1920 and 1950.

Limiting our survey here to the years from 1920 to about 1950, we will first of all examine some of the individual theologies produced during this period. In the next section, we will comment generally on the typological approaches evident in these works. Then, we shall outline the nature and characteristics of what has been called, rightly or wrongly, the Biblical Theology movement. By about 1950 biblical studies and biblical theology had reached a status in academic and theological—and even ecumenical—circles which they had not enjoyed for years. This condition was to last for about a decade or so before some of the presuppositions on which it rested were to be seriously challenged and the legitimacy of the "movement" questioned.

EDUARD KÖNIG

Four years after the conclusion of the first World War, the first tangible embodiment of the reviving interest in the study of Old Testament theology came with the publication of König's work. Its author had, a decade earlier, followed the lead of the historical school by issuing a history of Old Testament religion and so had, outwardly at least, conformed to the dominant pattern. As we noted, however, in the same work he made a valiant effort to retain an emphasis on the concept of revelation by drawing a distinction between Israel's "legitimate" religion and its "illegitimate" religions. König, in other words, was one of the few conservatives left in the wake of historicism's victorious advance who sought to preserve some of the theological interests of earlier scholars.

If one were to read no more than his introductory chapter, one would be inclined to rank him among the *Religionsgeschichtler* themselves. His rather ordinary definition of Old Testament theology reads: "It is the biblical and, therefore, historically oriented presentation of the religious and ethical content of the Old Testament writings" (p. 1). Source material for such a theology was to be taken from both canonical and non-canonical books. His method of interpretation he described as grammatico-historical. For this reason he repudiated all "spiritual" or "pneumatic" exegesis which, he felt, "was only a kind of allegorizing exegesis which lets the actual words say something else than what they literally mean" (p. 17). When one adds to these foregoing principles the phrases "critical" and "comparative" mentioned in the title, his affinities to the *Religionsgeschichtler* would seem to be all but complete. These outward appearances are, nevertheless, deceptive.

Like so many of the theologians of the nineteenth century, König divided his study into two major sections, the first containing a "history of Israel's religion," the second the "theology" proper. The historical portion was motivated by the same purpose as his earlier *History*, namely (1) to point out Israel's "legitimate" religion and (2) to show that it had been in existence since the days of Abraham. For him, too, the Pentateuch had chronological priority over the Prophets and was to be respected, in its entirety, as a record of actual historical events. It is also characteristic of his point of view that he insisted on explaining such a distinctive feature of Hebrew religion as prophecy not by historical and psychological methods, but instead as the outgrowth of "actual disclosures from beyond" (p. 87).

In the theological part his approach was systematic, with the usual topics, borrowed from Christian dogmatics, of God, Man, Sin, and Salvation appearing as the major items of his outline. Yet, even here the historical perspective was apparent. The heading which he gave to this entire section reads "History of the Unfolding of the Individual Factors of Israel's True Religion." To be sure, the history with which he was concerned was actually *Heilsgeschichte*. The very last sentence of his work makes this quite clear: "God's plan for the education and redemption of mankind, in its movement towards fulfillment, could not be retarded by any opposition which was not of his [God's] own doing" (p. 317). Elsewhere he speaks of "God's plan of salvation" and "ways of bringing back wayward humanity." It comes as no surprise, therefore, to find that in this *Theologie* one seems to be moving again in the world of von Hofmann and Oehler with their peculiar viewpoints and emphases.

WALTHER EICHRODT

The long years of preparation and readjustment which were required of a generation trained to think in historical rather than in theological terms finally came to an end in 1933 with the publication of two works on Old Testament theology, one by Walther Eichrodt (1890–1978), the other by Ernst Sellin (1867–1945). To appreciate the larger significance of this event it is well to remember that in that same year Germany came under National-Socialist control and thus entered into a period of its history when the Old Testament was relegated to the category of condemned books. Earlier in this chapter we noted the virulent attacks which were made on the Hebrew Scriptures as part of the Nazi anti-Jewish movement. In spite of this factor, or perhaps partially because of it, the year 1933 opened the door to a spate of works concerned with Old Testament theology.

As we have already seen, Eichrodt, who was a native German but later taught in Basel, Switzerland, was concerned over Old Testament theology and the revelatory character of the Bible long before his magisterial three-volume work began to appear. As early as 1925 he had written a work entitled "Is the Old Israelite National Religion a Religion of Revelation?" (*Ist die altisraelitische Nationalreligion Offenbarungsreligion?* [Gütersloh: C. Bertelsmann]). Four years later he had argued against Eissfeldt's proposal to separate *Religionsgeschichte* and Old Testament theology. Without any doubt Eichrodt's theology has been one of the most significant works of its genre produced in the twentieth century. Many would still say that it is the most important single work on Old Testament theology.

Eichrodt's work has been frequently analyzed and critiqued (see Gottwald; Nesbit, pp. 11–173; and Spriggs). In the opening chapter of his study he described two approaches to the theology or religion (the terms seem to be used synonymously on occasion) of the Old Testament which he repudiated as legitimate theological approaches. One was the attempt to organize biblical materials according to the outlines of dogmatic theology. The second was the historical treatment of the religious thought which he argued "fostered the idea that once the historical problems were clarified everything had been done" (I, p. 30). For the latter approach he had harsh words declaring that it was "high time that the tyranny of historicism in OT studies was broken and the proper approach to our task re-discovered." He proceeds in the next sentence to the real issue as he saw it:

> This is no new problem, certainly, but it is one that needs to be solved anew in every epoch of knowledge—*the problem of how to understand the realm of OT belief in its structural unity and how, by examining on the one hand its religious environment and on the other its essential coherence with the NT, to illuminate its profoundest meaning*. Only so shall we succeed in winning back for OT studies in general and OT theology in particular that place in Christian theology which at present has been surrendered to the comparative study of religions (I, p. 31).

His program thus called for an exposition of Old Testament belief in its structural unity but an exposition that was sensitive both to the ancient Near Eastern religious environment and to the later New Testament as well. Throughout his methodological statements, frequent reference is made to the New Testament, its revelation, and an expression of Old Testament faith that is analogous to it: "the OT religion, ineffaceably individual though it may be, can yet be grasped in this essential uniqueness only when it is seen as completed in Christ" (I, p. 27). This connection in his own mind between the Old and New Testaments can be seen in his statement of what was needed in the field.

> It is not just a matter of describing the all-round expansion of OT religion, or the phases through which it passed, but of determining to what extent . . . it ties up with NT revelation and is analogous to it. But this can only be done by taking a cross-section of the realm of OT thought, thus making possible both a comprehensive survey and a sifting of what is essential from what is not. In this way both the total structure of the system and the basic principles on which it rests can be exposed to view. In other words we have to undertake a *systematic examination* with objective classification and rational arrangement of the varied material. This does not in any way imply that the historical method of investigation is worthless, nor that it should be set aside. We ought rather to build deliberately on its conclusions and make use of its procedures. Nevertheless developmental analysis must be replaced by systematic synthesis, if we are to make more progress toward an interpretation of the outstanding religious phenomena of the OT in their deepest significance (I, pp. 27–28).

The hallmark of Eichrodt's program was to present a comprehensive survey and a systematic ordering of the material. Eichrodt was confident that it was possible "to present the religion of which the records are to be found in the Old Testament as *a self-contained entity exhibiting, despite ever-changing historical conditions, a constant basic tendency and character*" (I, p. 11). Eichrodt argued that this had to be done topically, by a "cross-cut" (*Quer-*

schnitt), rather than chronologically, by a "long-cut" (*Längsschnitt*). In order to present a cross-section of this constant self-contained entity, Eichrodt chose the idea of the covenant which he felt could be shown to cut across all the various divisions and strata of the Old Testament and which was a concept expressive of the divine-human relationship in Israel from the time of Moses onward. Already in the first edition of his work it is clear that "covenant" for him was understood in rather broad categories. In the preface to the fifth edition his response to his critics shows rather clearly that the term and its reference is even further weakened in its specificity in order to defend it as the key for providing a summary of the unchanging entity of Israelite religion.

> In the face of all objections, the 'covenant' has been retained as the central concept, by which to illuminate the structural unity and the unchanging basic tendency of the message of the OT. For it is in this concept that Israel's fundamental conviction of its special relationship with God is concentrated. The decisive consideration on this point is neither the presence nor absence of the actual term *berit*, as certain all too naive critics seem to imagine, but the fact that every expression of the OT which is determinative for its faith rests on the explicit or implicit assumption that a free act of God, consummated in history, has raised Israel to the rank of the People of God, in whom the nature and will of God are to be revealed. The word 'covenant', therefore, is so to speak a convenient symbol for an assurance much wider in scope and controlling the formation of the national faith at its deepest level, without which Israel would not be Israel. As an epitome of the dealings of God in history the 'covenant' is not a doctrinal concept, with the help of which a complete corpus of dogma can be worked out, but the characteristic description of a living process, which was begun at a particular time and at a particular place, in order to reveal a divine reality unique in the whole history of religion. Reference to this living process in every single paragraph of this work will not escape the attentive reader (I, pp. 13–14).

Believing that we "must plot our course as best we can along the lines of the OT's own dialectic," Eichrodt argued that there are "three principal categories, within which to study the special nature of the Israelite faith in God: *God and the People*, *God and the World* and *God and Man*" (I, p. 33). This general outline and its three components (borrowed from his teacher Otto Procksch) then became the three parts of his theology. The sections of his three volumes equal to these three parts bore the following outline:

Part One: God and the People

The Covenant Relationship
The Covenant Statutes
    The Secular Law
    The Cultus
The Name of the Covenant God
The Nature of the Covenant God
    Affirmations about the Divine Being
    Affirmations about the Divine Activity

The Instruments of the Covenant
     The Charismatic Leaders
     The Official Leaders
Covenant-Breaking and Judgment
Fulfilling the Covenant: The Consummation of God's Dominion

Part Two: God and the World

The Forms of God's Self-Manifestation
The Cosmic Powers of God
     The Spirit of God
     The Word of God
     The Wisdom of God
Cosmology and Creation
     The Place of Man in the Creation
     The Maintenance of the World
     The Celestial World
     The Underworld

Part Three: God and Man

The Individual and the Community in the Old Testament God-Man Relationship
The Fundamental Forms of Man's Personal Relationship with God
The Effect of Piety on Conduct (Old Testament morality)
Sin and Forgiveness
The Indestructibility of the Individual's Relationship with God (Immortality)

A moment's reflection shows that these major sections were based, for their part, on the distinction between *particularism* and *universalism*, with the first volume describing the thought patterns which arose out of the relationship between Yahweh and the Israelite people, and the other two dealing with the relationship between God, the universe, and humanity as such. The religion of the Old Testament thus assumed, in his treatment, a Janus-like character as it faced into these two directions, and Eichrodt did little to alleviate the tension or to suggest ways whereby a *rapprochement* might be effected. We may wonder, therefore, whether in his basic classification, he did not already—tacitly, of course—admit failure in his efforts to depict "the religion . . . of the Old Testament as an integrated quantity."

There are other signs of the difficulty he had in carrying out an otherwise thoroughly commendable purpose. It is worth noting, for instance, that his discussion of the two religious outlooks, the particularistic and the universalistic, presents each one as though it were complete in itself. Each has its own doctrine of God, its own conception of sin, and its own interpretation of salvation. It is, however, when we turn to what is also the most distinctive feature of his work, namely, the use of the covenant-idea as the central concept of Old Testament theology, that the trouble he experienced in accomplishing his intention becomes especially apparent.

In the first volume the concept of the covenant served him quite admirably as the integrating or centralizing factor *par excellence* to which every other idea could be related. For this reason, this portion of his theology exhibits "structural unity" beyond any doubt, as even a quick glance at its outline will convincingly show. The basis on which he rested his case for placing the covenant-idea at the very heart of his system was his assertion that the concept of the covenant established *a priori* the pecularity of Israel's understanding of God. In the other volumes, however, he not only did not use that idea as a co-ordinating factor but also did not make use of any integrating idea whatever, so that his outline at this point actually comes close to a stringing together of short essays.

For thoroughness of treatment, for range and amount of material discussed, and for persistence in trying to give Old Testament thought some form of systematic coherence, Eichrodt's monumental study knows no superior. Most of its principles and the application it makes of them are sane. Its greatest service to Old Testament theology is, perhaps, its insistence on the importance of discovering the "interrelatedness" of the various religious concepts. Its major interest is system, and to that interest all other considerations are definitely subordinated. Although he gave some lip service to historical development and historical change, the body of his discussion does not often pay attention to this historical perspective. Two of the few instances where he does are (1) in his comparison of the Hebrew and Babylonian worldviews (II, pp. 93–96) and (2) in his account of the development of Israel's charismatic leadership (I, pp. 289–339).

Two issues require additional comment. The first is his use of the covenant-idea as the central feature of Old Testament thought. The selection of that idea for such a position was, of course, not novel to Eichrodt. One could think back to Johannes Cocceius, the Puritans, or some of the persons influenced by the Erlangen theology. What was new in Eichrodt's treatment was the singularly conceptualized and static character he gave the idea. For him its chief value lay in the fact that it was a concept to which he could relate other concepts, whereas for Cocceius and others whose theologies had a strong *heilsgeschichtliche* orientation, the covenant concept's importance was mainly historical and could be understood genetically. That is to say, they looked upon the covenant or series of covenants as the cardinal events in the outworking of the divine plan for the redemption of humanity. Eichrodt's emphasis on the covenant-idea as a conceptual, static entity was, of course, also completely in line with his dominant interest in system instead of in history and development.

While one may grant the novelty of his use of the covenant-idea, the fact remains that he was able to apply it as an organizing principle only to a part of the religious thought contained in the Old Testament. As we look for reasons for his failure to reduce all of Old Testament religion to this single common denominator, the one that carries the greatest cogency is that the covenant and the peculiar viewpoint it represented was not commonly recognized by the Hebrew thinkers as the fundamental ingredient of their thought. The word itself did not enter into the vocabulary of the prophets in any appreciable degree until the exilic era, even though the basic assertion contained in the covenant-idea, namely, that Yahweh and Israel stood in a special relationship to one another, may be found in all the prophetic writings. It is good to keep in mind the objection raised by Ludwig Köhler against Eichrodt's use of the covenant, because it serves as a word of caution for all future efforts to discover there the quintessence of the religion of the Old Testament. Köhler's point is simply that there is no place where "the covenant is called, with the clarity of a definite program, the fundamental pattern of the Old Testament understanding of God" (1935, p. 272).

The second issue which Eichrodt's work raises for Old Testament theology is the question of the relationship between particularism and universalism. This question and the preceding one are, of course, in the final analysis akin to one another. The covenant was the symbol of the special ties between Yahweh and Israel and, as such, also represented particularism. In those instances where the thought of the Old Testament transcended this nationalistic framework and began to consider religion in more universalistic terms as a relationship between God and the World or between God and Humanity, the covenant had either no bearing whatever (especially in the wisdom literature) or was expected to be superseded by a new covenant (Jer. 31:31). This two-directional outlook is, therefore, responsible not only for the fact that Eichrodt found it mandatory to treat the theology of the Old Testament from two varying viewpoints but also for his inability to focus that theology entirely on the covenant-idea.

ERNST SELLIN

Sellin (1867–1945) divided his theology into two volumes, the first dealing with the history of Israelite-Judean religion and the second with Old Testament theology proper. The title of his work as a whole, *Old Testament Theology on a History-of-Religion Basis*, could on first sight be taken to offer the promise that here at last one might find a serious attempt to solve the complex questions involved in the relationship between the historical and the systematic viewpoints. Anyone expecting such an integration, however, would be disappointed. For, somewhat after the manner of Ewald, Dillmann, and Schultz, what Sellin did was to divide his study into two major parts, each having a high degree of autonomy.

His justification for allowing history and theology to go their own separate ways was contained in the two definitions of the function he ascribed to each. The history of the religion, he thought, had as its purpose to picture "the development and growth of the religion of the Israelite-Jewish nation both in terms of the divine revelation which pulsated and found expression here and of the multiform, natural-human influence, development, shaping, and piety from the beginnings to the coming of Jesus Christ." The objective of a theology of the Old Testament, on the other hand, was to describe "systematically the religious teachings and the faith which were fashioned in the Jewish community on the basis of the sacred writings during the fifth to the second pre-Christian centuries, but only in so far as they were recognized by Jesus Christ and his apostles as the presupposition and the foundation of their gospel, in so far as they, therefore, to use Luther's phrase in its widest sense, 'deal with Christ'" (I, p. 1). In other words, whereas the historical approach had as its purpose the description of Israel's religious development during its entire Old Testament period, the theological form of discussion was to concern itself only with the phases when the religion had reached maturity. In addition, where the former was to show not only the whole history of the divine revelation as it expressed itself in Israel's faith but also the human conditioning found there, the latter was to consider the permanently valuable elements alone, the criterion for determining this permanent value being in each case the New Testament. Other definitions which he offered tend in the same direction: "The theology of the Old Testament is the crown of the history of the Israelite-Jewish religion because it presents, from the standpoint of the Gospel, in systematic synthesis what has been the divine goal in the multiform historical development of the Old Testament religion" (I, p. 2). "Old Testament theology is the scientific presentation of this teaching which was presupposed by Jesus and the apostles as basic and upon which they wanted to build further" (II, p. 3).

For Sellin, as for Eissfeldt and Eichrodt, Old Testament theology thus required a peculiarly Christian orientation. "We are interested," he stated at one point, "only in the long line which found its fulfillment in the Gospel" (II, p. 1). One of the most striking ways in which he sought to apply this Christian perspective—perhaps, it would be better to be more specific and speak of it as a Pauline perspective—was the distinction he drew, on the basis of Paul's suggestion that the Old Testament contained both Law and Promise (Grace), between the national, cultic religion and the prophetic-ethical-universal-eschatological religion of the Hebrew Scriptures. In many areas of Old Testament thought these two forms of religion were interpenetrated, especially as far as the doctrines of God and Humanity were concerned, but on the question of Salvation they had, he argued, gone separate ways. The national cultus had shown itself singularly interested in the present and past and thus was akin to Judaism; the prophetic religion, on the other hand, had focused its attention primarily on the future, having "viewed the entire present from the point of view of the coming, of the approaching God who, as the Holy One, brings both misfortune (i.e., judgment) and salvation" (II, p. 77) and thus was preparatory and akin to Christianity.

Sellin's approach was, therefore, frankly eclectic and distinctively Christian. Whatever did not fit the twin categories of national cult religion and prophetic-ethical-universal-eschatological religion and did not belong to the "long line" which led to the gospel of Jesus and the apostles was left aside. In so doing he, at least superficially, cut the Gordian knot of Old Testament theology and worked with a fairly homogeneous mass of material capable of systematization. By picking and choosing among the changing and the relative, he sought to restore to the Bible something of the unity it had lost in the *religionsgeschichtliche* treatment. We may wonder, however, as we have wondered before in the case of similar conceptions of the nature and purpose of Old Testament theology, whether he did not buy his answer to the study's problems at too high a price, a price which involved (1) a major distortion of the Old Testament and (2) the disavowal of material which is innately of great value and a legitimate part of Israel's religious guest, namely, for example, the wisdom literature.

In the volume on the theology proper his method was almost entirely a systematic one and followed the usual outline of God, Man, and Salvation. In the second volume historical considerations are only slightly evident. One of the few instances where Sellin introduced such historical considerations is found in his discussion of the "media of revelation." In this case he organized his material to show a development from primitive to "highest, purest, and most immediate" (II, pp. 45–47). Although he was writing, fundamentally, a theology as background to the New Testament, his source material was derived primarily from the Old Testament canon. The Apocrypha he used only secondarily and the Pseudepigrapha not at all although it had been argued for years that the context of Christian origins was as much the Jewish/ Hellenistic world as the Old Testament.

LUDWIG KÖHLER

From a methodological standpoint, the simplest plan by all counts was that of the third of the German-language theologies to be published during the thirties, the *Theologie des Alten Testaments* by Köhler (1880–1956). It consisted of a simple and straightforward enumeration with a strong philological orientation of the statements made in the Old Testament about God, Man, and Judgment and Salvation and did not concern itself, therefore, with anything like Eichrodt's interest in a logically cohesive system or with Sellin's problem of the relationship between Israel's empirical religion and the theology of the Old Testament. His foreword, one of the briefest on record, has little to say on the question of correct method.

His definition of the study's purpose asserts that a work can be called Old Testament theology "if it manages to bring together and to relate those ideas and thoughts which are or can be important" (p. 9). He thus stresses the correct relationship between ideas and concepts. We surmise that the "correct relationship" of which he spoke refers to a kind of logical progression which he followed in treating the major topics of his theology. In the case of the teachings about God, for example, he began with God's existence ("The assumption that God exists is the Old Testament's greatest gift to mankind"; p. 19) and from this central point moved out in an ever-enlarging circle to God's nature, divine activity, and divine self-revelation. Similarly, we are left in the dark about the standard of judgment which is involved in the last part of his definition, "which are or can be important." He informed us that he had found it impossible to derive from the Old Testament itself the framework and the organization of the theological content of the Old Testament since "the Old Testament itself does not offer any scheme for that compilation we call its theology" (p. 9). Cryptic though it be, this statement may, perhaps, help us to understand why he preferred to organize his work as a "synthesis" based on the usual topics of theology, anthropology, and soteriology.

In the same foreword, Köhler expressed his agreement with literary and historical criticism and also accepted the need for comparative study of religion—"without it the Old Testament can be appreciated neither in its uniqueness nor in its dependence" (p. 9). Abraham's God, for example, belonged to the "pre-history" of Israel's religious thought and was of no great consequence for Old Testament theology. Similarly, he pointed out the existence of Persian angelology in Daniel but, because the book lay at the extreme edge of the Old Testament revelation, it could not be used as normative of the mainstream of Old Testament thought. On the whole, however, Köhler's practice was to leave historical considerations, such as development, social influences, and the impact of various historic personalities, out of the picture. Such matters, he thought, could be served better in a separate treatment (*TRu*, 1935, p. 265).

Before leaving Köhler, a word should be said about his complete denigration of the ancient Israelite cult. "Only one chapter, that on the cult, was difficult to place," he tells us (p. 9) and then discusses the topic as a subdivision of anthropology under the heading: "Man's Expedient for His Own Redemption: The Cult" (pp. 181–98).

WILHELM AND HANS MÖLLER

Eichrodt, Sellin, and Köhler had one thing in common. All believed that the task of Old Testament theology consisted in describing the religious ideas found in Israel's sacred writings. They placed their emphasis, in other words, on the conceptual content of the Old Testament. In the last work to appear in Germany before the outbreak of the second World War that empha-sis was shifted, for its intent was to exhibit not a system of thought but the history of the divine economy of salvation. As such, the work of the Möllers represented another example of the viewpoint of *Heilsgeschichte*. Its authors belonged to the extremely conservative wing of German theology and an-swered the question of their theological heritage themselves by claiming thorough agreement with the principles established by von Hofmann (p. 5).

They were quite explicit about the rules which, they thought, Old Tes-tament theology should adopt. In the first place, they demanded "theological understanding" as an essential ingredient of the approach and immediately defined that to mean "pneumatic theology" (p. 5). In the second place, they also wanted it to be understood that Old Testament theology was not a sepa-rate, autonomous discipline but that it formed a part of the wider field of "biblical theology" and must always be studied from a "christocentric view-point." "For practical reasons," they wrote, "and for the sake of a division of labor one might write a separate theology of the Old Testament, but it will receive its meaning only in a christocentric point of view" (p. 3). Their third principle was that of verbal inspiration: "Christocentric viewpoint and verbal inspiration are the two viewpoints which correct theological treatment of the Old Testament must presuppose" (p. 4). All results of higher criticism were, accordingly, to be rejected. Genesis, for example, contained no myths but actual, historical fact and divinely revealed truth. "Every critical word and every doubting interpretation concerning it would be blasphemy, unbelief, and treason to our cause and to all that is sacred" (p. 41). For this reason there was also "no more urgent task than to clear away, once and forever, all the rubbish of Gunkel's notions" (p. 30). Only by an unquestioning accept-ance of the value and the truth of all the biblical declarations could one write a "scientifically satisfying" (*sic*) theology of the Old Testament (p. 16).

Their fourth rule embodied their justification for the *heilsgeschichtliche* form of treatment they adopted in their work. Because the divine revelation had been given in *heilsgeschichtliche* terms, the organization or plan of an Old Testament theology could only be one of historical sequence. It may come as a surprise to discover that they took great pains to record their agree-ment with Gabler on this point and insisted on "a strict carrying out of Gabler's principle" but one may question whether they would have been very happy to accept the spirit which motivated Gabler in the first place to advocate the use of the historical method (p. 6). It is no surprise, however, to find them repudiating Eichrodt and Hempel—who had attempted to cull from Israel's sacred literature an integrated pattern of thought—and acclaiming Vischer's *Christuszeugnis* (pp. 14–16).

The outline they followed was designed to make clear the history of the economy of salvation as it appeared in the Old Testament. It distinguished six different stages, of which four were found in the book of Genesis. Their outline runs as follows:

(1) Gen. 1—2:3: The Foundation for All History and *Heilsgeschichte*
(2) Gen. 2:4—4:26: Oldest History of Mankind; the Fall
(3) Gen. 5:1—11:26: The Condition of Humanity Sinking Stage by Stage
(4) Gen. 11:27—50:26: The Patriarchs
(5) The Covenant at Sinai
(6) The Post-Mosaic Development
   A. The Prophetic Line (Early and Later Prophets)
   B. The Writings
(7) Brief Concluding Reflections from the Standpoint of the New Testament

Fully one-half of their discussion was devoted to the Pentateuch, a characteristic which offers silent commentary on the question of where they placed the emphasis of Old Testament theology. Frequent use of typology to bring out the relations between the two Testaments underscores their kinship with von Hofmann and Hengstenberg. For example, the famine in Egypt during Joseph's time is a type which points ultimately to Jesus who, quoting Hengstenberg (*Christologie*, II, p. 380), is the "true Joseph who brings an end to the hunger and thirst of the People of God by offering the true food and the true drink" (p. 137). Finally, that they meant to take seriously their earlier contention that a christocentric viewpoint was indispensable to their task is indicated by their concluding chapter which considered the place of the Old Testament in the whole economy of salvation culminating in Christ and Christianity.

There is one last remark which needs to be made about this book. In its final pages we are told, in words which were typical of the day when it was written but which also destroy whatever intrinsic merit it might have, that higher criticism must have been the handiwork of Jews. Even Wellhausen, the archetype of this "Ferment der Dekomposition," must have come under Jewish influence. For the present, however, one can only lament that "the Jewish influence, which otherwise has been broken among our people, is still allowed in this field to exert itself with disastrous effects" (pp. 514–17). Certainly, nothing more needs to be said except to register one's disappointment in a study of biblical religion which shows how singularly its authors have failed to capture, even for themselves, the spirit of the Bible at its best.

PAUL HEINISCH

The first example of modern Roman Catholic participation in the production of Old Testament theologies was the work of Heinisch (1878–1956), a Dutch professor at Nijmegen (see Harrington, pp. 77–88). His work appeared in German in 1940, just three years prior to the encyclical *Divino afflante Spiritu* of Pope Pius XII which removed the strictures placed on Catholic biblical scholars and the Modernist Movement by Pope Pius X in

1907. While it is true that M. Hetzenauer had published an Old Testament theology in 1908, his work, especially the second part, was primarily written along the lines of the old *dicta probantia* although it did grant some concessions to *Religionsgeschichte* by providing, in the first part, a history extending from Adam to Christ. Part of Hetzenauer's program was to oppose the critical scholarship of such Catholic liberals as M.-J. Lagrange.

Heinisch's work, primarily a student's handbook, was translated into English in 1950. For him, a theology and a history of religion were to be clearly distinguished. The history of the religion of ancient Israel was understood as radically different from the orthodox religion expounded in Scripture. He concluded that popular folk religion in Israel was unorthodox throughout most of its history and this is frequently noted in the Old Testament: "Nevertheless, it is not numbers which decide the truth and worth of a religion. We must restrict the content of Old Testament religion to the tenets advanced by men divinely illumined, viz., Moses and the prophets, the psalmists, the wisdom teachers and the Old Testament historians" (p. 21). How he differentiated between the history of religion and a theology is expounded in his introduction and is best quoted rather than described in order to preserve the flavor of the author's description.

> A "History of the Religion of Israel" would show how the people responded to the directives of their religious teachers, how environment and cultural progress affected the development of spiritual ideas; it would describe religious conditions, recount the ups and downs in the moral life of the people, note defections from Yahweh, growing immorality, persecutions, and indicate the distinctive character of each successive historical period.
>
> On the other hand a "Theology of the Old Testament" should present in a systematic manner what those leaders who were raised up by God and the writers whom God inspired required as to faith and morals. A theology can present more clearly than a history what is fundamental and accordingly permanent, what is merely transitional, and what preparation New Testament revelation had had in the Old. Old Testament theology points out what religious ideas and moral requirements were defended by enlightened souls, what the masses *should* have accepted, while a "History of the Religion of Israel" shows what the religious and moral conditions among the people actually were.
>
> The relationship between a theology of the Old Testament and a history of Israel's religion may in various respects be compared to the relationship between dogmatic theology and the history of dogmas. Dogmatic theology has as its purpose to propound the Church's teaching, to extract this teaching from the sources; history of dogmas has as its purpose to survey the battle of the Church's doctrine against conflicting opinions, to trace deviations, to indicate clearly the errors which in the course of centuries threatened to obscure the Church's teaching. But just as dogmatic theology cannot disregard the heresies, although it does not treat them *ex professo*, so also a systematic presentation of the theology of the Old Testament must take into consideration the development of doctrine; if a doctrine suffered no modification it may show

this by placing pertinent texts from various historical periods alongside one another (pp. 22–23).

When it came to his exposition of Old Testament theology, Heinisch basically presented his discussion around the central issues of dogmatic theology: God, creation, human acts (morality), life after death, and redemption. At numerous places, the tenets of scholastic theology were read into the Old Testament material, for example, in his discussions of God's immateriality (pp. 64–68), of preparation for the mystery of the most holy trinity (pp. 105–27), and of the privileges of Adam and Eve in paradise (pp. 164–65). At the same time, he acknowledged the gradual development of several ideas, utilized historical perspectives, and was willing to draw upon non-biblical parallels.

OTTO PROCKSCH

Although the Old Testament theology by Procksch (1874–1947) was published posthumously—three years after his death—his work in the field greatly influenced the authors of what are the most influential Old Testament theologies of the twentieth century—those of Eichrodt, who was his student, and von Rad, who aided in the preparation of Procksch's lectures for publication. The book is composed of lectures which Procksch gave several times throughout his career but whose final editing and publication were delayed by the war. He was a man of faith who believed that a faith perspective or existential involvement was necessary for a real depth relationship to and understanding of the biblical material.

Procksch divided his work into two parts. The first—the world of history—was concerned with the history of Israelite religion from patriarchal times until the late postexilic period (pp. 48–419). The second part—the world of thought—presented his systematic account or theology. Three main headings—God and World, God and People, and God and Man—served as organizing principles (pp. 420–713). The similarity to Eichrodt's scheme, with the reversal of the first two parts, is obvious but the priority of the scheme belongs to Procksch (see Eichrodt, I, p. 33 n. 1 and Procksch, p. 421 n. 1). His work is somewhat repetitious since similar material is frequently treated in both halves. The idea of the covenant plays an important role (pp. 512–31) but is not used as an organizing principle of the entire work.

Under "God and World," he discusses revelation, creation, and the cosmic structure; under "God and People" are treated the choice of Israel, the cult, the moral order, and the messianic hope; and under "God and Man," appear the topics of faith, atonement, and communion with God. For him the movement is from the more general and universal to the more particular, and from creation to the historical and the individual.

Procksch was especially interested in history and its relationship to revelation (see pp. 1–19), a topic with a long past and one we will encounter in more detail later. As we noted earlier, Procksch was one of the earlier proponents of pneumatic or spiritual exegesis and there is a strong Christian and christological emphasis to his work. The volume opens with the statements: "All theology is Christology. Jesus Christ is the only figure in our world of experience in which the revelation of God is complete." With such a view, it is surprising how little overt christianizing one finds in the substance of his work and exegesis.

MILLAR BURROWS

Finally, we turn our brief survey to focus on three discussions of Old Testament theology that were products of American biblical scholarship. The first to appear was *An Outline of Biblical Theology* by Burrows (1889–1980) whose occupancy of a chair of "Biblical Theology" at the Divinity School of Yale University represented in itself a landmark in the history of the discipline's progress in this country.

It is of first importance to keep in mind that this work was a "biblical" theology and that, consequently, its scope, its viewpoint, and its purpose were not precisely those of Old Testament theology. They come, rather, from the New Testament and from Christian theology, so that, in the nature of things, the Old Testament becomes to a large degree a record furnishing the antecedents to the teachings of Christianity.

Burrows's description of the purpose of biblical theology called for a concern with "the essential nature and basic features, the real fundamentals of biblical religion" (p. 3). In addition to this first purpose, which would seem to be primarily descriptive, he had also another, in this case, a normative one. For biblical theology also "asks what was God's judgment on that (i.e., the Hebrew and early Christian) religion, and what significance it has for us" (p. 4). It is at this point worth noting, however, that in his work the second purpose is decidedly overshadowed by the first for only in the first and the last chapters, which respectively deal with the questions of "Authority and Revelation" and the "Nature of Biblical Religion," does one find this normative aspect discussed to any appreciable degree.

Burrows was careful to point out that his interpretation of biblical theology does not contain a demand for a complete, logically articulated system of doctrine derived from the Bible. This is because there is in the Bible no theology in the sense of a systematic elaboration of doctrine but, rather, a living historical movement of religion with a "majestic, dramatic sweep of the divine revelation in history" where "the word becomes flesh, with spirit and life." The very form in which biblical religion is presented requires, therefore, a historical point of view. His definition of the historical point of view is worth repeating, not only because it contains in a concise statement the essential elements of historical criticism but also because it shows how integral a part of his method historical perspective was.

> Our point of view in interpreting it [biblical religion] must therefore be historical. This means not only distinguishing earlier from later stages and tracing developments, but also studying the religion at each stage in its cultural setting and in connection with the whole life of the people. Only such study can avoid misunderstanding and false modernization. The historical point of view emancipates us from the errors of the old proof-text method. It shows the organic growth, structure, and relationships of ideas and practices, and so helps to make clear the proportions and relative importance of the various elements of religion (p. 4).

This leads us directly to his conception of the relationship between theology and history of religion. While he nowhere differentiated the two as radically as did Eissfeldt and, on the contrary, believed that history of religion can be most beneficial to theology, he was also convinced that they were not identical. For the biblical theologian who looks at biblical religion from the standpoint of the New Testament, many aspects of biblical religious history have no significance and may be ignored. For example, "large areas of Hebrew religion, such as animal sacrifice or the veneration of sacred places, require relatively little attention, because they ceased to be important for the religion of the New Testament" (p. 5), a point similar to the basis Gabler propounded for distinguishing between the merely historically time-bound and true biblical concepts.

As far as the related problem of unity and diversity in biblical religion is concerned, he made some equally pertinent suggestions. He acknowledged that it might seem more appropriate to speak of the religions than of the religion of the Bible. He also argued, however, that "with all its variations, the Hebrew-Christian tradition runs true to type" and that "there is an underlying unity." This is so partly because "for Christian faith the focus and principle of unity appear in Christ" and partly because there is an intrinsic character common to all biblical religion (pp. 5, 325–28). For him, we always find the one God speaking to his people as the creator and ruler of all. The interpretation of human nature is by and large a constant one. The fact of human sin is maintained throughout, and, correspondingly, the need for a divinely wrought salvation is continuously asserted. There is always the expression of faith and trust in the inexhaustible and eternal goodness of God. Everywhere the claim is made that real faith must overflow into some form of moral living. These are a few of the factors which he considered to be common to the whole Bible and to produce a definitely unified religious outlook.

His actual method of treatment provided for a combination of the topical and historical methods. The framework for his study consists of a series of topics, each divided, in turn, into a number of subsidiary subjects, but the discussion of each topic was for the most part historical in form. The structure of his volume can be seen from the following list of major topics he discussed:

(1)	Authority and Revelation	(10)	Eschatology and the Future Life
(2)	God	(11)	The Way of Salvation
(3)	Christ	(12)	The Christian Life
(4)	The Universe	(13)	Special Offices and Functions
(5)	Man	(14)	Public Worship
(6)	The People of God	(15)	Christian Service
(7)	The Divine Requirement	(16)	Moral and Social Ideals
(8)	Sin	(17)	The Nature of Biblical Religion
(9)	Judgment and Salvation		

Here is how he described the treatment of each topic:

> To prevent a false impression of uniform, unchanging ideas, each topic will here be considered in its chronological development and with reference to the historical background. To prevent distortion of the picture by bringing our own questions to the material and imposing our categories upon it, the outline of topics has been derived, so far as possible, from the Bible itself. To avoid sacrificing proportion by putting all subjects upon the same level of importance, or by stressing those that are most interesting to us, we shall try to observe the scale of proportion and emphasis indicated by the main trend and ultimate outcome of the biblical development (p. 6).

There is a superficial resemblance between his list of topics and those selected by the earlier Protestant dogmatists (see above, pp. 6, 16–17). That, however, is about as far as the similarity goes. For, to use his own words, "instead of starting with a doctrinal system and supporting it with texts adduced as having equal authority and relevance regardless of date, authorship, or original historical connection, we seek here to gather up the results of competent, unprejudiced, inductive study, and to find the real meaning of the Bible, whether or not what we find supports our own theological views or can be accepted by us as true" (pp. 6–7).

In evaluating Burrows's work it is, of course, only fair to recognize and to take into account (1) that it is a discussion of biblical theology, not of Old Testament theology alone, and (2) that it is also peculiarly designed as a student manual to serve the needs of ministerial training. This second purpose explains why it is mainly a catalogue of statements about what the Bible says on the various topics under examination and why it does not seek either to explore points of view in depth or the inner relationships of biblical religious thought. It also explains why so many of the topics have a decidedly modern sound. This modern flavor can be seen in the wording of the following subjects: Religious Education; Evangelism and Missions; Social Action; Sex, Marriage, and the Family; Political Relations; International Relations: the Use of Force; Interracial Relations: the Unity of Mankind. This last characteristic may bring with it "the peril of modernizing" the Bible, but it helps as well to indicate the relevance of the Scripture for certain problems of contemporary religious thinking and practice. With these provisos, the book offers many suggestive illustrations of the manner in which the historical and theological viewpoints may be integrated.

OTTO JUSTICE BAAB

The work of Baab (1896–1958) had the distinction of being the first volume produced by an American during this period which focused specifically on Old Testament theology in the more technical sense. Like Burrows, Baab came to his interest in theological questions from an earlier background of historical criticism and a "liberal" conception of religion. He was fully aware, therefore, of the problems involved in treating the theology of the Old Testament in an age in which the historical viewpoint had come to reign supreme. His *Theology* had been preceded two years earlier by an article in which he had examined the issues connected with the discipline, and it was here that he had already set forth in programmatic form the methodological principles of his larger work.

Starting with the observation that Old Testament theology has in the past usually been discussed either dogmatically or historically and that both ways contain legitimate values as well as serious shortcomings, he attempted to develop a conception of the task facing the theologian which would bring together what might be considered to be the good features of both. As he saw them, the merits and demerits of the two forms of study were as follows. The drawbacks of the dogmatic treatment are "its lack of interest in the historical method," also its opposition to "freedom of inquiry." On the other hand, it rendered a valuable service by insisting on the "continuity of historical revelation" and on the "true insight" that history can have no meaning apart from God. The historical approach was (1) scientific and verifiable and (2) vivid because it provided "social concreteness and vitality." But it was also inclined to dissipate the idea of the religious unity of the Old Testament (1947, pp. 405–10). For him the task was, first, a matter of inductive and objective description for which one must draw on every one of the "scientific techniques peculiar to objective research" (1947, p. 413). There is, however, also a normative side to this task. This is so (1) because theology as a discipline is not only descriptive but normative as well and (2) because the Old Testament itself, through such statements as "Thus saith the Lord" or "The Word of the Lord is like burning fire in my bones," makes demands which are normative. On the normative aspect of theology in general he had this to say: "Yet it cannot be denied that theology—when it is not confused with biblical criticism—is the systematic formulation of religious ideas held to be true representations of ultimate reality as that reality affects the life and destiny of men. Theology always claims to be unique, exclusive, and final in its pronouncements" (1947, p. 411).

Few would quarrel with Baab's emphasis on the descriptive function of Old Testament theology. For that has been, more or less, a universally recognized function of the study since the days when Gabler sought to free it from its bondage to dogmatics. The problem of whether it should also include a normative interest was and still is, however, sufficiently debated to warrant a closer look at the use he makes of it.

Generally speaking, this normative function involves the demonstration that "Old Testament theology has relevance for an understanding of religious realities which are inherent in the structure of the universe," lest "the religion of tomorrow be severed completely from the biblical revelation which gave it birth" (1947, p. 418). To do so means, first, that the theologian, "by a thorough absorption in the spirit and viewpoint of the biblical records themselves," must make the presuppositions of biblical religion one's own. One should not, instead, look at that religion in terms of presuppositions originally derived from some form of contemporary philosophy, as has been the case with the "objective" study of Hebrew religion (1947, p. 412). Second, it means also that one should take seriously the claim to validity asserted in the Old Testament itself, for that, too, is a "substantial datum with which he is compelled to reckon" and which one should not try to "explain away" (1947, pp. 413–14).

In determining the normative value of the theology of the Old Testament, three specific tests must be used according to Baab. (1) There is the criterion of *logical consistency* according to which we may judge whether "the elements within any one religious concept and the several concepts in their relation to one another are made to fit together as parts of a whole" (1947, pp. 414–15). The chief issue here would seem to be whether one can speak of a single unified theology, for such unity is of prime importance if Old Testament theology is to have any normative value. (2) Another is that of *empirical verification*. This means that the theologian should test whether "the basic concepts of Old Testament religion correspond with experience so meaningfully that their truth may be validated thereby" (1947, p. 415). At this point Baab had in mind, for example, the correspondence between Hebrew faith and the empirical facts of the nation's historical experience and of the individual's own experience as an individual person. (3) Related to the test of empirical verification in terms of Israel's own experiences is a third test, namely, that of *conformity with discoveries of the scientists*, in order to show whether biblical views agree with what is today scientifically known about humanity and the social order (1947, p. 418).

Despite the importance he attached to the normative character of Old Testament theology in his discussions of method, it is also true that this aspect of his thinking constituted only a singularly small part of his actual *Theology*, and, furthermore, that it is present in any appreciable degree only in the second half of his concluding chapter. The bulk of his study is descriptive and is concerned with setting forth, under certain subsidiary headings, what the Old Testament says about God, Man, Sin, Salvation, the Kingdom of God, Death and the Hereafter, and the Problem of Evil. His discussion, on the whole, proceeds along systematic lines and does not follow, as did Burrows's study, precise chronological sequence, but historical considerations are not lacking. Again and again he mentions primitive antecedents, points out the relation between social factors and the faith of the Hebrews, and calls attention to the religions of the cultural areas within which the Hebrews lived.

In conclusion, one should add three other elements which figured in Baab's methodological principles. (1) He was convinced that the religion of the Old Testament is substantially a single entity. The trouble in the past, for him, has been with the critics who have overemphasized differences "to the point of distortion."

> As soon as the critic abandons his insistence upon the progressive development of the religion of the Old Testament through gradual stages, each of which is higher than that which preceded it, and permits the text to speak for itself, he may be in a position to discern a logically self-consistent ethical monotheism in much of the Old Testament (1947, pp. 415–16).

(2) The central and all-controlling concept of the Old Testament is the idea of God. It is the experience of the living and personal God which runs through this literature as its all-dominating theme. This should, therefore, be the starting point of any theology of the Old Testament. It also becomes "the clue to knowledge" to which all other concepts of Hebrew religion must be related (1949, p. 22). (3) His final principle comes in the form of a word of caution. One should not look for a "complete theology," for it cannot be found in the Old Testament. That "literature deals with other matters, although it is full of theological material." The theologian must abstract the theological material from its concrete, history-bound context and organize it according to logical principles derived from the investigator's own scientific training.

> This dynamic, activistic religion of Israel does not easily yield to this treatment. In view of this problem, one can only try to preserve the vital, organic quality of the biblical ideas by constantly viewing them in their historical setting and by seeking to describe them from the point of view of the men

who held them, with the hope of permitting the Old Testament itself to state its faith to the modern reader (1949, p. 22).

ROBERT CLAUDE DENTAN

Originally presented as a Ph.D. dissertation to the graduate faculty of Yale University, Dentan's *Preface to Old Testament Theology* shows many points of contact with the *Biblical Theology in Outline* by Millar Burrows under whose direction Dentan prepared his study. Some of his major objectives, he says in his foreword, included, along with the natural concern "to define Old Testament theology," a desire to take into account "the requirements of the theological curriculum" and "to define the more general term 'biblical theology'" (p. 9).

His book opens with a survey of the history of the discipline from the period of Protestant Scholasticism onward and, in its second half, attempts the formulation of proper methodological principles. Obviously it is in this second half that he advances his own perspectives as well as in his much later work: *The Design of the Scriptures: A First Reader in Biblical Theology* (New York: McGraw-Hill, 1965). Dentan's starting point is with "biblical theology" for it constitutes in his opinion the larger context within which Old Testament theology takes its subordinate place. Biblical theology is to be regarded—this likewise has been the common understanding of the matter since the days of Gabler—as "primarily a *historical discipline* . . . and it follows, incidentally, that its method must primarily be that of other historical sciences, viz., empirical and inductive" (p. 88). In essence, it is "*the study of the religious ideas of the Bible in their historic context*" (p. 90). This minimum definition, since it places its major emphasis on the historical character of biblical theology, immediately raises the question of the difference between it and the history of biblical religion. The answer to that question Dentan found in Eichrodt's differentiation which describes the essential distinction in terms of the difference between a "long-cut" and a "cross-cut," the one treating the religion in chronological sequence, and the other setting forth its persistent and distinctive principles in some kind of logical or systematic order. This, in fact, is the only legitimate distinction, even though it has sometimes been suggested that there is also another basic difference according to which a *History* is "coldly objective and 'scientific' in its handling of the material" while a *Theology*, on the other hand, "deals with the material as *Revelation* and seeks to determine its relevance to Christian theology and to the contemporary scene" (p. 46). This second form of differentiation is not entirely without justification when seen especially against the background of the excesses of the *religiongeschichtliche Schule*, but it does not belong to the essential differentiae. There is, fundamentally, no reason why a *History* should not deal, as König's, Kittel's, and Sellin's books have dealt, "with the

Old Testament as Revelation and be concerned with the theological significance of its subject-matter" (p. 93).

Because Old Testament theology is located within this framework which is provided by biblical theology, it is to be regarded as "*a Christian-theological discipline* and, as such, does not deal with the Old Testament in isolation, but always has some concern for its relation to the New." It is important to remember that "while in theory it might have originated in Judaism or amongst scholars with no religious convictions, it did in fact originate in the Christian theological curriculum" (p. 94). Dentan reinforces his point about the intimate relationship which he believes should exist between Old Testament theology and the New Testament—in effect making that relationship one of the chief cornerstones of his position—by establishing the proposition according to which Old Testament theology should not only deal with the structural unity of Old Testament religion but also give "due regard to the historical and ideological relationship of that religion to the religion of the New Testament" (p. 95). The discipline is to be regarded, therefore, in a special sense as "a preparatory exercise for the study of the New Testament," not because there happens to be an external, historical connection between the two parts of the Bible, but rather because "for Christian faith the connection . . . is integral and organic so that the two together form an indissoluble unity, the one being the necessary completion and fulfillment of the other" (pp. 98–99).

As a "Christian-theological discipline" Old Testament theology also stands in close relationship to the other broad fields into which the total organism of theological study is divided. For Dentan, it constitutes the point of departure for *historical theology* and can be regarded as the "first long section" of the first chapter (i.e., the chapter which treats biblical theology) in the history of dogma, with the proviso, however, that "since biblical theology deals with the period which is normative for faith, there is also a qualitative difference between it and the later chapters" (pp. 101–2). *Systematic theology* also has a vital stake in biblical and Old Testament theology, even though they are no longer related to one another as mistress to servant and have been properly treated as different areas of theological expression since the days of Gabler. From these biblical disciplines systematic theology receives its basic materials without which it would cease to be "in any distinctive sense *Christian* theology" (p. 102). Furthermore, it derives from them a norm by which its own theological formulation may be judged and with the help of which "its own false or eccentric emphases may be corrected" (p. 103). The third theological field for which biblical disciplines bear a responsibility is the area commonly described as *practical theology*. In the first place, they can be of great benefit to the minister in the preparation of sermons by providing a synoptic understanding of the whole biblical religion. A second value which may be gained from the study of the theology of the Bible is that it should serve as "an instrument for the cultivation of personal piety, especially amongst the clergy" (p. 104).

Another of the fundamental problems of Old Testament theology is that of its *scope*. This suggestion involves, for example, the use of non-canonical materials, a matter on which there has been considerable disagreement in the history of the discipline. Dentan's position here is one which favors the strict observance of the limits provided by the canon and "the exclusion of any *comprehensive* attempt to deal with the intertestamental literature" (p. 105). A far more complex question is that concerning the extent to which one should attempt to deal with *all* the Old Testament material. The general rule which one should follow at this point, he believes, is that "Old Testament theology should deal only with distinctive and characteristic religious ideas of the Old Testament" (p. 106). What this rule means in greater detail is made clear in the following propositions:

> (1) It [Old Testament theology] should exclude mere archaeological information.
> (2) Its primary concern should be with ideas, not with history or institutions.
> (3) Its concern should be the normative religion of the Old Testament. [Dentan elaborates on this crucial point by describing it as the effort "to discover what were the essential elements in the religious world view which was actually current in Israel during her great creative period." Merely popular religion and superstitions should be used only when they "illuminate the basic inner core of Israel's faith." Two criteria help to determine this normative religion: (1) persistence or pervasiveness and (2) distinctiveness; pp. 108–9.]
> (4) It should include all the major tendencies of normative Hebrew religion.
> (5) It should include a general discussion of ethical principles.
> (6) It should include a discussion of the nature of Hebrew piety (or religious psychology) (pp. 106–12).

Against this background of the nature and scope which belong to Old Testament theology Dentan finally draws the basic outlines of the method itself. By his own admission his interest is confined to two matters, exegesis and organization. On the first point, the question of the *method of interpretation*, he speaks out resolutely against all types of special "theological" interpretation, whether they be in the form of allegory, typology, or pneumatic exegesis, and instead states with great insistence that the grammatical-historical method must continue to be regarded as the only legitimate and proper one.

> The *primary* function of the Old Testament theologian is not to answer the question, "What does the Old Testament mean to me or to my sect?" but, "What did the religious concepts found in the Old Testament mean to the men of Old Testament times?" (p. 114).

It is, however, essential that one not confuse such a historical and critical approach with the cold, external, disinterested, and impersonal attitude which was fostered, for example, by historicism. For in addition to the requirement for objective, i.e., honest and unbiased, interpretation, there is also placed upon the Old Testament theologian a demand for sympathy, insight, and a sense of personal participation—what Gunkel noted as empathy—a requirement which, for that matter, is made of all good historiography if it is to be more than mere chronography and if it is to accomplish "the imaginative recreation of the stream of history with all its richness of human life and feeling" (p. 115). This admittedly subjective but necessary element of sympathy and insight can be furthered, in the case of Old Testament theology, by faith since "it is difficult to see how one could write sympathetically of the theology of the Old Testament who did not in some way share the Old Testament faith" (p. 116). Dentan is properly careful to make clear, however, that in speaking of the Old Testament theologian as a person of faith he does not regard that faith as "a miraculous new organ for the attainment of knowledge," but simply as an endowment which puts such a person "*within* the stream of which the Old Testament is a part" (p. 117).

The other question raised by the problem of the nature of the method, according to Dentan, relates to the *form of organization* which is best adapted to the needs of Old Testament theology. This vexing question has led to many attempted solutions and we will examine this issue a bit further in the next section. For Dentan, the center of the religion is located in its doctrine of God, for it is this doctrine "which gives to the Old Testament that structural and organic unity which it is the task of Old Testament theology to describe and discuss" (p. 118). While the centrality of the Idea of God, for Dentan, justifies one in speaking of a *theo*–logy, one should not expect to find "a closely articulated system of doctrine," but only "a complex of religious ideas which center in certain basic ideas about God" (pp. 118–19).

> Consequently, we are forced to seek for some method of organization which (1) will be simple, and (2) will present the material in a form meaningful to *us*. For this purpose it seems difficult to think of a better outline than that which is used by systematic theology, since this outline arose from an attempt to answer the basic questions concerning human life: What is the nature of God in his perfection? (theology); what is the nature of man in his weakness? (anthropology); what is the nature of that dynamic process by which man's weakness becomes reconciled with God's perfection? (soteriology) (pp. 119–20).

METHODS AND APPROACHES

David Stow **Adam**, "Theology," *ERE* 12(1922)293–300; James **Barr**, "The Problem of Old Testament Theology and the History of Religion," *CJT* 3(1957)141–49; Friedrich **Baumgärtel**, "Erwägungen zur Darstellung der Theologie des Alten Testaments," *TLZ* 76(1951)257–72; Hendrikus **Boers**, *What Is New Testament Theology?* (Philadelphia: Fortress Press, 1979); William A. **Irwin**, "The Reviving Theology of the Old Testament," *JR* 25(1945)235–46; *idem*, "The Interpretation of the Old Testament," *ZAW* 62(1949/50)1–14; *idem*, "Trends in Old Testament Theology," *JBR*

19(1951)186–88; Johannes **Lindblom**, "Zur Frage der Eigenart des alttestamentlichen Religion," *BZAW* 66(1936)128–37; James **Muilenberg**, "The Faith of Ancient
Israel," *The Vitality of the Christian Tradition* (ed. by George F. Thomas; New York:
Harper Brothers, 1944)1–35; M. E. **Polley**, "H. Wheeler Robinson and the Problem
of Organizing an Old Testament Theology," *The Use of the Old Testament in the New
and Other Essays* (ed. by James M. Efird; Durham: Duke University Press, 1972)149–
69; H. Wheeler **Robinson**, "The Place of the Old Testament in Christian Education,"
RelEd 2(1935)63–77; Krister **Stendahl**, "Biblical Theology, Contemporary," *IDB*
1(1962)418–32.

In our survey of interest in and works on Old Testament theology, and
to a lesser extent Old Testament religion, during the first half of the twentieth
century, the diversity of approaches and disparities of opinions on both the
method and content of such studies seem to be the characteristic traits. What
constitutes such a genre of scholarship, what its purpose is, whether it should
be merely descriptive or move toward the prescriptive and normative, how
one organizes a presentation to provide the most synthetic and comprehensive coverage of the totality of Israelite faith or belief, how one balances
historical and systematic concerns, have all been recurring issues.

The overall diversity in the field, or one could say the lack of uniformity, both in form and viewpoint can be illustrated by noting some of the
various points of concentration or centers of focus which provided the leitmotifs and organizing schemes for the various presentations. In these works
one finds *Heilsgeschichtler* who described the history of the "divine economy of salvation," and one finds those who considered their task to consist
in presenting the ideas of Israel's religion in some systematic form or in
tracing the course of monotheism. Some wanted a theology which was either
exclusively normative or confessional (Eissfeldt) or partially so (Sellin, Burrows, and Baab), while others stressed the descriptive function of Old Testament theology (Eichrodt, Köhler). A number demanded a New Testament
point of view (Eissfeldt, Sellin, Burrows, König, Procksch, and the two
Möllers), or were strongly influenced by Christian dogmatics (Heinisch); others,
again, ignored such perspectives (Köhler, Baab) or confined themselves to
pointing out the connections between Old and New Testament ideas after
having determined, in the first place, what the Old Testament has to say about
these ideas (Eichrodt). Finally, there were those who attempted to integrate
Israel's faith around a central concept (Eichrodt's idea of the covenant) or at
least used such a central concept as the focal point to which all other ideas
must be related (Baab's and Dentan's idea of God), and there were those who
denied the possibility of a logically cohesive system of thought (Eissfeldt,
Köhler, and Burrows).

Many issues were thus completely unsettled or were matters of great
debate. A similar situation in the 1970s would be taken as an obvious signal

that biblical or Old Testament theology was in a state of extreme crisis if not suffering from a sickness unto death. Diversity and lack of uniformity, however, may be indicative of vim and vitality if there is movement and life and not merely the reflex and traumatic jerkings of a dying organism. Frequently, the diversity and differences are at the surface rather than at a deeper level or else they indicate the genuine embodiment of authentic differences of opinion and methodologically distinct but nonetheless valid approaches.

The lack of uniformity on many matters in the works published between 1920 and 1950 should not blind us to the fact that there existed a widely held consensus on many fundamental matters. Particularly, all of the authors offered testimony of one kind or another to the difficulties they had experienced in systematizing the thought of the Old Testament, but practically all were confident that such systematization was a necessity and a possibility. The chief obstacle encountered seems to have been in every case the problem of determining some means for discovering or providing unity to the biblical material and thought, and it is not at all surprising, therefore, to discover that practically all of them paid considerable attention to this issue. The answer, in most instances, admitted the presence of diversity but also insisted that one should not abandon trying to find in Israel's religion a common outlook and that the historical method of presentation had magnified differences out of proportion. Only two in the group proposed solutions which would have to be considered extremely radical and have involved a limitation of the material to be included in the province of Old Testament theology. Sellin suggested the elimination of everything which had not been accepted by Jesus and the apostles as the "presupposition" of their thinking, while Eissfeldt went even farther and proposed to restrict the area of discussion to those elements which could be related to the standpoint of the theologian's own confessional or sectarian point of view.

One of the most prominent and common characteristics of their treatment of the theology of the Old Testament was the marked preference for a form of presentation which was almost entirely systematic and which gave little attention to changes in, and the evolution of, Hebrew religion except where this was done in a separate division of a work. In this matter it is, therefore, possible to detect a significant difference between them and the majority of their nineteenth-century counterparts, including the conservative ones. Whether this disposition is to be explained as a reaction against the history of religion type of study or because of an aversion to anything which might detract from the unity of Old Testament thought, the fact remains that most of these theologies made little room for a historical arrangement of the material. The only exceptions to this rule were Burrows, Fosdick, and the Möllers whose methods of organization provided for a combination, of one kind or another, of system and history and Kaufmann's work which was really a history of the religion. Historical criticism and history of religion were granted, to be sure, an important place among the investigations a theologian must undertake before passing over to theological formulation, and it is also true that no one followed Eissfeldt in denying all connection between theology and history of religion. Nevertheless, it is difficult not to gain the impression, as one reads the majority of these discussions, that the religion of the Old Testament was practically uniform from its beginning on.

While there had been, in other words, a marked tendency to modify Gabler's emphasis on the historical principle in this one important respect, his other principle, the need for systematization to produce a true biblical theology, enjoyed greater favor. By and large, the Old Testament theologians of this period appear to have tried sincerely and seriously to set forth the faith of the Old Testament as it is in itself and to avoid, as much as possible, the mistake of reading their own religious views into the religion of Israel. Their own theological beliefs do shine through, of course, but that is quite different from permitting a foreign system of thought to determine what the content of Old Testament theology should be, as was the case in earlier Protestant Orthodoxy. The most conspicuous violation of this principle was Eissfeldt's demand for a confessional orientation, and Sellin was perhaps not very far behind him. They do not, however, speak for the majority.

This concern for honest and unbiased description is in line with another striking feature of the theologies. Despite the inclination, which existed in some Christian circles, to substitute so-called theological, pneumatic, allegorical, or mystical types of exegesis for the grammatical-historical method of interpretation, these theologies remained almost completely free from the urge to find in the Bible meanings which were different from the actual sense of the words. Baab's insistence on letting the Old Testament "speak for itself" is typical of the general attitude, even König's. Only the Möllers went other ways in order to make use of pneumatic interpretation and typology.

In spite of the rather widespread discussion of revelation in general theology, the topic was of very little prominence in most of the Old Testament theologies during this first wave of the twentieth century (although see Procksch, pp. 421–54 and Burrows, pp. 8–53). The word "Revelation" and the parallel term "Word of God" do have a place, it is true, in their vocabulary, but that is as far as they go. In this they differ considerably from many of the nineteenth-century theologians who, one recalls, gave the matter of a normative statement of the doctrine of Revelation substantial attention. One Old Testament scholar in England, H. Wheeler Robinson, whom we have quoted extensively on this issue earlier (see pp. 148–49), was very concerned about this topic. His posthumously published prolegomena to an Old Testament theology, *Inspiration and Revelation in the Old Testament* (Oxford: Clarendon Press, 1946), treats in a preliminary fashion the following main topics: God and Nature, God and Man, God and History, The Inspiration of the Prophet, Revelation through the Priest, and Revelation in "Wisdom." Such a scheme reminds one of Procksch or Eichrodt but shows a far greater emphasis on inspiration and revelation than any of the studies noted in this chapter (see Polley).

Thus in spite of the great differences among the individual treatments, there were also many general commitments held in common. It should be recalled that the one period in biblical theology when there was widespread agreement and general uniformity in assumptions, methods, and manner of presentation was the period of Protestant Scholasticism as we have noted. Biblical theologians at that time took seriously the Reformation adage that the Bible was both *fons* and *judex*, source and norm, for theology (Diestel, pp. 233–34) and then proceeded to turn the book into a homogeneous apologetic source of divinely given proof-texts. The early critical Rationalists and the Pietists tried to shatter this consensus in their search for a biblical theology that could be used not as an apologetic support of but as a potent weapon against dogmatic orthodoxy. The nineteenth century, however, bequeathed to the twentieth century a Bible with contours that the mainline religious establishments of the eighteenth century could hardly have imagined. The Old Testament was seen as the product of over a millennium of human history rather than a divinely revealed compendium or holy thesaurus. Instead of a unified content and perspective with direct reference to transcendental reality, the Old Testament was seen as comprised of many documents without "temporal, formal, and factual unity" (Duhm, *Theologie der Propheten*, pp. 27–28). Instead of being viewed as a book with a structure and content identical to the best of dogmatic systems, the Old Testament was seen as a book more religious than theological, or at least as a book without a theological center and offering little or no clue to the means for its own systematization.

If this be the case, then what were those who wrote Old Testament theologies in the first half of the present century really doing? First of all, most of the Old Testament theologies which we have examined so far are primarily composed of systematic exegesis. Barr has described the basic activity of such works in the following terms:

> Of those works which have appeared under the title of "Theology of the Old Testament" and which have approved themselves to Old Testament scholars as responsible work, the criticism might be made that they are in fact, and perhaps in spite of their title, systematic exegesis. Instead of the familiar consecutive exegesis chapter by chapter as presented in commentaries, the "Theologies" present a systematic exegesis, collecting the material under various themes, displaying under each theme the disparities and similarities of opinion in various passages, seeking to assess them as a whole, and relating the themes one to another. This criticism would seem to have a considerable amount of foundation. It is not in itself a criticism against the books involved, but rather

a clarification of what they are really doing, and therefore of what is in this case involved in the title "Theology." If this is true, the "Theologies" do not form a radical break with the historical-critical discipline; they represent rather a different principle of organization. Within the synthetic organization of the "Theologies" there remains ample room for recognition of and attention to the separateness of sources and periods as discussed by historical-critical study, including the critical history of religion. The synthetic work accepts without any reservation the priority to itself of philological, literary and historical research. The synthetic principle of organization will be derived from the nature of the subject-matter, i.e. the totality of Israelite religious thought (p. 141).

A second activity involved, in fact an activity prior to the systematic exegesis, is the determination of some scheme or arrangement for presenting the exegesis. Unless one merely engages in a pure commentary form of exegesis, then the organizing scheme has to be imposed on the material from the outside. Some of these schemes, certainly, seem to allow a greater ease than others for the integration of multiple and diverse biblical materials and the diverse religious traditions of the Old Testament. The function of the scheme is, of course, to make as complete and comprehensible a coverage as possible but above all to offer a synthesis of the material. Such syntheses may be attempted either in logical terms, as was the case with the old proof-text method which followed the loci or topics of dogmatic theology or some scheme set up according to certain cardinal subjects (theology, anthropology, soteriology, etc.), or according to some assumed underlying principle or center from which the interpreter could work outward to the more peripheral. Or the synthesis could be historical as were the histories of Israelite religion.

While it might appear that some forms of the logical synthesis were more difficult to arrive at and follow than their historical counterparts, it should be noted that even historical approaches require some prior decisive choices. Where did one begin a history of Israel's religion? With the opening chapters of Genesis? With the patriarchs? With Moses? With the monarchy? All of these options—like their logical synthetic counterparts—presented the interpreter with the need to weigh evidence for and against various possibilities and then to sustain a description of the religion in such a form as to show how the various periods of history and the developments in the religion were integrally related. One might say that the logical synthesis—the theological form—regardless of the organizing principles used sought to produce a vertically conceived and constructed system or paradigm. The historical synthesis—whether a theology or a history of religion—sought to produce a horizontally conceived and constructed paradigm. Once the form of the synthesis was arrived at, the exposition of the material was basically similar—the systematic exegesis of texts brought together in conformity with the structural scheme.

Within each of the syntheses, there remained the possibility of integrating diverse perspectives—in addition to the overall scheme—which were not the direct consequence of systematic exegesis. In the logical synthesis, for example, the way one viewed the interrelationships of the schematic parts, the choice of texts, deductions from the texts and so forth meant that more was involved than merely exegesis. Similar considerations were factors in the historical synthesis but, especially in the *heilsgeschichtliche* approach, a further component becomes of major significance, namely, the course of the history itself as a history of redemption pointing beyond itself. In such historical schemes, the interpreter's philosophy of history becomes exceedingly important since it provides the interpretative clue for much of the exegesis and the interpretative glue holding the scheme together. In his great Old Testament theology written in a *heilsgeschichtliche* mold Oehler had already pointed out that "the theology of the Old Testament cannot limit itself to the directly didactic matter in the Old Testament. It must embrace the essential factors of the history of the divine kingdom in the Old Testament" (p. 6): that is, it must go beyond the text in the search for meaning or at least see the narrative aspect of the Bible as equal to or more important than the didactic aspect.

One final issue needs to be noted about these Old Testament theologies. This concerns their general avoidance of normative or evaluative statements about the texts and their referents in favor of a purely descriptive stance. This raises the question as to whether these works are really "theologies." By its very nature theology is concerned with truth, truth claims, and the evaluative aspects of thought. If we return to Gabler's original proposal, he argued that there should be two types of biblical theology—true and pure. These two forms of biblical theology which we have noted before but which deserve reemphasis have been succinctly described by Boers as follows:

> The second [the production of a true biblical theology] phase was to identify all the general concepts and to order them, giving close attention to differences due to the particular historical, geographic, and religious settings to which they belonged. The object was to produce a comprehensive system of biblical theology. As a model for such a system, Gabler commended the system of Stoic thought which had been produced by a certain Tiedemann. What Gabler had in mind was not a mere historical *re*presentation of the biblical religion but a systematic *presentation* of it in such a way that one could understand what it had been all about as an historical phenomenon. It should be noted that this was not yet a theology but a systematic historical presentation of the biblical religion. . . .
>
> Biblical theology in the narrower sense, that is, pure biblical theology, had the task of presenting the unchanging biblical teaching which was valid for all times, purified of those concepts that were limited to particular circumstances. It had to proceed by first identifying the latter concepts and then eliminating them from further consideration. The procedure was obviously not to try to collect the unchanging concepts from the comprehensive system imme-

diately but, by a process of elimination, that is, of the contingent concepts, to let them emerge as the purified concepts that remained. He probably assumed that this would have been a more reliable procedure. The purified system of these unchanging, divine concepts would then have formed a firm foundation on which the philosophical reflection in dogmatic theology could take place.

If the comprehensive theological task was performed in this way, Gabler was confident, it would be possible to distinguish between the areas of divine and of human wisdom in dogmatic theology, between the unchanging biblical concepts provided by biblical theology and the human philosophizing on the basis of them. In that way the objective of a biblically based dogmatic theology would have been achieved (pp. 34–35).

This twofold aspect—true and pure, descriptive and evaluative—has been widely recognized in religious studies. For example, writing in 1922, D. S. Adam described matters in the following way:

> Religion as an object of investigation has two aspects: (a) a historical aspect, under which it is to be regarded as a historical phenomenon appearing under various forms among various peoples with characteristics which furnish ample material for historical inquiry and investigation; and (b) a normative aspect, under which it appears as a present inner power of life making claim to truth and to the right to regulate individual and social life (p. 296).

According to Adam, biblical theology belongs in the first category since it

> is a purely historic discipline, aiming at the accurate presentation of historic fact and recorded thought in an impartial and objective way, without meantime taking into account the bearing of that on permanent normative religious truth. The methods to be used in Biblical theology are those of sound philology and impartial scientific exegesis or interpretation, so as to make sure that the ideas or doctrines set forth are those of the various Bible writers themselves, unmodified by any subjective theological bias of the interpreter. The work of adjusting the scheme of thought faithfully gathered from the Scriptures by sound impartial exegesis to a comprehensive scheme of normative systematic theology is the important task of the Christian systematic theologian (p. 297).

The acceptance of this descriptive role is characteristic of practically all the Old Testament theologies produced in the first half of this century. That is, they set out more to describe "what it meant" rather than "what it means" (see Stendahl, pp. 418–19), attempting as a rule to be scientifically neutral rather than admonitory or advocatory. The majority of those who undertook to state the proper methodological principles of this discipline limited its function to description. The only voice which was raised on behalf of an abandonment of description in favor of evaluation was that of Eissfeldt, whereas Burrows and Baab adopted the more intermediate position which called for a co-joining of the two but which actually gave far more attention to the task of describing the religious ideas and views contained in the Old Testament-than to that of evaluating them. All of this could, of course, be understood to mean that even the so-called "theologies" were in reality not theologies but actually systematic descriptions of Israelite religion following something resembling a theological scheme.

It could, of course, be argued that an Old Testament or biblical theology should be evaluative or should assume a normative stance. (As we shall see in the next section, there were definite movements in that direction already underway but these did not make much direct impact on the discussion until the late 1940s and the 1950s.) Several arguments could be made and were already hinted at in support of an evaluative function in this area. In the first place, one might argue that if a work is going to be a theological inquiry then it should have, in addition to its concern for the phenomenological or purely descriptive aspects of religion, also a definite and legitimate interest in the problem of ultimate truth and value. Accordingly, it was contended that what is legitimate for theology in general ought to be valid for Old Testament theology as well and that, therefore, to use Baab's words, "a consideration of the question of validity is a legitimate task for the Old Testament theologian" (p. 19). The second reason may be traced back to the wholly laudable desire to demonstrate the relevance of the Old Testament. "Biblical theology," Burrows asserted, "asks what was God's judgment on the ancient Hebrew and early Christian religion, and what significance it has for us" (p. 4). Finally, there is the matter of the Old Testament's own claims to validity which, as Baab believed, ought to be "given the same weight as that attached to matters of text and historical event" (p. 20).

One of the major questions about biblical theology, and a ground for opposition to the development which was raised during this period, was the fear that biblical theology would attempt to take on a normative role (see Irwin, 1945, p. 246; Lindblom; and Barr, pp. 143–45). At any rate, some evaluative and normative decisions seem inevitable in such study: some texts and concepts have to be isolated as more significant than others; that is, there has to be some selection of material, and most theological and even historical study has been pursued under the assumption that the material being treated had some relevance to the contemporary situation and the life of the church and synagogue.

THE SO-CALLED BIBLICAL THEOLOGY MOVEMENT

D. L. **Baker**, *Two Testaments, One Bible: A Study of Some Modern Solutions to the Theological Problem of the Relationship between the Old and New Testaments* (Leicester/Downers Grove: InterVarsity Press, 1976); James **Barr**, *The Semantics of Biblical Language* (London: Oxford University Press, 1961); *idem, The Bible in the Modern World* (London/New York: SCM Press/Harper & Row, 1973); *idem*, "Biblical Theology," *IDBSup*, pp. 104–11; *idem*, "Revelation in History," *IDBSup*, pp. 746–49; Brevard S. **Childs**, *Biblical Theology in Crisis* (Philadelphia: Westminster

210 The Rebirth of Old Testament Theology

Press, 1970); William G. **Dever**, "Biblical Theology and Biblical Archaeology: An Appreciation of G. Ernest Wright," *HTR* 73(1980)1–16; H. and H. A. **Frankfort** (eds.), *The Intellectual Adventure of Ancient Man* (Chicago: University of Chicago Press, 1946) = *Before Philosophy* (Harmondsworth: Penguin Books, 1949); Connolly **Gamble**, Jr., "The Literature of Biblical Theology: A Bibliographical Study," *Int* 7(1953)466–80; R. Lansing **Hicks**, "Present-day Trends in Biblical Theology," *ATR* 32(1950)136–53; A. R. **Johnson**, *The One and the Many in the Israelite Conception of God* (Cardiff: University of Wales Press, 1942); *idem, The Vitality of the Individual in the Thought of Ancient Israel* (Cardiff: University of Wales Press, 1949); David H. **Kelsey**, *The Uses of Scripture in Recent Theology* (Philadelphia/London: Fortress Press/SCM Press, 1975); James **Muilenberg**, "Return to Old Testament Theology," *Christianity and the Contemporary Scene* (ed. by R. C. Crump and H. H. Squires: New York; Morehouse-Gorham, 1943)30–44; Johannes **Pedersen**, *Israel: Its Life and Culture, I–IV* (London: Oxford University Press, 1926–1940); Alan **Richardson** and W. **Schweitzer** (eds.), *Biblical Authority for Today: A World Council of Churches Symposium on 'The Biblical Authority for the Churches' Social and Political Message Today* (London/Philadelphia: SCM Press/Westminster Press, 1951); J. W. **Rogerson**, *Anthropology and the Old Testament* (Oxford/Atlanta: Basil Blackwell/John Knox Press, 1978/1979); H. H. **Rowley**, *The Relevance of the Bible* (London/New York: J. Clarke & Co./Macmillan Company, 1942–1944); James D. **Smart**, *The Past, Present, and Future of Biblical Theology* (Philadelphia: Westminster Press, 1979); Study Department of the World Council of Churches (ed.), *From the Bible to the Modern World* (Geneva: World Council of Churches, 1947); *idem,* "Guiding Principles for the Interpretation of the Bible," *ER* 2(1949)81–86; *idem, The Bible and the Church's Message to the World* (Geneva: World Council of Churches, 1949); Oliver S. **Tomkins**, *The Church in the Purpose of God* (London: SCM Press, 1950); G. Ernest **Wright**, "The World Council of Churches and Biblical Interpretation," *Int* 3(1949)50–61; *idem, The Old Testament Against Its Environment* (London: SCM Press, 1950); *idem, God Who Acts: Biblical Theology as Recital* (London: SCM Press, 1952).

In the decade and a half following the second World War, the Bible and biblical theology came to occupy a place of prominence and authority in theological studies which they had not enjoyed for years, probably not since the days of the Reformation period. The prominence of the Bible during this period has led people to speak of a biblical theology movement. The importance assigned to the Bible during this time was in many respects an international phenomenon that was actually the culmination of many factors which had been operative in various ways in both the church and in theological scholarship for some time. Thus the movement, or better, the theological spirit of the era, cannot be viewed as a particular manifestation of theological conditions within any limited culture. It cannot be related or confined, for example, merely to the American scene, although it did take on different configurations in different cultural contexts.

The international character of the development can be seen in conferences and study groups sponsored by the World Council of Churches, such as those held in London (10–12 August 1946) and at Bossey (5–9 January

1947). The report of these discussions, held prior to the meeting of the WCC in Amsterdam in 1948, appeared under the title *From the Bible to the Modern World*. The expectation of results to be derived from biblical theology in these deliberations can be seen in the following quotes from this publication:

> In order to apply God's Design rightly to Man's Disorder, so as to diagnose the disease of our age, and prepare the way for its healing, it is necessary to become clear about the relationship between the Bible and the modern world. Has the Bible any "social and political message" at all? If so, is it a message that is relevant to the modern situation, or is it so conditioned by ancient thought-forms, ancient social customs and ancient political systems that it casts no light on modern perplexities? If it does cast light, is the light clear and unwavering, like God, "the Father of Lights, with whom is no variableness, nor any shadow that is cast by turning", or does it flicker and smoke like human lamps and candles? Just what does it mean for a modern man to find God's authoritative Word and Will in the Bible, and to conduct his social or political affairs in obedience to the divine commands which come to him through its pages? In short, *how do we get from the Bible to the Modern World*: over a bridge of some sort, or over a great chasm which has to be leaped by faith?
>
> At several points, there seems now to be much more agreement among Christians, concerning these fundamental issues, than there was a generation or two ago. Liberal Christians tended then to stress the historical criticism of the Bible in a manner which cast doubt upon the authority and relevance of large parts of it; conservatives generally felt they could maintain its full divine authority only by denying the validity of historical criticism. Liberals usually had a social and political message, but largely derived from extra-Biblical sources. When consciously referring to the Bible, they sometimes fell into what their critics called an "illicit modernizing" of Bible teaching. Conservatives, sticking closely to the text of Scripture, found in it a Gospel of personal salvation through Christ's death and resurrection, but no such Gospel of social salvation as that proclaimed by the liberals.
>
> It would be an exaggeration to say that these conflicts of thought have now entirely disappeared; but reports from many parts of the world indicate that the old liberal-orthodox antithesis has been considerably modified. Many Americans are finding a middle way between Fundamentalism and Modernism; on the Continent of Europe, Barth, Brunner, and the fresh appreciation of Luther's original teachings have led the way to a new reverence for the Bible as God's Word, compatible with respect for the historico-critical method, and concern for social and political problems. The historical criticism of the Bible has moved into a new phase, less preoccupied with the date, authorship, sources and circumstances of particular passages, and more concerned with the message of the Old and New Testaments as a whole (Biblical Theology). Above all, in the struggle between Church and State which assumed such dramatic and heroic forms in certain European countries during the rise and progress of Hitlerism, two positive emphases emerged in which liberals and conservatives stood together, so far as they remained loyal Christians: (1) *The Bible* as the "sword of the Spirit", by which Christians are enabled to withstand all assaults of their enemies; (2) *Social responsibility* as part of the Church's task, defined in the Bible itself. A great revival of Bible-reading and Bible-study, implying in some sense faith in its divine authority, is sweeping round the world, af-

fecting Roman Catholics and Eastern Orthodox as well as Protestants. And in
the name of the Lordship of Christ—whose universal sway over all earthly and
heavenly powers is part of the central message of the Bible—many Christians
hitherto indifferent to social problems are undertaking to reconstruct and re-
Christianize the crumbling structure of modern society (pp. 1–2).

While the Conference thus generally stood opposed to all dogmatic reactions against historical criticism, it by no means reverted to "pre-Barthian"
liberal methods of interpreting Scripture. In interpreting the "mind of Christ",
it did not confine itself to the "historically authentic words of Jesus", as liberal
critics used to do, but found this mind expressed in the whole plan of salvation
to which the Hebrew prophets and the early Church Fathers testify, and of
which Jesus is the centre, not the sum. As to "Biblical Theology", then, there
was wide agreement that a more or less unified message runs through the
Bible, centring in *Heilsgeschichte* or the history of the divine-human covenant
in its various forms and phrases; . . . (pp. 33–34).

The above quotes illustrate something of the hopes and expectations
that were associated with the biblical theology movement in general. Similar
affirmations of the role and importance of the Bible are to be found in the
later publications of the World Council of Churches Study Department and
in the work edited by Richardson and Schweitzer which was again the result
of initiative by the WCC. In the enthusiasm of the period, international scholars
and theologians were even able to agree on guiding principles for biblical
interpretation (see the report of the conference held at Wadham College,
Oxford, 28 June—6 July 1949 in *ER*, pp. 81–86 and Richardson/Schweitzer,
pp. 240–44).

Among the broader theological interests that came to expression in the
movement or that were embodied in the biblically-oriented spirit of the age,
the following certainly seem noteworthy. (1) Many felt that the centrality of
the Bible would lead to a reintegration of the total theological enterprise by
giving theology a center from which to work outward in addressing "Man's
Disorder" and in proclaiming "God's Design." (2) It was hoped that the role
of the Bible and biblical theology would provide a perspective and rallying
point for overcoming the divisions within the church universal. The Bible, it
seemed, was a shared entity around which diversity within the church and in
academic scholarship might find unity and commonality. (3) Barthian or neo-
orthodox theology with its focus on the Word of God had inclined theological
studies toward a focus on the Bible. (4) In the movement there was a strong
reaction to the way in which the Bible had been interpreted by liberal, historical critics whose work was seen as disinterested, analytic, existentially
unengaging, exegetically dry, and theologically sterile. Focusing on the theological aspects of the biblical materials was seen not only as a countermove
against liberal criticism but also as a recovery of a true dimension of the
biblical text (see Smart, p. 11). (5) The historical pessimism of the Bible as

well as its anthropological realism with their strong emphasis on human sinfulness and historical corruption were found especially meaningful by those who sought to make some sense of a war-torn world. (6) In a fashion, the biblical theology movement was the culmination of the effort to stress the relevance of the Bible which had been a serious concern, at least in Germany, since the anti-religious and anti-Old Testament expressions of the late nineteenth century. The issue of the relevance of the Bible had, of course, earlier concerned the non-German world as well (see above, pp. 144–51), but now it certainly became a more overt and international concern and topic of discussion (see Rowley's work as an example). It was widely believed that biblical theology or theology formulated and dependent upon the Bible would combine theological inquiry, concern for the existential life of the church and Christians, and the needs of preaching and thus be relevant across the entire field of Christian concerns.

The impact of the biblical theology movement can be seen across the spectrum of the theological activity of the late 1940s and throughout the 1950s. In some ways, the direct impact of the movement is less obvious in works which sought to expound Old Testament theology systematically than in the occasional monographs and essays which were less comprehensive and less methodologically rigorous than a standard theology. New publications, such as the journals *Theology Today* (Princeton Theological Seminary) and *Interpretation* (Union Theological Seminary in Virginia) and the series *Studies in Biblical Theology* (SCM Press), became organs and outlets for the movement (see Childs, pp. 14–17) and thus helped to contribute to its popularity and its more popular character.

A number of features were characteristic of many of the works which fell into the category of biblical theology during the period and which reflected certain features of hermeneutics and interpretation, many of which had been present for years in various aspects of the discipline. Childs in his book *Biblical Theology in Crisis* (pp. 32–50) and Barr in his *IDBSup* article have isolated various features reflective of the movement.

(1) In many ways, biblical theology saw itself in terms somewhat reminiscent of the Pietism of the eighteenth century; that is, it viewed itself as being anti-philosophical and opposed to the philosophical orientation of theology (also a characteristic of Barthianism) just as the Pietists had seen themselves as offering an alternative to rationalistic Orthodoxy. In fact, it was argued that biblical theology could not really be reduced to a system because of the "dramatic" quality of the biblical faith (so already, Gunkel, in *RGG* 1[1927], p. 1090) or because of the fact that biblical faith was a living organism uncapturable in a closed system.

(2) Strong emphasis was placed on the unity of the Bible. It was assumed and argued that this unity of the Scriptures was characteristic not only

of the two testaments separately but also that this unity transcended the division of the Bible into Old and New Testaments. Such a unity of the testaments could be expressed in terms of the sacred history (*Heilsgeschichte*) which bound together the Hebrew and Christian Scriptures, in terms of a comprehensive view of time in which Old Testament history was preparatory to the Christ-event which stood at the "chronological" center of history, in terms of shared concepts and interests, in terms of a shared pattern of thought, and so forth (see Baker).

(3) Another feature was the emphasis on the "Hebrew" quality and character of biblical thought and the contrast between Hebrew and Greek thought. Hebrew thought, it was argued, was concrete, dynamic, particularistic, etc., while Greek thought was described as abstract, theoretical, and rationalistic (for a description of the Hebrew-Greek contrast, see Barr, 1961, especially pp. 8–20). The emphasis on the value and authenticity of "Hebrew thought" led to such conclusions as the argument that although the New Testament was written in Greek, its authors were really Hebraic and that common, ancient Greek words could be filled with new and radically different meanings when they were used in a special Hebraic rather than their normal Greek sense. In broader categories, it was argued that there was a special Hebrew mentality and psychology which shared many characteristics of the thought of primitive peoples so that in order to understand the Bible, one had "to creep out of one's Western and twentieth-century skin and identify oneself with the feelings and thought-patterns of the past" (Stendahl, p. 418). This emphasis on the importance of Hebrew mentality can be seen in many publications from the period and in its more restrained form was given classical expression by Johannes Pedersen (1883–1977) and Aubrey Rodway Johnson (1901–; see Rogerson, pp. 46–65).

(4) A further characteristic of many works in biblical theology was related to a particular linguistic approach to the Bible. Here the emphasis was on word studies based on the assumption that the ancient's world of thought was reflected in the vocabulary and other linguistic features of the language. Words were assumed to function as technical concepts generally with the essence or distinctive aspect of the concept being reflected in the root meaning of a term. Greek words when used in Christian writings were often assumed to take on Hebraic content and thus to reflect not the Greek "concept" but the Hebriac. Kelsey has described how this approach, which had been employed rather extensively in biblical studies for years, tended to operate:

> [The interpreter] proceeds as though a concept, biblical or otherwise, were (a) a kind of container that lugs the selfsame meaning-content into every context, and (b) a kind of onion that accumulates layers of meaning from its several contexts of use in the past, interrelates them systematically, and thereafter

bears them in all contexts whatsoever, so that all uses of the concept are present when any one is explicitly used. . . . Furthermore, it suggests the view, . . . that a concept consists in some kind of ordered set of relationships that fall into a structure. . . . the Bible is tacitly treated as a system of concepts (p. 27).

(5) The Old Testament or the central features of Old Testament faith were considered as distinctive over against the ancient Near Eastern environment out of which it came. The title of a book by George Ernest Wright (1909–74), *The Old Testament Against Its Environment*, illustrates the general perspective of this approach. In the book Wright argues for the existence of "central elements of Biblical faith which are so unique and *sui generis* that they cannot have developed by natural evolutionary process from the pagan world in which they appeared . . . the faith of Israel even in its earliest and basic forms is so utterly different from that of the contemporary polytheisms that one simply cannot explain it fully by evolutionary or environmental categories" (p. 7).

Highly influential in the arguments for the uniqueness of Israelite faith and religion in the English-Speaking world was the book, *The Intellectual Adventure of Ancient Man* (published in England as *Before Philosophy*), edited by H. and H. A. Frankfort and based to some extent on the thought of E. Cassirer concerning the nature of primitive mentality (see Rogerson, pp. 59–63). The contributors to the Frankfort volume argued, in some respects in a perspective analogous to the thought of Kaufmann, that ancient Near Eastern thought was characterized by mythology and mythopoetry. Mythopoeic thought was assumed to be unanalytical and holistic in its understanding of the world of gods and humans. In such a world, the gods are understood as personifications and embodiments of cosmic and natural phenomena. Israelite religion differed radically from this conception. Frankfort describes the difference as follows:

> When we read in Psalm 19 that 'the heavens declare the glory of God; and the firmament sheweth his handiwork', we hear a voice which mocks the beliefs of Egyptians and Babylonians. The heavens, which were to the psalmist but a witness of God's greatness, were to the Mesopotamians the very majesty of godhead, the highest ruler, Anu. To the Egyptians the heavens signified the mystery of the divine mother through whom man was reborn. In Egypt and Mesopotamia the divine was comprehended as immanent: the gods were in nature. The Egyptians saw in the sun all that a man may know of the Creator; the Mesopotamians viewed the sun as the god Shamash, the guarantor of justice. But to the psalmist the sun was God's devoted servant who is as a bridegroom coming out of his chamber, and 'rejoiceth as a strong man to run a race.' The God of the psalmists and the prophets was not in nature. He transcended nature—and transcended, likewise, the realm of mythopoeic thought. It would seem that the Hebrews, no less than the Greeks, broke with the mode of speculation which had prevailed up to their time (p. 363).

The emphasis on the distinctiveness of Israelite faith and religion was, of course, one way of claiming authority for the Scriptures since it was assumed that uniqueness carried with it authoritative status and that distinctiveness was equivalent to truthfulness. In addition, this assumption led to the acceptance of some and the denial of other positions of both the *religionsgeschichtliche Schule* and the myth and ritual approach. That is, those who stressed the distinctive quality of Israelite faith also still affirmed the connections between Israelite life and religion and that of neighboring cultures and insisted on the necessity of studying biblical religion in light of Near Eastern religion. This dialectical attitude, however, generally served as the means of demonstrating how Israelite religion differed from all others in the region.

(6) A final feature of this phase of biblical theology was the emphasis on history as the arena of divine revelation with its associated stress on God's acts in history. A focus on the importance of history was certainly nothing new in biblical studies since much of the Old Testament is historical literature and the *Heilsgeschichte* approach had made historical matters of central significance. In addition, history had become one of the basic academic disciplines in the nineteenth century and to speak of revelation in history was to relate the religious content of the Old Testament to a respectable discipline. Most of these factors, however, lay in the background of the concerns of the time which focused instead on two other matters.

(a) Revelation in history was, first of all, a means for denying legitimacy to two other understandings of God's self-revelation. Conservative thought had argued for generations that God was revealed in propositions and statements and that the Bible was a book of such matters. On the other hand, liberal interpreters tended to view revelation as the product of humanity's gradual progress in spiritual understanding in which insight moved always, although not necessarily directly, toward higher forms and nobler conceptions.

The stress on revelation through history contended that revelation came through historical events, not in ideas or propositions, but in events in which God intervened and was revealed (see the quotes from Richardson and Robinson above, p. 166). Thus the revelation came from outside the human and historical processes but utilized humans who could understand and interpret the intervention of God. The Bible per se was thus primarily a record of this revelation. It was conceived of fundamentally as a book of history. Note the following position of Wright:

> The primary means by which God communicates with man is by his acts, which are the events of history. These events need interpretation, it is true, and God provides it in his Word by chosen heralds or messengers. But the focus of attention is not upon the Word of God in and for itself so that it can be frozen, so to speak, within a system of dogmatic propositions. The Word

leads us, not *away from* history, but *to* history and to responsible participation *within* history. It is the accompaniment of history. The Bible thus is not primarily the Word of God, but the record of the Acts of God, together with the human response thereto (1952, p. 107).

This approach thus allowed one to affirm the close connection between the Bible and revelation but to deny that the Bible or the words of the Bible were revelation. It stressed both the objective and subjective aspects of revelation. Thus, it allowed for historical criticism of the Bible, took the Scriptures seriously, and yet did not commit one to any form of the inerrancy-of-Scripture doctrine. Thus the position was clearly intended to occupy middle ground between Fundamentalism and Liberalism (see Wright, 1949).

(b) The emphasis on history and revelation in history, at least in some circles, encouraged efforts to attempt external substantiation of the historical events reported in the Old Testament. This was more characteristic of American than British scholarship and even less characteristic of German scholarship although no blanket characterization covers the entire situation. Archaeological work came to be closely associated with the desire to offer substantiation for the historicity of biblical reports about events or about the events presupposed behind the texts. The students of William Foxwell Albright (1891–1971) of Johns Hopkins University, who came close to representing an American "school" of Old Testament interpretation in the 1950s and 1960s, gave archaeology a very significant role in understanding the Bible. The most theologically articulate of this group was G. Ernest Wright who published in both archaeological and theological areas (see Dever). For him and others, biblical theology and biblical archaeology not merely went, but had to go, hand in hand if an adequate comprehension of the biblical materials was to be achieved. Childs has outlined the logic of this position as follows:

> God has revealed himself in the real events of human life which are found in the Bible. The theologian who seeks this knowledge of God must therefore study history. Since archaeology is the best tool for the study of ancient history, biblical theology and biblical archaeology belong together (p. 42).

It should be noted, of course, that interest in archaeological excavations and research was no new phenomenon. Interest in this area had been a significant force in biblical studies since the mid-nineteenth century. Throughout this period conclusions based on archaeological evidence had been used to illuminate, clarify, and substantiate biblical narratives and reports of events. What was new in the so-called biblical theology period was the close association between archaeological and theological interests and the desire to see archaeological work as supportive of the biblical portrayal of Israelite history and thus, at least indirectly, supportive of the contentions that God acts and is revealed in historical events. German scholarship was certainly interested and engaged in archaeological research but on the German scene there never developed as close as alliance between archaeology and theology as in American scholarship.

In summary, the biblical theology movement must not be seen purely as a product of the post-war years. In many ways, it was merely the culmination of processes already under way and the intensification of theological drives already present. The various characteristics of the movement which have recently, and in the discussion above, been described rather negatively, all had their roots in earlier scholarship. Certainly not all the characteristics noted are reflected in any of the works on biblical theology in the period as we shall see in the next chapter. Certain of the features were clearly over-stressed in many publications. Thus a number of the presuppositions on which many volumes were based were, as we shall see, without foundation or were primarily rhetorical and emotive in quality.

V.

RECENT DEVELOPMENTS IN OLD TESTAMENT THEOLOGY

James **Barr**, "Trends and Prospects in Biblical Theology," *JTS* 25(1974)265–82; *idem*, "Biblical Theology," *IDBSup*, pp. 104–11; Christoph **Barth**, "Grundprobleme einer Theologie des Alten Testaments," *EvTh* 23(1963)342–62; J. J. **Burden**, "Methods of Old Testament Theology: Past, Present and Future," *ThEv* 10(1977)14–33; Ronald E. **Clements**, "The Problem of Old Testament Theology," *LQHR* Sixth Series 34(1965)11–17; *idem*, "Recent Developments in Old Testament Theology," *EpRev* 3(1976)99–107; John J. **Collins**, "The 'Historical Character' of the Old Testament in Recent Biblical Theology," *CBQ* 41(1979)185–204; Anton **Fridrichsen** et al., *The Root of the Vine: Essays in Biblical Theology* (Westminster/New York: Dacre Press/Philosophical Library, 1953); John **Goldingay**, "The Study of Old Testament Theology: Its Aims and Purpose," *TynB* 26(1975)34–52; Wilfrid **Harrington**, *The Path of Biblical Theology* (Dublin: Gill and Macmillan, 1973)50–113; Julien **Harvey**, "The New Diachronic Biblical Theology of the Old Testament (1960–1970)," *BTB* 1(1971)5–29; Gerhard **Hasel**, *Old Testament Theology: Basic Issues in the Current Debate* (Grand Rapids: William B. Eerdmans, 1972, ³1982); *idem*, "A Decade of Old Testament Theology: Retrospect and Prospect," *ZAW* 93(1981)165–84; Johannes **Hempel**, "Alttestamentliche Theologie in Protestantischer Sicht heute," *BO* 15(1958)206–14; Edmund **Jacob**, *Grundfragen alttestamentliche Theologie* (Stuttgart: W. Kohlhammer, 1970); Eva **Osswald**, "Theologie des AT—eine bleibende Aufgabe alttestamentlicher Wissenschaft," *TLZ* 99(1974)641–58; M.-L. **Ramlot**, "Une decade de théologie biblique," *RThom* 64(1964)65–96; 65(1965)95–135; H. G. **Reventlow**, "Grundfragen der alttestamentlicher Theologie im Lichte der neueren deutschen Forschung," *TLZ* 17(1961)81–98; *idem*, "Basic Problems in Old Testament Theology," *JSOT* 11(1979)2–22; *idem*, *Hauptprobleme der alttestamentlicher Theologie im 20. Jahrhundert* (Darmstadt: Wissenschaftliche Buchgesellschaft, 1982)65–202; Roland **de Vaux**, "Peut-on écrire une 'théologie de l'Ancien Testament'?" *Bible et Orient* (Paris: Cerf, 1967)56–71 = "Is It Possible to Write a 'Theology of the Old Testament'?" *The Bible and the Ancient Near East* (London/Garden City: Darton, Longman, & Todd/Doubleday & Company, 1971)49–62; Preben **Wernberg-Möller**, "Is There an Old Testament Theology?" *HibJ* 59(1960)21–29; Ernst **Würthwein**, "Zur Theologie des Alten Testaments," *TRu* 36(1971)185–208; Walther **Zimmerli**, "Erwägungen zur Gestalt einer alttestamentlicher Theologie," *TLZ* 98(1963)81–98; *idem*, "Biblische Theologie I. Altes Testament," *TRE* 6(1980)426–55.

Since the mid-twentieth century a number of significant developments have taken place in the study of Old Testament theology and new issues and questions of methodology have arisen. After a period of vigorous activity in the 1950s, which may be seen as the second wave of Old Testament theologies in the twentieth century, the writing of theologies almost ceased in the 1960s, a decade which saw a renewed concern with the history of Israelite religion evident in the publication of major works by Pfeiffer (1961), Renckens (1962), Ringgren (1963), Vriezen (1963), and Fohrer (1968). This phenomenon was no doubt reflective, on the one hand, of the uncertain conditions in theological studies in general. This decade witnessed the collapse of theological movements which had dominated the field since the early post-war years and saw theological studies become much more introspective and more concerned with methodological problems than with dogmatic expositions. The cessation of the writing of Old Testament theologies was, on the other hand, also related not only to the impact of the appearance of von Rad's theology and the spectrum of methodological questions that followed the publication of his work but also to the reassessment of biblical theology as a discipline occasioned by the collapse of features in the consensus that had supported the movement. The recent production of literature concerned with methodological matters on the subject and the revival of writing Old Testament theologies in the 1970s—the third wave of the twentieth century—have become overwhelming as a quick glance at the bibliographical listings in the recent publications of Hasel (1982) and Reventlow (1982) clearly illustrate.

Many interpreters describing the developing conditions from about 1960 and assessing the contemporary situation suggest that the entire discipline of biblical theology is in crisis, to use the terminology of Childs's book. ("Old Testament theology today is undeniably in crisis," Hasel, 1982, p. 9.) Writing in 1971 Würthwein noted that a new phase in the discipline of Old Testament theology began following the first World War and that after fifty years there was even greater disagreement over matters relating to the subject than at the time the new phase began (p. 188). In our opinion, neither the dramatic outcry of "crisis" nor the judgment that there has been no advancement because the methodological disagreements continue really warrant serious consideration.

In this final chapter we shall survey in rather brief fashion most of the Old Testament theologies published between about 1950 and the present. The focus, however, will be primarily on three major issues: (1) the character and impact of Gerhard von Rad's theology; (2) the challenge to some of the presuppositions and methodological procedures of the so-called biblical theology movement which occurred primarily in the 1960s; and (3) the issues and concerns characteristic of scholarship since and as a consequence of the two previous factors.

OLD TESTAMENT THEOLOGIES OF THE 1950S

Peter R. **Ackroyd**, "Recent Biblical Theologies VII. G. A. F. Knight's 'A Christian Theology of the Old Testament,'" *ExpTim* 73(1961–62)164–68; William F. **Albright**, "Return to Biblical Theology," *CCen* 75(1958)1328–31; G. W. **Anderson**, "Recent Biblical Theologies V. Th. C. Vriezen's 'Outline of Old Testament Theology,'" *ExpTim* 73(1961–62)113–16; John **Bright**, "Recent Biblical Theologies VIII. Edmond Jacob's 'Theology of the Old Testament,'" *ExpTim* 73(1961–62)304–8; Ronald E. **Clements**, "Theodorus C. Vriezen, An Outline of Old Testament Theology," in Laurin, pp. 121–40; John I. **Durham**, "George A. F. Knight, *A Christian Theology of the Old Testament*," in Laurin, pp. 171–90; R. Lansing **Hicks**, "G. Ernest Wright and Old Testament Theology," *ATR* 58(1976)158–78; David A. **Hubbard**, "Paul van Imschoot, *Theology of the Old Testament*," in Laurin, pp. 191–215; Paul van **Imschoot**, *Théologie de l'Ancien Testament* (2 vols.; Tournai: Desclée et Cie, 1954–56); vol. 1 = *Theology of the Old Testament, I, God* (New York: Desclée, 1965); Edmond **Jacob**, *Théologie de l'Ancien Testament* (Neuchâtel: Delachaux et Niestlé, 1955) = *Theology of the Old Testament* (London/New York: Hodder & Stoughton/Harper & Brothers, 1958); David H. **Kelsey**, *The Uses of Scripture in Recent Theology* (Philadelphia/London: Fortress Press/SCM Press, 1975); George A. F. **Knight**, *A Christian Theology of the Old Testament* (London/Richmond: SCM Press/John Knox Press, 1959); Robert B. **Laurin**, "Edmond Jacob, *Theology of the Old Testament*," *Contemporary Old Testament Theologians* (ed. by R. B. Laurin; Valley Forge: Judson Press, 1970)141–70; J. Barton **Payne**, *The Theology of the Older Testament* (Grand Rapids: Zondervan Publishing House, 1962); J. N. **Schofield**, *Introducing Old Testament Theology* (London/Philadelphia: SCM Press/Westminster Press, 1964); Th. C. **Vriezen**, *Hoofdlijnen der Theologie van het Oude Testament* (Wageningen: H. Veenman & Zonen, 1949, ²1954, ³1966) = *An Outline of Old Testament Theology* (Oxford/Newton, MA: Basil Blackwell/Charles T. Branford Company, 1958, ²1970); G. Ernest **Wright**, *God Who Acts: Biblical Theology as Recital* (London: SCM Press, 1952); *idem*, "Reflections Concerning Old Testament Theology," *Studia biblica et semitica. Theodoro Christiano Vriezen . . . dedicata* (Wageningen: H. Veenman & Zonen, 1966)376–88; *idem*, *The Old Testament and Theology* (New York: Harper & Row, 1969); Edward J. **Young**, *The Study of Old Testament Theology Today* (London/Westwood, NJ: James Clark & Co./Fleming H. Revell Company, 1958/1959); *idem*, "What Is Old Testament Biblical Theology?" *EvQ* 31(1959)136–42.

During the 1950s a number of Old Testament theologies were published; in fact, this decade has been spoken of as the "golden age" of Old Testament theology. Some of these works were very similar to those of the 1930s but all show varying degrees of influence from the biblical theology movement. This decade also witnessed, at least in the United States, the reawakening of biblical conservatism which sought to identify its position over against both mainstream-liberal and neo-orthodox interpretations of the Bible.

In this section, we will analyze the main features of some of the Old Testament theologies published during the decade. Since von Rad's theology was such an epoch-making volume, his work will be treated in a section by itself.

THEODORUS CHRISTIAAN VRIEZEN

Of all the theologies published during this period, one of the fullest, the most methodologically oriented, and the most substantive in content is that by the Dutch Old Testament scholar Vriezen (1899–; see Anderson and Clements). First published in Dutch in 1949, the second edition was translated into English in 1958 and then followed by a second edition in 1970 which translates the third Dutch edition. (References are to the second English edition.) In the introduction, which comprises about one-third of the volume, Vriezen discusses (a) the Christian church and the Old Testament; (b) the historical character of the Old Testament revelation; fundamental and factual observations; (c) the spiritual structure of the Old Testament and of the Old Testament writings; (d) the Old Testament as the Word of God, and its use in the church; and (e) basis, task, and method of Old Testament theology. Within these sections a wide variety of topics are surveyed ranging from a brief history of Israelite religion to a discussion of Israelite literature to the history of the church's use of the Old Testament.

In his methodological section Vriezen is emphatic in his stress on Old Testament theology as a Christian undertaking: "we start from the view that *both as to its object and its method Old Testament theology is and must be a Christian theological science*" (p. 147). He argues that "only when Eissfeldt's line of thought is followed out consistently can we arrive at a definition of Old Testament theology which guarantees a science independent in name and content" (p. 148). Old Testament theology thus must be clearly distinguished from a history of Israelite religion.

> Old Testament theology is a form of scholarship differing from the history of Israel's religion in its object as well as in its method. In its object, *because its object is not the religion of Israel but the Old Testament*; in its method *because it is a study of the message of the Old Testament both in itself and in its relation to the New Testament. . . . its task is to define the characteristic features of the message of the Old Testament*, and for that reason many things can be left out of account which are of more importance in the study of the religion of Israel; as a theological branch of scholarship the theology of the Old Testament seeks *particularly the element of revelation in the message of the Old Testament*; it must work, therefore, with *theological standards* and must give *its own evaluation of the Old Testament message on the ground of its Christian theological starting-point*. In doing so it must guard against the error of tearing apart the *correlation between faith and revelation* by identifying revelation and canon. From the Christian point of view the canon, too, must be submitted to the judgement of the preaching of Jesus Christ (pp. 148–49).

Thus, Vriezen is quite willing to claim and stress the revelatory character of the Old Testament (p. 19), the necessity to make judgments about this revelation, and the place of Old Testament theology within the larger field of Christian theology (p. 149), standing between dogmatic and historical theology (p. 145).

In explicating the content of Old Testament theology, Vriezen focuses on the idea of communion with God arguing that the nature of the knowledge of God in the Old Testament is based on an intimate relationship between the holy God and humanity—a relationship which is existential: *"The basis of Israel's conception of God is the reality of an immediate spiritual communion between God, the Holy One, and man and the world"* (p. 157). This understanding of communion with God as the basic Old Testament religious principle provides Vriezen with the organizational principle for his work. Under the topic of "intercourse between God and man" he discusses the revelation of God, the cult, and human piety: that is, the means, nature, and intermediaries of revelation, which establish and sustain the communion; the cult which maintains, purifies, and integrates the communion between God and human beings; and piety which is the human reaction to the revelation. From this, he moves to discuss the community of God in terms of Yahweh, the God of the community, the forms of the community (social structures, leadership, and relationships), the standards of the community (ethics), and man in the community of God. The final section treats "the prospect of the community of God: God, man and the world in the present and the future."

In many ways, Vriezen's work bears comparison with those of Eichrodt and Procksch to which it has many parallels especially in the emphasis on seeing a pervasive theological continuity or a cross-sectional consistency in Old Testament theology with the central foci being the various relationships between God and Israel, God and humankind and the world, and the communion and its consequences which resulted. Unlike Eichrodt, he does not narrow the focus of that relationship or communion to any overly restrictive concept such as the covenant: "We cannot be certain that the communion between God and the people was considered from the outset as a *covenantal* communion" (p. 351). In the final edition of his work, he intensified his stress on the unity of the Old Testament at a time when this was being challenged (see p. 8). Unlike many other interpreters, Vriezen was able to integrate cultic matters as well as ethics into his discussion and to relate his understanding of revelation to the actual practices and concerns of Israelite religion. Although a strong Christian emphasis is asserted in his methodological section, perhaps a reflection of his background in reformed dogmatics, little of this appears in his discussion of the contents of the theology. He was still concerned with the substantive issues involved in the debates of the 1920s and 1930s over confessional and descriptive matters without opting for an easy solution. He came as close as any to claiming a normative role for

Old Testament theology in the whole of the theological enterprise but did not explain how this would function in actual practice.

GEORGE ERNEST WRIGHT

When we turn from the cautious and well thought out work of Vriezen to the programmatic essay *God Who Acts* by Wright (1909–74), we are confronted not with a major portrayal of Old Testament theology but with a prolegomena to a theology written, as the author himself later said, "with all the enthusiasm of fresh discovery and with the exaggeration which came from personal reaction against a view of theology [liberal idealism?] in which I had been reared" (1969, p. 11). As a student of Albright, Wright began his career in archaeology, was active in the early post-war ecumenical movement, and became one of the chief proponents of the biblical theology movement (for a sympathetic survey of his career and writings, see Hicks).

Wright advocated several major theses about the Old Testament and its theology. (1) The knowledge or doctrine of God in ancient Israel "was not derived from systematic or speculative thought, but rather in the first instance from the attempt to explain the events which led to the establishment of the nation" (1952, p. 44). Therefore God is "known by what he has done" (p. 84). "The Bible thus is not primarily the Word of God, but the record of the Acts of God, together with the human response thereto" (p. 107). (2) This knowledge of God was inferred from events which "actually had happened in human history" (p. 44):

> Now in Biblical faith everything depends upon whether the central events actually occurred. Biblical scepticism might doubt whether God was Director of the events (Jer. 5:12) but there was no doubt that there was an Exodus, that the nation was established at Mount Sinai, that it did obtain the land, that it did lose it subsequently, that Jesus did live, that he did die on a cross, and that he did appear subsequently to a large number of independent witnesses (pp. 126–27).

Wright thus argues that the revelation or knowledge of God is the product of "the attempt to explain the events which led to the establishment of the nation" (p. 44) or "inferences drawn from" historical events or what God has done (p. 106). A great deal of emphasis is placed on the facticity or objective reality of the historical events which can be established and studied through proper archaeological and historical method. In his later writings he sought to combine the actual historical occurrences and their interpretations as both constitutive of the "event."

> The historical happening and its interpretation, the deed and the word of God as its commentary, these constitute the Biblical event. . . . In other words, the event-centered mode of God's revelation cannot be systematized, for it in-

cludes both the confessional recital of God's activity and the inferences and deductions that a worshiping community draw from it in their own historical situations (1969, pp. 44–45).

(3) Biblical theology "is fundamentally an interpretation of history, a confessional recital of historical events as the acts of God" (p. 57), and theology is "the discipline by which the Church, carefully and with full knowledge of the risk, translates Biblical faith into the non-Biblical language of another age" (p. 108). (4) Certain doctrines were the product of inferences drawn from the historical events. These include the doctrines of election, of a covenant community responsible to God, and of divine creation (see pp. 38–50). (In his 1959 publication Wright, in a radical alteration of his position, speaks of God as Creator, Lord [Divine Monarch], and Warrior without much emphasis on these conceptions of God as the product of inferences drawn from historical events. They are noted as "primary assumptions and assertions about God in the Old Testament" [p. 70] which support the proposition "that what is basically Biblical is a special political understanding of the universe" [p. 10].)

Wright's theological work was influenced by a number of factors in addition to his concern for archaeological and historical reconstruction of ancient Israelite life learned from Albright whose basic program was to prove that we can "treat the Bible from beginning to end as an authentic document of religious [and political] history" (Albright, p. 1330). Among such influences (see Wright, 1969, pp. 39–69) were Brunner's understanding of revelation as encounter, C. H. Dodd's stress on the historical kerygma of the New Testament, and some of the early works of von Rad which we shall note later.

Since we shall examine the attack on features of the biblical theology movement and thus many of Wright's presuppositions and arguments in a later section, at this point it is sufficient to note that in spite of his emphasis on the authority of the narrative aspects of the Bible—its reports of the significant events or acts of God—"the *narrative* mode of biblical literature plays no role in shaping the theology" which Wright suggests should be expounded (Kelsey, p. 37). Kelsey continues:

> Once this is noted, Wright's initial stress on the narrative features of scripture at the expense of its openly didactic features seems quite misleading. The narrative *qua* narrative does not authorize proposals about God. It simply gives us the grounds for defining biblical concepts which the modern Christian is to take over as his own and restate. The concepts are what is authoritative for theological proposals today, and the narrative from which they are distilled is left behind. . . . it seems, ironically, that Wright himself has brought us back to biblical concept theology! (p. 37).

EDMOND JACOB

The work by Jacob (1909–), French professor of Old Testament at Strasbourg, represents an approach to Old Testament theology which uses a modified dogmatic scheme as the organizing principle (see Bright and Laurin). For Jacob, Old Testament theology is "defined as the systematic account of the specific religious ideas which can be found throughout the Old Testament and which form its profound unity" (p. 11). Elsewhere, however, he speaks not of pervasive and prominent ideas but of two themes—the presence and the action of God—as the dominant features of the Old Testament.

The content of the theology is then expounded according to the following three headings: (1) characteristic aspects of the God of the Old Testament, (2) the action of God according to the Old Testament, and (3) opposition to and final triumph of God's work. In general terms, the first two correspond to the presence and action of God seen as the two main themes. In reality, Jacob's scheme is much closer to the classical topics of dogmatic theology than immediately appears. Under section one, for example, there is the traditional topic of the doctrine of God and the various divine properties. Under the treatment of God's actions come the discussion of such issues as creation, anthropology, and history. The third part is really eschatology, being concerned with sin and redemption, death and the future life, and the final consummation. Significant features of the Old Testament are omitted: "Piety, religious institutions and ethics are not part of the Old Testament theology's specific domain" (p. 32).

Many statements in the volume illustrate the lack of coherence, consistency, and clarity in the author's thought. For example, in spite of the opening definition of the discipline, noted above, he remarks that "the Old Testament does not bring us ideas about God, but acts of God" (p. 32). No doubt one sees here some nodding accommodation to one of the emphases of the biblical theology movement. Jacob's book, like many works from the period, suffers from an overemphasis on the etymology and root meanings of terms as if these were the carriers of significant meaning in and of themselves. In his review of the work, Barr warned against this semantic weakness:

> One of the values of this book is the interest it takes in Hebrew words, and in this way it forms a good introduction for the student into what has been done recently in word-studies and lexicographical material as a basis for understanding Hebrew thinking and its modes of theological expression. But there is a limit to what you can prove this way, and the limit is set by strict linguistic method and by a strict clarity about when you are speaking of the thought processes which use these words; what you can prove of one does not necessarily and unambiguously apply to the other. You cannot, I think, argue as follows: "This aspect of miracles, as wide as it is diffuse, is confirmed by the language. The fact that Hebrew has not *one* but several terms to signify miracle

attests its frequency, but also its fluidity." By the same logic Germans must think more frequently and more variably about humanity because they have two words corresponding to English "man". And while we are talking about man, consider this argument: "If it is true that *'adam* insists on the human kind, *'enosh* on his feebleness, *'ish* on his power, *geber* on his strength, then we can say that added together they indicate that man according to the Old Testament is a perishable creature, who lives only as a member of the group, but that he is also a powerful being capable of choice and dominion. So the semantic enquiry confirms the general teaching of the Bible on the insignificance and greatness of man" (p. 157). Is it not too good to be true to suppose that by taking the Hebrew terms for something and adding their etymologies together we arrive at a pattern coinciding with the Israelite mode of thought about that thing? (*JSS* 5[1960]168).

Like most Old Testament theologians, Jacob felt that he had to give some statement about the Old Testament as Christian Scripture. He wrote: "A theology of the Old Testament which is founded not on certain isolated verses, but on the Old Testament as a whole, can only be a Christology, for what was revealed under the old covenant, through a long and varied history, in events, persons and institutions, is, in Christ, gathered together and brought to perfection" (p. 12). What he meant by this is not very clear but fortunately he made no attempt to operate on such an assumption in his description of the theology, and his patronage to Christianity appears to be little more than a swiftly executed genuflection.

PAUL VAN IMSCHOOT

The papal encyclical *Divino afflante Spiritu* issued by Pope Pius XII in 1943 removed the constraints which had been placed on Roman Catholic biblical scholars by Pope Piux X in 1907. The new ruling of the church urged Catholic scholars to pursue biblical scholarship and theology zealously as the following excerpt from the document indicates:

> With special zeal they should apply themselves not only to expounding exclusively those matters which belong to the historical, archaeological, philological and other auxiliary services—as, to our regret, is done in certain commentaries—but having duly referred to these, insofar as they may aid the exegesis, they should set forth in particular the theological doctrine in faith and morals of the individual books or texts so that their exposition may not only aid the professors of theology in their explanations and proofs of the dogmas of faith, but may also be of assistance to priests in their presentation of Christian doctrine to the people, and may help all the faithful to lead a life that is holy and worthy of a Christian.

The movement of Catholics into the mainstream of Old Testament studies progressed rapidly in the 1950s and 1960s (see Harrington, pp. 77–88). The first major Old Testament theology by a Catholic was the work by van Imschoot (1889–?) who was a long-time professor of exegesis at the Major

Seminary in Ghent, Belgium. His plans called for a three-volume work but only the first two appeared before his death and only volume one was translated into English (for a survey of his work and similar Catholic scholarship of the time, see Hubbard).

Van Imschoot consciously chose to expound the theology of the Old Testament in "a logical arrangement of the doctrines" so as to "bring into sharper focus the continuity and the likeness of the two revelations" [in the two testaments] and thus to "cast a clear light on the lacunas and the imperfections of the Old Law" (I, p. 2). For the structure of his presentation, he deliberately followed the old Christian tripartite approach—Theology-Anthropology-Soteriology—and pointed to Sellin and Köhler as practitioners of this method. Thus he divided his work into three volumes to fit the pattern:

   I. God and His relations with the world in general and with Israel in particular.
  II. Man, that is to say, ideas about nature and man's destiny, about his obligations and failings towards God and his neighbor, or the question of duty and sin.
 III. Divine judgment and salvation, in other words, the general eschatology of the Old Testament (p. 5).

In many ways, van Imschoot's work reflects the influence of Thomist theology. This can be seen especially in the first topic of his volume on God which discusses "God Considered in Himself" where he comments on the existence of God, the divine names and so forth including the divine metaphysical and moral attributes as well as God's sentiments. The rest of the volume treats "God and the world" and "God and His people." This movement from the more general topics to the more particular can be seen as reflective of a Catholic perspective and as the opposite of most Protestant approaches, such as Eichrodt's, which move from the more particular to the more general and universal—that is from election to creation.

The second volume of his work—"L'Homme"—provides van Imschoot the opportunity to give full coverage to religious life and practices as well as ethics since, after commenting on the law codes, he discusses human duties toward God ("Les devoirs religieux" and "Le culte") and humanity ("Les devoirs envers l'homme"). The section on sin ("Le péché") is deliberately brief since his program called for a full volume on judgment and salvation.

As a whole, van Imschoot took a conservative stance toward critical literary and historical matters and he expressed great confidence in the accuracy of the traditions about early Israelite life. Nonetheless, he was more open to critical positions than his Catholic predecessor Heinisch. His work, like Köhler's, is similar to "a compendium of brief essays on Old Testament subjects. Were the articles in alphabetical rather than logical order, they would come close to comprising a dictionary of Old Testament themes" (Hubbard, p. 202).

GEORGE ANGUS FULTON KNIGHT

The work by the Scottish theologian Knight (1909–) was the first major Old Testament theology to be written by a Britisher since the publication of Davidson's posthumous volume in 1904 (see Ackroyd and Durham). Without doubt, it has been one of the most controversial theologies since Vischer's christological interpretation of the Old Testament first made its appearance in the 1930s (see the summary of attitudes toward and reviews of Knight's work in Durham, pp. 175–77).

The title of Knight's work clearly expresses a major emphasis of the book, namely, its Christian orientation and its concern to interpret the material within the life of the church. Note his comments in the following quote:

> This Theology is written with the deliberate presupposition—and none of us can escape our presuppositions—that the Old Testament is nothing less than Christian Scripture. Therefore it is what the Germans would call a *Kirchliche Theologie* of the Old Testament. It is written by one who assumes that the Church believes the Old Testament to be the Word of God, just as surely as it believes it of the New Testament. A Theology of the Old Testament must arise out of the combined thinking of the church, and not merely from the disciplined studies of scholars who may not necessarily be committed to a Christian obedience. . . . The Old Testament is a book that must be read within the walls of the Christian Church, since 'the Church has received the Old Testament from the hand of Jesus'. Therefore an exposition of the Old Testament cannot confine itself to a critical and historical analysis either of its books or of its teaching (p. 7).

Knight's tendency to read the Old Testament in a christianized perspective is evident in many of his other publications although in his theology he declares that "the assumption that the Old Testament is the Word of God to the Church, however, is not the same thing as the inference that may be drawn therefrom, viz., that the Old Testament must be understood christologically" (pp. 7–8). His earlier work, *A Biblical Approach to the Doctrine of the Trinity* (Edinburgh: Scottish Journal of Theology, 1953), had sought to argue that the Christian doctrine of the Trinity was anticipated in the Old Testament in its Hebraic emphasis on the diversity in unity in regard to the nature of God (see 1953, pp. 16–20). This emphasis can be found throughout his discussion of the doctrine of God (see especially 1959, pp. 65–83).

For Knight, "the central theme of the Old Testament is nothing less than the revelation of the redemptive activity of God in and through the Son, Israel" (p. 9), a theme which clearly has connotations drawn from the New Testament. The outline of his work is as follows: God, God and Creation, God and Israel, and the Zeal of the Lord. Much of his exposition of various topics under the major headings attempts to bring out what he calls the "pictorial thinking" of the material which "is the essence of the whole biblical revelation" (p. 80). Thus his work has numerous imaginative and often insightful discussions of what he calls "figures"—such as the figures of the vine, son of God, son of man, bride, rock, and servant used in the "interpretation of Israel by Israel." The work has many similarities to the typological and almost allegorical reading of Scripture found in the works of A. G. Hebert (see Ackroyd, p. 164).

The full impact of Knight's Christian reading of the Old Testament is best seen in his section on the "Five 'Moments' in Israel's Experience" (pp. 202–17). Three of these "moments" are parallel to the three important moments in the life of all persons—birth, marriage, and death (p. 202). Birth (Israel's being called into existence as God's child), marriage (which occurred at Mt. Sinai when Israel was wedded to its God), and death (at the fall of Jerusalem in 587 BC and the subsequent deportations) for Israel were extended in two further moments. The fourth moment—after the "Easter Saturday of the soul of Israel" was experienced in the Exile—consists of the resurrection of Israel to new life, that is "the *Body of Israel*, no less, arising from the death of the Exile" (p. 208). The fifth and final moment is promised

> in the story of redemption when even the ruins and the waste places (Ezek. 36.36) would be built, when the desert would rejoice and blossom as the rose (Isa. 35.1), and when, after the resurrection of the Bride and her reconciliation with her divine Lover, even the land that was under a curse consequent upon the sin of Adam (Gen. 3.17) would be married to God and share in the total reconciliation of the cosmos (Isa. 62. 1–4) (p. 213).

The five moments in the life of Israel are then seen as parallels to the moments in the life of Christ.

> The five 'moments' in the life of Israel, which the Hebrew Old Testament Canon is sufficient to give us, correspond exactly with a like five 'moments' in the work of Christ ["birth, marriage (including the giving of the new Torah), death, resurrection and exaltation"]. Therefore, any doctrine which we may discover in the Apocrypha that is nowhere paralleled by a similar doctrine in the full 'five-moment' period in the story of Christ as it is revealed in the NT, is not likely to be an authentic element in the total biblical revelation (p. 213).

The inspirational or homiletical thrust of Knight's work can be seen in how he applies the "five-moments" to the life of the contemporary Christian:

> The 'five-moment' interpretation of the story of Israel renders the OT the divinely given commentary upon the NT which aids the believer to understand more profoundly how God deals with his own individual soul. The adopted Son, Israel, is described in the OT as a sinner redeemed by God's grace. The story of Israel is thus the story of 'me' writ large, and painted on an extensive canvas, covering a period not just of three-score years and ten, but of a thou-

sand years. With such a large canvas, he who runs may read. Each facet of the truth of God can now be more nearly observed. And since the individual most surely knows in the secret of his heart the reality of the first three 'moments' which Israel knew, he is now presented with a significant hope as well. This is because the story of this other sinful and adopted Son did not end with death. The Christian believer has already discovered that in his baptism he has passed beyond the moment of death and has entered into eternal life. This is true for him, because he is already 'in Christ', the second Israel. The first Israel, too, however, is 'in Christ', since 'before Abraham was, I am' (John 8.58). More-over we now know that the first Israel waited in confident hope for the fifth 'moment' to dawn. The Christian believer today, then, assured by the witness of the Holy Spirit himself, can also look forward with joy to that fifth 'mo-ment' when he too will enter into the glory which is laid up for those who love their Lord (p. 215).

Enough has been said to give some insight into the approach and content of Knight's work as well as to indicate why the book was so controversial.

EDWARD JOSEPH YOUNG

Neo-orthodoxy in general theology and certain emphases in biblical theology during the 1940s and 1950s had certainly given hope, especially in the United States, that the Old modernist-fundamentalist or liberal-conservative bifurcation could be overcome and a new moderate position could be pro-duced (see Childs, pp. 20–22). The impact of a critical-historical study of the Bible had polarized American scholars a generation after matters had tended to settle down elsewhere. Conservatives, however, never bought into the new approaches and saw neo-orthodox theology as just as "unbiblical" and a lot more devious than older forms of liberalism.

During the 1950s conservative or evangelical theology became more self-conscious and more aggressive in its opposition to other positions. This resurgence can be seen in the formation of the Evangelical Theological So-ciety in the United States (1949), in the inauguration of the journal *Christian-ity Today* (1956), and in the growing influence of the Tyndale Fellowship in the British Commonwealth.

The writings of Young (1907–68), while not producing a theology per se, attacked current scholarly attitudes and proclaimed the need for a con-servative approach to biblical theology which would assert the historic, or-thodox position. Such a position, he argued, would have to be based on theistic presuppositions—that God genuinely acted in the way the Bible says he did—and on a view of the Bible as the authoritative revelation of God. The following quotes illustrate his position:

> The study of Old Testament theology, therefore, if it is to do justice to the phenomena, will recognize the Scriptures as a special Divine revelation. It will operate upon the principles of Christian theism. It will also seek to do full justice to the character of special revelation as progressive. It will not seek to

discover Christian doctrine where that doctrine is not to be found, but it will keep in mind the fact that all Scripture was spoken by the God of truth. It will, therefore, not shy away from this revelation, but will recognize that it is truly a preparation for the final revelation in Jesus Christ. Most earnestly, and based upon sober grammatico-historical exegesis, will it endeavour to do full justice to the progressive character of the Old Testament revelation.

It will also remember the great epochs of revelation, and, seeking to discover these epochs, will be guided alone by the Scriptures. And lastly, it will pay full heed to the words of the Bible and to the background against which these words were spoken (p. 58).

Old Testament theology is concerned with the study of genuine revelations which the true God gave to Israel. These revelations had to do with His purposes in the salvation of mankind. His plan of salvation may be subsumed under the word covenant. It is, therefore, with the covenant of grace that Old Testament theology is concerned. This is its true content; this is its true subject-matter. In Old Testament theology we study God who has come to man, not man who, on his own initiative, comes, or has come, to God (p. 84).

JOHN BARTON PAYNE

An example of an Old Testament theology written from an evangelical or "Bible-believing" perspective can be seen in the work of Payne (1922–79) and although published in 1962 may be discussed at this point. This massive and learned volume is structured around the idea of the covenant or testament. After presenting a history of the discipline and a discussion of revelation and inspiration ("revelation makes truth known, but inspiration provides for its infallible recording"; p. 63), Payne outlines the essential features of the testament relationship taking his point of departure from Hebrews 9:

On the basis of Hebrews 9, "testament" may be defined as a "legal disposition by which qualified heirs are bequeathed an inheritance through the death of the testator." Five major aspects to the testamental arrangement appear: *the testator*, who gives and is styled "the mediator" (Heb. 9:15); *the heirs*, who receive and are also referred to as "the called" (9:15); *the method of effectuation*, namely, by a gracious bequeath that is executed upon the death of the testator (9:16); *the conditions*, by which the heir qualifies for the gift, for as Hebrews 9:28 puts it, the testament is "to them that wait for Him" (cf. its being "commanded," 9:20); and *the inheritance* which is given, namely, "eternal salvation" (9:15, 28) (p. 87).

On the basis of these five testamentary aspects, Payne then organizes the theology in the following fashion: The Testator: God (which contains discussion of the personality, works, names, attributes, and persons of God); The Heir: Man (which treats election, the sinful race, the origin of sin, and the nature of man); The Effectuation: Grace (which treats regenerating monergism, the death of the testator, the person and work of the Messiah, and other supernatural agents); The Conditions: Commitment (repentance, faith, morals, and ceremonial places, actions, and times); and The Inheritance: Reconciliation (redeemed life, life after death, the New Testament, and the testament of peace).

Payne sees six successive revelations of the testament in the Old Testament which give structure to the anticipatory history that would be fulfilled in Christ (see p. 95). These are the Edenic (Gen. 3:15), the Noachian (Gen. 9:9), the Abrahamic (Gen. 15:18), the Sinaitic (Exod. 19:5–6), the Levitical (Num. 25:12–13), and the Davidic (2 Sam. 7:13). Features of all of these are typologically representative as well as expectations of the New Testament and the final testament of peace at the consummation of time.

GERHARD VON RAD

James **Barr**, "Recent Biblical Theologies VI. Gerhard von Rad's Theologie des Alten Testaments," *ExpTim* 73(1961–62)142–46; Friedrich **Baumgärtel**, "Gerhard von Rad's 'Theologie des Alten Testaments,'" *TLZ* 86(1961)801–16, 895–908; J. L. **Crenshaw,** *Gerhard von Rad* (Waco, TX: Word Books, 1979); G. Henton **Davies**, "Gerhard-von Rad, Old Testament Theology," in Laurin, pp. 63–90; Erhard **Gerstenberger**, "Psalms," *Old Testament Form Criticism* (ed. by J. H. Hayes; San Antonio: Trinity University Press, 1974)179–223; A. J. **Greig,** "Some Formative Aspects in the Development of Gerhard von Rad's Idea of History," *AUSS* 16(1978)313–31; J. W. **Groves,** *Actualization and Interpretation in the Old Testament* (Ph.D. dissertation, Yale University, 1979); W. G. **Nesbitt**, *A Study in Contemporary Old Testament Biblical Theologies* (Ph.D. dissertation, Marquette University, 1969); Gerhard **von Rad**, *Das formgeschichtliche Problem des Hexateuch* (Stuttgart: W. Kohlhammer, 1938) = *The Problem of the Hexateuch and Other Essays* (Edinburgh/New York: Oliver & Boyd/McGraw-Hill, 1966)1–78; *idem*, "Grundprobleme einer biblischen Theologie des Alten Testaments," *TLZ* 68(1943)225–34; *idem*, "History and the Patriarchs," *ExpTim* 72(1960–61)213–16; *idem, Theologie des Alten Testaments*. I. *Die Theologie der geschichtlichen Überlieferungen Israels*; II. *Die Theologie der prophetischen Überlieferungen Israels* (Munich: Chr. Kaiser, 1957–61) = *Old Testament Theology*. I. *The Theology of Israel's Historical Traditions*; II. *The Theology of Israel's Prophetic Traditions* (Edinburgh/New York: Oliver & Boyd/Harper & Row, 1962–65); *idem*, "Offene Fragen im Umkreis einer Theologie des Alten Testaments," *TLZ* 88(1963)401–15; *idem, Weisheit in Israel* (London/Nashville:SCM Press/Abingdon Press, 1972); D. G. **Spriggs,** *Two Old Testament Theologies: A Comparative Evaluation of the Contributions of Eichrodt and von Rad to Our Understanding of the Nature of Old Testament Theology* (London: SCM Press, 1974); G. Ernest **Wright**, "Modern Issues in Biblical Studies: History and the Patriarchs," *ExpTim* 71(1959–60)292–96; Walther **Zimmerli**, "Gerhard von Rad, 'Theologie des Alten Testaments,'" *VT* 13(1963)100–111.

In his theology, with its challenge of previous methodologies and with its new proposals, von Rad (1901–71) inaugurated a new epoch in the study of Old Testament theology. He argued against any organization of Old Testament theology along the lines of central concepts, pervasive topics, assumed structures of Israelite thought or world of faith, or systematic theological categories which had been characteristic, in one way or another, of all the theologies of the twentieth century since this was to impose an alien structure on the material. As an alternative, he proposed that "the subject matter which concerns the theologian is . . . not the spiritual and religious world of Israel and the conditions of her soul in general, nor is it her world of faith, all of which can only be reconstructed by means of conclusions drawn from the documents: instead, it is simply Israel's own explicit assertions about Jahweh" (I, p. 105).

A number of basic principles underlie von Rad's attempt to handle Old Testament material simultaneously in both historical and theological fashion. The fundamental principle which he was asserting is that the Old Testament itself must set the agenda for writing a theology not some scheme or ideas imposed from the outside. A second principle for him was the conclusion that the Old Testament is primarily a book of history concerned with the divine acts in history: "The Old Testament writings confine themselves to representing Jahweh's relationship to Israel and the world in one aspect only, namely as a continuing divine activity in history. This implies that in principle Israel's faith is grounded in a theology of history" (I, p. 106; a position already formulated by him in 1943). A third principle affirms that the traditions about Israel's sacred history or God's acts in history were formulated as testimonies or credal confessions which were the products of Israel's thinking about itself and thus were used in differing ways and contexts since "Israel constantly fell back on the old traditions connected with the great saving appointments, and in each specific case she actualised them in a very arbitrary, and often novel, way." Thus the same traditions could be "actualised in a different way at different times and probably also at different places" (II, p. 413). A fourth principle is the recognition that the Old Testament does not contain a single, unified theology:

> The unity of the Old Testament is even more open to question than before, for traditio-historical analysis has disclosed a number of theologies which differ widely both in their conception of the fundamental events of the saving history and in the way they understand the theology of history, the divine action (II, p. 412).

> Unlike the revelation in Christ, the revelation of Jahweh in the Old Testament is divided up over a long series of separate acts of revelation which are very different in content. It seems to be without a centre which determines everything and which could give to the separate acts both an interpretation and their proper theological connexion with one another (I, p. 115).

Fifthly, the relationship and tension between promise and fulfillment provided von Rad with perspectives for viewing the way in which actualization of older traditions functioned in the life of Israel.

If we seek to extract from the bewildering number of these actualisations some characteristic, common, and continuing feature, it is this—in one way or another (the specific tradition determines the way) Israel was always placed in the vacuum between an election made manifest in her history, and which had a definite promise attached to it, and a fulfilment of this promise which was looked for in the future. Each successive generation had the task of understanding itself as Israel in Jahweh's eyes. Israel therefore had many possible ways of understanding her position before Jahweh as an elect nation; for she had different election traditions which she actualised. The common element in all of these was that Israel was poised between promise and fulfilment and that she saw herself as walking along a road which led from a particular promise to a particular fulfilment. . . .

This continual actualisation of the data of the saving history, with its consequence that every generation saw itself anew on the march towards a fulfilment, occupies such a prominent position in the Old Testament that a "Theology of the Old Testament" must accommodate itself to it (II, p. 414).

Finally, since the basic content of the Old Testament is the sacred history or *Heilsgeschichte*, "re-telling remains the most legitimate form of theological discourse on the Old Testament" (I, p. 121). That is, since Israel made its confession in the form of historical statements, the rehearsal of these should form the basic content of Old Testament theology which in its own way becomes a contemporary actualization of the biblical traditions.

Von Rad saw his theology as the product of a "surprising convergence—indeed the mutual intersection—which has come about during the last twenty or thirty years between introductory studies and Biblical theology" (I, p. v). That this was the case is one of the primary reasons for the widespread popularity of his work. The introductory studies which von Rad referred to were centered in German form-critical and traditio-historical work with their more immediate roots ultimately going back to Gunkel. The latter had argued that most of the various traditions of the Old Testament, analyzable into their various genres according to their content, mood, and *Sitz im Leben* (life-situation), originally existed as independent units and then were gradually brought together and shaped to form cycles of larger complexes. Gunkel, however, had little to say about the institutional contexts in which such collection and usage took place—he spoke of scenes around the camp-fires and of professional storytellers. It remained for Albrecht Alt (1883–1956) and Martin Noth (1902–68) to attempt a reconstruction of early Israelite institutional structures in which the tradition-building took place. They emphasized early Israelite tribal structures, centered in the so-called amphictyony, and sacred places and cultic occasions as the contexts in which traditions were used, reformulated, and combined. Von Rad's early work also belonged in this endeavor though he was concerned more with literary than institutional reconstruction.

A second line of research, ultimately going back to Romanticism and especially Johann Gottfried Herder (1744–1803), focused on the issue of how ancient traditions could be contemporized or actualized in later cultures. Also significant in this endeavor were Gunkel and Mowinckel (see Groves, pp. 8–71). The latter was especially concerned with actualization of traditions in cultic contexts. Von Rad's 1938 essay on the form-critical origin and development of the Hexateuch was a major significant contribution to the study of the history of traditions and already contains many of the perspectives found in his theology. In this work he sought to illustrate how the final form of the Hexateuch developed by arguing that its final form was the outgrowth and intricate elaboration of early brief credos or confessional creeds such as those found in Deut. 26:5b–9; 6:20–24; Josh. 24:2b–13. These creeds were comprised of historical traditions focusing on (1) the patriarchs to whom the land was promised, (2) the exodus from Egypt accompanied by manifestations of divine power, and (3) the settlement in the promised land. Von Rad concluded that the absence of any mention of Sinai in these credos suggested that "the canonical redemption story of the exodus and settlement in Canaan on the one hand, and the tradition of Israel's experiences at Sinai on the other, really stand over against each other as two originally independent traditions" (1966, p. 13). Von Rad located these two independent complexes, and their annual actualization, in two early festivals. The first he located in the context of the spring Festival of Weeks originally celebrated at the ancient shrine at Gilgal. The Sinai complex was understood as the cult-legend of the fall Feast of Tabernacles at Shechem. Eventually, these traditions were loosed from the cult, elaborated, combined, and prefaced with the primeval history (Gen. 1—11) to produce the final form of the Hexateuch. Thus von Rad argues that in its shaping and utilization of these traditions, ancient Israel continuously confessed its faith and proclaimed its kerygmatic message.

Von Rad divided his theology into two volumes. The first treats the theology of Israel's historical traditions and the second discusses the theology of Israel's prophetic traditions. In both volumes the central concern is with the historical traditions. The prophets are understood as dialoguing with Israel's sacred traditions and as proclaiming new divine actions which will bring Israel's previous history to an end and inaugurate a new stage. The following lengthy passage is worthy of quoting in full since it provides insight into both von Rad's understanding of Old Testament theology and his approach to the prophets:

> The most accurate test of the starting-point and arrangement of a theology of the Old testament is, however, the phenomenon of prophecy. At what point has it to be dealt with, and in what connexion? If we are resolved on giving a systematic and connected presentation of the religious ideas, then we shall have occasion to speak about prophecy throughout—in dealing with the holiness of Jahweh, the beliefs about creation, the idea of the covenant, etc. But

in so doing would we do justice to its message? We should also, however, do it an injustice if we reserved treatment of it for a special section dealing with Israel's thought about her own and the nations' future. This is not the way to bring the message of the prophets into organic connexion with the religious ideas of Israel. However overpoweringly diverse it may be, it nevertheless has its starting-point in the conviction that Israel's previous history with Jahweh has come to an end, and that he will start something new with her. The prophets seek to convince their contemporaries that for them the hitherto existing saving ordinances have lost their worth, and that, if Israel is to be saved, she must move in faith into a new saving activity of Jahweh, one which is only to come in the future. But this conviction of theirs, that what has existed till now is broken off, places them basically outside the saving history as it had been understood up to then by Israel. The prophets' message had its centre and its bewildering dynamic effect in the fact that it smashed in pieces Israel's existence with God up to the present, and rang up the curtain of history for a new action on his part with her. So prophecy needs separate treatment in a theology of the Old Testament (I, p. 128).

In volume one of the theology, von Rad first provides "A History of Jahwism and of the Sacral Institutions in Israel in Outline" which corresponds to a brief survey of the history of Israelite religion. Following a discussion of methodology, he then analyzes the traditional complexes of the Hexateuch—primeval history, history of the patriarchs, deliverance from Egypt, divine revelation at Sinai, the wandering in the wilderness, the conception of Moses and his office, and the granting of the land of Canaan. The second main portion of the volume analyzes the topic of Israel's anointed (primarily concerned with Davidic issues) and here von Rad focuses on the books of Judges—2 Kings and the work of the Chronicler. Finally, there is a section on "Israel Before Yahweh (Israel's Answer)" which is presented primarily as Israel's response in psalms and wisdom to Yahweh's acts and to its life before Yahweh: "This answer of Israel's . . . shows us how these acts affect Israel, and how Israel on her side accepted and understood this existence in immediacy with Jahweh and in proximity to him, that is, the steps which, in this proximity to Jahweh, she took to justify or to be ashamed of herself, in her own eyes and before Jahweh" (I, pp. 355–56). The second volume provides a discussion of general considerations about prophecy as well as a treatment of most of the prophets primarily in terms of their relationship to the old sacred traditions and of their proclamation of new events to come. A major section on the relationship of the Old Testament to the New—in terms of the latter's re-actualization of the former—concludes the volume.

To criticize such an overpowering work as von Rad's is difficult since it is a work from which one can learn so much. Perhaps simply some general assessments bordering on critique can be the most informing way to summarize this discussion of his work. (1) Von Rad's attempt to utilize a form of *Heilsgeschichte* but without the insistence on the factual historicity of the events in the form they were actually narrated represents a radical break with earlier *Heilsgeschichte* approaches and with the conservative-fundamentalist emphasis. In their approach, which of course raises numerous issues as we shall see, Wright (who seems to us to have been heavily dependent on von Rad's early works) and von Rad represent somewhat similar interests but radically different attitudes as their exchange in the *Expository Times* indicates. Von Rad was willing to remain at the level of the theological significance of a tradition and to elucidate this through literary and exegetical work whereas Wright argued that one must push back behind the text itself through archaeological and historical research to the actual event itself which supposedly lay behind the tradition. Von Rad's conclusion was that

> Wright in his discovery of the historical background leaves the realm of the witness to this history behind him and pushes back to an area which is theologically speechless. . . . in a Biblical-theological respect, the authenticity of these stories can never be said to be based on any eventual enlightenment which can be attained from this direction. At the most certain details could become clearer (*ExpTim* 72, p. 215).

(2) In some respects von Rad utilizes aspects of methodological approaches to Old Testament traditions but with a loss of some of their substantial underpinning. Gunkel, for example, was highly cognizant of the sociological dimensions of the biblical traditions and the role of these in their interpretation. Mowinckel relied upon cultic-mythical dimensions in his approach which took the functional re-actualization of mythic drama seriously. Both of these factors are missing from von Rad who utilizes aspects of their methods but who appears to have been greatly influenced by a Barthian-homiletical approach to traditions and the Bible. To say that von Rad represents the wedding of the perspectives of Gunkel and Mowinckel with a Barthian approach to Scripture may be saying too much but it seems to reflect the situation (so also Gerstenberger, pp. 184–88). It is uncertain how influential Barth was on von Rad but their early careers show many similarities in their combating of Nazi propaganda (see Crenshaw, pp. 15–21, 26–41).

(3) Von Rad's insistence that Old Testament theology is merely the re-telling or rehearsal of Israel's self-interpretations would, of course, be naive if it were true of his approach. Such a position reminds one of certain Barthian simplisticisms. Von Rad, of course, interpreted the traditions in terms of the views of modern scholarship, especially in terms of traditio-historical perspectives. To understand and explicate Deuteronomy, for example, in light of its being a re-interpretation of Israel's traditions in the seventh century is, of course, not to re-tell the story the way ancient Israel told it since the ancients assigned the book to the era of Moses not Josiah.

(4) His assessment of the importance and the role of Israel's historical traditions in its own life looks much like theological romanticism. Surely

such traditions were not as prominent and all important in Israelite life as von Rad suggests. In his interpretation of the prophets in this manner, he almost completely abandons any concern for their personhood and individuality in thought and experience.

(5) His overemphasis on history and the Old Testament as a book of history led to his underplaying of the importance of creation thought in the Old Testament (a judgment not applicable to Mowinckel although Mowinckel never produced an Old Testament theology). In addition, von Rad, although he made penetrating and revolutionary comments on Old Testament wisdom, had, like Wright, almost to consider it "non-biblical." His later book on wisdom, however, rectified the position taken in his theology.

(6) Finally, in spite of his creative combination of theological and historical interests, von Rad did not completely avoid the sort of systematized theological discussions which he criticized so strongly in persons like Eichrodt (who thought von Rad had only written a history of Israelite religion rather than an Old Testament theology). Von Rad's discussions of such matters as Hebrew thought about time and the righteousness of Yahweh illustrate that he too broke with his own program and often tilted toward the systematic and the conceptual modes of organization and discourse (see Barr's review, pp. 143–44).

THE RE-EVALUATION OF FEATURES OF THE BIBLICAL THEOLOGY MOVEMENT

Bertil **Albrektson**, *History and the Gods: An Essay on the Idea of Historical Events as Divine Manifestations in the Ancient Near East and in Israel* (Lund: C. W. K. Gleerup, 1967); James **Barr**, "Revelation Through History in the Old Testament and in Modern Theology," *Int* 17(1963)193–205; *idem, Old and New in Interpretation: A Study of the Two Testaments* (London/New York: SCM Press/Harper and Row, 1966); *idem,* "Old Testament Scholarship in the 1960s," *CQ* 2(1969–70)201–6; *idem, The Semantics of Biblical Language* (London: Oxford University Press, 1961); *idem,* "Biblical Theology," *IDBSup*, pp. 104–11; *idem,* "Revelation in History," *IDBSup*, pp. 746–49; *idem,* "Story and History in Biblical Theology," *JR* 56(1976)1–17 = *Explorations in Theology 7* (London: SCM Press, 1980)1–17 = *The Scope and Authority of the Bible* (Philadelphia: Westminster Press, 1980)1–17; John **Bowden**, *What About the Old Testament?* (London: SCM Press, 1969); James R. **Branton**, "Our Present Situation in Biblical Theology," *RelLife* 26(1956–57)5–18; Walter **Brueggemann**, *In Man We Trust: The Neglected Side of Biblical Faith* (Atlanta: John Knox Press, 1972); Brevard **Childs**, *Biblical Theology in Crisis* (Philadelphia: Westminster Press, 1970); J. J. **Finkelstein**, "The Bible, Archaeology, and History: Have the Excavations Corroborated Scripture?" *Commentary* 28(1959)341–49; Anton **Fridrichsen** et al., *The Root of the Vine: Essays in Biblical Theology* (Westminster/ New York: Dacre Press/Philosophical Library, 1953); Hartmut **Gese**, "Geschichtliches Denken im Alten Orient und im Alten Testament," *ZTK* 55(1958)127–45 = "The Idea of History in the Ancient Near East and the Old Testament," *JTC* 1(1965)49–

64; Langdon **Gilkey**, "Cosmology, Ontology and the Travail of Biblical Language," *JR* 41(1961)194–205; *idem, Naming the Whirlwind: The Renewal of God-Language* (Indianapolis: Bobbs-Merrill Company, 1969)73–106; Franz **Hesse**, "Die Erfor-schung der Geschichte als theologische Aufgabe," *KD* 4(1958)1–19; *idem*, "Keryg-ma oder geschichtliche Wirklichkeit?" *ZTK* 57(1960)17–26; William A. **Irwin**," "The Study of Israel's Religion," *VT* 7(1957)113–26; *idem*, "A Still Small Voice . . . Said, What Are You Doing Here?" *JBL* 78(1959)1–12; David H. **Kelsey**, *The Uses of Scripture in Recent Theology* (Philadelphia/London: Fortress Press/SCM Press, 1975); Winston L. **King**, "Some Ambiguities in Biblical Theology," *RelLife* 27(1957–58)95–104; Robert H. **Pfeiffer**, "Fact and Faith in Biblical History," *JBL* 70(1951)1–14; H. D. **Preuss**, "Erwägungen zum theologischen Ort alttestamentlicher Weisheits Literatur," *EvTh* 30(1970)393–417; John F. **Priest**, "Where Is Wisdom to Be Placed?" *JBR* 31(1963)275–82; Morton S. **Smith**, "The Common Theology of the Ancient Near East," *JBL* 71(1952)135–47; *idem*, "The Present State of Old Testament Stud-ies," *JBL* 88(1969)19–35; Krister **Stendahl**, "Biblical Theology, Contemporary," *IDB* 1(1962)418–32.

Earlier, we noted some of the features which characterized most ap-proaches to biblical theology in the post-World War II period (see above, pp. 213–18). Among these were emphases on the unity of the Bible, the unique-ness of the biblical faith, history as the locus of God's revelation, the distinc-tive quality of Hebraic thought, the focus on word studies, and so forth. Many of these emphases and works which stressed such features came under increasing criticism with the passage of time (for surveys of the critique, see especially Childs, pp. 61–87, and Barr, *IDBSup*).

Even in the 1940s and early 1950s, when biblical theology was at its apogee and there was widespread optimism throughout the Christian world that biblical theology was the wave of the future with regard both to theolog-ical exposition itself and to the hoped-for healing of divisions within the church, the movement already had come under attack. Various scholars charged that the new movement was characterized by a mood of the irrational, a desire to revert to a pre-critical or confessional approach to the Bible, and a surrender of the academic historical-critical approach to biblical studies (see Childs, pp. 25–26). With the passage of time the attacks became more pointed although they initially made little impact. Here we can only note some of such early criticisms. In 1952 Morton Smith sought to show that biblical faith rather than being radically distinctive from actually had much in common with general Near Eastern religion. A collection of articles by several Swed-ish scholars called for a descriptive rather than a normative task for biblical theology (see Fridrichsen). This descriptive task of biblical theology—to de-scribe "what it meant" rather than "what it means"—was echoed by Stendahl in his later, highly influential article in the *Interpreter's Dictionary of the Bible*. Irwin attacked the perspectives of the movement as these had found expression in statements of the WCC, particularly, the argument that "every biblical interpretation has to set out from Jesus Christ." He described the movement as "too often of a less rigorous thinking than the scholarship of a generation ago. With a few pious platitudes it is prone to skim lightly over serious and basic issues which the former age would have insisted must first of all be seriously faced" (1957, p. 116). He characterized it as "mingling of homiletics with hermeneutics" (p. 122) which frequently "arrives only at superficiality when attempting edification, and in the interest of relevance exhumes old errors" (1959, p. 5).

The emphasis on revelation through history received the severest blows. This theme which was basic to much of the approach came to fullest expression in the early writings of von Rad and Wright. The attack on this position centered on several features.

(1) An uneasiness was felt with this approach because of its inability to integrate the wisdom literature (Proverbs, Job, Ecclesiastes, and many of the Psalms) into what was considered the mainstream of Old Testament faith (see Preuss for a negative approach to wisdom's place in Old Testament theology and Brueggemann for a positive approach). It was argued that if the primary focus of the Old Testament is on the revelation of God through historical events, then the wisdom literature which is little if at all concerned with history—either in its secular or sacred form—sits like an alien block of material in the Bible. In *God Who Acts*, Wright wrote:

> It is the wisdom literature which offers the chief difficulty because it does not fit into the type of faith exhibited in the historical and prophetic literature. In it there is no explicit reference to or development of the doctrine of history, election, or covenant (p. 103).

Proponents of revelation through history were forced to recognize that excluding wisdom, or seeing it as Israel's response to Yahweh's acts in history (so von Rad in his *Theology*), meant that a major area of the Old Testament could not be easily fitted into such a scheme. Surely no adequate theology could do justice to the Old Testament unless this material could be made an integral part of the picture (see Priest).

(2) Theologians who spoke of "God acting in history" were accused of equivocation on the issue. Conservatives had long pointed out that neo-orthodox theology had evaded the question of the real historicity of God's intervention in history and had created a smokescreen by using terminology taken over from the realism of the biblical narratives which their descriptions of events in naturalistic categories denied. So long as only conservatives were making this point, it was given little attention. In 1961 Gilkey, from a liberal theological position, made a devastating analysis of speech about God's acts in history as this was used in biblical theology. He accused biblical theology of being "half liberal and modern, on the one hand, and half biblical and orthodox, on the other, i.e., its world view or cosmology is modern, while its

theological language is biblical and orthodox" (p. 194). By this, he meant that such scholars as Wright spoke about God acting and speaking in history, especially in the exodus event, as if they accepted a world view which allowed for direct intervention of God in history in miraculous form, but in reality when they described these events they did so in terms of a modern world view in which events are understood within a natural and causal space-time continuum. That is, the events are considered as explicable in normal scientific terms and the biblical depiction is emptied of its claims about the divine. Thus the interpreter, according to Gilkey, is actually forced to speak about God's acts in meaningless, abstract language or else to see them as part of a faith-response to or faith-construct of an event occurring according to normally accepted world processes. The action of God in special events is taken, therefore, as merely a subjectively produced religious belief and not an objective occurrence.

(3) In his 1962 inaugural lecture at Princeton Theological Seminary, Barr challenged "the assertion that 'history' is the absolutely supreme milieu of God's revelation" (1963, p. 193). He argued that the biblical materials themselves do not presuppose what the revelation through history position assumes. That is, the texts frequently assign as much or more significance to the self-declaration, the speaking, of God than to the acts of God. In addition, he argued that the biblical narrative is more story than history. Elsewhere, he has clarified this point by emphasizing that the Old Testament narrative material is "not generated out of an antecedent 'history', but is rather a cumulative story into which later events are fitted" (1976, p. 108). Thus the narrative is more of a cumulative tradition in which communication takes place rather than an historical account which is concerned to present revelation as the consequence of God's acts in events or a series of events. In addition, the Old Testament speaks of Yahweh's actions without relating these to historical events.

> In (the wisdom literature), while it is known that God may and does act in human affairs, there is no impression that any particular series of historical acts are the sole or even the central foundation for all knowledge of him. On the contrary, it seems rather that God is knowable or known without appeal to such a source of revelation. Something analogous can be said of many materials which have a cultic setting, mainly in the Psalms (Barr, 1966, pp. 72–73).

(4) If, as Wright and others argued, revelation is the product of inferences drawn from events, then the idea that such inferences constituted revelation was called into question. Kelsey posed and critiqued this issue in the following way:

> Wright argues that in the biblical view God reveals who he is and what he is like in acts in history. He glosses this by saying that man's understanding of

God is *inferred* from historical events. That seems an odd use of "reveal." When Sherlock Holmes infers from the details of a skillfully concealed crime what the nature of its agent was, one hardly says that the culprit "revealed" himself by committing the criminal act. Surely one says rather that Holmes "discovered" him or "found him out." Yet it seems odd to say that ancient Israelites "discovered" God or "found him out" in the things he did to the citizens of Ai, or to citizens of Jerusalem for that matter (p. 38).

(5) Especially in American scholarship, the emphasis on God's revelation in history was closely associated with archaeological research which, certainly in the popular mind, was assumed to be supportive of the historicity of biblical events and the trustworthiness of biblical traditions and thus of the "revelatory" character of such events. Voices such as Finkelstein, however, began to challenge the argument that archaeology corroborated the Bible and to insist that archaeology was a neutral discipline whose primary task was the illumination of the cultural and general historical background of the biblical narratives rather than a discipline whose purpose was to support the facticity of specific events. Excavations at numerous places, but especially at the ancient sites of Jericho and Ai, produced evidence that not only did not corroborate Old Testament narratives but also in fact called into question the historicity of the events reported about these places and thus undercut the conclusion that "external evidence" derived from archaeological research and cultural studies verified the "internal evidence" of the Bible.

(6) The emphasis on revelation through history and the emphasis on salvation history tended to exacerbate the tension between the history of Israel as reported in the Old Testament and the history of Israel as reconstructed through historical-critical scholarship. Above all, it was German scholarship and especially von Rad's theology which forced consideration of this phenomenon. (As a rule the issue was more acute in German scholarship, where the standard history of Israel by Martin Noth differed considerably from the biblical account, than in English-language scholarship, where the widely used history by John Bright tended to follow the biblical narratives more closely.) Von Rad had admitted the differences between these two "histories" of Israel and sought not to overplay the distinction between the two while arguing that Old Testament theology has to be based on the kerygmatic or confessional version of the history:

> Historical investigation [in historical-critical studies] searches for a critically assured minimum—the kerygmatic picture tends towards a theological maximum. The fact that these two views of Israel's history are so divergent is one of the most serious burdens imposed today upon Biblical scholarship. No doubt historical investigation has a great deal that is true to say about the growth of this picture of the history which the faith of Israel painted: but the phenomenon of the faith, which speaks now of salvation, now of judgment, is beyond its power to explain.

> It would not do, however, simply to explain the one picture as historical and the other as unhistorical. The kerygmatic picture too (and this even at the points where it diverges so widely from our historical picture) is founded in the actual history and has not been invented (I, p. 108).

Various scholars, but especially Hesse, opposed von Rad's position and argued that Old Testament theology must be based on the actual history as reconstructed by critical scholarship.

(7) A subordinate postulate to revelation in history was the argument that other and contemporary nations lacked any great interest in history and thus did not view history as the arena of divine activity and revelation. Sometimes this was presented in terms of a contrast between the assumed cyclical focus of Greek thought and the linear interests of Hebrew thought and, at other times, as distinctively Israelite perspective that set the biblical materials apart from other Near Eastern literature and thought whose orientation was supposedly toward nature rather than history.

As early as 1958 Gese pointed out that movements toward a historical viewpoint and the writing of history were already present in the Near East, especially among the Hittites, prior to the rise of Israel. A major blow to the supposed exclusive character of Israel's conception of divine action in history was the work of Albrektson who demonstrated that the belief that gods acted in history was a widespread Near Eastern tenet: "The Old Testament idea of historical events as divine revelation must be counted among the similarities, not among the distinctive traits: it is part of the common theology of the ancient Near East" (p. 114).

A second feature of biblical theology, in addition to revelation in history, which was challenged was the emphasis on the unity of the Bible. Earlier biblical scholarship, having divided biblical materials into sources, layers of tradition, original components, and later redactions, had seen the materials as products of different writers, different interests, and different periods, and thus tended to stress the diversity of biblical perspectives. This tendency had been one of the elements reacted against so negatively by biblical theologians who swung the pendulum far in the other direction. Even people like Wright who superimposed a God-who-acts theology across most of the Bible was incapable of integrating the wisdom literature into such a scheme. One of the strongest blows against the unity of the Old Testament was leveled by von Rad who suggested that the Old Testament contains not just one but a large number of theologies which differ considerably from one another. As we shall see in a later section efforts to find a unity or unifying center to the Old Testament have not been very successful.

Also coming under attack in the 1960s was the widespread practice of constructing theology on the basis of word studies, etymologies, and linguistic arguments (for the practice, see above, pp. 214–15, 229–31). Many of the products of this approach were incorporated in bible dictionaries and wordbooks such as Kittel's *Theological Dictionary of the New Testament*. In his book on semantics (1961) and subsequent works, Barr criticized the widespread misuse of linguistic evidence which he argued was based on poor or no linguistic theory. Kelsey has since criticized this approach dubbing it the "biblical concept theology" (pp. 24–30).

In summary, many factors operative in biblical theology in the decade and a half following the second World War were seriously challenged and contested during the 1960s. Many weaknesses and inconsistencies in the movement were exposed but the critiques were not necessarily so much an attack on biblical theology per se as an attack on certain ways of going about the task (see Barr, *IDBSup*, p. 107 where he says his critique "was not an attack on biblical theology in itself"). In addition, the challenge or "crisis" was one paralleled in systematic theology as well and thus was part of a much broader crisis extending throughout the theological disciplines (see Gilkey, 1969).

THE RECENT QUEST FOR
AN ADEQUATE THEOLOGY

Walter **Brueggemann**, "A Convergence in Recent Old Testament Theologies," *JSOT* 18(1980)2–18; Ronald E. **Clements**, *Old Testament Theology: A Fresh Approach* (London/Atlanta: Marshall, Morgan & Scott/John Knox Press, 1978); Alfons **Deissler**, *Die Grundbotschaft des Alten Testaments. Ein theologischer Durchblick* (Freiburg/Basil/Wien: Herder, 1972); William **Dyrness**, *Themes in Old Testament Theology* (Leicester/Downers Grove: InterVarsity Press, 1979); Georg **Fohrer**, *Theologische Grundstrukturen des Alten Testaments* (Berlin: Walter de Gruyter, 1972); Maximiliano **García Cordero**, *Teología de la Biblia: vol. 1, Antiguo Testamento* (Madrid: Editorial Católica, 1970); Paul **Hanson**, *Dynamic Transcendence: The Correlation of Confessional Heritage and Contemporary Experience in a Biblical Model of Divine Activity* (Philadelphia: Fortress Press, 1978); Gerhard F. **Hasel**, "A Decade of Old Testament Theology: Retrospect and Prospect," *ZAW* 93(1981)165–83; David F. **Hinson**, *Theology of the Old Testament* (London: SPCK, 1976); Walter C. **Kaiser**, Jr., *Toward an Old Testament Theology* (Grand Rapids: Zondervan Publishing House, 1978); Chester K. **Lehman**, *Biblical Theology: vol. 1, Old Testament* (Scottsdale, PA: Herald Press, 1971); John L. **McKenzie**, *A Theology of the Old Testament* (Garden City: Doubleday & Company, 1974); Samuel **Terrien**, *The Elusive Presence: Toward a New Biblical Theology* (San Francisco: Harper & Row, 1978); idem, "The Play of Wisdom: Turning Point in Biblical Theology," *HBT* 3(1981)125–53; Claus **Westermann**, *Theologie des Alten Testaments in Grundzugen* (Göttingen: Vandenhoeck & Ruprecht, 1978) = *Elements of Old Testament Theology* (Atlanta: John Knox Press, 1982); Walther **Zimmerli**, *Grundriss der alttestamentlichen Theologie* (Stuttgart: W. Kohlhammer Verlag, 1972 = *Old Testament Theology in Outline* (Atlanta/Edinburgh: John Knox Press/T. & T. Clark, 1978).

After the prodigious production of Old Testament theologies in the decade of the 1950s and particularly the appearance of von Rad's work, the following decade was a period of introspection and critical analysis. Only three theologies made an appearance: the restatement of the conservative position by Payne (1962; see above pp. 232–33), the modest volume by Schofield (1964) intended for a popular readership; and Wright's volume (1969) which set out to offer a restatement of his views but in fact actually constituted a reformulation stressing the concept of the covenant and thus a position more in line with the position of Eichrodt than that of von Rad.

The production of new theologies began again in the 1970s and in fact this decade witnessed the appearance of over a dozen such works—a number unprecedented in any ten-year period since the development of Old Testament theology as an independent discipline. The number of such works, however, does not in itself either suggest substantial advancement in the discipline or imply that major methodological problems have been overcome.

In this section we shall examine some of the theologies produced during this decade but will treat them in terms of patterns in the approaches in a manner similar to that found in the work of Hasel. Such an examination of the material can illustrate both the diversity of approaches which have been used in organizing and presenting the material as well as some of the methodological problems involved.

(1) In many works which we have surveyed, we have noted the use of a dogmatic scheme borrowed from Christian dogmatics or systematic theology, a scheme which organizes the material according to the broad topics of Theology, Anthropology, and Soteriology (God, Man, and Salvation). This pattern of following the outline of theology has, of course, been used since the early days of biblical theology during the period of Protestant Scholasticism though, of course, in the earlier days the dogmatic topics were far more detailed (see above, pp. 6, 16–17). The work by the Spanish Catholic scholar García Cordero falls into this scheme and thus fits the pattern which we have seen in the works of other Catholics, for example, Heinisch and van Imschoot (see above, pp. 189–91, 227–29). García Cordero provides some variety on the older scheme dividing his work into the topics of (a) God, (b) Divine Manifestations, (c) Angelic Spirits, and (d) Anthropology which comprise part one. The second section is a discussion of hope while part three discusses religious and moral obligations to God and human beings, and the final section concerns the fall and rehabilitation of humanity. In Catholicism one can obviously see the continuing influence of the church's dogmatic teachings influencing the method of presentation. That such a pattern, whose simplicity is inviting and whose structure seems to promise an immediate relationship to and usability by systematic theologians, is not limited to Catholic scholars can be seen in the study guide by Hinson who treats the

material around the following topics: God, Other Spiritual Beings, Man, The Fall, Salvation, New Life, The Ultimate Goal, and The Old Testament in the New Testament. The work of Dyrness although called "Themes in Old Testament Theology" also follows a modified systematic theology form as can be seen in his outline—the self-revelation of God, the nature of God, creation and providence, man and woman, sin, the covenant, the law, worship, piety, ethics, wisdom, the spirit of God, prophecy, and the hope of Israel.

Such an approach to the material has been criticized frequently throughout the twentieth century, most notably by Eichrodt and von Rad. More recently, Terrien has written the following of such a method:

> It is now recognized that such attempts, inherited in part from Platonic conceptual thinking and Aristotelian logic, were bound to translate the *sui generis* thrust of biblical faith into the alien idiom of didactic exposition (p. 34).

Such a verdict seems overly harsh. As we noted in our treatment of biblical theology in Protestant Scholasticism (see above, pp. 15–19), the organizational categories in such an approach are certainly dominated by theological interests imposed from outside the biblical thought world itself. Nonetheless, the organization of the material along such lines can contribute to the integration of biblical perspectives into both the confessional life of religious communities and the more academic pursuit of theology proper and it does so in categories and structures that are certainly at home in both of these areas. Those who treat the material from such a dogmatic-didactic perspective could certainly argue that their presentations have a structural relevance to the way in which contemporary religious thought, especially Christian thought, has chosen to structure its discourse and, at the same time, it addresses and brings to bear biblical perspectives on universal concerns. Further, proponents of such an approach could argue that since the Bible itself proposes no particular approach for organizing its own theological perspectives, then any systematization or scheme is alien to the Bible itself and thus the employment of a scheme other than that of systematic theology introduces further complications by presenting the material in a form alien to contemporary theological perspectives.

(2) Since the early nineteenth century which saw the beginning dominance of historical issues in biblical studies, the impact of developmental schemes or models based on historical progression has been characteristic of many treatments of Old Testament religion and theology. Such schemes have also drawn upon *heilsgeschichtliche* perspectives in which the Bible is viewed as the record of the gradual fulfillment of the divine purpose in history finding its culmination in the Christ-event. In addition, such an approach would seem to have roots in at least the pentateuchal and prophetical books of the Old Testament.

This sort of progressive-historical approach characterizes the work of Lehman who acknowledges his debt to the thought and approaches of Vos, Eichrodt, and Oehler (pp. 7–8, 26–27, 35–38). Lehman's work, like that of García Cordero, is a biblical theology covering both testaments. For him, biblical theology is "determined in the main by the principle of historic progression" (p. 38). The progressive revelation of God is then seen manifesting itself in a continuous unfolding in the various covenants throughout history beginning with that of Noah. While Lehman works with this scheme he also employs other schematic divisions. He attempts to structure the material along the lines of the Hebrew canon—Pentateuch, Prophets, and Hagiographa (or Writings). In places, the theology of individual biblical books is treated and the thought of each outlined around certain topics such as God, election, covenant, and so forth. In places this division interrupts the canonical division. For example, Isaiah 40—66 is treated as a separate work although this is clearly not the case in the present canonical form of the book of Isaiah. Here Lehman is dependent upon historical considerations that do not follow upon canonical conclusions. In addition, utilization of a canonical scheme breaks with the effort to follow out the progressive revelation approach unless one assumes that the canon has been structured on historical principles.

The focus of the progressive-historical approach to Old Testament theology has some attractive features about it. First of all, it does give the impression of working within and out of a canonical structure especially in so far as the first two parts of the canon are concerned. The Pentateuch does give the impression of being structured around a series of covenants culminating in the Mosaic period. The second part of the canon—the prophets—does deal with how the Mosaic covenant was implemented in the history of Israel in the land and presents as centrally important the additional covenant of God with David. The second part of the prophets—the classical prophets per se—is oriented toward the future and concerned with the coming situation under the new conditions of God's future activity. Problems with the progressive-historical approach are (a) the fact that the third part of the canon is difficult if not impossible to fit within such a scheme and (b) the fact that historical-critical research has called into question whether Israel's faith and the Scriptures originated and originally functioned in the order in which they now appear in the canon. Lehman thus is occasionally forced, as we noted also with von Rad, to depart from the biblical scheme and to interpret on the basis of historical-critical considerations.

(3) A number of scholars have chosen to expound their theologies in terms of a dialectic or polar structures rather than to use a single concept or some overriding principle. Such an approach can be seen in the presentation of Claus Westermann whose work, like that of his former Heidelberg colleague von Rad, is influenced by form-criticism, traditio-historical criticism,

and Barthian theology. One also sees in Westermann a significant interest in structural studies, an interest reflected in many of his earlier works. Westermann sees the basic structure of the Old Testament as "story," thus "the structure of an Old Testament theology must be based on events rather than concepts" (p. 9). Verb structures thus must dominate over noun structures. The dialectic in his discussion can be seen in numerous ways: God speaks and acts; the story narrates God's speaking and acting but also incorporates human response in both word and deed and in praise and confession; the prophets and their works are structured around judgment oracles and their opposites, salvation oracles; and the psalms as part of the human response contain lament and praise. Westermann explicates the dominant dialectic in terms of deliverance/blessing or the dynamic tension between history and creation. The first focuses on the intervention of Yahweh to save and the latter concerns the constant action of Yahweh in what might be called providence. These two poles are discussed in the chapters entitled "The Saving God and History" and "The Blessing God and Creation." This is followed then by a discussion of God's judgment and compassion and finally by a treatment of the diversity of the human response to the polarities of God's actions of salvation and sustaining.

Westermann's work assigns little place to wisdom literature because "wisdom has no place within this basic framework of an Old Testament theology, since it originally and in reality does not have as its object an occurrence between God and man; in its earlier stages wisdom is overwhelmingly secular." Unlike von Rad who saw wisdom as part of the human response, Westermann understands it in terms of creation: "The theological home of wisdom can be found within the context of human creation; the creator gives humanity the ability to understand its world and to become oriented within it" (p. 11).

Another work which utilizes dialectical concerns is the theology by Terrien which takes as its central theme or perspective for both the Old and New Testaments, "the presence of God" which, he says, stands at the center of biblical faith" (for predecessors who stressed this emphasis, see Terrien, 1981, pp. 131–32). The divine presence is elusive; it is a presence that partakes of hiddenness: "To recognize the centrality of the theology of presence and the integral mutuality of cultus and faith in ancient Israel opens up the possibility of a new approach to the study of biblical religion" (1978, p. 4). For Terrien, cultus and presence have dominance over covenant.

> It is the Hebraic theology of presence, not the covenant ceremonial, that constitutes the field of forces which links—across the biblical centuries—the fathers of Israel, the reforming prophets, the priests of Jerusalem, the psalmists of Zion, the Jobian poet, and the bearers of the gospel. The history of

biblical religion hinges upon the growth and transformation of the Hebraic theology of presence (p. 31).

Terrien discusses the theme of the divine presence within the Old Testament in terms of the epiphanic visitations to the patriarchs, the Sinai theophanies, the presence in the temple, the prophetic vision, the psalmody of presence, the play of wisdom, and the final epiphany. The presence in the New Testament is treated under the rubrics "presence as the word" and "the name and the glory." Throughout much of his discussion various polarities can be seen. Most dominant is the ethical/aesthetic but one finds also the polarities of ear/eye, north/south, name/glory, passion/contemplation, etc. (see Brueggemann, p. 5). The following quotation provides in a nutshell a taste of his explication of the material:

> The Yahweh purists of North Israel, followed by the great prophets from Amos to Jeremiah and by the Deuteronomists, stressed the theologoumenon of presence through the hearing of the name, as shown by the analysis of this particular cluster of traditions concerning the Mosaic theophanies, the tent of meeting and the temple. Judah, on the contrary, from the Yahwist narrators to the Jerusalem priests and Ezekiel with his school, emphasized the theologoumenon of presence through the seeing of the glory, as shown by the analysis of this particular cluster of traditions concerning the Mosaic theophanies, the ark and, again, the temple.
>
> The theologoumenon of presence through hearing ascribes a *sine qua non* significance to obedience, and therefore to ethical behavior and a passion for social justice. The theologoumenon of presence through seeing concentrates its concern upon ritual acts of communion, expiation sacrifices, sacramental meals and para-mystical contemplation. It stresses the correct cult more than social morality. Influenced in part by the Zion myth, postexilic Judaism rebuilt the temple and returned to Jerusalem, but a great many Jews chose to reside in foreign lands, although they maintained their loyalty to the faith of their fathers. The persistence of Diaspora communities besides the temple congregation in Jerusalem reflects conflicting theologies.
>
> The first of these theologies implies a mode of divine presence which is independent from the myth of space, the *hagios topos*. It democratizes a prophetic sense of communion with Yahweh which raises the election of Israel to a universal responsibility. It also maintains the conditionality, hence the historical relativity, of the Mosaic covenant. The second of these theologies implies a mode of divine presence which is indissolubly dependent upon temple ideology and ritual. It has not succeeded, in spite of the prophetic notion of time and the rise of apocalyptic, in overcoming the myth of the *omphalos* [the navel or center of the world] which Judah inherited through the Canaanites from the Northwest Semitic fertility cults. It tended to view the election of Israel in terms of a Davidic, eternal, and therefore mythical, covenant (1981, p. 132).

Of all the recent theologies, Terrien's provides one of the fullest integrations of wisdom into his discussion. For him, the figure of wisdom, especially wisdom at play, provides the key for mediating the unresolved tension between Torah and Prophets: "Between the Mosaic theophany [in the Torah] and the final epiphany [in the Prophets and apocalyptic], the God of Israel does not manifest himself in history. Through wisdom, however, the *Deus absconditus* still remains the *Deus praesens*" (1981, p. 137). Terrien argues that the major dialectics are brought together and overcome in wisdom: "The figure of personified Wisdom brings together the theologoumenon of the name, with its response of the ear, and the theologoumenon of the glory, with its response of the eye" (1978, p. 473). Finally, wisdom is seen as the key for moving from the Old to the New Testament and as the means for producing a coalescence of the dialectic between masculine and feminine:

> The importance of the theme of wisdom as a major factor in the birth of the theological thinking of the early church brings to sharp focus the need to re-evaluate the masculine aspect of christology and to affirm a new equilibrium predicated upon the masculine-feminine qualities of the *Sophia-Logos* complex (1981, pp. 140–41).

> In their attempts to interpret the person of Jesus of Nazareth, the early Christians "saw" in him Sophia, Logos, and Nomos incarnate (John 1:14). . . . As Sophia and Logos, the figure of Jesus combined for the primitive church the masculine and feminine elements of the human understanding of the Godhead, without allowing for the alien mythology of an androgynous deity (1978, p. 473).

Another work, although not a full-blown theology, which sets out a series of dialectical relationships or perspectives is the work by Hanson. A number of dialectics are noted or hinted at in his work: cosmic/teleological (or eschatological), synchronic/diachronic, particularity of events/cosmic providence, confessional heritage/subsequent appropriation, tradition/experience, consolidation/creativity, visionary/pragmatic, hierocratic leaders/disenfranchised. All of these are posed more as probes than explored in depth and are obviously ultimately pointing to ways in which Scripture may be appropriated in the present.

A final work which may be seen as posing a dialectical way of looking at the Old Testament is the work by Clements. One of the main concerns of this work, which is more of a prolegomenon than a full-blown treatment of Old Testament theology, is its interest in how different understandings of the Old Testament have resulted from Jewish and Christian readings of the material. Clements argues that an Old Testament theology should serve both Judaism and Christianity and provide a platform for conversation.

> In the interests of a better mutual understanding, and of a dialogue which is more than merely an entrenched polemic, there are very good reasons why Christians and Jews should study the Old Testament together, and should seek to understand how each has drawn from the older faith and writings of ancient Israel. If an Old Testament theology is to be justified as a modern theological

discipline, and is to continue to have a place in the theological curriculum of
colleges and universities, it must surely be on the grounds that it can provide
a place of useful theological encounter between Jewish and Christian faith. In
this each should have the opportunity to view its intellectual convictions in the
light of the distinctive ancient religion from which they both sprang, and with
a reference to the sacred literature which they both continue to use liturgically
(p. 10).

Although Clements argues that "it is the nature and being of God himself which establishes a unity in the Old Testament" (p. 23) and then explicates the theme of the God of Israel (pp. 53–78) and its consequent counterpart,
the People of God (pp. 79–103), these are not the primary focus of his work.
His focus is on the Old Testament as both law and promise and how the
material has been read by the two manifestations of the people of God (Judaism and Christianity) in these two diverse ways, both building upon interests inherent in the work itself.

> . . . the early Christian claim that the whole Old Testament is a book of pro-
> phetic promise cannot be regarded as something imposed on the literature from
> outside. Rather it reflects an understanding which exists within the Old Testa-
> ment canon itself. We find, therefore, that the Old Testament is presented to
> us with two major themes governing its form and establishing a basis of under-
> standing from which all its writings are to be interpreted. It is a book of *tôrâh*—
> of the 'law' of the covenant between God and Israel. Yet it is also a book of
> promise, for it recognises the tensions that have arisen within this covenant
> relationship and the fact that Israel stands poised between the election of God,
> with all the promises that this entails of land, national life, and the task of
> bringing blessing to the nations, and its fulfilment. The law itself is both a gift
> and a goal. While we can see that historically the theme of 'law' belongs
> primarily to the Pentateuch and that of 'promise' to the Prophets, in practice
> all parts of the literature could be interpreted from the perspective of both
> themes. However, their mutual interrelationships, and the questions of priority
> between them, do not appear with any rigid fixity. In their own ways, both
> Judaism and Christianity saw the relationships differently as they built upon
> the Old Testament and established their own priorities in interpreting its de-
> mands upon the continuing 'Israel of God' (pp. 153–54).

The treatment of the Old Testament material in terms of the dialectical
relationship of various themes and emphases represents an attempt both to
overcome the current stalemate in methodology and to come to grips with
the diversity within the Old Testament. To this extent, the approach moves
away from trying to locate a single perspective or concept for elucidating the
theology, a problem to which we shall return in a later section.

(4) The desire to locate a single concept which runs throughout the
material and could be used like Eichrodt's emphasis on the covenant in order
to present a cross-section of the entire Old Testament is still held as a goal
by some interpreters. Kaiser locates this in the theme of "promise" which is
understood broadly enough to include the idea of blessing as well: "Scripture

presents its own key of organization. The OT does possess its own canonical inner unity which binds together the various emphases and longitudinal themes. This is not a hidden inner unity. It lies open and ready for all: The Promise of God" (p. 69). Kaiser traces this theme of the promise throughout eleven different periods beginning with the pre-patriarchal period (Gen. 3:15) and extending into post-exilic prophecy. He concludes that the biblical writers themselves in the various periods made "connections between the various blocks of materials and sections of Israel's history. Often the linkage was made in a critical speech, pronouncement, or in a repeated refrain . . . with familiar reference to the repeated blessing and promise of a seed, a land, a world-wide blessing, a rest, a king, a dynasty, and a God dwelling with His people" (p. 69). Such an effort to find a longitudinal concept that cuts through all facets of the Old Testament always tends to encounter difficulties, and Kaiser is forced to conclude that "all mere historigraphic, cultic, institutional, or archaeological studies ought to be relegated to other (?) parts of the body of theology" (p. 15), and such matters as law and wisdom are only forcibly related to promise.

(5) Many interpreters opt for selecting various topics or themes without trying to employ these in any connected fashion. Fohrer, for example, works with a dual concept or two focal points in an ellipse, namely, the rule of God and the communion between God and humanity which he calls "the unity in the variety" (chapter 4). He also focuses on various forms of existence found in the Old Testament—magic, cultic, legal, national-religious, and prophetic—and argues that only the latter combines believing submission and obedient service (p. 94) while the others are judged to be based on human efforts to build and maintain communion with God. Fohrer is not only concerned with a descriptive account of Old Testament theology but also with its application to modern life and this explains some of his emphases and judgments.

McKenzie's work, the first Catholic volume to break with the traditional systematic theology outline, has set out to structure a theology around the "ways Israel, according to its literary records, experienced Yahweh" (p. 32). On this basis, McKenzie focuses on the cult, revelation through authentic spokespersons of Yahweh, history, nature, wisdom, institutions, and the future of Israel although he thought the last not to be a real topic of Old Testament theology (see his summary, pp. 32–35). For McKenzie, the primary principle for the selection of topics is the amount of coverage they receive in the text and in the totality of the experience of Israel in addition to their "profundity": "Not every biblical experience of Yahweh, not every fragment of God-talk, is of equal profundity; and it is only the totality of the experience that enables us to make these distinctions" (p. 35).

Zimmerli has focused much of his work and his theology around the name of Yahweh or the self-asserration "I am Yahweh." It is Yahweh, who, for him, is the central focus and which provides the inner and authentic continuity of the Old Testament witness (p. 14). His first chapter thus focuses on the fundamentals, namely, the revelation and description of Yahweh in the Pentateuch. This is then followed by chapters on Yahweh's gifts and commandments. Life before God in light of the gift and the command is then analyzed with wisdom being treated, as in von Rad, as part of the human response to the divine. His final chapter on crisis and hope describes the "ultimate depth that reveals fully the nature of Yahweh" in Yahweh's reaction to the crisis in the life of humanity produced by humanity's failures, a reaction that signals both judgment and salvation. Even here, as in most of his discussion, Zimmerli focuses on the divine. Perhaps no modern interpreter takes *theology* as speech about God so seriously as Zimmerli!

CONTINUING AND CONTEMPORARY ISSUES IN OLD TESTAMENT THEOLOGY

Throughout this survey of the history of Old Testament theology, we have noted the various problems and issues which have been part of the movement. Before looking at some of the specific issues still debated in contemporary research, a general summary of larger issues and concerns seems in order.

(1) First of all, the relationship of biblical theology to dogmatics and systematic theology and thus the authority of the Bible have been continuous concerns. Biblical theology was spawned during the post-Reformation period of Protestant Scholasticism as a discipline subordinate to and in the service of systematic theology and confessional dogmatics. During this period it was widely assumed by Protestants that the Bible was the unique and infallible authority whose contents were made up of doctrinal statements awaiting exposition and organization. Subsequently, the dual influence of Pietism and Rationalism sought to free the Bible and biblical theology from the influence of dogmatics. Many wished to use the simplified biblical faith as a weapon against Scholasticism. Others, like Gabler, hoped that a description of pure biblical theology could provide a compendium of the universally and eternally binding ideas of the Bible which had been revealed to the inspired individual authors of Scripture and which would in turn serve as a basis for unity in the church and also be of service to dogmatic theology. (Gabler's program, in many ways, anticipated the interests of the modern Biblical Theology Movement which in most cases worked with biblical concepts very similar to Gabler's understanding of biblical ideas.)

The rise of historical approaches to the study of the Bible in the nineteenth century introduced a certain relativism in claims about the Bible, revelation, and its authority and tended to force the conclusion that the biblical faith was one stage in the history of religious thought and theology rather than the final and normative expression of such thought and theology. This historical approach reached its zenith in the history-of-religion interpretations at the turn of the century which tended to give up on any significant emphasis on inspiration and revelation and thus normativity. The recovery of biblical theology after the first World War was an attempt to break with this liberal-historical approach with its stress on evolution and relativism. After the second World War—in the so-called Biblical Theology Movement—attempts were made to assert a more normative and authoritative role for the Bible in theology. By this time, however, the commonly accepted view of revelation had shifted from an emphasis on revealed doctrines and propositions made known to inspired individuals to a view of revelation as encounter and thus to a focus on the interaction between God and humanity in history. With the collapse of this emphasis, a more subdued attitude has come to prevail in which the Bible forms again one but not necessarily the dominant source and authority for theology.

(2) A second major issue has been more internal, namely, the question of methodology. How does one go about writing a theology of the Old Testament? Here a wide range of answers has been given. On the one extreme is the purely or primarily historical approach, a product of the nineteenth century, which ended up as the history of Israelite religion. Here biblical thought and practices are discussed within a scheme and in light of conclusions drawn from historical research. On the other extreme, there continues the pattern of utilizing dogmatic schemes within which the biblical material is analyzed or made to fit. Between these extremes, scholars have experimented and continued to work with diverse modifications of the two dominant patterns. Since the the Old Testament itself is so diverse in its contents and provides no clear clue as to how its thought might be structured, it has come to be recognized that no methodological approach can claim to be "the biblical approach" nor necessarily the most satisfactory. In a way, pragmatic standards seem to come into play in judging between various methods—whether an approach seems to handle the material adequately.

(3) Whether Old Testament theology should be written as primarily a descriptive discipline or whether it should also attempt to interpret the material and faith for the contemporary situation has been a recurring issue, although coming to focus primarily in the nineteenth century since prior to that time there was little question in the main about the contemporary "relevance of the Bible." A historical and descriptive approach to the Old Testament argued that the materials must be understood in the light of their original contexts, that is, one must describe as objectively as possible "what it meant." The movement to statements about "what it means," its relevance and rela-

tionship to the contemporary, was supposed to be a secondary move and procedure. Obviously any assumption that one can readily determine "what it meant" has itself serious methodological flaws and is based on the views of the *religionsgeschichtliche Schule* that felt the modern interpreter could, in some fashion, become contemporary with the ancient and sense and feel what the ancients sensed and felt. This may be partially true but it certainly remains an ideal never fully realizable. Again, the assumption that one can say "what it means" in the modern situation is rather naive if taken overly realistically. "What it means" has varied throughout the centuries and varies today depending upon the interpreter, the mode of reading and appropriating the material, and the process by which one clarifies what it means. For many, it means what it says; for others, its meaning must be "translated," "transposed," or "re-described" in modern terms. Even when some such step as this has been taken, "what it meant" may not be transferrable to the modern situation or else may prove to be distasteful in the present as, for example, some of the Old Testament attitudes toward war, slavery, and women.

(4) A constant factor in Old Testament theology has been the relationship of biblical studies to contemporary philosophical, theological, and other currents of thought. As we have tried to point out throughout this work, biblical interpretation has always taken place within a contextual setting in which the issues and positions of the day—philosophical, theological, scientific, ecclesiastical, and cultural—have exerted enormous pressures on the interpretation of the Bible. At the same time, how the Bible has been approached and studied has greatly influenced the shape of the biblical theology produced in such a context. Two examples will suffice. The rationalistic presentation of Old Testament theology in the late eighteenth and nineteenth centuries sought to discover ideas and ideals in the Bible which were congenial to a rationalistic understanding of the world. Thus references to miracles and other divine interventions and manifestations of the divine in history were dismissed as products of an ancient but incorrect understanding of the world. More recently, von Rad acknowledged that his theology and the modern methods of studying the Bible—namely form- and traditio-historical criticism—fit together like hand and glove. Thus his approach to Old Testament theology was possible only because of the confluence of several developments both within biblical studies and within theology in general, that is, the Old Testament understood as the product of the growth of tradition and the emphasis in theology on its kerygmatic or preaching quality.

This mutual relationship between these larger concerns and biblical studies cannot really be overcome even when clearly recognized and attempts are made to be objective. The posture and presuppositions of the interpreter cannot be avoided even if it were desirable. Ebeling's description of the two meanings of biblical theology, namely, (a) a theology which is based on and rooted in the Bible and (b) the theology which the Bible itself contains, is perhaps a helpful distinction to make but in some ways implies a dichotomy and a sharpness of differentiation that is difficult if not impossible to maintain in practice.

At this point, let us turn to the consideration of some more specific and ongoing issues in the contemporary study of Old Testament theology.

The Problem of a Center of the Old Testament

G. **Fohrer**, "The Centre of a Theology of the Old Testament," *NGTT* 7(1966)198–206; *idem*, "Der Mittelpunkt einer Theologie des Alten Testaments," *TZ* 24(1968)161–72; Gerhard **Hasel**, "The Problem of the Center in the Old Testament Theology Debate," *ZAW* 86(1974)65–82; Siegfried **Herrmann**, "Die Konstruktive Restauration. Das Deuteronomium als Mitte biblischer Theologie," *Probleme biblischer Theologie* (ed. by H. W. Wolff; Munich: Chr. Kaiser, 1970)155–70; Günther **Klein**, "'Reich Gottes' als biblischer Zentralbegriff," *EvTh* 30(1970)642–70; D. J. **McCarthy**, "Covenant in the Old Testament: The Present State of Inquiry," *CBQ* 27(1965)217–40; A. D. H. **Mayes**, *Israel in the Period of the Judges* (London: SCM Press, 1974); G. E. **Mendenhall**, *Law and Covenant in Israel and the Ancient East* (Pittsburgh: Biblical Colloquium, 1955); Lothar **Perlitt**, *Bundestheologie im Alten Testaments* (Neukirchen-Vluyn: Neukirchener Verlag, 1971); F. C. **Prussner**, "The Covenant of David and the Problem of Unity in Old Testament Theology," *Transitions in Biblical Scholarship* (ed. by J. C. Rylaarsdam; Chicago: University of Chicago Press, 1968)17–41; H. H. **Rowley**, *The Unity of the Bible* (London: Carey Kingsgate Press, 1953); H. H. **Schmid**, "Ich will euer Gott sein, und ihr sollt mein Volk sein. Die sogenannte Bundesformel und die Frage nach der Mitte des Alten Testaments," *Kirche. Festschrift für Günther Bornkamm* (ed. by D. Lührmann and Georg Strecker; Tübingen: J. C. B. Mohr, 1980)1–26; W. H. **Schmidt**, *Alttestamentlicher Glaube in seiner Geschichte* (Neukirchen-Vluyn: Neukirchener Verlag, 1968, [4]1982) = *The Faith of the Old Testament: A History* (Oxford/Philadelphia: Basil Blackwell/Westminster Press, 1983); *idem*, *Das erste Gebot. Seine Bedeutung für die Alte Testament* (Munich: Chr. Kaiser Verlag, 1970); Rudolf **Smend**, *Die Mitte des Alten Testaments* (Zurich: EVZ-Verlag, 1970); E. **Zenger**, "Die Mitte der alttestamentliche Glaubensgeschichte," *KatBl* 101(1976)3–16; Walther **Zimmerli**, "Zum Problem der 'Mitte des Alten Testaments'," *EvTh* 35(1975)97–118.

The effort to isolate a center, kernel, core, or middle (German *Mitte*) of the Old Testament or a comprehensive, unifying principle according to which a presentation of the material might be organized has long occupied Old Testament theologians. In his monograph on the topic, Smend has surveyed the efforts, beginning in the nineteenth century, to discover a "Grundidee" or "Grundprinzip" in Israelite religion. The diversity of the suggested possibilities is almost legion (for recent suggestions, see Reventlow, 1982, pp. 138–47; Hasel, 1982, pp. 117–43). Proposals include the holiness of God, the lordship of God, God's rulership, the kingdom of God, election, presence, divine sovereignty, promise, or simply the topic "God."

This particular issue was pushed to the forefront by the work of Eichrodt who chose the concept of covenant as an integrating principle for his synthetic approach (see above pp. 179–84; a similar but not as all-encompassing an emphasis on covenant is already found in the seventeenth-century Federalism and in the nineteenth-century works of Kayser and Oehler). For a time a number of factors tended to coalesce in support of Eichrodt's position. (1) First of all, major portions of the Old Testament do seem to be structured around various covenants. As we noted earlier, this is especially the case with the Pentateuch. (2) The reconstruction of early Israelite history by Alt and Noth argued for the existence of a tribal league or amphictyony in which the twelve tribes were joined together with one another and with Yahweh in a covenant relationship. (3) The laws of the Old Testament could be seen as conditional requirements for the maintenance of the covenant. (4) The prophets and their messages also seemed to be understandable as functioning within the theological frame of covenant thought even if the prophets were not actually covenant mediators themselves. (5) When Mendenhall and others pointed to parallels between Old Testament texts and ancient Near Eastern treaties from as early as the thirteenth century BCE, it was assumed that these extra-biblical texts supported an early date for covenant thought in ancient Israel. (A similar but little-noticed comparison of biblical and non-biblical covenants had already been made years earlier in *Geschichte des Bundesgedanken im Alten Testament* [Münster: Aschendorffschen Buchhandlung, 1910] by Paul Karge.) Thus one finds that in the 1950s and 1960s the concept of covenant became widespread in most literature on the Old Testament.

Several factors called into question the dominance of covenant in the life of ancient Israel including challenges to the reconstruction of early Israel as an amphictyony, to the parallels drawn between biblical and non-biblical covenantal texts, to the association of law and prophecy with covenant, and to the early date both for the role of covenant in ancient Israel and for its appearance in biblical literature (see McCarthy, Mayes, and Perlitt). Even the diversity in the biblical use of covenant became a problem. Eichrodt, of course, had built his case primarily on the Mosaic or Sinaitic covenant and tended to downplay the radically different but equally important Davidic covenant (see Prussner). In addition, of course, there was always the question of whether the covenant concept, however understood, was broad enough to include all portions of the Old Testament.

In more recent times dual principles have been suggested as foci for structuring the central content of the Old Testament. Smend argues for a return to the old formula noted by Wellhausen: "Yahweh the God of Israel, Israel the people of Yahweh." The so-called covenant formula—"I will be your God and you shall be my people"—has many parallels to Wellhausen's old suggestion (see Schmid). As we have seen, Fohrer works with two foci—the lordship of God and the communion of God with humanity.

Other scholars such as Zimmerli and Schmidt emphasize the name of Yahweh and the self-asservation or self-revelation of Yahweh—"I am Yahweh," and its response "You Yahweh" as well as the assertion "I am that I am"—in addition to an emphasis on certain of the commandments especially the first and the second as leitmotifs for approaching the material (see Schmidt, 1983, pp. 49–88). Finally, Herrmann has suggested a much broader base for looking at the center of the Old Testament. He suggests that the book of Deuteronomy should be viewed and treated as the center of Old Testament thought since so many biblical themes are found in this work, that is, "the basic issues of Old Testament theology are concentrated *in nuce*" in the book (p. 156). In addition, Deuteronomy's perspectives and influence are quite pervasive in other Old Testament materials. Another broad suggestion recently made by Schmid is "creation faith" which, as we shall see below, has been a neglected area in Old Testament theology. As we have seen, many recent theologies have tended to work with dual points or foci rather than a single concept (see above, pp. 248–51).

The search for a center for the Old Testament has always been encouraged by the need to provide some organizational principle to give structure to the treatment of the subject-matter. The emphasis on the unity of the Bible in the period following the second World War encouraged the quest for a ruling and dominant perspective since it was assumed that a unified Bible should have an obvious core manifesting this unity. However, if one goes back to such a work as that by Rowley, it becomes obvious that the emphasis on the unity of the Bible was more enthusiastic than realistic. Rowley's highly influential work was simply based on the commonality of certain themes traceable throughout the Old and New Testaments and thus focused on a unity that was superficial to say the least.

Several factors have raised questions about finding a center or middle for the Old Testament. The influence of von Rad's theology and his attack on Eichrodt's approach was highly significant since he frequently argued against any principle under which all the material could be subsumed: "The Old Testament contains not merely one, but quite a number of theologies which are widely divergent both in structure and method of argument" (II, p. 414). He questioned whether one should even use the term theology in the singular when speaking of the Old Testament.

> So we have seriously to ask ourselves whether and in what sense we may still claim to use the title "Old Testament theology" in the singular. Where is its focal point? Of course, it can be said that Jahweh is the focal point of the Old Testament. That is, however, simply the beginning of the whole question: what kind of Jahweh is he? Does he not, in the course of his self-revelation, conceal

himself more and more deeply from his people? Have we not relied for far too long on our illusory idea of the unity of the Old Testament, an idea which must now be refounded? . . . Israel certainly tried continually to understand herself and her history as a unit: but such a unity existed only during the particular period in her faith with which she was at the moment concerned. It was not something demonstrable in her political and cultic history, nor was it to be found there: it was a *credendum*. Israel's knowledge of her own future also formed part of this unity for her (II, pp. 415–16).

In spite of von Rad's vehemence against finding a "basic structure" or "basic tendency," it seems that his arguments were mostly polemical and he himself actually worked with a principle of unity or synthetic approach, namely, Israel's continuous integration of her history in confessional form:

Israel was ready to see herself embodied in the most out-of-the-way traditions of one of her component parts, and to include and absorb the experience there recorded in the great picture of the history of Israel. Here at last we come upon one unifying principle towards which Israel's theological thinking strove, and with reference to which it ordered its material and thought; this was "Israel," the people of God, which always acts as a unit, and with which God always deals as a unit (I, p. 118).

Thus it appears that even those who seem to deny a principle of unity assume some structure for approaching the material. This is to be expected and will probably continue to function, in one form or another, in any presentation of Old Testament theology.

History, Tradition, and Story

James **Barr**, "Revelation in History," *IDBSup*, pp. 746–49; *idem*, "Story and History in Biblical Theology," *JR* 56(1976)1–17 = *Explorations in Theology 7* (London: SCM Press, 1980) = *The Scope and Authority of the Bible* (Philadelphia: Westminster Press, 1980)1–17; John J. **Collins**, "The 'Historical Character' of the Old Testament in Recent Biblical Theology," *CBQ* 41(1979)185–204; Hartmut **Gese**, "Tradition and Biblical Theology," in Knight, pp. 301–26; *idem*, *Zur biblischen Theologie. Alttestamentliche Vorträge* (Munich: Chr. Kaiser Verlag, 1977) = *Essays on Biblical Theology* (Minneapolis: Augsburg Publishing House, 1981); Douglas A. **Knight**, (ed.), *Tradition and Theology in the Old Testament* (Philadelphia: Fortress Press, 1977); Werner E. **Lemke**, "Revelation through History in Recent Biblical Theology: A Critical Appraisal," *Int* 36(1982)34–46; Hiroshi **Obayashi**, "Pannenberg and Troeltsch: History and Religion," *JAAR* 38(1970)401–19; Norman **Porteous**, "Old Testament and History," *ASTI* 8(1970–71)21–77; J. J. M. **Roberts**, "Myth *Versus* History: Relaying the Comparative Foundations," *CBQ* 38(1976)1–13; Rudolf **Smend**, *Elemente alttestamentlichen Geschichtsdenkens* (Zurich: EVZ-Verlag, 1968); Thomas L. **Thompson**, *The Historicity of the Patriarchal Narratives: The Quest for the Historical Abraham* (Berlin: Walter de Gruyter, 1974).

Since the seventeenth century, when historians were forced to admit that the biblical version of history, beginning with Adam and Eve, could no longer accommodate the accumulating evidence of a divergent picture of world history, the biblical history of the world and Israel presented in the Old Testament has been a matter of contention (see our treatment of Isaac de La Peyrère, above pp. 26–27). Throughout the intervening centuries biblical scholars have sought to defend, modify, and explain biblical history, recognizing that the final editors of the biblical material were concerned, at least in a minimum fashion, with producing what we would call "history" in several major blocks of Old Testament material, Genesis—2 Kings being the most obvious example. That is, the material was structured in a more or less continuous narrative, causes for events were stipulated, and the storyline follows a chronological outline. When it became obvious that the history of Israel produced by critical research differed from the history as written by the biblical writers, this matter proved an enormous problem. At the beginning of the nineteenth century, for example, de Wette was willing to give up on writing a history of Israel and its religion because he denied that we possess sufficient reliable biblical evidence. His contemporary, Vatke, wrote in 1835:

> The Hebrews did not at all raise themselves to the standpoint of properly historical contemplation, and there is no book of the Old Testament, however much it may contain material that is otherwise objectively historical, that deserves the name of true historiography (*Die biblische Theologie I*, p. 716; translation from Barr, 1976, p. 13).

Theologians like Gottfried Menken (1768–1831), Johann Tobias Beck (1804–78), and especially von Hofmann (see above, pp. 82–84) who followed a *Heilsgeschichte* approach sought to argue for the identity of the salvation history with ordinary history. As early as 1875, however, the historian August Köhler (1835–97) "distinguished between a secular and theological discipline of biblical history, claiming that it is the theologian's task 'to study and to retell the course of OT history as the authors of the OT understood it'" (Hasel, 1982, p. 99).

In spite of such positions and difficulties nineteenth-century biblical scholars and theologians generally seized upon the historical character of the Bible and its religion as a strong apologetic argument since during the century practically all areas of cultural and intellectual life were explored in historical form. That biblical religion was "a historical religion" seemed to support its authenticity in an age greatly concerned with history; just as the moderns were concerned with history so were the biblical writers. The revelation-in-history movement was only the logical outgrowth of this position. Wright and others argued that the value of the "history" depended upon its correlation with the factual course of events (see also de Vaux). Although von Rad declared that "the Old Testament is a history book" (II, p. 357), he was willing to elucidate the theology along the lines of the "confessional" history or *Heilsgeschichte*.

The clash of views over the two forms of history and the problem of revelation in history has been noted above (see pp. 241–44) and nothing final on the matter has been concluded. The efforts of Hesse and others to anchor theological discussions in the course of history as reconstructed by critical scholarship has had little fruitful results and few followers, although Wolfhart Pannenberg has abandoned the idea of two histories and sought to argue that "revelation is history" and to extend the concept of history to include "reality in its totality." Such a view, however, places revelation in the totality and thus at the end of history (see Hasel, 1982, pp. 108–11; Obayashi).

In light of the stalemate in the discussion over confessional and critical history, two developments in recent discussion are noteworthy. (1) First of all, much attention has shifted to focus on tradition and the way in which traditions and streams of tradition have been shaped in the Old Testament (see the volume edited by Knight). The term tradition has been used, as it was by von Rad, in order partially to bypass the issue of the historicity of events. Gese has argued that "theology must be understood essentially as an historical process of development" (1977, p. 303). His program has been called "theology as tradition building." He describes his program, which in some ways simply carries von Rad's approach to its logical conclusion, as follows:

> We are advocating that biblical theology has the task of determining the theology of the whole tradition and that it can accomplish this neither by iso- lating a dogmatic doctrine as the unifying factor of the whole, nor by descrip- tively rendering historical diversity as the assemblage of the whole, but only by attempting to grasp the totality as a cohesion. Consequently, this task con- fronts (a) the individual text with its preliterary antecedents, (b) the develop- ment of the text as literature with its own literary classification, and (c) the growth of the text tradition into a corpus embracing the whole (1977, p. 308).

Those who advocate doing theology in terms of tradition building or the formation of tradition have yet to produce a major theology along these lines although Gese has produced several essays on the topic. He wishes to trace the process of tradition building on into the New Testament and thus produce a total biblical theology. This seems very difficult since many Old Testament traditions are not utilized in the New and in fact reached their final form and shape with the Old Testament itself. In addition, certainly many portions of the Old Testament are not the product of a prior tradition nor have they a tradition history except as they became part of the canon of Old Testament Scripture.

(2) A second development is the treatment of the narrative material as a story rather than as history although it may be history-like in many places. Such an approach obviously would not take in all the parts of the Old Testa- ment but only those narrative portions which have some similarity to history

per se—a unitary form, chronological framework, and so forth. Barr has argued:

> The long narrative corpus of the Old Testament seems to me, as a body of literature, to merit the title of story rather than that of history. Or, to put it in another way, it seems to merit entirely the title of story but only in part the title history (1980, p. 5).

> This narrative spirals back and forward across what we would call history, sometimes coming closer to it and sometimes going far away from it (1976, p. 748).

To call the Bible or at least its narrative portions "a storybook" certainly avoids many of the difficulties of calling it "a history book." The former takes the narrative as creative literature rather than as historical record. Thompson earlier made the point this way:

> Salvation history is not an historical account of saving events open to the study of the historian. Salvation history did not happen; it is a literary form which has its own historical context. In fact, we can say that the faith of Israel is not an historical faith, in the sense of a faith based on historical event; it is rather a faith within history. It is a faith that is structured by the experience of Israel's history, and as such has the freedom and openness to the future which is characteristic of reflection on historical experience. It is a faith, however, which has its justification, not in the evidence of past events, for the traditions of the past serve only as the occasion of the expression of faith, but in the assertion of a future promise. The promise itself arises out of an understanding of the present which is attributed to the past and recreates it as meaningful. The expression of this faith finds its condensation in an historical form which sees the past as promise. But this expression is not itself a writing of history, nor is it really about the past, but it is about the present hope. Out of the experience of the present, new possibilities of the past emerge, and these new possibilities are expressed typologically in terms of promise and fulfillment. Reflection on the present as fulfillment recreates the past as promise, which reflection itself becomes promise of a future hope. What is historical and there-fore very much open to the historical-critical disciplines are the events and the historical situation in which Israel's past traditions achieve significance as promise, but prior to this new understanding, the traditions do not have signif-icance for the understanding of faith (pp. 328–29).

The consequences of reading the narrative as story or as a literary form are several. (a) It allows one to dispense with or hold in abeyance the issue of whether events happened as they were told. (b) The locus or dynamics of revelation, if one chooses to use this word, can be seen as associated primar-ily with the people and the process which produced the story and secondarily with the story rather than with the events it tells about. (c) The story can be seen as one of the ways in which Israel chose to give order and cohesion to its life by producing a symbolic context for its present and a basis for its future. (d) The story, not the actual history of Israel, can be viewed as what

Israel wished to express about its own self-understanding. (e) The Old Testament story may be read by the contemporary person as paradigmatic and as informing just as any other meaningful story in world literature.

Exactly how such an approach to the Old Testament as story will work itself out has yet to be demonstrated in Old Testament theology. Does it mean that theology will consist of merely retelling the story or merely reading the story? If theology deals in some fashion with truth claims, how does this factor impact upon reading the narrative as if it were fiction or no more than history-like? Can the modern person, or could the ancient person, listen to and learn from a history-like story without becoming engaged in the question of the facticity of its episodes? Is the resort to story as a description merely a means to avoid the issues over which the debates about history, salvation-history, God's acts in history, and other matters have so long raged?

The History of Israelite Religion and Old Testament Theology

G. W. **Anderson**, "Hebrew Religion," *The Old Testament and Modern Study: A Generation of Discovery and Research* (ed. by H. H. Rowley; London: Oxford University Press, 1951)283–310; James **Barr**, "The Problem of Old Testament Theology and the History of Religion" *CJT* 3(1957)141–49; *idem*, "Trends and Prospects in Biblical Theology," *JTS* 25(1974)265–82; Otto **Eissfeldt**, "Israelitisch-jüdische Religionsgeschichte und alttestamentliche Theologie," *ZAW* 44(1926)1–12; Hermann **Gunkel**, "Biblische Theologie und biblische Religionsgeschichte: I. des AT," *RGG* 1(1927)1089–91; Herbert F. **Hahn**, "Wellhausen's Interpretation of Israel's Religious History: A Reappraisal of His Ruling Ideas," *Essays on Jewish Life and Thought* (ed. by J. L. Blau et al.; New York: Columbia University Press, 1959)299–308; William A. **Irwin**, "The Study of Israel's Religion," *VT* (7(1957)113–26; C. R. **North**, "Old Testament Theology and the History of Hebrew Religion," *SJT* 2(1949)113–26; Werner H. **Schmidt**, *The Faith of the Old Testament: A History* (Oxford/Philadelphia: Basil Blackwell/Westminster Press, 1983); Walther **Zimmerli**, "The History of Israelite Religion," *Tradition and Interpretation* (ed. by G. W. Anderson; London: Oxford University Press, 1979)351–84.

During the past two centuries, the relationship between the disciplines of the history of Israelite religion and Old Testament theology has been a most controverted issue. The roots of both disciplines can already be seen, as we noted earlier (see above, pp. 62–64), in the proposals of Gabler. His "true biblical theology" was intended to be a comprehensive description and summary—that is, a presentation—of the biblical materials with their contents arranged in chronological order and presented irrespective of whether they still retained any value or relationship to the life and theology of the present or were merely historically conditioned and human in origin. (It should be recalled that, as a rationalist, he was primarily although not completely concerned with the "ideas" of the various periods.) This approach closely corresponds to what later came to be called a history of Israelite religion. His "pure biblical theology" was to be a compendium—or a representation—drawn from the true biblical theology retaining those ideas and insights with permanent, universal, and divinely ordained values. Here then we have the basis for what later became Old Testament theology.

The relationship between these two approaches has, of course, been a problem ever since. At various times the two have been in competition and proponents of each approach have argued for the superiority of one over the other. Generally, even theologies have had to resort to some utilization of historical perspectives, either as an introduction or else as a structuring factor within particular discussions.

There are a number of reasons why the tension between the two disciplines exists and why they overlap at points. (1) Conservatively speaking, the literature of the Old Testament originated over a period probably spanning a millennium of time. If that be the case, then one would be foolish not to admit that changes in thought, practice, and perspective varied over the years and thus one must allow for some forms of historical development however the material is presented. (2) The Old Testament literature is enormously diverse. This is the case even if one confines the consideration merely to the different genres of literature involved. In addition, the material treats such a variety of issues and was written and edited by an enormous number of different people at different times. Somehow, this variety and its different historical contexts must be taken into consideration. (3) The final editing of the Old Testament material was carried out late in history and the canonical order of the material hardly corresponds to the historical origin of the material. If this important observation is to be a factor in writing a theology then historical issues have to be taken into consideration or at least the conclusions of historical critical scholarship have to be presupposed. (4) The Old Testament possesses no real center, or to say it differently, the various genres and blocks of material are not all concerned with the same issues, and thus historical and sociological factors have to be utilized to appreciate the interests which are found diffused through the volume. (5) Large portions of the Old Testament are narratives and documents concerned with historical developments—this is the case even if one chooses to employ a more neutral term like story rather than history—and therefore involve even the theologian in a discussion of matters of history. (6) Finally, many have felt that histories of Old Testament religion dealt with "religion" while Old Testament theologies dealt with "revelation." This sort of argument was widely expounded in Barthian circles because of Barth's disdain for religion, which he characterized as humanity's efforts at self-salvation. This division between religion and revelation really plays no role in the Old Testament. Practically all of the Old Testament literature merely assumes the fact of God's self-revelations, and since this is practically a given dictum there is no great interest in the Old Testament about the potentiality and method of divine revelation. No real dividing line is drawn between revelation and the practice of religion. To some extent, the bifurcation between religion (the concern of historical studies) and revelation (the concern of theology) has been the continuation of the old concept of theology as being equal to ideas and religion as being equal to practice. Since there is no such line drawn in the Old Testament itself then both theologies and histories have to deal with both ideas and practices.

The nineteenth century saw the triumph of the history-of-religion approach over the theological approach. In many ways, Wellhausen's work was the culmination of forces operative throughout the century (see Hahn). The dominance of the historical approach was countered beginning in the 1920s but with a diversity of programs suggested, the most radical being Eissfeldt's argument that the two disciplines should go their separate ways. The biblical theology movement deprecated the historical approach. In more recent years there seems to have been something of a truce struck between the two approaches. Some scholars, such as Eichrodt, Vriezen, Fohrer, and von Rad (in the first section of his theology), have written both histories of Israelite religion and Old Testament theologies. This mutual recognition of separate and equal but interrelated disciplines is as it should be. Both are necessary and beneficial to the other and probably some of the methodologies of each are required by the other.

Many attempts have been made to distinguish between a history of a religion and a theology (see for example the comments of Eissfeldt, Heinisch, and Dentan, above, pp. 158–60, 190–91, 198–201). The following seem to be noteworthy although the distinctions should not be assumed to be rigidly applicable since there is much overlapping (see especially, Barr, 1974, pp. 275–78).

(1) First of all, the two types generally differ in terms of their intentionality. A history of religion seeks to provide a historical and chronological presentation or a purely descriptive account of the religion of ancient Israel whereas a theology seeks to single out and explicate the features and ideas that are central to the Old Testament and to relate these in some fashion to normal theological concerns and processes of thought. Theology is concerned, in a way, to expound the thought of a particular body of literature (namely the Old Testament) while the intention of a history of religion is to describe religion as part of the ongoing dynamic of a historical people (namely the people of ancient Israel and Judah).

(2) A history of religion is generally much more inclusive in scope than a theology. Such matters as the pre-Israelite origin of ideas and practices, peripheral issues, characteristics and ideas that disappeared in the course of time, relationships to non-biblical religion, and so on fall into the purview of

the discipline. Old Testament theology is generally more concerned with those factors and issues which dominate in the texts and which were characteristic and normative or at least which the final editors of the Scriptures chose to preserve and highlight. A history of religion would be as interested in the prophets which the biblical traditions now condemn as in those whom the traditions now canonize. A history of religion is more apt to draw on non-biblical evidence, therefore, such as that derived from archaeological research, than is a theology.

(3) As we have seen, Old Testament theology has sought to find some organizing principle, central concepts, or officially sanctioned positions in the Bible to use as a structuring center or middle from which to work. To use Eichrodt's phrase, theology is more interested in the cross-section of the material which can be used to integrate and produce a central focus or foci (see the previous discussion on the center of the Old Testament, above, pp. 257–60). Historical treatments have been much more willing to use historical frameworks as the structuring principle and thus settle for a more diffused presentation which is content with tracing the progress of ideas and practices rather than resorting to value judgments.

(4) This last point means that theology has been more concerned with the normative rather than with the antiquarian aspects of the Bible. That is, Old Testament theologies, whether explicitly stated or not, are more concerned with the relationship of their material to contemporary and theological thought than are histories of religion. They tend to be more systematic and didactic rather than merely descriptive. To use terminology we have employed earlier, theologies seek to be vertically and synthetically organized whereas histories of religion seek to be horizontally or longitudinally organized. A history may be said to be written to be read and used in association with the study of the history of the people whereas a theology may be said to be written to be read and used in association with general theological study or perhaps as a frame of reference for reading the Old Testament.

It should be emphasized, however, that such distinctions as we have made are rather theoretical and superficially descriptive. In reality, the two approaches frequently overlap. One person's theology may appear to another as merely a history of religion. (This was Eichrodt's view of von Rad's work.) Since the two disciplines have many areas in which they overlap and frequently employ very common methodologies, both should be pursued and both are validly worthwhile in seeking to understand both the Old Testament and the total faith and practices of ancient Israel as well as the historical and faith contexts out of which the Old Testament traditions originated and were employed. Attempts to integrate the two, as in the recent work of Schmidt, also have their place and make their contribution.

The Canon and Old Testament Theology

James **Barr**, *Holy Scripture: Canon, Authority, Criticism* (London/Philadelphia: SCM Press/Westminster Press, 1983); Joseph **Blenkinsopp**, *Prophecy and Canon* (Notre Dame, IN: University of Notre Dame Press, 1977); Brevard S. **Childs**, *Biblical Theology in Crisis* (Philadelphia: Westminster Press, 1970); *idem*, "The Old Testament as Scripture of the Church," *CTM* 43(1972)709–22; *idem*, *The Book of Exodus* (London/Philadelphia: SCM Press/Westminster Press, 1974); *idem*, *Introduction to the Old Testament as Scripture* (London/Philadelphia: SCM Press/Fortress Press, 1979); James D. G. **Gunn**, "Levels of Canonical Authority," *HBT* 4(1982)13–60; S. E. **McEvenue**, "The Old Testament, Scripture or Theology?" *Int* 35(1981)229–42; James A. **Sanders**, *Torah and Canon* (Philadelphia: Fortress Press, 1974); *idem*, "Adaptable for Life: The Nature and Function of Canon," *Magnalia Dei: The Mighty Acts of God* (ed. by F. M. Cross, et al.; Garden City: Doubleday, 1976)531–60; *idem*, "Hermeneutics," *IDBSup*, pp. 402–7; *idem*, *Canon and Community: A Guide to Canonical Criticism* (Philadelphia: Fortress Press, 1984).

Since the early centuries of the synagogue and church, both have possessed a collection of sacred writings to which the term canon has been applied. The term, with its basic meaning of "list," was used to designate the list of sacred books which were considered as authoritative writings. The term, used in this form, seems to have been employed primarily within the Christian community and applied only secondarily to the Jewish collection of writings. The limits of the two canons seem to have been arrived at through a number of considerations: the widespread usage of the works, certain criteria about date of origin and authorship, and the basic agreement or usability of the books' contents to support the generally accepted structures of faith held to be normative and orthodox within the mainstream of the two religions. So far as the Hebrew Scriptures or Old Testament were concerned, the two communities came to use two different canons—the Septuagint or Christian Old Testament was more extensive than the Hebrew canon and the books held in common were differently ordered. Both the synagogue and the church utilized and interpreted the Scriptures against faith systems which were located outside of or deduced from the canons. For Judaism, the secondary collection of texts—the Talmud—as an embodiment of rabbinic exegesis and faith served as a lens for reading and understanding the primary, that is, the biblical, texts. For Christians who, like the Jews, recognized differences within their sacred texts, external controls also served as the lens for reading the texts. For Christianity this role was played by the so-called rule of faith—"what has always been believed everywhere by everyone"—and the later creeds and confessions of the community. Thus the two canons of Scripture functioned primarily as the "fountainhead" or "basis of appeal" for the ongoing, living, and developing tradition of the communities.

At the Protestant Reformation, the question of the canon, in conjunction with Luther's principle of *sola scriptura*, came again into prominence because if the Reformers were going to appeal to the Bible against the church and its authority and tradition, then it had to be certain about what composed the canon. In this endeavor the Reformers gave up the more extensive Christian canon of the Old Testament and classified as canonical only those works in the Hebrew Bible but retained the old Christian ordering of the books. As is well known, Luther tended to narrow further the central authority by appealing to what might be called "a canon within the canon" (see above, pp. 8–10).

With the rise of first critical and then historical approaches to Scripture, the widely held assumptions about how the canon was believed to have come into being was challenged (see on Spinoza, above, pp. 32–34). With the challenge to the divine inspiration of the Scriptures by such people as Semler, the differences between canonical and non-canonical began to fade. The older view that the canon was the basis and creator of the faith and tradition of the communities was reversed so that, even in Protestantism, the canon was seen as the product of the faith and tradition of the communities. While the old paradigm had spoken in terms of God—revelation—Scripture—community, the new approaches tended to work with a paradigm of God—community—tradition—Scripture. As we noted at the end of chapter III, historical and comparative studies further eroded the role of the canon by focusing on the origin and growth of traditions prior to their becoming scriptural and authoritative much less canonical (see above, pp. 138–39). In spite of such erosion of canonical authority, the canonical works were still given a special consideration and role not accorded non-biblical works, although in New Testament studies non-biblical works and thought became as highly influential as the Old Testament in understanding the origins of Christianity and its systems of faith.

In recent years a renewed stress on the canon and what has broadly been called "canonical criticism" has surfaced. This approach, especially associated with Childs and Sanders although with significant differences between them, is characterized by several features. (1) The process which produced, along with the contents of, the final canonical form of the text are given a special significance. To some extent, this is similar to the development of new emphases in biblical studies in general, namely, redaction criticism, structuralism, and what is called "new criticism"—all three of which focus on analysis of the final form of the texts. (2) As in the old "biblical theology movement" of the 1940s, historical-critical scholarship becomes the object of intense flagellation and is blamed for many of the ills apparently besetting biblical theology as a whole. Some have described this hostility toward biblical criticism as a nostalgia for the sixteenth century when in Protestantism biblical studies and theology were practically identical. (3) Childs proceeds to speak of the need and shape of a new biblical theology which would not be limited to "the descriptive task" but which would overlap with dogmatic theology and thus create a genuine dialogue between the two (1970, p. 93).

Childs has outlined his approach, primarily in his *Biblical Theology in Crisis*, demonstrated his exegetical tendencies in his commentary on Exodus, and produced a *magnum opus* in his *Introduction to the Old Testament as Scripture*. The latter book, one of the most discussed and controversial among recent publications (see the numerous reviews in special issues of *JSOT* 16[1980]2–60 and *HBT* 2[1980] 113–211, with responses from Childs), was written to provide some of the groundwork to support a canonical biblical theology of both testaments. In terms of a biblical or canonical theology, he purposes, "when seen from the context of the canon both the question of what the text meant and what it means are inseparably linked and both belong to the task of the interpretation of the Bible as Scripture." Such an approach means the repudiation of the critical method which "set up an iron curtain between the past and the present" and "is an inadequate method for studying the Bible as the church's Scripture" (1970, pp. 141–42).

Among Childs's proposals for a new biblical theology are the following. (1) The canon must serve as the context for biblical theology (1970, pp. 99–106). (2) This means a canon including both Old and New Testaments which "together constitute Sacred Scripture for the Christian church" and which form a "normative body of tradition." (3) "The Scriptures must be interpreted in relation to their function within the community of faith that treasured them." (4) The Scriptures must be viewed as "a channel of life for the continuing church, through which God instructs and admonishes his people" (p. 99). (5) The Bible is thus "a vehicle of divine reality" (p. 100) and when "understood as the Scriptures of the church, functions as the vehicle for God's special communicating of himself to his church and the world" (p. 104). (6) The doctrine of biblical inspiration assumes a significant role and in fact Childs argues that "one of the major factors in the breakdown of the Biblical Theology Movement was its total failure to come to grips with the inspiration of Scripture" (p. 103). (7) Since the Old Testament makes use of and offers interpretations of the Old, how the New uses the Old can at least offer pointers for how the Old Testament should be interpreted within a biblical theology (pp. 114–18). (8) No normative role can be assigned to the pre-history or pre-canonical nor to the post-historical or post-canonical form of the text or its interpretation but only to the final canonical form.

> The reason for insisting on the final form of scripture lies in the peculiar relationship between text and the people of God which is constitutive of the canon. The shape of the biblical text reflects a history of encounter between God and Israel. The canon serves to describe this peculiar relationship and to define the

scope of this history by establishing a beginning and end to the process. It assigns a special quality to this particular segment of human history which became normative for all successive generations of this community of faith. The significance of the final form of the biblical text is that it alone bears witness to the full history of revelation. Within the Old Testament neither the process of the formation of the literature nor the history of its canonization is assigned an independent integrity. This dimension has often been lost or purposely blurred and is therefore dependent on scholarly reconstruction. The fixing of a canon of scripture implies that the witness to Israel's experience with God lies not in recovering such historical processes, but is testified to in the effect on the biblical text itself. Scripture bears witness to God's activity in history on Israel's behalf, but history *per se* is not a medium of revelation which is commensurate with a canon. It is only in the final form of the biblical text in which the normative history has reached an end that the full effect of this revelatory history can be perceived (1979, pp. 75–76).

While Childs and canonical critics have yet to produce a full-blown work of biblical theology, numerous questions and criticisms of the approach have developed especially because of its stress on the canon as the context and the boundary for doing biblical theology. The most devastating critique is found in the recent work by Barr. Some of the issues raised by Childs's program are the following.

(1) Was canonization as significant a phenomenon as is claimed? The early church seems to have gotten along for years without finally settling on the books to be part of the official list or canon of Scripture. The initial list of Old Testament canonical books was only set at the councils of Hippo (393) and Carthage (in 397 and 497). Again such churches as the Ethiopian decided on even a larger canon. When the Protestants returned to a greatly reduced canon composed of only the works found in the Hebrew Bible, one gets the impression that canonization per se was not of great consequence. Even without being canonized, works may be accepted as authoritative or "Scripture" and used as sources for formulating and judging the faith.

(2) Isn't stressing the canonical phase actually stressing simply one stage in the process of tradition building over against other stages? Since canonization was an action of the patristic age, emphasis on the canon assigns this period—a non-biblical time—a special status in history which is not shared by earlier and biblical periods. Why must the end of a process be more important than earlier periods?

(3) Were not some portions of the biblical material treated with just as much authority at earlier stages as they were after the canonical stage? Gunn, for example, has shown that one may speak of several levels of "canonical" authority—the tradition-history phase, the final author or final composition level, the canonical level, and the ecclesiastical level. Thus it is difficult to assign authority strictly to the canonical phase.

(4) How does one adjudicate in those cases where the original meaning

of a text appears to clash with the final canonical form? According to Childs, one would have to stress the final canonical form and where the New Testament interpretation differs from that of the Old Testament then presumably the former would have priority.

(5) Doesn't Childs's position have to argue not only for the inspiration of the final and canonical form but also for the process by which the final form developed? In his *Introduction* Childs attempts to show how the collecting, editing, and joining together of material was "divinely controlled." If the final editorial process was such a work of the Spirit but preliminary to the canonical stage, why should not the even earlier stages of the tradition be seen as inspired and thus in some fashion as authoritative?

(6) Does not Childs's program simply carry the old biblical theology movement to its logical conclusion even including some of its veneration for Barthian theology? In Barth's exegesis, like Childs's program, the goal was not really understanding the text so much as encounter and contact with the divine reality—namely, God—which is mediated by the text. If this is the case, then where does the real authority and certainty lie—in the canon or in the reality behind the canon, and if the latter then why should the divine be so restricted to the canon? Barr remarks: "The canon was the Grail for which the American Biblical Theology Movement had been the Quest" (p. 136).

(7) Does saying that the canon provides the context for biblical Scripture really allow one any vantage point for judging between various and diverse positions within the canon? Both Isaiah 2:4 and Joel 3:9–10 are canonical but how would one judge between the value of their two positions?

(8) If theology has to do with truth claims how can the appeal to canonical material really settle the matter? McEvenue has expressed the dilemma of the purely canonical approach in the following terms:

> It is simply erroneous to think that one can proceed to truth of any kind using the Bible or a deposit of faith as the sole criterion. Unless you are simply restating the explicit biblical statement, you are always using some criterion outside the Bible. . . . Theological truths are not reached by deduction or dialectic or any form of reasoning restricted to the canon or a deposit of faith. They are determined in judgments which have reflected on what scripture says and also on whatever other clearly relevant knowledge the theologian may possess. There is no single final norm. Theological truths are discovered by open minds passionately hungry for a contemporary, true understanding of God (pp. 236–37).

(9) If the canon is taken as the final boundary for doing biblical theology, is not a lot lost from the inability to draw upon the insights and conclusions of the history of religion? Surely, the New Testament cannot be fully understood merely by interpreting it within the canon. By limiting consideration to the canon, factors such as the apocryphal literature, other non-biblical intertestamental texts, the Qumran scrolls, and other matters would seem to

be excluded from any real functional role. Surely, many a text cannot be fully understood without recourse to matters that lie behind or outside of the text. "The universe of meaning, within which the language of the biblical books operated, was never one circumscribed by the canon of scripture, which did not then exist" (Barr, *IDBSup*, p. 110). If this was the case with the origin of the biblical books then it would seem that in their interpretation canonical walls should not function to exclude either the pre-history of the traditions or their setting in a larger universe of meaning.

Creation, Cosmology, and World Order

Bernhard W. **Anderson** (ed.), *Creation in the Old Testament* (London/Philadelphia: SPCK/Fortress Press, 1984); Joseph **Blenkinsopp**, "The Structure of P," *CBQ* 38(1976)275–92; R. L. **Cohn**, *The Shape of Sacred Space: Four Biblical Studies* (Chico: Scholars Press, 1982); James L. **Crenshaw** (ed.), *Studies in Ancient Israelite Wisdom* (New York: KTAV, 1976); Julien **Harvey**, "Wisdom Literature and Biblical Theology," *BTB* 1(1971)308–19; Hans-Jürgen **Hermisson**, "Observations on the Creation Theology in Wisdom," *Israelite Wisdom: Theological and Literary Essays in Honor of Samuel Terrien* (ed. by John G. Gammie et al., Missoula: Scholars Press, 1978)43–57; A. S. **Kapelrud**, "Die Theologie der Schöpfung im Alten Testament," *ZAW* 91(1979)159–70; Rolf **Knierim**, "Cosmos and History in Israel's Theology," *HBT* 3(1981)59–124; Baruch A. **Levine**, *In the Presence of the Lord: A Study of Cult and Some Cultic Terms in Ancient Israel* (Leiden: E. J. Brill, 1974); *idem*, "Priestly Writers," *IDBSup*, pp. 683–87; Jacob **Milgrom**, "Sacrifices and Offerings, OT," *IDBSup*, pp. 763–71; *idem, Cult and Conscience: The* Asham *and the Priestly Doctrine of Repentance* (Leiden: E. J. Brill, 1976); *idem, Studies in Cultic Theology and Terminology* (Leiden: E. J. Brill, 1983); Sigmund **Mowinckel**, *The Psalms in Israel's Worship* (2 vols.; Oxford/Nashville: Basil Blackwell/Abingdon Press, 1962); B. D. **Napier**, "On Creation-Faith in the Old Testament: A Survey," *Int* 16(1962)21–42; H. G. **Reventlow**, *Hauptprobleme der alttestamentlichen Theologie im 20. Jahrhundert* (Darmstadt: Wissenschaftliche Buchgesellschaft, 1982); H. H. **Schmid**, *Wesen und Geschichte der Weisheit* (Berlin: A. Töpelmann, 1966); *idem, Gerechtigkeit als Weltordnung* (Tübingen: J. C. B. Mohr, 1968); *idem*, "Schöpfung, Gerechtigkeit und Heil. 'Schöpfungstheologie' als Gesamthorizant biblischer Theologie," *ZTK* 70(1973)1–19; Werner H. **Schmidt**, *Die Schöpfungsgeschichte der Priesterschrift* (Neukirchener-Vluyn: Neukirchener Verlag, 1964); R. B. Y. **Scott**, "The Study of Wisdom Literature," *Int* 24(1970)20–45; Odil H. **Steck**, *Der Schöpfungsbericht der Priestschrift* (Göttingen: Vandenhoeck & Ruprecht, 1975); *idem, World and Environment* (Nashville: Abingdon Press, 1980); *idem*, "Alttestamentliche Impulse für eine Theologie der Natur," *TZ* 34(1978)202–11; Samuel **Terrien**, "The Play of Wisdom: Turning Point in Biblical Theology," *HBT* 3(1981)125–53; L. E. **Toombs**, "Old Testament Theology and the Wisdom Literature," *JBR* 23(1955)193–96; Wayne Sibley **Towner**, "The Renewed Authority of Old Testament Wisdom for Contemporary Faith," *Canon and Authority* (ed. by G. W. Coats and B. O. Long; Philadelphia: Fortress Press, 1977)132–47; David **Tracy** and Nicholas **Lash** (eds.), *Cosmology and Theology* (New York/Edinburgh: Seabury Press/T. & T. Clark, 1983); Claus **Westermann**, *Beginning and End in the Bible* (Philadelphia: Fortress Press, 1972); *idem, Elements of Old Testament Theol-*

ogy (Atlanta: John Knox Press, 1982); Jay **Wilcoxen**, "Some Anthropocentric Aspects of Israel's Sacred History," *JR* 48(1968)333–50.

Three important areas of Old Testament thought and literature have been proverbial step-children in the recent discipline of Old Testament theology. These are its teachings and interest in creation, the cult and its associated activities especially as this found embodiment in the so-called Priestly source of the Pentateuch (Hexateuch?), and the various manifestations of wisdom thought and literature. Two of these areas—creation and wisdom—have been noted as major problem areas now receiving considerable attention in the recent survey by Reventlow (1982, pp. 148–202 for full bibliographies). Here we can only note some of the reasons for this neglect of all three areas and enter a plea for their authentic integration into the substance of the discipline.

Creation thought in the Bible has had to take a backseat to the interest in history. Throughout the latter part of the nineteenth century historical language and methodology became the way of talking about and approaching the Old Testament. This emphasis on historical matters was fed by the development of the idea of history as the arena of revelation. In turn, Barthian theology with its disdain for natural religion and natural revelation further submerged any real concern for creation per se. Thus one finds exemplified in von Rad's work what became the dominant consensus:

> The Old Testament is a history book; it tells of God's history with Israel, with the nations, and with the world, from the creation of the world down to the last things, that is to say, down to the time when dominion over the world is given to the Son of Man (Dan. vii. 13f.). This history can be described as saving history because, as it is presented, creation itself is understood as a saving act of God (*Theology*, II, p. 357).

The consequence of this type of approach was to subordinate creation to history and thus to see creation thought as a late development, as subsidiary to and supportive of salvation history, and as part of an aetiology of aetiologies used to explain the existence of the historical Israel.

The deprecation of the cult and sacral orders—that is the P-material—has been a factor in much of Protestantism since its earliest days. In fact, throughout church history the ceremonial and cultic material of the Old Testament has been either downplayed or used merely as a vehicle for christological and eucharistic exposition. The priestly, sacerdotal emphases have been castigated since the days of Deism, and in the nineteenth century Protestants "turned" the prophets into reformers and equated the cultic life and priesthood of Israel with Catholicism just as Luther had earlier done with the New Testament portrayals of the Pharisees. In biblical studies it became fashionable to give as little attention as possible to the cultic legislation of the

Old Testament and to consider, as Köhler did, the sacrificial system as a human contrivance created for humanity's hope of self-salvation. To the benefit of such an approach, however, it must be noted that much of what went on in the Israelite cult, or most any ancient cult, is a world apart and thus strange to modern humans who would have trouble with connecting the slaughter of animals and their ritual disposition with the means of grace and restitution.

So far as wisdom as concerned, we have earlier noted in several places how difficult it has been to integrate it into the major Old Testament theologies (see above, pp. 241, 249). One of the significant features of the recent two decades of Old Testament research has been the increasing interest in wisdom thought, but few have been able to discuss it as a salient feature of a larger context. (Terrien's work and the *separate* volume by von Rad represent two of the better exceptions.)

Creation thought, priestly thought (cult and ceremonial), and wisdom thought have one major feature which they share in common: they order reality into meaning forms or create universes of meaning within which life can be viewed and understood without much special appeal to or reliance on historical thought categories or *Heilsgeschichte*. As we noted earlier, even a focus on history is simply one way of trying to order existence and explain realities within meaningful contexts. Thus in actuality all four biblical thought categories tend to serve a similar function each focusing on the task from a different perspective.

There are a number of arguments to support the significant importance of all three of these areas in Old Testament thought and Israelite religion. (Most of the works noted in the bibliography at the beginning of this section assume positive attitudes toward the three areas and their importance for biblical thought.) If one takes creation, for example, it can be argued as Schmid has done, that creation faith or the faith that God has created and maintains the world along with its manifold orders is not a marginal theme of biblical theology, but its basic theme as such (1973, p. 15). This is the theme with which the Bible opens; Israel's festivals were fundamentally nature oriented and only secondarily history oriented; creation was a far more dominant interest and concern of the cult and temple architecture than covenant and *Heilsgeschichte*; and even Israelite eschatology spoke as much of a new heaven and a new earth as of a new history and a new Israel. The old myth and ritual approach (see above, pp. 168–71), so disdained in German and most English-language scholarship, may have gone overboard in some of its emphases but its stress on creation and re-creation in the cult certainly deserves more merit than it has received.

Probably no major stream of tradition in the Old Testament is more theologically reflective and integrated than the P-source. This material is organized and structured so as to present a total worldview and a structure of time, geography, cultural roles, weekly, seasonal, and multiyear cycles, a view of the proper orders of life and how they interrelate, ritual and routine for overcoming the disruptions in life and for the restoration of proper relationships both between persons and between humans and the divine. It should be noted that the priests, not the prophets, were the real custodians of the care of souls in ancient Israel and priestly theology created a universe of meaning which could deal with the totality of life in its many dimensions and exigencies. There was certainly nothing less spiritual about cultic and legal piety than about prophetic proclamation; in fact, probably the opposite was the case.

Finally, wisdom sought to advise and admonish on the basis of human experience, world orders, and creation thought without much reliance either on cultic and sacral considerations or on the ordering given to existence through historical developments. Nonetheless, an authoritative status was claimed for the insights gained from wisdom's reflections and observations on the world and human life and for the directives for living deduced from such observation and reflection. The wisdom books clearly demonstrate that radical differences of opinion and universes of meaning could be based on this type of observation and reflection. Also, it is interesting to note that it is only in these books that theological reflection of the type fairly characteristic of modern times really occurs in the Old Testament.

Early Judaism and Old Testament Theology

James **Barr**, "Le Judaïsme postbiblique et al théologie de l'Ancient Testament," *RTP* 18(1968)209–17; *idem*, *Judaism—Its Continuity with the Bible* (Southampton: Southampton University, 1968); Joseph **Blenkinsopp**, *Prophecy and Canon* (Notre Dame: University of Notre Dame Press, 1977); *idem*, "Interpretation and the Tendency to Sectarianism: An Aspect of Second Temple History," *Jewish and Christian Self-Definition*, vol. 2: *Aspects of Judaism in the Graeco-Roman Period* (ed. by E. P. Sanders, et al.; Philadelphia: Fortress Press, 1981)1–26; George Foot **Moore**, "Christian Writers on Judaism," *HTR* 14(1921)197–254; E. P. **Sanders**, *Paul and Palestinian Judaism: A Comparison of Patterns of Religion* (London/Philadelphia: SCM Press/Fortress Press, 1977).

Throughout this volume we have noted the low esteem in which postexilic and early Judaism have been held by biblical theologians and interpreters. This anti-Judaism has its roots in the New Testament and in the early church and has been a cancerous sore on the church throughout history. At the end of the eighteenth century the deprecation of Judaism became a feature in the way biblical history was subdivided. The pre-exilic period was looked upon favorably and the postexilic or post-Deuteronomic period, the time of the origins and development of Judaism as a stateless community, was seen as a time of deterioration and degeneration when spontaneous and unmediated, prophetic-type religion with its emphasis on ethical individualism and personal experience was supposedly replaced with a legalistic system of life and faith (see above, pp. 140–41). With the passage of time this view only intensified and was fed by the growing anti-Semitism in Germany. Moore characterized this depiction of postexilic Judaism as "a system of theology, and not an ancient Jewish system but a modern German system" superimposed on the late biblical period and the early thought and life of Judaism (p. 229).

Unfortunately, this negative trend in the evaluation of the period has continued and become a part of the most influential theologies of the twentieth century, those of Eichrodt and von Rad. The following quotes illustrate their positions with Eichrodt talking about later Judaism and von Rad about the impact and eventual consequences of the Deuteronomic reformation:

> . . . in the rabbinism of the first century . . . *fear and love* are now recognized as *two different types of piety*, which can be understood as coexisting, but can never be brought together in a unified view. Before long fear is characterized as the lower stage of piety, because it produces obedience only from compulsion and desire for reward, while love keeps the Torah for its own sake, without thinking of any egoistic purpose. But because the genuineness of piety is seen not in the mental attitude but in the doing of the Law, even the keeping of the Law from fear cannot be held worthy of reproach. Soon, too, a right coexistence of fear and love in the heart of Man is regarded as the normal attitude toward God, fear seeming necessary to guard one from contempt for the Law, while love helps one to overcome the weariness, indeed hatred, inspired by its oppressive burden and compulsion. The essence of the Jewish religion of the Law may therefore be seen as a regulation of the God-Man relationship which exhausts itself in endless casuistry, and leaves the heart empty; which because of its exact knowledge of the heart of Man strives to incorporate even the lower motive as necessary, and yet at the same time seeks to restrain and combat unbridled desire for reward with the motive of love. It is impossible to find clearer evidence of the lack of a unified religious attitude. The fact that Jesus and his Apostles had recourse to the Old Testament in their description of the right attitude toward God witnesses plainly to the fact that in them the inner schizophrenia of Jewish piety had been overcome, and that the liberation of Man for willing surrender to God had once more emerged into the light of day (Eichrodt, *Theology*, II, p. 315).

> In the post-exilic age . . . Israel now no longer appeared as a people determined by nature and history; it was the law which more and more began to define who belonged to her and who did not. . . . what was Israel and what was not became a matter of the interpretation of the law . . . [The] flexibility of Jahweh's revelation, allowing it to gear itself to the place and time and condition of the Israel at the time addressed, ceases. The law becomes an absolute entity, unconditionally valid irrespective of time or historical situation. But this made the revelation of the divine commandments something different from what it had been hitherto. This was no longer the helpful di-

recting will of the God who conducted his people through history: rather it is now beginning to become the "law" in the theological sense of the word. Up to now the commandments had been of service to the people of Israel as they made their way through history and through the confusion occasioned by heathen forms of worship. But now Israel had to serve the commandments. Certainly the old way of looking at the commandments was still preserved in the postexilic community for a considerable period. We do not as yet see any legal casuistry proper. But when the law was made absolute, the path to such a casuistry, with its intrinsic consequences, had to be followed out. But the most serious aspect of this whole process was that in understanding the law in this way Israel parted company with history, that is, with the history which she had hitherto experienced with Jahweh. She did not part company with her relationship to Jahweh. But once she began to look upon the will of Jahweh in such a timeless and absolute way, the saving history necessarily ceased moving on. This Israel no longer had a history, at least a history with Jahweh (von Rad, *Theology*, I, pp. 90–91).

Unfortunately such misunderstandings and caricatures of the postexilic period and early Judaism have continued to dominate Christian reading of the evidence (see Sanders).

Until this sort of depiction can be overcome in biblical studies, Old Testament theology will be seriously handicapped by its failure to offer an adequate and appreciative assessment of the religion and thought of postexilic times. It also endangers and hampers the cooperation between Jewish and Christian scholars. Numerous arguments might be marshaled against what has become this classical Christian representation of early Judaism.

(1) The emphasis on Israel's loss of a sense of history during the postexilic period is probably a misunderstanding of the true situation. Von Rad depicts earlier Israel as being historically oriented, a sentiment subsequently lost. Two factors mitigate against this position. (a) The confessional creeds or credos emphasizing historical events, which von Rad isolated and used as the primary data for his depiction of the history of salvation tradition, may in reality be late and not early and therefore more the product of late rather than early Israelite life. (b) Much of the literature of the Hebrew Bible, in its final form, was the product of the exilic and postexilic community. This has long been recognized in the case of the Deuteronomistic literature but more recent studies argue a similar case for much of the material of the Pentateuch as well. This would certainly not suggest a loss of interest in history during this period but would suggest that the significant and formative historical events were merely placed in the distant past so that antiquity and authority were treated as correlative.

(2) The depiction of Judaism as a legalistic, degraded spirituality certainly appears as a caricature and such a description of the religion is based on Christian perspectives rather than actual assertions and positions found within late Old Testament books and Jewish texts themselves.

(3) Judaism must be seen as just as legitimate a continuation and interpretation of the Hebrew Scriptures as is Christianity. They are both legitimate daughters of the same earlier mother.

(4) The postexilic period was not a time which saw the end of prophecy and the diversity of spiritual vitality within Judaism. The continuation of prophecy in various forms and the development of apocalyptic as well as the existence of various parties and sects testify against any understanding of Judaism as a monolithic, legalistic system.

(5) The anti-institutional, anti-cultic sentiments noted in the previous section have greatly influenced attitudes toward the late biblical period and early Judaism. As we have noted, such an attitude fails to appreciate fully the spiritual dimensions and values in institutional life and ceremonial practices. Behind many Protestant depictions of Jewish life lie an antagonism toward Catholicism and the Lutheran overemphasis on the dichotomy between Gospel and Law.

(6) Many of the factors criticized in later periods were probably already features in Israelite life even prior to the Exile. There was never a time when Israelite life failed to have a cultic and institutional orientation. Part of the difference between the time before and after the Exile was the consequence of political realities. Prior to the Exile, Israel was a monarchical state in which citizenship was based on territorial and political factors—but nonetheless institutionalized and celebrated in the cult. The situation after the Exile, with the loss of political independence, required a structuring of the community and its life around institutions which were primarily religious but which in their way were probably not as hierarchical and authoritative as the political structures of the pre-exilic period. That is, self-definition had to assume a different character, and certain laws and characteristics came to assume a greater role while other features and factors disappeared. In addition, many of the same features of early Judaism are already found in Deuteronomy and other works; thus to distinguish radically between the biblical and non-biblical is unjustified.

SUBJECT INDEX

allegory, 22, 135, 230
Amyraldism, 42, 43–44
Anabaptists, 14
archaeology, 89, 128, 217–18, 224, 238, 243
Arminianism, 42–43
authority (of OT), 10–11, 13, 18, 24, 29, 43, 45, 76, 136, 151, 216, 254–55

Barthianism, 90, 154–58, 166, 171, 211–12, 213, 238, 249, 272, 274

canon, 33, 34, 59, 76, 138–39, 200, 222, 248, 268–73
Counter-Reformation, 8, 14
covenant, 20–23, 32, 181–84, 191, 212, 223, 232–33, 246, 248, 258
creation, 239, 249, 273–76

Deism, 21, 38, 44, 45–47, 48, 57, 59, 99, 274
dicta probantia (or *classica*), 5, 7, 18, 22, 54, 58, 60, 67, 160, 190

Enlightenment, 38, 47–49, 53, 56, 87
exegesis, 3, 19, 21, 23, 43, 58, 60, 61, 68, 76, 135, 142, 153–54, 162–65, 200, 205–6
experience, 39–40, 48, 75, 86, 137, 139–40

Federal theology (see also covenant), 5, 19–23, 34, 83, 258
form criticism, 132, 168, 235, 248

Hegelianism, 77–80, 87, 98, 100–4, 173
Heilsgeschichte, 22, 33, 82–84, 87, 106, 108, 110, 115–16, 122, 126, 140, 179, 188, 212, 216, 235, 237–38, 247, 261, 275

historical criticism, 12, 25–26, 37, 38, 51, 56, 83, 104, 127, 135–36, 141, 143, 144–45, 147–48, 156, 211, 217
historicism, 80, 87–90, 139, 180, 200
history (see also *Heilsgeschichte*), 3, 34, 42, 56, 70–71, 78, 87–89, 132, 159, 161, 216–17, 237–39, 241–44, 255, 260–64, 274, 275
history of religion (*Religionsgeschichte*), 66, 69, 71, 77, 89, 91, 127–28, 131–37, 145, 158–59, 168, 175, 190–91, 193, 216, 256, 264–67
humanism, 11–12, 37

Idealism, 49–51, 75, 78, 98
inerrancy, 14, 18, 217
inspiration, 9, 30, 44, 58, 59, 61, 70, 77, 81, 85, 113, 146–47, 156–57, 163, 188, 205, 232, 255, 270, 272

Judaism, 34, 47, 50, 70, 76, 95–96, 99–100, 122, 140–41, 150–51, 185, 251–52, 276–79

law, 9–10, 21, 32, 46, 64, 102, 127, 175, 252, 277–78

Messiah (Messianism), 26–27, 81, 161–62
monotheism, 69, 96–97, 102, 112, 139, 175
myth and ritual school, 168–71, 216, 275
mythology, 52, 68, 176, 215

Nazism, 151, 164, 179, 211

Orthodoxy (see also Scholasticism), 5, 10, 13, 17, 24, 36, 38, 42, 44, 52, 54, 67, 70, 75, 81, 109

Pan-Babylonian school, 150, 169

philosophy, 3, 29–33, 37, 49
Pietism, 38–41, 52, 54, 58, 81, 82, 83,
   137, 205, 213, 254
pre-Adamism, 26–27
prophecy, prophets, 30, 94, 103, 105,
   106, 115, 118, 122, 128, 129–30,
   139–40, 178

Rationalism, 38, 41, 48, 51, 52, 54,
   66, 70–71, 75, 81, 90–91, 205, 254,
   256
reason, 24, 29–34, 37, 38, 46, 48, 50,
   53–54
Reformation, 8, 24, 80
Religionsgeschichte (see history of
   religion)
Renaissance, 24, 37, 87
revelation, 19, 29–32, 46–47, 48–49,
   61, 71, 96, 101, 107, 112–13, 115,
   119, 121, 127, 133, 136, 148–49,
   155–56, 159, 166, 178, 204, 216–17,
   231–32, 241–44, 255
Romanticism, 38, 51–52, 75, 235

Scepticism, 14, 24, 50, 88

Scholasticism, 8, 12–15, 17–18, 21, 23,
   24, 34, 40, 54, 56, 160, 205, 247,
   254
science, 14, 25, 41–42, 86–87
sensus plenior, 164–65
social sciences, 75, 86–87, 127
Socinians, 14, 42, 44–45, 50
systematic (dogmatic) theology, 2–4, 7,
   29, 38, 55–56, 64–65, 142, 199,
   246–47, 254

traditio-historical criticism, 234–36,
   248
typology, 22, 108–9, 116, 135, 164–
   65, 189, 230, 233

universal ideas (notions), 3–4, 30–31,
   46–47, 64

wisdom (literature), 117, 184, 186,
   239, 241, 249–51, 274–76
Word of God, 9, 14, 18, 24, 30–32, 59,
   155–56
World Council of Churches, 210–12

PERSON INDEX

Abramowski, Rudolf, 144
Achtemeier, Paul J., 74
Ackroyd, Peter R., 221, 229, 230
Adam, David Stow, 201, 208
Addis, William Edward, 133
Agricola, Rudolf, 16
Albrektson, Bertil, 239, 244
Albright, William Foxwell, 217, 221, 224, 225
Allen, Don Cameron, 1, 25, 26, 27, 44
Alt, Albrecht, 235, 258
Ames, William, 20
von Ammon, Christoph Friedrich, 66–68
Amyraut, Moses, 43
Anderson, A.A., 143
Anderson, Bernhard W., 273
Anderson, G.W., 166, 168, 221, 222, 264
Applegate, Kenneth W., 35, 47
Aquinas, Thomas, 12
Aristotle, 12, 16, 37, 41, 78, 86
Arminius, Jacob, 43
Arndt, Johann, 39
Arnold, Matthew, 144, 147
Astruc, Jean, 69

Baab, Otto Justice, 176, 195–98, 202, 204, 208, 209
Bacon, Francis, 25, 28, 41
Bahrdt, Carl Friedrich, 2, 55
Baier, Johann Wilhelm, 7, 65
Baille, John, 166, 167
Baker, D. L., 209, 214
Barr, James, 167, 168, 201, 205, 209, 213, 214, 219, 226, 233, 239, 240, 242, 245, 260, 262, 264, 266, 268, 271, 272, 273, 276

Barth, Christoph, 219
Barth, Karl, 151, 154–58, 162, 163, 171, 211, 238, 265, 272
Barton, George Aaron, 168
Basedow, Johannes Bernhard, 57, 60, 61
von Baudissin, Wolf Wilhelm Friedrich, 133
Bauer, Bruno, 103–5
Bauer, Georg Lorenz, 66, 68–70, 71, 90, 91, 98, 129
Baumgartel, Friedrich, 167, 201, 233
Baumgarten, Michael, 84
Baumgarten, Siegmund Jakob, 41, 48, 60
Baumgarten-Cruisius, Ludwig Friedrich Otto, 105–7, 108, 112
Baur, Ferdinand Christian, 107
Bayle, Pierre, 37
Beck, Johann Tobias, 261
Beck, Lewis White, 35
Benecke, Heinrich, 73, 101
Bengel, J.A., 41, 82, 107, 115
Bennett, William Henry, 124, 125, 133
Berkeley, George, 47
Berlin, Isaiah, 35, 51
Bertheau, Ernst, 119
Bertholet, Alfred, 168
Bettenson, Henry, 1, 23
Betz, O., 143
Bevan, E.R., 144
Beza, Theodore, 12
Blau, J.L., 264
Blenkinsopp, Joseph, 268, 273, 276
Boers, Hendrikus, 35, 62, 136, 201, 207
Bollandus, John, 37
Bonhoeffer, Dietrich, 151, 162, 163–64
Bonus, Arthur, 150

Bornkamm, Günther, 257
Bousset, Wilhelm, 89
Bowden, John, 239
Boyle, Robert, 28
Bozeman, Theodore Dwight, 73, 142
Braaten, Carl, E. 154
Branton, James R., 239
Briggs, Charles Augustus, 124, 125
Bright, John, 221, 226, 243
Bromiley, Geoffrey W., 151, 155
Brown, Jerry Wayne, 73, 123
Brown, Raymond E., 151, 165
Bruce, F.F., 143
Brueggemann, Walter, 239, 241, 245, 250
Brunner, Heinrich Emil, 155, 211, 225
Buber, Martin, 167, 168
Budde, Karl Ferdinand Reinhardt, 133, 152
Bullinger, Johann Heinrich, 20
Bunyan, John, 39
Burden, J. J., 219
Burrows, Millar, 176, 192–95, 197, 202, 203, 204, 208, 209
Buss, Martin J., 73, 132, 144, 147
Büsching, Anton Friedrich, 55, 57
Butler, Joseph, 47
Buxtorff, Johannes, 44

Calov, Abraham, 7, 15, 65
Calvin, John, 8, 10, 11, 13, 14, 24, 34, 157, 158
Cappel, Louis, 43, 44
Carpenter, Edward, 35
Carpenter, Joseph Estlin, 73
Carpenter, S. C., 167
Cassirer, Ernst, 35, 37, 215
Causse, S. T., 73
Chadwick, Henry, 35, 49, 52
Chamberlain, Houston Steward, 150
Chemnitz, Martin, 15, 65
Cheyne, Thomas Kelly, 73, 98, 100, 103, 118, 121, 125, 133
Childs, Brevard S., 209, 213, 217, 220, 231, 239, 240, 268, 269–72
Christmann, Wolfgang Jacob, 7
Cicero, 16
Clements, Ronald E., 143, 219, 221, 222, 245, 251–52
Coats, George W., 273
Cocceius, Johannes, 4, 5, 19–23, 83, 183

Cohn, R. L., 273
Colenson, William John, 129
Collins, Anthony, 46
Collins, John J., 219, 260
von Cölln, Daniel George Conrad, 94–98, 99
Columbus, Christopher, 36
Comte, Auguste, 86
Cornill, Carl Heinrich, 172
Craig, Clarence T., 151
Crenshaw, J. L., 233, 238, 273
Cross, F.M., 268
Crowther, M. A., 73, 123
Crump, R. C., 210
Cullmann, Oscar, 74

Danielou, Jean, 151, 165
Darwin, Charles, 86, 87
Davey, Francis N., 151, 165
Davidson, Andrew Bruce, 124–26, 131, 173, 229
Davies, G. Henton, 233
Davies, T. W., 73, 118, 119
Day, G. E., 118
Deissler, Alfons, 245
Delitzsch, Franz Julius, 84, 111, 150
Delitzsch, Friedrich, 144, 150
Dentan, Robert Claude, 35, 55, 92, 143, 176, 198–201, 266
Descartes, René, 24, 28, 37, 43
Deutschmann, Johann, 54
Dever, William G., 210, 217
De Vries, John Simon, 73, 123
Diest, Henricus à, 7
Diestel, Ludwig, 35, 55, 92, 109, 205
Dillmann, Christian Friedrich August, 96, 119, 122–23, 130, 173, 184
Dinsmore, Charles Allen, 147
Dodd, C.H., 225
Donner, Herbert, 1, 30
Dorner, Isaak August, 77
Drews, Arthur, 149
Duff, Archibald, 124, 125, 133
Duhm, Bernhard, 130–31, 171, 173, 205
Durham, John I., 221, 229
Durkheim, Emile, 149
Dyrness, William, 245, 247

Ebeling, Gerhard, 35, 54, 256
Eerdmans, Bernardus Dirk, 168
Efird, James M., 202

Eichhorn, Albert, 89
Eichhorn, Johann Gottfried, 51, 56, 68, 69, 99, 170
Eichrodt, Walther, 151, 158, 160–61, 176, 177, 179–84, 185, 186, 187, 191, 198, 202, 205, 223, 228, 233, 239, 246, 247, 248, 251, 252, 257, 258, 259, 266, 267, 277
Eissfeldt, Otto, 151, 158–60, 161, 185, 193, 202, 203, 204, 208, 222, 264, 266
Eldredge, Laurence, 1, 2, 62, 64
Erasmus, Desiderius, 24
Ernesti, Johann August, 58, 60
Ewald, Heinrich George August, 100, 110, 111, 118–21, 124, 130, 173, 184

Faulenbach, Heiner, 1, 19
Faustus, 44
Feldman, Burton, 35, 52
Feuerbach, Ludwig, 80, 149
Fichte, Johann Gottlieb, 78
Finkelstein, J. J., 239, 243
Fohrer, Georg, 220, 245, 253, 257, 259, 266
Ford, David, 151
Forsyth, Peter Taylor, 154
Fosdick, Harry Emerson, 174, 203
Fowler, Henry Thatcher, 133
Francke, August Hermann, 40
von Frank, F. R., 82
Frankfort, H. & H. A., 210, 215
Franklin, Benjamin, 47
Frazer, James, 170
Frederick the Great, 41
Frei, Hans, 1, 19, 47, 52, 58, 59
Freiday, Dean, 35, 43
Freud, Sigmund, 149
Fridrichsen, Anton, 219, 239, 240
Friedlander, Michael, 141
Friedman, Jerome, 1, 24
Fries, Jakob Friedrich, 98
Fritsch, C. T., 143
Furnish, Victor Paul, 1, 25

Gabler, Johann Philipp, 2–5, 56, 62–66, 67, 70, 71, 91, 95, 105, 106, 109, 128, 129, 134, 159, 160, 170, 171, 188, 193, 196, 198, 199, 204, 207, 208, 254, 264
Galileo, 25, 37

Gamble, Connolly Jr., 210
Gammie, John G., 273
García Cordero Maximiliano, 245, 248
Gay, Peter, 35, 47, 49
George, Johann Friedrich Ludwig, 93, 102, 129
Gerhard, Johann, 15, 17
Gerstenberger, Erhard, 233, 238
Gese, Hartmut, 239, 244, 260, 262
Gesenius, Wilhelm, 92, 94, 100
Gilkey, Langdon, 240, 241, 245
Gillispie, Charles Coulston, 73, 87
Girgensohn, Karl, 151, 153
Glover, Willis B., 73, 123, 154
von Goethe, Johann Wolfgang, 78
Goeze, Johan Melchior, 57
Goldingay, John, 219
Gottwald, Norman K., 177, 179
Graf, Karl Heinrich, 74, 111, 115, 120, 127, 129
Gramberg, Carl Peter Wilhelm, 92–94, 100, 102, 129, 172
Greenberg, Moshe, 175
Greig, A. J., 233
Gressmann, Hugo, 73, 131, 132
Griffith, Gwilym O., 151, 154
Grønbech, Vilhelm, 168
Grossgebauer, Theophilus, 39
Grotius, Hugo, 26, 43
Groves, J. W., 233, 236
Gruehn, Werner, 151, 153
Gunkel, Hermann, 73, 89, 131–32, 134, 137, 138, 140, 144, 145, 147, 168, 188, 201, 213, 235, 236, 238, 264
Gunn, James D. G., 268, 271
Gunneweg, Antonius Hermann Joseph, 35, 152

Hahn, H. A., 109, 143
Hahn, Herbert F., 73, 89, 264, 266
Hammond, Henry, 57
Hänel, Johannes, 167
Hanson, Paul, 245, 251
von Harless, Adolf, 82
von Harnack, Adolf, 136, 151, 153, 154, 174
Harper, William Rainey, 147
Harrelson, Walter, 152
Harrington, Wilfrid J., 143, 177, 189, 219, 227

Hartlich, Christian, 167, 170
von Hartmann, Eduard, 149
Harvey, Julien, 219, 273
Hasel, Gerhard F., 219, 220, 245, 246, 257, 261, 262
Hävernick, Heinrich Andreas Christoph, 91, 105, 112
Harvey, Julien, 219, 273
Hayes, J. H., 144, 233
Haymann, Carl, 4, 54
Hazard, Paul, 35, 57
Hebert, Arthur Gabriel, 152, 165, 230
Hegel, Georg Wilhelm Friedrich, 50, 77–80, 87, 98, 100, 105, 122
Heinisch, Paul, 177, 189–91, 202, 228, 246, 266
Hempel, Johannes, 144, 147, 158, 167, 188, 219
Hengstenberg, Ernst Wilhelm, 80–84, 95, 101, 105, 109, 161, 189
Herbert, A. Gabriel, 165, 230
Herbert of Cherbury, Edward Lord, 46
von Herder, Johann Gottfried, 4, 35, 51–52, 98, 236
Hermission, Hans-Jürgen, 273
Herrmann, Siegfried, 257
Herrmann, Wilhelm, 154, 155, 259
Hesse, Franz, 240, 244, 262
Hetzenauer, M., 7, 190
Heyne, Christian Gottlob, 52, 69
Hicks, R. Lansing, 210, 221, 224
Hinson, David F., 245, 246
Hobbes, Thomas, 25, 26, 28, 46
Hodge, Charles, 142
von Hofmann, Johann Christian Konrad, 62, 80–84, 111, 114, 116, 120, 147, 179, 188, 189, 261
Hofmann, J. G., 62
Hölscher, Gustav, 168
Hooke, Samuel Henry, 167, 168, 169, 170
Hornig, Gottfried, 35, 56
Hubbard, David A., 221, 228, 229
Huffmon, Herbert H., 144, 150
Hufnagel, Wilhelm Friedrick, 55, 62
Hülsemann, Johann, 7
Hume, David, 47
Hummel, Horace D., 152, 161, 163
Hupfeld, Hermann, 121
Hutter, Leonhard, 15
Huxley, Thomas Henry, 87

Ilgen, Karl David, 68
van Imschoot, Paul, 221, 227–29, 246
Irwin, William A., 152, 159, 167, 201, 209, 240, 264

Jacob, Edmond, 219, 221, 226–27
Jefferson, Thomas, 47
Jensen, Peter, 150
Jeremias, Alfred, 150
John of Damascus, 16
Johnson, A. R., 210, 214

Kähler, Martin, 152, 154, 155
Kaiser, Gottlieb Philipp Christian, 74, 91–92, 98
Kaiser, Otto, 35, 58, 152
Kaiser, Walter C., 192, 245, 252–53
Kant, Immanuel, 35, 49–51, 53, 67, 69, 75, 76, 78, 98
Kapelrud, A. S., 273
Karge, Paul, 258
Kaufmann, Walter, 73, 79, 203, 215
Kaufmann, Yehezkel, 175–76
Kautzsch, Emil Friedrich, 133, 144, 147
Kayser, August, 133, 258
Kelsey, David H., 210, 214, 221, 225, 240, 242, 245
Kennett, Robert Hatch, 144
Kent, Charles Foster, 144, 148
Kepler, Johann, 25, 37
Kierkegaard, Søren, 155
Kimbrough, S. T. Jr., 73, 123
King, Winston L., 240
Kittel, Gerhard, 245
Kittel, Rudolf, 122, 133, 152, 153, 168, 198, 245
Klatt, Werner, 73, 132
Klein, Günther, 257
Knierim, Rolf, 273
Knight, Douglas A., 73, 128, 140, 260, 261, 262
Knight, George A. F., 221, 229–31
Knudson, Albert Cornelius, 171–74
Köberle, Justus, 144, 147
Köhler, August, 261, 275
Köhler, Ludwig, 152, 158, 177, 184, 186–87, 202, 228, 275
König, Eduard, 133, 152, 158, 177, 178–79, 198, 202, 204
Kraeling, Emil Gottlieb Heinrich, 35, 50, 76, 143, 150, 153, 154, 161, 162

Kraus, Hans-Joachim, 35, 60, 62, 67, 76, 81, 82, 99, 143
Kuenen, Abraham, 127, 129–30, 131
Kuske, Martin, 152, 163, 164

de Lagarde, Paul Anton, 88, 150
Lagrange, Marie Joseph, 148, 190
Lampe, G. W. H., 152, 165
La Peyrère, 23, 25, 26–27, 28, 34, 37, 261
Lash, Nicholas, 273
Laurin, Robert B., 177, 221, 226
Lehman, Chester K., 245, 248
Leibniz, Gottfried Wilhelm, 38, 48
Lemke, Werner E., 260
Lenin, Nikolai, 84
Lessing, Gotthold Ephraim, 4, 48, 49, 52, 67
Levine, Baruch A., 273
Lindblom, Johannes, 167, 168, 202, 209
Locke, John, 43, 46, 47, 56, 57
Löhr, Max Richard Herman, 133
Loisy, Alfred Firmin, 133, 148
Lombard, Peter, 15, 16
Long, Burke O., 273
Lotz, David W., 1, 9
Lotz, Wilhelm, 144, 147
Lowth, Robert, 51
Luhrmann, D., 257
Luther, Martin, 8–13, 15, 23, 34, 40, 81, 99, 151, 154, 155, 162, 185, 211, 269, 274
Lütkens, Franz Julius, 54
Lyell, Charles, 86

Mabillon, Jean, 39, 86
McCarthy, D. J., 257, 258
McCoy, Charles S., 1, 19
McEvenue, S. E., 268, 272
McFadyen, John Edgar, 144, 148
McKane, William A., 73, 132
McKee, David R., 1
McKenzie, John L., 245, 253
McKim, Donald D., 1, 8, 9
McLellan, Joseph C., 1, 20
Maimonides, 27
Maius, Johann Heinrich, 7
Major, Georg, 11
Manasseh ben Israel, 28
Manuel, Frank E., 35, 52
Marheineke, Philipp Konrad, 100

de Marolles, Michel, 27
Marti, Karl, 147
Martin, Hugh, 167
Marty, M. E., 152
Marx, Karl, 80, 84, 149
Matthews, Isaac George, 168
Mayes, A.D.H., 257, 258
Melanchthon, Philipp, 5, 8, 10, 11, 15–17
Mendenhall, G. E., 257, 258
Menken, Gottfried, 261
Merk, Otto, 1, 60, 62, 68
Michaelis, C. B., 41
Michaelis, J. D., 51
Milgrom, Jacob, 273
Minear, Paul S., 167
Mollenauer, Robert, 36
Möller, Wilhelm and Hans, 177, 187–89, 202, 203, 204
Montefiore, Claude Joseph Goldsmid, 132
Moore, George Foot, 73, 140, 168, 276, 277
Morus, Samuel Friedrich, Nathanael, 64
von Mosheim, Johann Lorenz, 57
Moulton, Richard Green, 144, 147
Mowinckel, Sigmund, 167, 168, 170, 236, 238, 239, 273
Muilenberg, James, 202, 210
Müller, Max, 136

Napier, B. D., 273
Napoleon, 80
Neander, Johann August Wilhelm, 77
Nesbit, W. G., 177, 179, 233
Newton, Isaac, 41, 42
Niebuhr, H. Richard, 167
Nietzsche, Friedrich Wilhelm, 149
Nineham, D. E., 35
Nöldeke, Theodor, 119
North, Christopher R., 152, 264
Noth, Martin, 235, 243, 258

Obayashi, Hiroshi, 260, 262
Oden, Robert A., Jr., 73, 132
Oehler, Gustaf Friedrich, 107, 110, 114–18, 117, 120, 121, 124, 125, 126, 173, 179, 207, 248, 258
Oehler, Theodor, 114
Oesterley, William Oscar Emil, 131, 168

van Oldenbarneveldt, Johann, 43
Orr, James, 144
Osswald, Eva, 219

Pace, Edward George, 168
Pahncke, Karl, 121
Paine, Thomas, 47
Pannenberg, Wolfhart, 262
Pascal, Blaise, 39
Paterson, J. A., 111
Pauck, Wilhelm, 1, 16, 152, 155, 156
Payne, J. Barton, 221, 232–33, 246
Peake, Arthur Samuel, 144, 148
Pedersen, Johannes, 210, 214
Pelikan, Jaroslav, 1, 9
Perlitt, Lothar, 74, 257, 258
Peters, John Punnett, 133
Pfeiffer, Robert H., 220, 240
Piepenbring, Charles, 124, 133
de la Place, Joshua, 43
Plato, 75, 78
Polley, M. E., 202, 205
Pope Alexander, 41
Pope Leo XIII, 148
Pope Pius X, 148, 189, 227
Pope Pius XII, 189, 227
Popkin, Richard H., 1, 24, 26, 27, 28,
   34, 46
Porteous, Norman W., 143, 152, 260
Preus, Christian, 74, 83, 144
Preus, James Samuel, 1, 10
Preuss, H. D., 240, 241
Priest, John F., 240, 241
Procksch, Otto, 152, 154, 177, 181,
   191–92, 203, 204, 205, 223
Prussner, F. C., 257, 258
Pyrrho of Elis, 24

von Rad, Gerhard, 164, 177, 191, 220,
   225, 233–39, 241, 243, 244, 246,
   247, 248, 249, 254, 256, 259, 260,
   261, 266, 267, 274, 275, 277, 278
Ramlot, M.-L., 219
von Ranke, Leopold, 84, 87
Rauschenbusch, Walter, 84
Reimarus, Hermann Samuel, 48, 50, 91
Renckens, Henricus, 220
Reuss, Eduard Wilhelm Eugen, 101,
   123, 127, 129, 139
Reventlow, Henning Graf, 36, 45, 48,
   57, 143, 151, 152, 153, 161, 219,
   220, 257, 273, 274

Richardson, Alan, 152, 165, 166, 210,
   212
Richardson, Robert D., 35, 52
Richter, Matthaeus, 6
Riehm, Eduard Karl August, 121–22,
   130, 173
Ringgren, Helmer, 220
Ritschl, Albrecht Benjamin, 84–86, 88,
   114, 127, 155
Ritschl, Dietrich, 36, 56, 58, 59
Roberts, J. J. M., 260
Robertson, James, 141, 152, 166
Robinson, Henry Wheeler, 144, 148,
   149, 152, 165, 202, 204
Robinson, James M., 152, 157
Robinson, Theodore Henry, 131, 157,
   165, 168, 169
Rogers, Jack Bartlett, 1, 8, 9
Rogerson, John William, 36, 69, 74,
   99, 111, 141, 167, 168, 169, 170,
   210, 214, 215
Rosweyde, Herbert, 37
Rousseau, Jean-Jacques, 52
Rowley, H. H., 143, 152, 166, 210,
   213, 257, 259, 264
Rylaarsdam, John Coert, 167, 257

Sachs, Walter, 167, 170
Salmond, S. D. F., 125, 126
Sanders, E. P., 276, 278
Sanders, James A., 268, 269
Sandys-Wunsch, John, 1, 2, 36, 57, 60,
   61, 62, 64, 74, 91, 92
von Schelling, Friedrich Wilhelm Jo-
   seph, 78
von Schiller, Johann Christoph Fried-
   rich, 78
Schleiermacher, Friedrich Daniel Ernst,
   50, 52, 66, 75–77, 79, 80, 83, 90,
   98, 100, 101, 137
Schmid, H. H., 257, 259, 273, 275
Schmidt, Sebastian, 4, 5–7, 14–18
Schmidt, Werner H., 257, 259, 264,
   267, 273
Schofield, John N., 177, 221
Scholder, Klaus, 1, 14, 44
Schopenhauer, Arthur, 149
Schultz, David, 94, 121, 124
Schultz, Ernst Andreas Heinrich Hermann, 96, 109, 110–14, 115, 117,
   119, 124, 184

Schütte, H. W., 1, 74, 144, 150
Schwaiger, Georg, 36
Schwarzbach, Bertram, 36, 47
Schweitzer, W., 210, 212
Scott, R. B. Y., 273
Sellin, Ernst, 96, 177, 179, 184–86, 187, 198, 202, 203, 204, 228
Semler, Johann Salomo, 4, 41, 54, 57, 58, 67, 70, 269
Servetus, Miguel, 25
Shaffer, E. S., 74, 123
Silberman, Lou H., 140
Simon, Richard, 26, 37, 57
Simpson, Cuthbert, A., 177
Singer, Charles, 144
Smart, James D., 152, 159, 210, 212
Smend, Rudolf (Sr.), 131, 136
Smend, Rudolf, 36, 49, 62, 74, 96, 99, 119, 140, 257, 258, 260
Smith, E. D., 118
Smith, George Adam, 144, 148, 149
Smith, Henry Preserved, 133, 136
Smith, Morton S., 240
Smith, William Robertson, 131, 137, 142, 169
Sozzini (Socinus), Fautus, 44
Sozzini (Socinus), Lelio, 44
Spencer, Herbert, 86
Spener, Philip Jacob, 36, 39
Spinoza, Benedict, 5, 23, 25, 27–34, 37, 46, 59, 75, 99, 269
Spriggs, D. G., 177, 179, 233
Squires, H. H., 210
Stade, Bernhard, 111, 133, 136, 141
Staerk, Willy, 152, 158
Steck, Karl Gerhard, 74, 82
Steck, Odil H., 273
Stendahl, Krister, 202, 208, 214, 240
Stephen, Leslie, 36, 47
Steudel, Johann Christian Friedrich, 96, 105, 107–9, 112, 114
Steuernagel, Carl, 152, 158
Strauss, Emil, 72
Strauss, David Friedrich, 100, 107
Strauss, Leo, 1, 28
Strecker, Georg, 257
Stuart, Moses, 58
Sykes, S. W., 74, 123, 141

Tappert, Theodore G., 36, 39
Taylor, S., 118

Teelinck, Willem, 39
Teller, Wilhelm Abraham, 7, 54
Tennent, Gilbert, 39
Terrien, Samuel, 245, 247, 249–51, 273, 275
Tholuck, Friedrich August Gottreu, 77
Thomas, George F., 202
Thomasius, Christian, 40
Thomasius, Gottfried, 40, 82
Thompson, R. J., 74, 141
Thompson, Thomas L., 260, 263
Tillich, Paul, 36, 38, 44, 52, 56
Tindal, Matthew, 46, 47, 49
Tittmann, C.C., 2
Toland, John, 46, 52
Töllner, J. G., 2
Tomkins, Oliver S., 210
Toombs, L.E., 273
Towner, Wayne Sibley, 273
Tracy, David, 273
Trillhaas, Wolfgang, 1, 74
Troeltsch, Ernst, 74, 80, 86, 88–89
Turretin, Francis, 12, 14

Vatke, Johann Karl Wilhelm, 74, 79, 98, 100–103, 104, 105, 111, 129, 260
de Vaux, Roland, 219, 261
Vermigli, Peter Martyr, 12
Vischer, Wilhelm, 152, 158, 162–63, 164, 188, 229
Vitringa, Campegius, 57
Vollborth, J.C., 60
Voltaire, 38, 47
Volz, Paul, 167, 170
Vos, Geerhardus, 248
Vriemoet, Emo Lucius, 7
Vriezen, Theodorus Christiaan, 220, 221, 222–24, 266

Warfield, Benjamin Breckinridge, 142
Wasserman, E. R., 35
Weber, Max, 88
Weidmann, Helmut, 144, 150
Weisman, Christian Eberhard, 7
Wellhausen, Julius, 73, 74, 119, 120, 127, 129, 130, 131, 132, 137, 140, 141, 146, 153, 169, 171, 173, 175, 189, 258, 266
Wendte, Charles W., 144
Wernberg-Möller, Preben, 219
Wesley, John, 39

Westermann, Claus, 245, 248–49, 273
de Wette, Wilhelm Martin Leberecht,
    81, 93, 95, 96, 98–100, 102, 261
Widengren, Geo, 168
Wigand, Johann, 6
Wilbur, Earl Morse, 36, 44
Wilcoxen, Jay, 274
Willey, Basil, 1, 25, 36, 37, 42, 46
Willi, Thomas, 36, 51
Willoughby, H. R., 167, 176
Winckelmann, Johann Joachim, 52
Winckler, Hugo, 150
Wintzer, F., 1, 74
Wolff, Johann Christian, 48, 49, 60, 75
Wolff, H.W., 257
Woollcombe, K. J., 152, 165
Wrede, William, 89

Wright, George Ernest, 210, 215, 216,
    217, 221, 224–25, 233, 238, 239,
    241, 242, 244, 246, 261
Würthwein, Ernst, 152, 177, 219, 220

Young, Edward Joseph, 221, 231–32

Zachariä, Gotthelf Traugott, 2, 41, 56,
    60–62, 67
Zanchi, Girolami, 12
Zenger, E., 257
Zickler, Friedrich Samuel, 7
Zimmerli, Walther, 74, 139, 219, 233,
    245, 253, 257, 259, 264
Zinzendorf, Nicholas, 39
Zwingli, Ulrich, 8, 10, 11